Give Your CPA Exam Score a Boost with these Essential Study Tools

Cram Course

Boost your score by 8-10 points!

- Get a final review with this condensed CPA Exam Review supplement – the perfect complement to your full review course

- Reinforce your understanding of the most heavily tested topics on the CPA Exam

- Take the Cram Course leading up to Exam Day to refresh your mind on important topics

Audio Lectures

Maximize every minute leading up to the exam!

- Easy MP3 download – ideal for Apple or Android devices

- Turn any moment into a study opportunity! Listen to lectures on your commute, at the gym, or even as you nod off to sleep

- Immerse yourself in the most important CPA Exam topics

CPA Exam Flashcards

Make studying portable, accessible, and fun!

- Harness overarching CPA Exam concepts

- Create important connections to actual CPA Exam usage and application

- Make studying more exciting by involving family & friends – pull out your flashcards for a quick & interactive study method.

Upgrade your course package at

www.rogercpareview.com/cpa-courses/study-materials

BEC

Business Environment and Concepts

Written By:

Roger Philipp, CPA, CGMA

Roger CPA Review
P.O. Box 590059
San Francisco, CA 94159
www.rogercpareview.com
(877) 764-4272
(415) 346-4272

Permissions_____

The following items are utilized in this volume, and are copyright property of the American Institute of Certified Public Accountants, Inc. (AICPA), all rights reserved:

- Uniform CPA Examination and Questions and Unofficial Answers, Copyright © 1991, 1992, 1993, 1994, 1995, 1996, 1997, 1998, 1999, 2000, 2001, 2002, 2003, 2004, 2005, 2006, 2007, 2008, 2009, 2010, 2011, 2012, 2013, 2014, 2015, 2016, 2017, 2018
- Audit and Accounting Guides, Auditing Procedure Studies, Risk Alerts, Statements of Position, and code of Professional Conduct
- Statements on Auditing Standards, Statements on Standards for Consulting Services, Statements on Responsibilities in Personal Financial Planning Practice, Statements on Standards for Accounting and Review Services, Statements on Quality Control Standards, Statements on Standards for Attestation Engagements, and Statements on Responsibilities in Tax Practice
- Accounting Research Bulletins, APB Opinions, Audit and Accounting Guides, Auditing Procedure Studies, Risk Alerts, Statements of Position, and Code of Professional Conduct
- Uniform CPA Examination Blueprints
- Independent Standard Board (ISB) Standards

Portions of various FASB and GASB documents, copyright property of the Financial Accounting Foundation, 401 Merritt 7, PO Box 5116, Norwalk, CT 06856-5116, are utilized with permission. Complete copies of these documents are available from the Financial Accounting Foundation. These selections include the following:

Financial Accounting Standards Board (FASB)
- *The FASB Accounting Standards Codification* ™ and Statements of Financial Accounting Concepts
- FASB Statements, Interpretations, Technical Bulletins, and Statements of Financial Accounting Concepts

Governmental Accounting Standards Board (GASB)
- GASB Codification of Governmental Accounting and Financial Reporting Standards, GASB Statements, GASB Concepts Statements, and GASB Interpretations
- GASB Statements, Interpretations, and Technical Bulletins

The following items are utilized in this volume, and are copyright property of the International Financial Reporting Standards (IFRS) Foundation and the International Accounting Standards Board (IASB), all rights reserved:
- IASB International Reporting Standards (IFRS), International Accounting Standards (IAS) and Interpretations

ABOUT THE AUTHOR

Roger S. Philipp, CPA, CGMA
CEO, Founder, and Instructor, Roger CPA Review

Roger Philipp, CPA, CGMA, is one of the most celebrated motivators and instructors in the accounting profession. Roger believes you should enjoy what you do – in life, business, and learning. Guided by this philosophy, he strives to create dynamic and engaging instruction that makes learning concepts enjoyable. This focus has helped aspiring accountants across the globe reach career success for almost 30 years.

Roger launched Roger CPA Review in 2001 with the goal to create a CPA review course that would alter the landscape of accounting education. He continues to act as a key inspiration and spark for company innovation. Roger CPA Review's success is fueled by his unique approach to teaching, in which he breaks down and simplifies complex topics, with support from memory aids and mnemonic devices, to help students understand and retain information.

Roger's early career began in public accounting at Deloitte & Touche, where he earned his CPA designation, before transitioning to educational instruction. He was a lead instructor at Mark Dauberman CPA Review, before starting Roger CPA Review. Roger attributes his entrepreneurial success to the many doors his CPA license opened, as well as his passion for making professional education engaging and relevant for optimum effectiveness. In recent years, Roger was featured as one of Accounting Today's Top 100 Most Influential People in Public Accounting.

Today, Roger is a member of the AICPA, CalCPA, and is on the Board of Directors for the American Professional Accounting Certification Providers Association (APACPA). He resides in San Francisco with his wife and co-founder of the company, Louisa, and their three children. He enjoys traveling with his family, enjoying the arts, and volunteering at his local food bank.

Acknowledgements

This course textbook and the associated questions would not be possible without the contributions of our team of experts: **Jae Johnson**, CPA (our lead content developer), **Eva Arnold**, CPA, and **Wendy Urka**, CPA. Jae in particular has been the driving force behind the updates and improvements for this year's textbooks.

Roger and the company also recognize and appreciate the many contributions **Mark Dauberman** has made to the textbooks over the many years we have worked together.

Business Environment & Concepts

Table of Contents

Introduction

Table of Contents

Section – Introduction

Table of Contents

Lecture 0.01 – Course Introduction

Welcome to your Roger CPA Review Course!

Greetings Student,

It is an honor to be your partner on your CPA Exam journey. Your success is our success, which is why we are 100% dedicated to providing you with a learning experience that inspires, delights and delivers results with optimum efficiency. With the power or our new SmartPath Predictive Technology™, paired with the profession's leading video lectures and course materials, you'll be on your way to CPA in no time.

The course is structured for a variety of student types. Each topic is broken down from the beginning and taught as if the student has little to no prior knowledge of the particular topic at hand. Therefore, whether you are a first-time review student who has never attempted an exam part, or a seasoned professional returning to the exam after an earlier attempt, you will be prepared.

As you work through the material, you will be able to gauge your competency on each topic using the SmartPath platform, which is integrated into your Interactive Practice Questions. SmartPath provides recommended targets that are based on the performance of previous students who have passed the CPA Exam. We highly recommend you aim to reach each target so that you will know that you have reached a point of adequate readiness to take the exam.

Ultimately, you control your destiny. As your instructor Roger Philipp, CPA, CGMA always says, "The CPA Exam is not an IQ test. It is a test of discipline. If you study, you will pass!" To get the most out of your course, please **read through this Introduction** to understand more about the CPA Exam, course content, and study strategies. You will also find on the next page our **"Guide to Using Your Roger CPA Review Course".** This will provide you with our recommended approach to preparing with this course and its support features.

We wish you all the best on this journey and are here to guide you along the way.

Sincerely,

The Roger CPA Review Team
#TaketheSmartPath

Follow Roger CPA Review on social media for CPA Exam tips and tricks at @RogerCPAReview.

Subscribe to our blog to get the most up-to-date CPA Exam information as well as plenty of advice on careers, education and the CPA Exam at ROGERCPAREVIEW.COM/BLOG.

GUIDE TO USING YOUR ROGER CPA REVIEW COURSE

Plan Learn Practice Review

I. Plan – Stick to a plan, and you are more likely to succeed!

- Choose the 3, 6, 9 or 12-month study planner, and customize to meet your needs.
- Stay on track and make up any missed days.

II. Learn – Build a solid foundation in core concepts.

- **Lectures**
  - Watch all lectures within a section. You may find it helpful to follow along with the *Course Textbook* and take notes along the way.
  - Take advantage of course player tools like Closed Captioning, Add Note and Adjustable Playback Speed (faster for quick review, slower for new or challenging topics).
- **Course Textbooks**
  - Read the *Course Textbook* section thoroughly to solidify concepts.
  - Take advantage of eTextbook capabilities in your course, such as easy navigation, search and highlighting.
- **Class Questions**
  - Watch *Class Question* lectures for coaching on specific questions.
  - Follow along with the *Class Questions* in your *Course Textbook*.

> **Tip:** Work through the topics and questions within one course section at a time.

III. Practice – Apply concepts using the *Interactive Practice Questions* Software.

- **SmartPath Predictive Technology™**
  - Use the *SmartPath* platform to compare your progress to students who have passed.
  - Aim to hit both *SmartPath* targets per section: (1) number of question attempts, (2) score.
  - Take *Smart Quizzes*, which use adaptive technology to serve you the multiple-choice questions (MCQs) and task-based simulations (TBSs) you need to hit your targets.
- Click *New Quiz* to create customized practice sessions. Select the number of MCQs and TBSs to include, specify course sections covered, and apply other helpful filtering options.
- Take advantage of question software tools like note-taking and links back to related lectures.
- After any practice session, review your work and read through all answer explanations to understand *why* you were correct or incorrect.

IV. Review – Get ready for exam day.

- Ensure you have hit all *SmartPath* targets and revisit sections marked "Needs Improvement."
  - The *View Lectures* button in *SmartPath* provides easy access to relevant lectures.
- Take a full-length practice exam in the CPA Exam Simulator to hone your test taking strategy, time management and self-discipline under exam-like conditions.
- Revisit lectures and rework any questions you have bookmarked or noted for review.
- Take the *Cram Course* for a final review of the most heavily tested topics.

Need more help with accounting topics? Search for answers from real CPAs in the *Homework Help Center*.

Application, Scheduling, & Taking the Exam

** All information regarding AICPA, NASBA and Prometric rules and regulations in this introduction are up to date as of September 2018. Please see aicpa.org and nasba.org for the most current information.

To ensure that the Uniform CPA Examination keeps pace with the evolution of the accounting and business worlds, the examination is a computer-based test (CBT). The computerized exam:
- Enables testing of higher-level cognitive skills.
- Permits integration of real-world entry-level requirements.
- Provides flexibility and convenience to candidates.
- Offers greater consistency in evaluation.
- Helps save time in administration, grading, and reporting.
- Provides added exam security.

A tutorial that reviews the examination's format and navigation functions is available at aicpa.org. Choose the "Become a CPA" tab and then pick "CPA Exam" from the options in the list. From there, candidates can find the tutorial and sample tests. All exam candidates are encouraged to review this prior to sitting. The tutorial is intended to familiarize candidates with the functionality and types of questions and responses used in the examination format. The tutorial does not focus on examination content and is not intended as a replacement for study materials.

EXAM APPLICATION

State boards strongly urge candidates to apply online as the processing time is reduced. The applications for the CPA Exam are available online, and the link for the individual states can be found on our website at RogerCPAreview.com. Qualified candidates who have met all of the educational requirements may apply at any time. See individual state boards or NASBA.org for their specific application process. It is the candidate's responsibility to understand their jurisdiction's requirements to sit for the CPA exam and applicants are encouraged to familiarize themselves with licensure requirements prior to applying for the CPA exam.

Depending on the jurisdiction, candidates will apply directly through either their state board of accountancy or CPAES (CPA Examination Services, a division of NASBA). Some states have specific rules regarding coursework, applications and transcripts so candidates should contact their board if they are unsure on or unclear about any requirements. If candidates do not follow instructions and forget to submit required information with their application (fingerprint cards, photographs, etc.), the candidate will be rejected to sit in their state, forfeit application fee(s) and must re-apply.

Candidates in the following states must apply through **NASBA's CPA Examination Services** and may call **800-CPA-EXAM** for further information on application requirements and procedures:

Alaska, Colorado, Connecticut, Delaware, Florida, Georgia, Hawaii, Indiana, Iowa, Kansas, Louisiana, Maine, Massachusetts, Michigan, Minnesota, Missouri, Montana, Nebraska, New Hampshire, New Jersey, New Mexico, New York, Ohio, Pennsylvania, Puerto Rico, Rhode Island, South Carolina, Tennessee, Utah, Vermont, Washington, or Wisconsin.

Candidates in the following states must apply with their **Board of Accountancy**. See a full list of boards of accountancy and contact information at the end of this Introduction.

Alabama, Arizona, Arkansas, California, District of Columbia, Guam, Idaho, Illinois, Kentucky, Maryland, Mississippi, Nevada, North Carolina, North Dakota, Oklahoma, Oregon, South Dakota, Texas, U.S. Virgin Islands, Virginia, West Virginia, or Wyoming.

Application Steps

STATE BOARD OF ACCOUNTANCY

1. Meet requirements and submit educational documents to Board
2. Create client account and obtain password from Board
3. Complete application using client account (print Application Remittance Form)
4. Submit signed Application Remittance Form and fee
5. Receive Board approval and select exam section(s)

NASBA

6. Receive Payment Coupon from NASBA
   - If you do not receive the Payment Coupon within 10 business days after section selection, visit NASBA's Web site at *nasba.org* to pay online.
7. Pay NASBA Exam Section Fee(s)
   - NASBA's Online Credit Card Payment Form: Answer only the required fields when paying online. In accordance with the Board's Privacy Policy, NASBA does not collect or require exam applicants to fill in the Mother's Maiden Name field on NASBA's form. Please enter the word UNKNOWN in the Mother's Maiden Name field. This will allow you to continue processing your online payment. For additional payment information, telephone 1-866-696-2722.
8. Receive Notice to Schedule (NTS) from NASBA
   - If you do not receive the NTS within 10 business days after you pay the section fee(s), notify the Board or NASBA. Your NTS is valid in most states for 6 months, in others it can be good for 3, 6, 9, or 12 months.

PROMETRIC

9. Schedule with Prometric
10. Take CPA Exam at a Prometric Testing Center
    - You MUST bring your NTS with you to the testing center. You will be denied entry to the CPA Exam if you do not present the NTS.

BOARD

11. Receive Score Report from Board

Additional Information

For additional information on how to get answers to common questions, consult this table.

For questions about:	Contact:
• Eligibility to take the examination • Special testing accommodations • Completing application forms • Name and/or address changes • Examination scores • Your Board of Accountancy's fees	Write, call or send an e-mail to the appropriate Board of Accountancy. A complete list of Boards of Accountancy may be found at end of this Introduction.
• Receiving your Notice to Schedule (NTS) • Replacing a lost NTS • Payments to NASBA • General comments about the test center where you took your examination	Call NASBA at 1-800-CPA-EXAM (1-800-272-3926) or send an e-mail to cpaexam@nasba.org
For questions about:	**Contact:**
• Scheduling, rescheduling or canceling your examination appointment • Directions to your test center	All information and instant scheduling is available at prometric.com/cpa Additionally, candidates may contact the Prometric Candidate Services Call Center at 1-800-580-9648
• Content of the examination • Specific multiple-choice questions and/or task-based simulations on the examination • Questions about rescore requests	Visit the AICPA's CPA Page: aicpa.org, Career Guidance, Becoming a CPA, CPAExam Or send an e-mail to cpaexam@aicpa.org

Test Centers

Test centers move, new ones are opened, and some close from time-to-time. The most current list of test centers may be found on the Prometric website at prometric.com/cpa.

Testing Windows

The Uniform CPA Examination is offered the first two months plus 10 days of each calendar quarter. These months of testing are known as the "testing windows." The examination is given in these testing windows to allow for systems and database maintenance. The exam is not available during the following times: March 11-March 31, June 11-June 30, September 11-September 31, and December 11-December 31. It is important to plan accordingly; it is the candidate's responsibility to schedule the remaining un-passed sections of the examination or the candidate may risk losing credit for previously passed sections. Candidates will be able to take any or all sections of the examination during any testing window and in any order but will not be allowed to take the same section more than once during any testing window. If a section is failed, the candidate must wait for the next available testing window and submit a re-application to receive a new NTS.

Testing is Available	Testing is NOT Available
January, February, March 1-10	March 11 to end of month
April, May, June 1-10	June 11 to end of month
July, August, September 1-10	September 11 to end of month
October, November, December 1-10	December 11 to end of month

EXAM SCHEDULING

Eligibility to Test

In order to make appointments at test centers, candidates must have a valid Notice to Schedule (NTS). Candidates receive an NTS after they apply to take an examination and are deemed eligible by their state boards of accountancy. An NTS is provided for every section a candidate has been approved to take. The NTS is valid only for a specified period of time and cannot be used once it expires. Therefore, **it is important that candidates schedule their test appointments as soon as they receive the NTS.** The NTS is good for **6 months** in most jurisdictions except the following:

- Texas   90 days from date of application
- California   9 months from date NTS is issued
- Hawaii   9 months from date NTS is issued
- Louisiana   9 months from date NTS is issued
- Utah   9 months from date NTS is issued
- North Dakota   12 months from date NTS is issued
- South Dakota   12 months from date NTS is issued
- Virginia   12 months from date NTS is issued

Testing Centers

Prometric will administer the exam at authorized CPA Exam testing sites throughout the United States, Guam, Puerto Rico, the Virgin Islands, and the District of Columbia, as well as at international sites in Japan, Bahrain, Kuwait, Lebanon, the United Arab Emirates, and Brazil. Other international locations are on the horizon. Special citizenship requirements and fees apply to testing internationally.

Candidates are not required to take the CPA Exam at a Prometric site located in the state where they applied and may schedule their exams at any authorized Prometric site regardless of location.

After submitting an application, receiving approval by the State Board of Accountancy (Board), and submitting the required fees to NASBA, the candidate will be authorized to contact Prometric to schedule a specific testing date and time. The test sites are normally open six days each week. Candidates are encouraged to check Prometric's Web site at *prometric.com* to locate a testing site near them.

Schedule Early

Scheduling is available throughout the year, but candidates should schedule examination appointments as soon as possible after receiving their NTS. Being proactive about scheduling will help to secure the candidate's first choice of date and location of test centers. Tests are scheduled on a first come, first served basis. To ensure that candidates are able to take their examination section(s) on the first desired date and time, candidates should make their appointment(s) at least 65 days before the date they want to take the examination. **The earlier candidates schedule appointments, the better their chances are of obtaining the location, date, and time of their**

choice. Test appointments **cannot** be scheduled fewer than five days in advance of the desired test date. Walk-in testing is **not** allowed. The last two weeks of an exam window tend to fill up early, so candidates should plan ahead and schedule as early as possible.

Candidates may schedule examination sessions at *prometric.com/CPA* or by calling Prometric's Call Center at 1-800-580-9648. Candidates must have their Notice to Schedule available when making test appointments. Examination section(s) must be taken within the time period for which an NTS is valid (3-12 months depending on jurisdiction) and may not be rescheduled after the NTS has expired. Boards of Accountancy, NASBA and Prometric are not responsible if a candidate cannot schedule an appointment before deadlines in your jurisdiction; it is imperative to plan ahead.

Candidates have three scheduling options:

1. Visit prometric.com/cpa on the Internet

Candidates will find that the easiest and quickest way to schedule an examination appointment (as well as reschedule and cancel an appointment if necessary) is on the Internet. Using the Internet provides 24-hour access to scheduling and avoids any "on hold" waiting time. Because of this, candidates have the quickest and most direct access to preferred dates and test center locations. Additionally, they will quickly receive a detailed confirmation of exam appointments (on screen and via e-mail). Before making any appointments, candidates must have received a valid NTS and should have this available before beginning the scheduling process. Additionally, candidates must be ready to identify the dates, times and locations where they want to take each section. It is not necessary to make all appointments at one time and candidates may schedule one exam at a time even if they have paid for more than one on any particular NTS. During the scheduling process, candidates will be required to provide various pieces of information from the NTS. Online scheduling is done by completing the following easy steps:

1.   Go to prometric.com/cpa. Select SCHEDULE APPOINTMENT.
2.   Select CPA Exam and Country/State.
3.   Read all the information on the Information Review screen and click NEXT.
4.   After viewing welcome screen, click NEXT, read all of the policy information and click "I Agree" to proceed.
5.   On the Program Identifier Screen, enter your examination section identification number from your NTS (you have one identification number for each section of the examination—be sure to use the correct examination identification number for the section you are scheduling). Click "Next."
6.   Confirm proper section and click NEXT.
7.   Follow on-screen instructions to select the date and location you would like to schedule your section.
8.   Select COMPLETE REGISTRATION to finalize your scheduling. Print the confirmation number for your appointment and keep it for your records.

2. Call 1-800-580-9648 (Candidate Services Call Center)

Prometric's Candidate Services Call Center is open Monday through Friday from 8:00 a.m. to 8:00 p.m. Eastern time. (Hearing-impaired candidates using teletypewriter (TTY) may call 1-800-529-3590 to schedule appointments.) Candidates must schedule a separate appointment for each section of the examination that they are planning to take. If calling to schedule two or more sections, candidates should be prepared to identify the dates, times and locations they want to take each section. It is not necessary to make all appointments in one call and candidates may make one appointment at a time. Before calling, the candidate must have an NTS and should have access to it during the call as they will be required to provide the customer service representative with various pieces of information from the NTS.

Candidates will NOT receive written confirmation of their appointment so must write down the date, time, location, and confirmation number for each appointment. Candidates may also visit prometric.com/cpa to confirm their appointment(s). If the candidate is not familiar with the test center location they should ask the customer service representative for directions while they are making the appointment over the phone. There are multiple test centers in some metropolitan areas, so it is important for candidates to be certain of the correct test center location where they are scheduled to take their examination(s).

Those interested in a test run of the Prometric system may also use the telephone call center to schedule a 15-minute generic sample test at the facility prior to examination so they can familiarize themselves with the location and Prometric. There is a $30 fee for this *Test Drive* service.

3. Call the Local Test Center

Some candidates prefer to speak to a customer service representative at the local test center; if this is the case, candidates may call the center directly to make an exam appointment. Calls will only be accepted during business hours, which vary for each test center. Leaving a voicemail message at the local test center is NOT an acceptable method of scheduling. If calling to take two or more sections, candidates should be prepared to identify the dates and times they want to take each section. It is not necessary to make all appointments in one call and the candidate may schedule one appointment at a time. Before calling, the candidate must have an NTS and should have access to it during the call as they will be required to provide the customer service representative with various pieces of information from the NTS.

Candidates will NOT receive written confirmation of their appointment so must write down the date, time, location, and confirmation number for each appointment. Candidates may also visit prometric.com/cpa to confirm their appointment(s). If the candidate is not familiar with the test center location they should ask the customer service representative for directions while they are making the appointment over the phone. There are multiple test centers in some metropolitan areas, so it is important for candidates to be certain of the correct test center location where they are scheduled to take their examination(s).

TESTING INTERNATIONALLY

The international testing format follows the same state board licensure process and the current examination structure. The exam is still only offered in English and is available during the same four testing windows per calendar year as offered to US candidates. There are additional fees that applicants must pay if they wish to take the exam internationally.

Who is eligible?

U.S. citizens and permanent residents living abroad, and citizens and long-term residents of the countries in which the exam is being administered are eligible. In some cases, permanent residents or citizens of neighboring countries may test at international testing centers. The only form of identification that an applicant can use to test internationally is a passport.

Non-US Countries Offering CPA Exam Testing

Japan, Brazil, the United Arab Emirates, Lebanon, Kuwait, and Bahrain

| Citizenship Status | Eligibility to Test in These Countries | | | | | | |
C = Citizen PR = legal permanent or long term resident	U.S.	Japan	Brazil	UAE	Lebanon	Kuwait	Bahrain
U.S. C/PR	X	X	X	X	X	X	X
Japan C/PR	X	X					
Antigua/Barbuda C/PR			X				
Argentina C/PR	X		X				
Bahamas C/PR			X				
Barbados C/PR			X				
Belize C/PR			X				
Bolivia C/PR	X		X				
Brazil C/PR	X		X				
Cayman Islands C/PR			X				
Chile C/PR	X		X				
Colombia C/PR	X		X				
Costa Rica C/PR			X				
Dominica C/PR			X				
Dominican Republic C/PR			X				
Ecuador C/PR	X		X				
El Salvador C/PR			X				
French Guiana C/PR	X		X				
Grenada C/PR			X				
Guatemala C/PR			X				
Guyana C/PR	X		X				
Haiti C/PR			X				
Honduras C/PR			X				
Jamaica C/PR			X				
Mexico C/PR			X				
Nicaragua C/PR			X				
Panama C/PR			X				
Paraguay C/PR	X		X				
Peru C/PR	X		X				
St. Kitts/Nevis C/PR			X				
St. Lucia C/PR			X				
St. Vincent/Grenadines C/PR			X				
Suriname C/PR	X		X				
Trinidad & Tobago C/PR			X				
Uruguay C/PR	X		X				
Venezuela C/PR	X		X				
Bahrain C/PR	X			X	X	X	X
Egypt C/PR	X			X	X	X	X
Jordan C/PR	X			X	X	X	X
Kuwait C/PR	X			X	X	X	X
Lebanon C/PR	X			X	X	X	X
Oman C/PR	X			X	X	X	X
Qatar C/PR	X			X	X	X	X
Saudi Arabia C/PR	X			X	X	X	X
UAE C/PR	X			X	X	X	X
Yemen C/PR	X			X	X	X	X
India C/PR	X			X	X	X	X
Any other country in the world C/PR	X						

STEPS FOR APPLYING INTERNATIONALLY*

1. Students must first meet eligibility requirements and apply to a US 'State Board' as long as that state board is one that allows international testing. For states that allow this, please see the list on the next page.
2. Applicant receives their Notice to Schedule.
3. Once approved, the student would then need to complete a separate international registration process on the NASBA website.
4. The applicant must make a commitment to seek CPA licensure upon passing the CPA Exam, and thereafter maintain their status as licensees.
5. Meet citizenship/residency requirements in the jurisdiction in which they are sitting for their exams.
6. Pay additional fees (see below).

*For more on how to apply to sit for the CPA Exam in your non-US country please visit nasba.org/international/international-exam/.

Additional Exam Fees for Testing Internationally

Subject	Additional Amount
Auditing and Attestation (AUD)	$ 356.55
Business Environment and Concepts (BEC)	$ 356.55
Financial Accounting and Reporting (FAR)	$ 356.55
Regulation (REG)	$ 356.55

Changes for the International Exam

Scores for international candidates will be released on the same timeline as domestic scores.

You cannot take your test internationally without a passport. This is most relevant for people living within a testing country or area – in which they must STILL have a passport to demonstrate citizenship and nationality.

Students who are not eligible to test within an approved country's jurisdiction, but are still international (non-US applicant), must report to the United States only and cannot go to a different country to test.

US State Boards that Accept International Applicant Test-takers			
Alaska	Indiana	Nevada	South Carolina
Arizona	Iowa	New Hampshire	South Dakota
Arkansas	Kansas	New Mexico	Tennessee
Colorado	Louisiana	New York	Texas
Connecticut	Maine	North Dakota	Utah
District of Columbia	Massachusetts	Ohio	Vermont
Florida	Michigan	Oklahoma	Virginia
Georgia	Minnesota	Oregon	Washington
Guam	Missouri	Pennsylvania	West Virginia
Hawaii	Montana	Puerto Rico	Wisconsin
Illinois	Nebraska	Rhode Island	Wyoming

TAKING THE EXAMINATION IN GUAM

Regardless of which Board of Accountancy has declared a candidate eligible for the examination, if the candidate intends to take their examination in Guam, they must pay an additional $140 surcharge for each examination section. Residents of Guam who are able to pay at the Guam Computer Testing Center, will incur a reduced surcharge fee of $70. All Guam test-takers must schedule their appointments by either of the following two options:

1. Visit **nasba.org/exams/cpaexam/guam/** on the Internet

NASBA operates the Guam computer testing center in cooperation with the Guam Board of Accountancy and Prometric. Before visiting this website, candidates should have an NTS and credit card readily available. Once at the website, candidates will be asked to provide information from their NTS and will pay the surcharge using a credit card. After paying the additional surcharge for each examination section, the candidate will need to wait at least 24 hours before scheduling an appointment following the instructions described above.

2. Call the Guam Computer Testing Center: 855-CPA-GUAM or 671-300-7441

The Guam computer testing center is open Monday through Friday from 7:00 a.m. to 4:00 p.m. Guam time. Have your NTS and credit card in front of you when you call. Candidates will be asked to provide information from their NTS and will pay the surcharge using a credit card. After paying the additional surcharge for each examination section, the candidate will need to wait at least 24 hours before scheduling an appointment following the instructions described above.

For Pre-approved Special Testing Accommodations, Call 1-800-967-1139

International Locations Accommodations Phone Numbers:
Japan 0120-34-7737
Latin America 1-443-751-4990
Middle East 31-320-239-530

DO NOT CALL ANY OF THESE NUMBERS UNLESS YOU HAVE BEEN PRE-APPROVED FOR SPECIAL TESTING ACCOMMODATIONS BY YOUR BOARD OF ACCOUNTANCY.

If the Board of Accountancy has approved a candidate for special testing accommodations, the information regarding the nature of the accommodation will be sent to NASBA. The type of accommodation will be shown on the candidate's NTS and will be sent to Prometric. Neither the candidate nor the customer service representative may make any changes to the accommodations that have been approved. A candidate requiring special testing accommodations should contact their Board of Accountancy before proceeding if they believe there are any errors on the NTS. If you call to take two or more sections, be prepared to identify the dates, times and locations for each section you wish to take. It is not necessary to make all appointments in one call. If you prefer, you may make one appointment at a time.

Before calling, the candidate must have an NTS and should have access to it during the call as they will be required to provide the customer service representative with various pieces of information from the NTS.

Candidates may visit prometric.com/cpa to confirm their appointment(s). If the candidate is not familiar with the test center location they should ask the customer service representative for directions while they are making the appointment over the phone. There are multiple test centers in some metropolitan areas, so it is important for candidates to be certain of the correct test center location where they are scheduled to take their examination(s).

CHANGES TO APPOINTMENTS

After making an appointment for an examination section, the candidate may find it necessary to change or cancel an appointment. Candidates should be aware that they may be required to pay a penalty or forfeit examination fees, depending on when they notify Prometric of the change or cancellation.

Change the Date, Time or Location of an Appointment

There are three methods to reschedule or change an existing exam appointment:

- Use Prometric's Web scheduling tool located at prometric.com/cpa. The system is available 24 hours a day, seven days a week.
- Call the Prometric Candidate Services Call Center at 1-800-580-9648. The Center is open Monday through Friday from 8:00 a.m. to 8:00 p.m. Eastern time.
- Call the local test center where your appointment is scheduled. If you need to reschedule your appointment, review the table below to determine deadlines and associated fees. Please note that Saturday is considered a business day.

If calling to change an exam date, time or location, the candidate must speak with a staff member and cannot leave a message to reschedule. Candidates testing with special testing accommodations should call 1-800-967-1139 to reschedule. Candidates using a teletypewriter (TTY) should call 1-800-529-3590.

Some types of accommodations are only available at a limited number of test centers. A candidate's Board of Accountancy will have already notified the candidate of this before sending an NTS to a candidate who has requested special accommodations.

Ineligibility

If a candidate's Board of Accountancy informs NASBA that they are no longer eligible to take the Uniform CPA Examination for any reason, the NTS will be cancelled. The candidate will receive a copy of a canceled NTS by United States mail, fax or e-mail, depending on the method identified as the candidate's preferred method for receipt of information.

If the candidate has NOT scheduled an appointment, they do not need to take any other action. If they have scheduled an appointment, NASBA will contact Prometric to cancel the appointment and rescind eligibility. In the event that a candidate is determined to be no longer eligible to take the examination by their Board of Accountancy, examination fees will NOT be refunded.

Refunds

Under most circumstances, NASBA **will not** refund section fees. Additional information on payment of section fees can be found on NASBA's Web site at *nasba.org*.

Test Center Closings

If severe weather or other local emergency requires a test center to be closed, every attempt will be made to contact candidates scheduled to sit for the exam on that day. If a candidate is unsure of whether or not the test center will be open on their exam day due to inclement weather or other unforeseeable circumstance, the candidate may call their test center directly. If the center is open, it is the candidate's responsibility to keep the appointment. If the center is closed, the candidate will be given the opportunity to reschedule without penalty. If unable to contact the local test center, the candidate may check on the Web at prometric.com/cpa, or call the Candidate Services Call Center at 1-800-580-9648, Monday through Friday, from 8:00 a.m. to 8:00 p.m. Eastern time.

Fees

Fees for the 2017 Exam are as follows:

Application/Qualification Fee paid	(Varies by State)
First time Qualifying and Sitting	Approx. $50-$200
Previously Qualified and Sat (Repeat)	Approx. $25-$75
Section Fees to be Paid Directly to NASBA	(Uniform)
Auditing and Attestation	$208.40
Financial Accounting and Reporting	$208.40
Regulation	$208.40
Business Environment and Concepts	$208.40
Total fees paid to NASBA for all four sections	$833.60

Credit Status

The Exam utilizes a "rolling" 18-month credit status system. This replaced the conditional credit system of the paper-and-pencil exam. Credit status is established by passing one section of the examination. Once a candidate passes a section of the examination, the candidate will be allowed a maximum of 18 months to pass all remaining sections in order to retain credit on the passed section. If the candidate does not pass all four sections within that 18-month period, the candidate will lose credit for the first section of the exam passed. A new 18-month period will commence with a start date of the next section that was passed. There are state boards that offer exceptions to the above-described 18-month credit status period but for the majority of jurisdictions the 18-month rolling period applies and begins from the date the candidate sits for their first passed exam.

TAKE YOUR EXAMINATION

Arrive Early

Candidates must arrive at the test center at least 30 minutes before the scheduled appointment time for their examination. This allows time to sign in, have a digital photograph taken, be fingerprinted, review the security and test center policies and be seated at the workstation. If a candidate arrives for their scheduled testing appointment any time after the scheduled start time, they may be denied permission to test and will not receive a refund. Therefore, candidates should be sure to arrive at least 30 minutes before their scheduled appointment time to avoid forfeiting all fees for the examination section.

YOU MUST BRING YOUR NOTICE TO SCHEDULE (NTS) WITH YOU

The NTS contains an "Examination Password" that will be entered on the computer before starting the exam as a part of the log-in process. It is important to bring the correct NTS to the testing center as it is possible for a candidate to have more than one active NTS at a time. A candidate will not be admitted into the test center without the correct NTS and will forfeit all examination fees for that section if denied entry for this reason.

Personal Identification

The Uniform CPA Examination employs very strict security measures. One level of security involves identification. **The same form of the candidate's name must appear on the candidate's application, NTS, and on the primary identification presented at the test center.** It is important for candidates to spell and present their names correctly during the application process to assure the correct information is reflected on their Notice to Schedule. If the candidate's name is different from identifications presented at check-in, the candidate will not be permitted to test. Candidates must present two forms of identification, one of which must contain a recent photograph, to test center staff before being allowed into the examination. Each form of identification must bear the candidate's signature and must not be expired. Candidates who do not present a valid ID will be barred entry to the exam and exam fees will not be refunded.

You must present *one* of the following primary forms of identification:
- A valid (not expired) state- or territory-issued driver's license with photograph and signature.
- A valid (not expired) state- or territory-issued identification card with a recent photograph and signature (Candidates who do not drive may have an identification card issued by the agency which also issues driver's licenses.)
- A valid (not expired) government-issued passport with a recent photograph and signature.
- A United States military identification card with a recent photograph and signature.

Your secondary form of identification may be one of the following (or another item from the list above):
- An identification card issued by your Board of Accountancy which includes the same name that appears on the NTS (if applicable to your jurisdiction)
- A valid (not expired) credit card
- A bank ATM card
- A debit card

The following are *UNACCEPTABLE* forms of identification:
- A draft classification card
- A Social Security card
- A student identification card
- A United States permanent residency card (green card)

The secondary form of identification **does not** have to match the information on a candidate's NTS exactly. For example, if a candidate's middle name is printed on their driver's license and NTS but not on an unexpired ATM/debit card, the driver's license may be used as primary identification while the debit card can serve as secondary identification without issue. It is important to keep this in mind when applying to the state board so that the candidate's name is printed correctly on the NTS.

If the test center staff have questions about the identification presented, the candidate may be asked for additional proof of identity and, if staff are unable to verify identity, the candidate may be refused admission to the exam and will forfeit the examination fee for that section. Admittance to the test center and examination does not imply that the identification presented is valid or that the candidate's scores will be reported if subsequent investigations reveal impersonation or forgery.

Fingerprint Requirement

All CPA Exam candidates are required to have a digital fingerprint taken at Prometric that is used as primary identification for subsequent exam appearances as well as for re-admission to the test center after a break.

Digital fingerprint images will be encrypted and stored electronically together with candidate identification information. Fingerprint images will also be used to detect any attempt to impersonate CPA candidates.

Fingerprinting will be required every time a candidate reports to the test center. In addition, candidates returning to test rooms after breaks will be asked to have their fingerprints taken again for comparison with the fingerprints captured at the beginning of the session. Candidates should keep this in mind if they choose to take breaks during the exam.

At the Test Center

The staff at each test center have been trained in the procedures specific to the Uniform CPA Examination. The staff are there to guide candidates through the guidelines that have been developed by the Boards of Accountancy, NASBA and the AICPA.

1. You must arrive at the test center at least 30 minutes before your scheduled appointment. If you arrive after your scheduled appointment time, you may forfeit your appointment and will not be eligible to have your examination fees refunded.

2. Your examination should begin within 30 minutes of the scheduled start time. If circumstances arise that delay your session more than 30 minutes, you will be given the choice of continuing to wait or rescheduling your appointment.

3. You must place personal belongings, such as a purse or cell phone, in the storage lockers provided by the test center. You will be given the key to your locker which must be returned to the test center staff when you leave. The lockers are very small and are not intended to hold large items. Do not bring anything to the test center unless it is absolutely necessary. Test center personnel will not be responsible for lost or stolen items.

4. You will submit a digital fingerprint that will be used for identification purposes for future Prometric visits or to verify your identity if you leave the testing room for any reason during the exam (like a break or to put your sweater in your locker). Keep your photo ID on you at all times as well but expect your fingerprint to be used as your primary identification within the testing center.

5. You will have a digital photograph taken of your face. (If the digital camera equipment is not working, a Polaroid picture will be taken.)

6. You will be required to sign the test center log book. Each time you exit and re-enter the testing room, you will be required to sign the log book and present your identification.

7. You will be escorted to a workstation by test center staff. You must remain in your seat during the examination, except when authorized to get up and leave the testing room. Except for a standard break at the halfway point of the Exam, any breaks taken (e.g. to use the restroom) will count against the clock.

8. Candidates will be provided with two double-sided, laminated, colored sheets called "noteboards," as well as a fine point marker for making notations. This has replaced the paper and pencil scratch paper provided in the past. You will be directed to write your examination Launch Code (from your NTS) on your noteboards. You will be required to return the noteboards to the test center staff when your exam is complete. If more writing space is required, you may request additional noteboards from the test center staff once you have turned in the original noteboards you received. You must not bring any paper or pencils to the workstation in the testing room.

9. Notify the test center staff if:
    a. You experience a problem with your computer
    b. An error message appears on the computer screen (do not clear the message)
    c. You need additional noteboards
    d. You need the test center staff for any other reason

10. When you finish the examination, leave the testing room quietly, turn in your noteboard and sign the test center log book. The test center staff will dismiss you after completing all necessary procedures.

Test Center Regulations

A standardized environment is necessary to ensure that candidates take equivalent but different exams. For this reason, all candidates must follow the same regulations.
- Papers, books, food or purses are not allowed in the testing room.
- Eating, drinking or use of tobacco is not allowed in the testing room.
- Talking or communicating with other candidates is not allowed in the testing room
- Calculators, tablets or other computer devices are not allowed in the testing room.
- Communication devices (e.g., cell phones, pagers, two-way radios, wireless internet connections to personal digital assistant devices) are not allowed in the testing room.
- Recording devices (audio and video) are not allowed in the testing room.
- You must not leave the testing room without the permission of the test center staff.
- You must be fingerprinted to re-enter the room after any breaks.

A complete list of prohibited items can be found on the AICPA website.

Breaks

Each examination section contains units known as testlets. Each testlet is comprised of either a group of multiple-choice questions or several task-based problems known as simulations. After each testlet, the candidate will be asked if he or she would like to take a non-standardized break (see below for information about the standardized break). Those who do choose a break must indicate in the software that they will take an optional break and will be asked to leave the testing room quietly and sign the test center log book. Test center staff will confirm that the candidate has completed a testlet before allowing a break. Remember: you do not have to take a break and the clock will keep running if you do (for a non-standardized break)! Therefore, it is recommended that you use break time wisely. Leaving the testing room at any time without exiting the testlet and selecting the break option will result in the candidate being barred from reentry into the testing room and information regarding the candidate's absence will be reported to their Board of Accountancy.

Exam candidates are given a standardized break after the third (of five) testlets. This standardized break is up to 15 minutes and does NOT count against the candidate's time in the Exam. **We recommend that you take this break** to refresh before continuing with the exam.

The standardized break will not count against a candidate's time on the exam, but any other break will count against the time on the exam.

Examination Confidentiality and Break Policy

All candidates must accept the terms of the confidentiality and break policy statement before beginning their examination. The statement must be accepted or the test will be terminated and any exam fees will be forfeited.

Candidate Misconduct, Cheating, Copyright Infringement

The Boards of Accountancy, NASBA and the AICPA take candidate misconduct, including cheating on the Uniform CPA Examination, very seriously. If a Board of Accountancy determines that a candidate is culpable of misconduct or has cheated, the candidate will be subject to a variety of penalties including, but not limited to: invalidation of grades, disqualification from subsequent examination administrations, and civil and criminal penalties. In cases where candidate misconduct or cheating is discovered after a candidate has obtained a CPA license or certificate, a Board of Accountancy may rescind the license or certificate. If the test center staff suspects misconduct, a warning will be given to the candidate for any of the following situations:

- Communicating, orally or otherwise, with another candidate or person
- Copying from or looking at another candidate's materials or workstation
- Allowing another candidate to copy from or look at materials or workstation
- Giving or receiving assistance in answering examination questions or problems
- Reading examination questions or simulations aloud
- Engaging in conduct that interferes with the administration of the examination or unnecessarily disturbing staff or other candidates
- Grounds for confiscation of a prohibited item and warning the candidate include: Possession of any prohibited item (whether or not in use) inside, or while entering or exiting the testing room. This includes use of any prohibited item during a break in a manner that could result in cheating or the removal of examination questions or simulations

Prohibited items include, but are not limited to:

- Books
- Briefcase
- Calculator/Computer
- Camera, Photographic or Scanning Device (still or video)
- Cellular Phone

- Cigarette/Tobacco Product
- Container of any kind
- Dictionary
- Earphones
- Electronic devices of any kind
- Eraser
- Eyeglass Case
- Food or Beverage
- Handbag/Backpack/Hip Pack
- Hat or Visor (except head coverings worn for religious reasons)
- Headset or Earphones (if not provided by Testing Center). You may bring soft, foam earplugs with no cords or wires attached for your use. TCAs will inspect the earplugs
- Jewelry – Pendant Necklace or Large Earrings
- Newspaper or Magazine
- Non-Prescription Sunglasses
- Notebook
- Notes in any written form
- Organizer / Day Planner
- Outline
- Pager / Beeper
- Paper (if not provided by Test Center)
- Pen / Pencil (if not provided by Test Center)
- Pencil Sharpener
- Plastic Bag
- Purse/Wallet
- Radio/Transmitter/Receiver
- Ruler/Slide Ruler
- Study Material
- Tape/Disk Recorder or Player
- Umbrella
- Watch
- Wearable technology
- Weapon of any kind

In addition, jackets, coats, and sweaters are also prohibited; however, if you require a separate sweater or a jacket due to room temperature, it must be worn at all times.

The Boards of Accountancy, NASBA, the AICPA and Prometric use a variety of procedures to prevent candidate misconduct and cheating on the examination. Test center staff are trained to watch for unusual behavior and incidents during the examination. In addition, all examination sessions are audio/videotaped to document the occurrence of any unusual activity and candidate misconduct is reported to Boards of Accountancy on a daily basis.

All examination materials are owned and copyrighted by the AICPA. Any reproduction and/or distribution of examination materials, including memorization, without the express written authorization of the AICPA, is prohibited. This behavior infringes on the legal rights of the AICPA and, in addition to the penalties listed above, the AICPA will take appropriate legal action when any copyright infringements have occurred.

Please see the AICPA's website at _aicpa.org_ for a complete list of prohibited items and current information on examination policies.

Grounds for Dismissal

Test center staff may dismiss candidates from the examination or may have scores canceled by the candidate's Board of Accountancy for engaging in misconduct or not following the test center regulations. The following are examples of behavior that will not be tolerated during the examination:

- Repeating acts of misconduct after receiving prior warning(s)
- Attempting to remove or removing examination questions from the testing room by any means
- Copying, writing or summarizing examination questions on any material other than the noteboards issued to you
- Tampering with computer software or hardware, or attempting to use a computer for any reason other than completing the examination session
- Intentional refusal or failure to comply with instructions of the test center staff
- Attempting to have an impersonator gain admission to the testing room or to substitute for you after a break
- Conduct that may threaten bodily harm or damage to property

RECEIVE YOUR SCORE(S)

Generally, Boards of Accountancy will report scores on a numeric scale of 0-99, with 75 as a passing score. This scale does NOT represent "percent correct." A score of 75 reflects examination performance that represents the knowledge and skills needed to protect the public. A few Boards of Accountancy have elected to report a pass or fail status instead of numeric scores. All questions contained in the examination, including BEC written communication task-based simulations, are formatted to allow responses to be scored electronically. Human graders score selected written communication responses. Candidates receive points for each correct answer to a multiple-choice question.

Similarly, responses to the questions asked in the simulations receive points based on correct answers or correct completion of the presented task. Points are not subtracted for incorrect responses. The points are accumulated according to the relative contributions of each question, which are weighted (see the Uniform CPA Examination Blueprints and skills definition documents for specific content areas and weights, or go to aicpa.org). Overall scores are then adjusted to ensure scores for all candidates (even those who test in different administrations with different examinations) are comparable and equivalent.

When You Should Expect Your Scores

The AICPA sends candidate scores to NASBA. The AICPA will release scores for the exams taken in a window on a specific target date according to the schedule below. However, distribution of scores to the exam takers is the responsibility of the Boards of Accountancy. Each Board of Accountancy sets its own schedule regarding the frequency with which it will approve and release scores.

The AICPA target dates are not guaranteed and may be pushed back due to unforeseen issues. Additionally, BEC scores may be subject to longer delays due to the scoring of Written Communication. Candidates who do not receive their scores should call NASBA at 866-MY-NASBA.

Day of Exam in Testing Window*	Target Release Date Timeline
Day 1-20	11 business days following day 20 of the testing window
Day 21-45	6 business days following day 45 of the testing window
Day 46-Close of Window	6 business days following the close of the testing window
After Close of Window	6 business days after receiving all scoring data for the window

*date the records are received by the AICPA

The Score Review and Appeal Processes

Score Review

Score Review is an independent verification of a candidate's Uniform CPA Examination score, and NOT a re-grading or reconsideration of the candidate's responses on the examination. Because all scores undergo several quality control checks before they are reported, the likelihood of a score change following score review is exceedingly small, **or less than 1%** of all requested score reviews since the inception of the computer-based test. However, the score review option is available to candidates who would like to have their scores checked one more time. Fees apply.

Appeals

If allowed in a candidate's jurisdiction, an option to appeal a failing score may exist. This option enables the candidate to view the questions that he or she answered incorrectly as well as their responses. Such viewing takes place only in an authorized location, under secure conditions, and in the presence of a representative of the candidate's Board of Accountancy. In order to qualify for a score appeal, the candidate must submit a formal request to their Board of Accountancy within 30 days of the date printed on the score report, obtain the Board of Accountancy's approval, and pay the required fee. Contact your Board of Accountancy for specific instructions on the score appeal process. If a candidate is allowed a score appeal, they will be given the opportunity to view the questions they answered incorrectly as well as their responses to those questions. The AICPA will respond to any comments made by the candidate, rescore appealed responses and forward the results to NASBA. NASBA will then forward the scores to the candidate's Board of Accountancy.

RETAKING THE EXAMINATION

Candidates who fail any section of the CPA Exam may retake that section in a future testing window but are not allowed to repeat a failed section within the same two-month testing window. Information on how to retake a failed examination section will be sent to the candidate from their Board of Accountancy with a score report detailing the candidate's performance in each area of that particular exam section. This information may be helpful when preparing to retake any examination sections or in planning for near-term continuing professional education needs. For any questions on retake policies and fees, contact your Board of Accountancy.

ETHICS EXAM

Some jurisdictions require CPA Exam candidates to successfully complete an ethics examination as a requirement of CPA licensure, generally after the candidate has passed all four sections of the exam. The ethics portion is either administered through the AICPA or through continuing education (CPE) provided by your state society of CPAs. Check with your state board for more information on ethics requirements for your jurisdiction.

The CPA Exam

STRUCTURE

The Uniform CPA Examination spans 16 hours and consists of four separate exam parts.

The Uniform CPA Exam
Auditing & Attestation (AUD - 4 hours)
Financial Accounting & Reporting (FAR - 4 hours)
Regulation (REG - 4 hours)
Business Environment & Concepts (BEC - 4 hours)

Examination Content

The content areas for each exam part, along with skills tested, are outlined in the Uniform CPA Examination Blueprints published by the AICPA. For more information about the examination blueprints, visit aicpa.org and choose the "Become a CPA" tab.

Uniform CPA Examination Blueprints

Starting with the 2017 exam the AICPA introduced a set of Uniform CPA Examination Blueprints, which document the minimum level of knowledge and skills needed for initial licensure in content areas and in representative tasks. The blueprints are organized by content AREA, content GROUP, and content TOPIC. Each topic includes one or more representative TASK(s) that a newly licensed CPA may be expected to complete. Each representative task is linked to a SKILL tested in the exam.

Skills are based on Bloom's Taxonomy of Educational Objectives. Critical thinking skills range from the lowest level (Remembering and Understanding) to the highest level (Evaluation), as summarized in the following table.

Skill Levels (beginning with the highest)	
Evaluation	The examination or assessment of problems and use of judgment to draw conclusions.
Analysis	The examination and study of the interrelationships of separate areas in order to identify causes and find evidence to support inferences.
Application	The use or demonstration of knowledge, concepts or techniques.
Remembering and Understanding	The perception and comprehension of the significance of an area utilizing knowledge gained.

The AICPA conducted a Practice Analysis from 2014 to 2015 in which one main finding was clear: firms expect newly licensed CPAs on their staff to perform at a higher level. The AICPA raised the bar with the revamped 2017 CPA Exam that more authentically tests candidates on the tasks and skill levels that will be required of them as newly licensed CPAs.

Types of Questions

Your score on each exam part is determined by the sum of points assigned to individual questions and simulation parts. Thus, you must attempt to maximize your points on each individual item. To familiarize yourself with the examination's format, functions, and question and response types, review the examination tutorial at aicpa.org. A sample test that contains a few sample multiple-choice questions and simulations for each applicable section is currently available. Neither the tutorial nor the sample test will be available at the test centers and candidates are encouraged to familiarize themselves with the test format prior to taking their first examination.

Multiple Choice Questions

A format is considered objective when it can be graded without subjectivity. Grading objective examinations is a mechanical process that requires little judgment. Any format that can be graded by machine is generally considered objective. Objective formats result in very consistent scores because the acceptability of particular responses is determined before grading begins. The most widely used objective format is multiple-choice (i.e., 4-option questions) because it has a restricted set of alternatives from which the correct answer must be selected. Multiple-choice questions (MCQs) make up 50% of FAR, AUD, REG and BEC.

The multiple-choice questions within each exam part are organized into two groups which are referred to as testlets. The first two testlets of each exam section will contain 31-38 multiple-choice questions per testlet, which are together worth up 50 percent of the exam part. The multiple-choice testlets vary in overall difficulty. A testlet is labeled either 'moderate' or 'difficult' based on its makeup. The questions in a 'difficult' testlet have a higher average level of difficulty than those in a 'moderate' testlet; however, questions of higher difficulty carry a higher point percentage rate therefore fewer must be answered correctly to pass. Every candidate's first multiple-choice testlet in each section will be a 'moderate' testlet. If a candidate scores well on the first testlet, he or she will receive a 'difficult' second testlet. Candidates that do not perform well on the first testlet receive a second 'moderate' testlet. Because the scoring procedure takes the difficulty of the testlet into account, candidates are scored fairly regardless of the type of testlets they receive.

Each multiple-choice testlet contains "operational" and "pretest" questions. The operational questions are the only ones that are used to determine your score. Pretest questions are not scored; they are being tested for future use as operational questions. However, you have no way of knowing which questions are operational and which questions are pretest questions. Therefore, you must approach each question as if it will be used to determine your grade. Of the multiple-choice questions, there are 72 operational and 12 pretest questions in the AUD exam, 66 operational and 11 pretest questions in the FAR exam, 76 operational and 12 pretest questions in the REG exam, and 62 operational and 10 pretest questions in the BEC exam.

Task-Based Simulations

Task-based simulations (TBSs) make up 50% of the FAR, AUD, and REG exams, but only 35% of the BEC exam (with written communications problems taking up the remaining 15%). Each operational TBS in the FAR, AUD, and REG exams is worth approximately 7.1% of the exam score. Each operational TBS in the BEC exam is worth approximately 11.7% of the exam score. The FAR, AUD, and REG sections of the exam each contain 8 task-based simulations. The BEC section includes 4 simulation problems as well as 3 written communication problems, of which 2 are graded. Each of these 2 graded written communications problems is worth approximately 7.5% of the exam score. The actual percentage of total score assigned to each requirement will vary according to its difficulty. Each TBS should be allotted about 10 to 20 minutes to complete, depending on difficulty. Candidates will be required to demonstrate their ability to apply certain skills (application, analysis, or evaluation) in each part of the CPA Exam using task-based simulations. These skills will be tested in a variety of methods such as simulation, or relational case studies, which will test candidates' knowledge and skills using work-related situations. Simulations will require candidates to have basic computer skills, knowledge of common spreadsheet and word processing functions, the ability to use a financial calculator or a spreadsheet to perform standard financial calculations, and the ability to use electronic tools such as databases for research. Therefore, you need to become proficient in the use of these tools to maximize your score on the task-based simulation component of each applicable exam section.

In the exam software, TBSs are often accompanied by exhibits containing documents and sources for the user's reference during the exam. All exhibits are arranged above the problem. When opened, they appear on the right side of the screen, where they can be moved and organized for optimal viewing. Up to eight exhibits can be open at one time. To watch a video prepared by the AICPA giving an orientation to this functionality, go to:

https://www.aicpa.org/becomeacpa/cpaexam/forcandidates/tutorialandsampletest.html.

Document Review Simulations

Document Review Simulation, or DRSs, are designed to simulate tasks that the candidate will be required to perform as a newly licensed CPA (based on up to two years' experience as a CPA). Each DRS presents a document that has a series of highlighted phrases or sentences that the candidate will need to determine are correct or incorrect. To help make these conclusions, numerous supporting documents, or exhibits, such as legal letters, phone transcripts, financial statements, trial balances and authoritative literature will be included. The candidate will need to sort through these documents to determine what is, and what is not, important to solving the problem. Please see the Appendix at the end of this book for more information about DRSs.

Written Communication – BEC

Written communication will be assessed through the use of responses to essay questions, which will be based upon the content topics as outlined in the Blueprints. Candidates will have access to a word processor, which includes a cut-copy-paste feature. Candidates are encouraged to use the "Help" tab for more information on the word processor functionality as it is similar to but not exactly like popular word processor programs the candidate may already be familiar with.

Research Task Format

FAR, AUD and REG will each contain at least one research problem. If a candidate's exam contains two research problems, it is likely that one of them is a problem being pre-tested.

Candidates will be asked to search through the database to find an appropriate reference that addresses the issue presented in the research problem. A scenario is presented in which the candidate must find his or her answer in the authoritative literature using a pre-determined list of codes (such as Professional Standards or federal taxation code). The candidate will choose the appropriate code title from the drop-down list and then enter a specific reference number applicable to their given scenario.

Authoritative literature for each section appears as follows:

FAR: Candidates will search the FASB ASC (Accounting Standards Codification) for their responses; this section does not have a dropdown menu to select from.

REG: IRC - Internal Revenue Code

AUD: AU-C - Clarified U.S. Auditing Standards
PCAOB – AS - PCAOB Auditing Standards
AT-C - Attestation Services
AR-C - Statements on Standards for Accounting and Review Services
ET - Code of Professional Conduct
BL - Bylaws
VS - Statements on Standards for Valuation Services
CS - Statement on Standards for Consulting Services
PFP - Personal Financial Planning
CPE - Continuing Professional Education
TS – Tax Services
PR – Peer Review Standards
QC - Quality Control

For example, a candidate may be asked the following question:

> A client has entered into an interest rate swap and just learned that it is considered a derivative. The cost was negligible and the entity is trying to determine at what amount to report it on its balance sheet. Identify the location in professional standards that indicates how derivatives should initially be measured.

Using the Authoritative Literature icon at the top of the screen, the candidate will search for keywords associated with the question using the search box, which will pull up all references within the literature to those keywords. From there, the candidate should use the "search within" function to find specific instances of keywords within each subsection. Keywords will be highlighted in the text and the candidate can go through them to find the relevant text that answers the research problem.

In this case, a search for "derivative" and a more detailed search within all references to that topic using the *search within* button would likely bring up FASB ASC 815-10-30-1, which reads:

> All derivative instruments shall be measured initially at fair value.

Using the provided drop-down menu, the candidate would then select the appropriate literature reference from the list (in this case, FASB codification) and enter the codification numbers in the blank boxes. It will look something like this:

> A client has entered into an interest rate swap and just learned that it is considered a derivative. The cost was negligible and the entity is trying to determine at what amount to report it on its balance sheet. Identify the location in professional standards that indicates how derivatives should initially be measured.

Enter your response in the answer fields below.

FASB ASC	815	10	30	1

Research questions will also alert the candidate if they have correctly formatted their answer by displaying a message like "Examples of correctly formatted sections are shown below" or "A correctly formatted IRC subsection is a lower case letter" in a box above the candidate response.

To master research type questions, you can either practice at the below NASBA website, or you can use the Interactive Practice Questions software included in your course.

CPA Exam Candidates: Free Online Access to Professional Literature Package

CPA Exam candidates can get a free six-month subscription to professional literature used in the CPA Examination. This online package includes AICPA Professional Standards, FASB Current Text and FASB Original Pronouncements. Only candidates who have applied to take the CPA Exam and have been deemed eligible by state boards of accountancy will receive access to this package of professional literature. NASBA will verify that a candidate has a valid NTS (Notice to Schedule). A candidate must be in receipt of a valid NTS prior to receiving authorization to the professional literature.

To subscribe visit: https://nasba.org/proflit/

Another good source for Researching Tax Codes for the **Regulation Exam**:

https://www.irs.gov/tax-professionals/tax-code-regulations-and-official-guidance

Testlets

Each section of the exam is presented in 5 testlets. The first 2 testlets contain multiple-choice questions (MCQs) and the last 3 testlets contain task-based simulations. (In the BEC exam, 2 of the last 3 testlets contain task-based simulations and 1 contains written communication problems.) Candidates can go back and forth between different questions within a testlet but cannot go back to previous testlets or review their questions once they have submitted their exam as complete.

Additional facts about the Exam

- You may take 1 part at a time.
- Results are released at various times throughout the exam window.
- In most jurisdictions, candidates must pass all four parts of the Uniform CPA Examination within a "rolling" eighteen-month period, which begins on the date that the first section(s) passed is taken.
- Generally, any credit for any exam part(s) passed outside the eighteen-month period will expire and that section(s) must be retaken.
- Candidates will not be allowed to retake a failed exam part(s) within the same quarter (examination window)
- Candidates will take different, equivalent exams.

Effective Date of Pronouncements (AICPA, 11/12/2015)

Accounting and auditing pronouncements are eligible to be tested on the Uniform CPA Examination in the later of: (1) the first testing window beginning after the pronouncement's earliest mandatory effective date or (2) the first testing window beginning six (6) months after the pronouncement's issuance date. In either case, there is a simultaneous introduction of content related to the new pronouncement and removal of content related to the previous pronouncement.

For the federal taxation area, the Internal Revenue Code and federal tax regulations in effect six months after the enactment date or the change's effective date, whichever is later, are eligible for testing.

For all other subjects covered in the Regulation (REG) and Business Environment and Concepts (BEC) sections, materials eligible to be tested include federal laws in the window beginning six months after their effective date, and uniform acts in the window beginning one year after their adoption by a simple majority of the jurisdictions.

Lecture 0.02 – BEC Introduction

Business Environment and Concepts – 4 Hours

Content Allocation

The content areas tested in the BEC exam, as well as the weight given to each content area, are summarized in the following table.

Content Area		Weight
Area I	Corporate Governance	17-27%
Area II	Economic Concepts and Analysis	17-27%
Area III	Financial Management	11-21%
Area IV	Information Technology	15-25%
Area V	Operations Management	15-25%

Skill Allocation

The skills tested in the BEC exam, as well as the weight given to each skill, are summarized in the following table.

Skill	Weight
Evaluation	-
Analysis	20-30%
Application	50-60%
Remembering and Understanding	15-25%

Remembering and Understanding is tested in all five areas of the BEC section. Remembering and understanding tasks focus on the knowledge necessary to demonstrate an understanding of the general business environment and business concepts, such as those involving enterprise risk management.

Application is also tested in all five areas of the BEC section. Application tasks focus on general topics such as those found in the subjects of economics and information technology, and the day-to-day financial management tasks that newly licensed CPAs perform, such as those involving calculations involving ratios, valuation and budgeting.

Analysis skills, tested in Areas II, III and V involve tasks that require a higher level of analysis and interpretation. These tasks, such as comparing investment alternatives using calculations of financial metrics, financial modeling, forecasting and projection, frequently require newly licensed CPAs to gather evidence to support inferences.

The representative tasks combine both the applicable content knowledge and the skills required in the context of the work that a newly licensed CPA would reasonably be expected to perform. The BEC section does not test any content at the Evaluation skill level as newly licensed CPAs are not expected to demonstrate that level of skill in regards to the BEC content.

Exam Structure and Time Allocation

There are five testlets in each section of the exam. The number of MCQs and TBSs in each testlet is shown below along with recommendations from Roger CPA Review for the amount of time you should devote to each testlet.

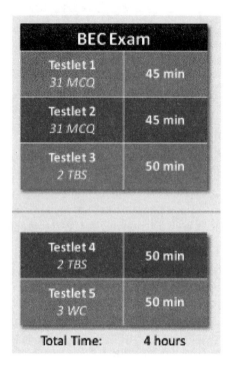

Things to consider:
- o   Allocate 75 seconds per multiple choice question
- o   Allocate 10 - 15 minutes for each written communication question
- o   Allocate 15-25 minutes for each task-based simulation, depending on complexity
- o   Plan to use no more than 10 minutes per research question (none in BEC)
- o   Take the standard 15-minute break after the 3rd testlet – it doesn't count against your time.

Uniform CPA Examination Blueprints
Effective January 1, 2019

BUSINESS ENVIRONMENT & CONCEPTS (BEC)

The AICPA gives candidates clear guidelines for the knowledge and skills that are tested on the CPA Exam. In the following excerpt we point to the most important information published by the AICPA describing the Exam sections.

The Business Environment and Concepts (BEC) exam tests knowledge and skills that a newly licensed CPA must demonstrate when performing:
- Audit, attest, accounting and review services
- Financial reporting
- Tax preparation
- Other professional responsibilities in their role as certified public accountants.

The content areas tested under the BEC exam encompass five diverse subject areas. These content areas are corporate governance, economic concepts and analysis, financial management, information technology, and operations management.

Area I of the BEC exam blueprint covers several topics related to Corporate Governance, including the following:
- Knowledge of the purpose and objectives of internal control frameworks and enterprise risk management frameworks
- Identifying the components and principles of internal control frameworks and enterprise risk management frameworks.
- Identifying key corporate governance provisions of the Sarbanes-Oxley Act of 2002

Area II of the BEC exam blueprint covers several topics related to Economic Concepts and Analysis, including the following:
- Knowledge of economic concepts and analysis that would demonstrate an understanding of the impact of business cycles on an entity's industry or business operation
- Determining market influences on the business environment, such as globalization
- Determining the business reasons for and the underlying economic substance of transactions and their accounting implications
- Understanding financial risks and the methods for mitigating the impact of these risks

Area III of the BEC exam blueprint covers several topics related to Financial Management, including the following:
- Assessing the factors influencing a company's capital structure, such as risk, leverage, cost of capital, growth rate, profitability, asset structure, and loan covenants
- Calculating metrics associated with the components of working capital, such as current ratio, quick ratio, cash conversion cycle, turnover ratios
- Determining the impact of business decisions on working capital
- Understanding commonly used financial valuation and decision models and applying that knowledge to assess assumptions, calculate the value of assets, and compare investment alternatives

Area IV of the BEC exam blueprint covers several topics related to Information Technology, including the following:

- Understanding the governance of the information technology operations of a business
- Identifying information systems that are used to process and accumulate data as well as provide monitoring and financial reporting information
- Determining whether there is appropriate segregation of duties, authorization levels, and data security in an organization to maintain an appropriate internal control structure
- Identifying business and operational risks inherent in an entity's disaster recovery/ business continuity plan

Area V of the BEC exam blueprint covers several topics related to Operations Management, including the following:

- Understanding business operations and use of quality control initiatives and performance measures to improve operations
- Application of cost accounting concepts and use of variance analysis techniques
- Utilizing budgeting and forecasting techniques to monitor progress and enhance accountability

References – Business Environment and Concepts

The Committee of Sponsoring Organizations of the Treadway Commission (COSO):

- Internal Control – Integrated Framework
- Enterprise Risk Management – Integrated Framework

Sarbanes-Oxley Act of 2002:

- Title III, Corporate Responsibility
- Title IV, Enhanced Financial Disclosures
- Title VIII, Corporate and Criminal Fraud Accountability
- Title IX, White-Collar Crime Penalty Enhancements
- Title XI, Corporate Fraud Accountability

Current Business Periodicals

Current Textbooks on:

- Accounting Information Systems
- Budgeting and Measurement
- Corporate Governance
- Economics
- Enterprise Risk Management
- Finance
- Management
- Management Information Systems
- Managerial Accounting
- Production Operations

Business Environment and Concepts

Area I - Corporate Governance
(17-27%)

Content group/topic	Skill				Representative task
	Remembering and Understanding	Application	Analysis	Evaluation	
A. Internal control frameworks					
1. Purpose and objectives	✓				Define internal control within the context of the COSO internal control framework, including the purpose, objectives and limitations of the framework.
2. Components and principles	✓				Identify and define the components, principles and underlying structure of the COSO internal control framework.
		✓			Apply the COSO internal control framework to identify entity and transaction level risks (inherent and residual) related to an organization's compliance, operations and reporting (internal and external, financial and non-financial) objectives.
		✓			Apply the COSO internal control framework to identify risks related to fraudulent financial and non-financial reporting, misappropriation of assets and illegal acts, including the risk of management override of controls.
		✓			Apply the COSO internal control framework to identify controls to meet an entity's compliance, operations and reporting (internal and external, financial and non-financial) objectives, throughout an entity's structure, from entity-wide through sub-units, down to the transactional level.
		✓			Apply the COSO internal control framework to identify an appropriate mix of automated and manual application controls, (e.g., authorization and approval, verifications, physical controls, controls over standing data, reconciliations and supervisory controls) to prevent and detect errors in transactions.
		✓			Describe the corporate governance structure within an organization (tone at the top, policies, steering committees, oversight, ethics, etc.).

Business Environment and Concepts

Area I - Corporate Governance
(17-27%) (continued)

Content group/topic	Skill				Representative task
	Remembering and Understanding	Application	Analysis	Evaluation	
B. Enterprise risk management (ERM) frameworks					
1. Purpose and objectives	✓				Define ERM within the context of the COSO ERM framework, including the purpose and objectives of the framework.
2. Components and principles	✓				Identify and define the components, principles and underlying structure of the COSO ERM framework.
	✓				Understand the relationship among risk, business strategy and performance within the context of the COSO ERM framework.
		✓			Apply the COSO ERM framework to identify risk/opportunity scenarios in an entity.
C. Other regulatory frameworks and provisions					
	✓				Identify and define key corporate governance provisions of the Sarbanes-Oxley Act of 2002 and other regulatory pronouncements.
		✓			Identify regulatory deficiencies within an entity by using the requirements associated with the Sarbanes-Oxley Act of 2002.

Business Environment and Concepts

Area II - Economic Concepts and Analysis (17-27%)

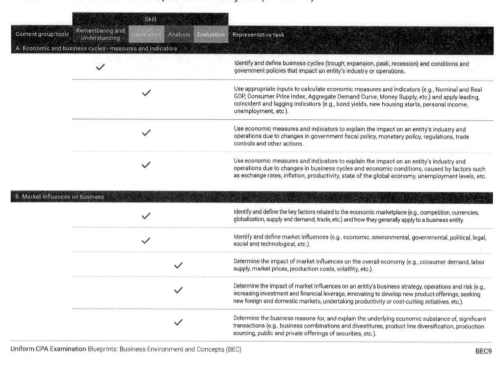

Content group/topic	Remembering and Understanding	Application	Analysis	Evaluation	Representative task
A. Economic and business cycles - measures and indicators					
	✓				Identify and define business cycles (trough, expansion, peak, recession) and conditions and government policies that impact an entity's industry or operations.
		✓			Use appropriate inputs to calculate economic measures and indicators (e.g., Nominal and Real GDP, Consumer Price Index, Aggregate Demand Curve, Money Supply, etc.) and apply leading, coincident and lagging indicators (e.g., bond yields, new housing starts, personal income, unemployment, etc.).
		✓			Use economic measures and indicators to explain the impact on an entity's industry and operations due to changes in government fiscal policy, monetary policy, regulations, trade controls and other actions.
		✓			Use economic measures and indicators to explain the impact on an entity's industry and operations due to changes in business cycles and economic conditions, caused by factors such as exchange rates, inflation, productivity, state of the global economy, unemployment levels, etc.
B. Market influences on business					
		✓			Identify and define the key factors related to the economic marketplace (e.g., competition, currencies, globalization, supply and demand, trade, etc.) and how they generally apply to a business entity.
		✓			Identify and define market influences (e.g., economic, environmental, governmental, political, legal, social and technological, etc.).
			✓		Determine the impact of market influences on the overall economy (e.g., consumer demand, labor supply, market prices, production costs, volatility, etc.).
			✓		Determine the impact of market influences on an entity's business strategy, operations and risk (e.g., increasing investment and financial leverage, innovating to develop new product offerings, seeking new foreign and domestic markets, undertaking productivity or cost-cutting initiatives, etc.).
			✓		Determine the business reasons for, and explain the underlying economic substance of, significant transactions (e.g., business combinations and divestitures, product line diversification, production sourcing, public and private offerings of securities, etc.).

Uniform CPA Examination Blueprints: Business Environment and Concepts (BEC) BEC9

Business Environment and Concepts

Area II - Economic Concepts and Analysis
(17-27%) (continued)

Content group/topic	Remembering and Understanding	Application	Analysis	Evaluation	Representative task
C. Financial risk management					
1. Market, interest rate, currency, liquidity, credit, price and other risks		✓			Calculate and use ratios and measures to quantify risks associated with interest rates, currency exchange, liquidity, prices, etc. in a business entity.
2. Means for mitigating/controlling financial risks		✓			Identify strategies to mitigate financial risks (market, interest rate, currency, liquidity, etc.) and quantify their impact on a business entity.

Uniform CPA Examination Blueprints: Business Environment and Concepts (BEC) BEC10

Area III - Financial Management
(11-21%)

Content group/topic	Remembering and Understanding	Skill: Application	Analysis	Evaluation	Representative task
A. Capital structure					
	✓				Describe an organization's capital structure and related concepts, such as cost of capital, asset structure, loan covenants, growth rate, profitability, leverage and risk.
	✓				Calculate the cost of capital for a given financial scenario.
			✓		Compare and contrast the strategies for financing new business initiatives and operations within the context of an optimal capital structure, using statistical analysis where appropriate.
B. Working capital					
1. Fundamentals and key metrics of working capital management	✓				Calculate the metrics associated with the working capital components, such as current ratio, quick ratio, cash conversion cycle, inventory turnover and receivables turnover.
			✓		Detect significant fluctuations or variances in the working capital cycle using working capital ratio analyses.
2. Strategies for managing working capital			✓		Compare inventory management processes, including pricing and valuation methods, to determine the effects on the working capital of a given entity.
			✓		Compare accounts payable management techniques, including usage of discounts, factors affecting discount policy, uses of electronic funds transfer as a payment method and determination of an optimal vendor payment schedule in order to determine the effects on the working capital of a given entity.
			✓		Distinguish between corporate banking arrangements, including establishment of lines of credit, borrowing capacity and monitoring of compliance with debt covenants in order to determine the effects on the working capital of a given entity.
			✓		Interpret the differences between the business risks and the opportunities in an entity's credit management policies to determine the effects on the working capital of a given entity.
			✓		Analyze the effects on working capital caused by financing using long-term debt and/or short-term debt.

Uniform CPA Examination Blueprints: Business Environment and Concepts (BEC)   BEC11

Area III - Financial Management
(11-21%) (continued)

Content group/topic	Remembering and Understanding	Skill: Application	Analysis	Evaluation	Representative task
C. Financial valuation methods and decision models					
	✓				Identify and define the different financial valuation methods and their assumptions, including but not limited to fair value, Black-Scholes, Capital Asset Pricing Model and Dividend Discount Model.
	✓				Identify and define the different financial decision models and assumptions involved in making decisions relating to asset and investment management, debt, equity and leasing.
	✓				Identify the sources of data and factors that management considers in forming the assumptions used to prepare an accounting estimate.
	✓				Describe the process and framework within which management exercises its responsibilities over the review and approval of accounting estimates.
		✓			Calculate the value of an asset using commonly accepted financial valuation methods.
			✓		Compare investment alternatives using calculations of financial metrics (payback period, net-present value, economic value added, cash flow analysis, internal rate of return etc.), financial modeling, forecasting, projection and analysis techniques.
			✓		Compare options in a lease vs. buy decision scenario.

Uniform CPA Examination Blueprints: Business Environment and Concepts (BEC)   BEC12

Business Environment and Concepts

Area IV - Information Technology
(15-25%)

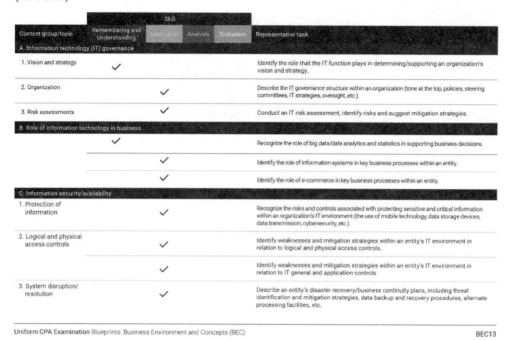

Content group/topic	Remembering and Understanding	Application	Analysis	Evaluation	Representative task
A. Information technology (IT) governance					
1. Vision and strategy	✓				Identify the role that the IT function plays in determining/supporting an organization's vision and strategy.
2. Organization		✓			Describe the IT governance structure within an organization (tone at the top, policies, steering committees, IT strategies, oversight, etc.).
3. Risk assessments		✓			Conduct an IT risk assessment, identify risks and suggest mitigation strategies.
B. Role of information technology in business					
	✓				Recognize the role of big data/data analytics and statistics in supporting business decisions.
		✓			Identify the role of information systems in key business processes within an entity.
		✓			Identify the role of e-commerce in key business processes within an entity.
C. Information security/availability					
1. Protection of information		✓			Recognize the risks and controls associated with protecting sensitive and critical information within an organization's IT environment (the use of mobile technology, data storage devices, data transmission, cybersecurity, etc.).
2. Logical and physical access controls		✓			Identify weaknesses and mitigation strategies within an entity's IT environment in relation to logical and physical access controls.
		✓			Identify weaknesses and mitigation strategies within an entity's IT environment in relation to IT general and application controls.
3. System disruption/resolution		✓			Describe an entity's disaster recovery/business continuity plans, including threat identification and mitigation strategies, data backup and recovery procedures, alternate processing facilities, etc.

Uniform CPA Examination Blueprints: Business Environment and Concepts (BEC)

BEC13

Business Environment and Concepts

Area IV - Information Technology
(15-25%) (continued)

Content group/topic	Remembering and Understanding	Application	Analysis	Evaluation	Representative task
D. Processing integrity (input/processing/output controls)					
		✓			Describe the role of input, processing and output controls within an entity to support completeness, accuracy and continued processing integrity.
		✓			Determine the appropriateness of the design and operating effectiveness of application controls (authorizations, approvals, tolerance levels, input edits, etc.).
		✓			Identify issues related to the design and effectiveness of IT control activities, including manual vs. automated controls, as well as preventive, detective and corrective controls.
E. Systems development and maintenance					
	✓				Identify different information system testing strategies.
		✓			Recognize the fundamental issues and risks associated with implementing new information systems or maintaining existing information systems within an entity.

Uniform CPA Examination Blueprints: Business Environment and Concepts (BEC)

BEC14

Business Environment and Concepts

Area V - Operations Management
(15-25%)

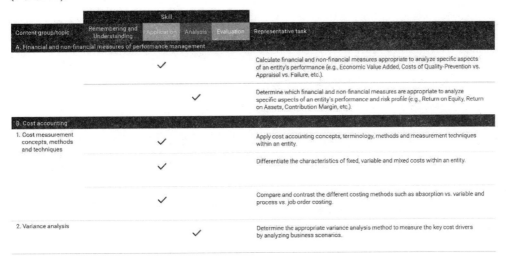

Content group/topic	Remembering and Understanding	Application	Analysis	Evaluation	Representative task
A. Financial and non-financial measures of performance management					
		✓			Calculate financial and non-financial measures appropriate to analyze specific aspects of an entity's performance (e.g., Economic Value Added, Costs of Quality-Prevention vs. Appraisal vs. Failure, etc.).
			✓		Determine which financial and non-financial measures are appropriate to analyze specific aspects of an entity's performance and risk profile (e.g., Return on Equity, Return on Assets, Contribution Margin, etc.).
B. Cost accounting					
1. Cost measurement concepts, methods and techniques		✓			Apply cost accounting concepts, terminology, methods and measurement techniques within an entity.
		✓			Differentiate the characteristics of fixed, variable and mixed costs within an entity.
		✓			Compare and contrast the different costing methods such as absorption vs. variable and process vs. job order costing.
2. Variance analysis			✓		Determine the appropriate variance analysis method to measure the key cost drivers by analyzing business scenarios.

Uniform CPA Examination Blueprints: Business Environment and Concepts (BEC)   BEC15

Business Environment and Concepts

Area V - Operations Management
(15-25%) (continued)

Content group/topic	Remembering and Understanding	Application	Analysis	Evaluation	Representative task
C. Process management					
1. Approaches, techniques, measures, benefits to process-management driven businesses	✓				Identify commonly used operational management approaches, techniques and measures within the context of business process management.
2. Management philosophies and techniques for performance improvement	✓				Identify commonly used management philosophies and techniques for performance and quality improvement within the context of business process management.
D. Planning techniques					
1. Budgeting and analysis		✓			Prepare a budget to guide business decisions.
			✓		Reconcile results against a budget or prior periods and perform analysis of variances as needed.
2. Forecasting and projection		✓			Use forecasting and projection techniques to model revenue growth, cost and expense characteristics, profitability, etc.
		✓			Prepare and calculate metrics to be utilized in the planning process, such as cost benefit analysis, sensitivity analysis, breakeven analysis, economic order quantity, etc.
			✓		Analyze results of forecasts and projections using ratio analysis and explanations of correlations to, or variations from, key financial indices.
			✓		Compare and contrast alternative approaches (such as system replacement, make vs. buy and cost/benefit) proposed to address business challenges or opportunities for a given entity.

Uniform CPA Examination Blueprints: Business Environment and Concepts (BEC)   BEC16

State	State Board Web Address	Telephone #
AK	commerce.state.ak.us/occ/pcpa.htm	(907) 465-3811
AL	asbpa.alabama.gov	(334) 242-5700
AR	state.ar.us/asbpa	(501) 682-1520
AZ	azaccountancy.gov	(602) 364-0804
CA	dca.ca.gov/cba	(916) 263-3680
CO	dora.state.co.us/accountants	(303) 894-7800
CT	ct.gov/sboa	(860) 509-6179
DC	pearsonvue.com/dc/accountancy/	(202) 442-4320
DE	dpr.delaware.gov/boards/accountancy/index.shtml	(302) 744-4500
FL	myfloridalicense.com/dbpr/cpa/	(850) 487-1395
GA	sos.state.ga.us/plb/accountancy/	(478) 207-1400
GU	guamboa.org	(671) 647-0813
HI	hawaii.gov/dcca/areas/pvl/boards/accountancy	(808) 586-2696
IA	state.ia.us/iacc	(515) 281-5910
ID	isba.idaho.gov	(208) 334-2490
IL	ilboa.org	(217) 531-0950
IN	in.gov/pla/accountancy.htm	(317) 234-3040
KS	ksboa.org	(785) 296-2162
KY	cpa.ky.gov	(502) 595-3037
LA	cpaboard.state.la.us	(504) 566-1244
MA	mass.gov/reg/boards/pa	(617) 727-1806
MD	dllr.state.md.us/license/occprof/account.html	(410) 230-6322
ME	maine.gov/pfr/professionallicensing/professions/accountants/index.htm	(207) 624-8603
MI	michigan.gov/accountancy	(517) 241-9249
MN	boa.state.mn.us	(651) 296-7938
MO	pr.mo.gov/accountancy.asp	(573) 751-0012
MS	msbpa.state.ms.us	(601) 354-7320
MT	publicaccountant.mt.gov	(406) 841-2389
NC	nccpaboard.gov	(919) 733-4222
ND	state.nd.us/ndsba	(800) 532-5904
NE	nol.org/home/BPA	(402) 471-3595
NH	nh.gov/accountancy	(603) 271-3286
NJ	state.nj.us/lps/ca/accountancy/	(973) 504-6380
NM	rld.state.nm.us/accountancy/index.html	(505) 841-9108
NV	nvaccountancy.com/	(775) 786-0231
NY	op.nysed.gov/cpa.htm	(518) 474-3817
OH	acc.ohio.gov/	(614) 466-4135
OK	oab.state.ok.us	(405) 521-2397
OR	egov.oregon.gov/BOA/	(503) 378-4181
PA	dos.state.pa.us/account	(717) 783-1404
PR	estado.gobierno.pr/	(787) 722-4816
RI	dbr.ri.gov/divisions/accountancy/	(401) 222-3185
SC	llr.state.sc.us/POL/Accountancy	(803) 896-4770
SD	state.sd.us/dol/Boards/accountancy/acc-home.htm	(605) 367-5770
TN	tn.gov/commerce/boards/tnsba/index.shtml	(615) 741-2550
TX	tsbpa.state.tx.us	(512) 305-7800
UT	dopl.utah.gov	(801) 530-6396
VA	boa.virginia.gov	(804) 367-8505
VI	dlca.gov.vi	(340) 773-4305
VT	vtprofessionals.org/opr1/accountants	(802) 828-2837
WA	cpaboard.wa.gov	(360) 753-2585
WI	drl.wi.gov/profession.asp?profid=60&locid=0	(608) 266-5511
WV	boa.wv.gov/Pages/default.aspx	(304) 558-3557
WY	cpaboard.state.wy.us	(307) 777-7551

Section 1 – Economic Concepts

Table of Contents

EXAM NOTE: *Please refer to the AICPA BEC Blueprint in the Introduction of this book to find a listing of the representative tasks (and their associated skill levels—i.e., Remembering and Understanding, Application, and Analysis) that the candidate should be able to perform based on the knowledge obtained in this section.*

Economic Concepts

Lecture 1.01 – Microeconomics: Demand Curve

Economics is the study of how we allocate scarce resources to satisfy unlimited wants.

Microeconomics is the study of the decisions of, and interactions among, various individual economic agents (households and firms). Both households and firms act as buyers in the economy, providing **demand** for products (or goods) and services (including labor). Both households and firms act as sellers in the economy, providing the **supply** of products and services. The interaction of demand and supply determine the price, quantity produced and consumed, and the allocation of products and services.

*D*emand (or Demand Curve)—Remember that the demand curve, starting with a D, slopes *Down*, also starting with a D

A **demand curve** shows the *inverse relationship* between the price and the quantity of a product or service that a group of consumers are willing and able to buy at a particular time (i.e., the quantity demanded). For instance, as the price of a product increases (e.g., from 10 to 20), the quantity demanded by buyers decreases (e.g., from 50 to 30).

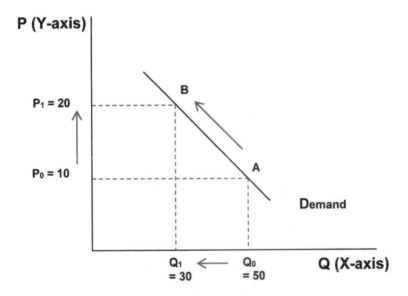

Important tip!!! Economists are very specific about the usage of the terms "demand" vs. "quantity demanded." The term "demand" refers to the demand curve that can be plotted on a graph with quantity demanded on the x-axis (horizontal) and price on the y-axis (vertical). The demand curve may also be thought of as a schedule listing multiple combinations of prices and quantities demanded (e.g., those for points A and B in the graph). Thus, economists would not say that higher prices decrease "demand." Instead, economists would say that at higher prices, "quantity demanded" is lower. As prices increase, one moves along the demand curve to find lower quantities demanded.

Price and quantity demanded have a reliably ***inverse relationship***; however, the precise placement of the demand curve on the graph may change regularly. These changes are known as **demand curve shifts**. A demand curve shifts if there are changes in relevant factors *other than a change in price*. Economists use a variety of terms to describe demand curve shifts:

- **Changes in the demand curve where quantity demanded becomes larger for each and every price** are described as "the demand curve shifted upward," "the demand curve shifted outward," "the demand curve shifted to the right," or "demand increased."

- **Changes in the demand curve where quantity demanded becomes smaller for each and every price** are described as "the demand curve shifted downward," "the demand curve shifted inward," "the demand curve shifted to the left," or "demand decreased."

Below we show an upward demand curve shift from D_0 to D_1. Note that at a price of 20, consumers are willing and able to purchase 50 instead of 30 units. Alternatively, for a quantity of 30, consumers are willing and able to pay a price of 27 instead of 20.

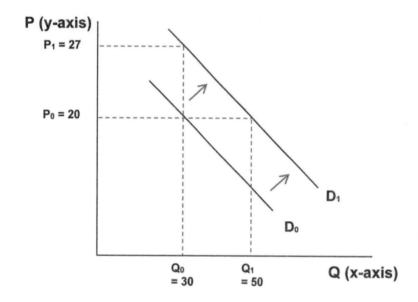

There are various reasons why demand curves may shift. Some factors exhibit a **direct relationship** with the demand curve, meaning that increases in that factor cause the demand curve to *shift upward* (or demand to increase). Examples are:

- **The price of a substitute good –** When product A may be an acceptable alternative to product B, an increase in the price of product A will make product B more attractive (e.g., some consumers will shift from buying product A to product B). For example, an increase in the price of hamburgers will increase the demand for hot dogs.

- **Expectations of price changes –** Consumers are more likely to buy now if they think prices will increase in the future. For example, if cigarette taxes are expected to double next year, some buyers will bring forward some of their purchases, increasing demand this year until the tax increase goes into effect.

- **Income (for normal goods) –** For many goods (e.g., cars or smartphones), when incomes increase (wealth increase), demand increases. Below we point out that not all goods are "normal goods."

- **Extent of the market –** New consumers may increase demand, therefore increasing the size of the market. For example, the removal of trade barriers by foreign governments will increase the demand for American products that can be exported. A baby boom will increase demand for baby food. A large inflow of immigrants from a country to the U.S. will increase demand for that country's ethnic food in the U.S.

Other factors exhibit an **inverse relationship** with the demand curve, meaning that increases in that factor cause the demand curve to *shift downward* (or demand to decrease). Examples are:

- **The price of a complement good** – When products are normally used together, an increase in the price of one of the goods decreases demand for the other. For example, an increase in the price of chips will cause a downward shift in the demand for salsa.

- **Income** (for **inferior goods**) – For some goods (e.g., used cars), when incomes increase (wealth), demand decreases as consumers shift their spending to other goods (e.g., new cars).

- **Consumer boycotts** – An organized boycott will, if effective, temporarily decrease the demand for a product. For example, members of unions commonly refuse to buy from businesses that are involved in labor disputes.

Changes in consumer tastes may, of course, affect demand but whether demand increases or decreases as a result depends on whether the change in tastes favors or disfavors the specific product. These are said to have an indeterminate relationship. The theory of *derived demand* predicts that demand for the resources used to produce product A is derived from the demand for product A.

Lecture 1.02 – Elasticity

In economics, elasticities measure the sensitivity of something (e.g., quantity demanded) to changes in something else (e.g., price). There are various types of elasticity, including price elasticity of demand, price elasticity of supply, income elasticity of demand, and cross elasticity of demand.

Barring shifts in the demand curve, a firm expects the quantity demanded for its product to decrease as the price increases. A smaller level of sales (i.e., quantity demanded) could reduce the firm's total revenue (= price * quantity). Alternatively, a higher price could increase the firm's total revenue. Whether total revenue will increase or decrease when prices change turns out to depend on the **Price Elasticity** of Demand. The concept of price elasticity of demand measures how responsive the quantity demanded (of a good or service) is to a change in price. Economists often refer to the "price elasticity of demand" simply as "elasticity of demand."

> **_Price Elasticity of Demand (Ed)_** = _Percentage change in **Quantity demanded**_
> _(Elasticity of Demand)_   _Percentage change in **Price**_

Elasticities are commonly computed using the "arc method" or relative to the midpoint (or average) between conditions before and after a change, instead of relative to conditions "before" the change.

$$Ed = \frac{\dfrac{Change\ in\ quantity\ demanded}{Average\ quantity\ demanded}}{\dfrac{Change\ in\ price}{Average\ price}}$$

Using the formula above, price elasticities of demand technically yield negative answers (either the change in quantity demanded or the change in price will be negative while the other is positive). When interpreting price elasticities of demand, it is customary to ignore the negative sign (or to report its absolute value).

If Ed is greater than 1, demand is **elastic**, and total revenue will decline if the price is increased. If Ed is less than 1, demand is considered **inelastic**, and total revenue will increase if the price is increased. If elasticity is equal to 1, demand is said to be "**unit elastic**," (unitary) and total revenue is not sensitive to price changes. For example, goods that represent a larger fraction of consumers' budgets tend to be elastic (automobiles) and those that represent a smaller fraction of consumers' budgets tend to be inelastic (table salt).

For example, assume a firm can sell (i.e., it faces a quantity demanded of) 110 units for a product that is priced at $9 per unit. Thus, its total revenue currently would be 110 × $9 = $990. The firm is considering a price increase of $2 per unit or 20% (under the arc method).

If the 20% price increase caused quantity demanded to decrease from 110 to 80 or by 30 units (30/95 (avg Q dem = 31.6%), price elasticity would be: 31.6% / 20% = 1.58, and demand would be elastic. Thus, total revenue would decline to 80 × $11 = $880.

If the price increase caused quantity demanded to decrease only from 110 to 100, or by 10 units (9.5%), price elasticity would be 9.5% / 20% = 0.48, and demand would be inelastic. Thus, total revenue would increase to 100 × $11 = $1,100.

		Elastic	Inelastic	Unit elastic
Unit price	$9	$11	$11	$11
X units	x 110	x 80	x 100	x 90
Total Rev.	$990	$880	$1,100	$990
% ch Qt % ch Pr		.316 .20 = 1.58	.095 .20 = .48	.20 .20 = 1.0

Elasticities are often larger if more time elapsed while the compared changes took place. For instance, in the short run, consumers may not be able to reduce their consumption of gasoline significantly when there is an increase in gasoline prices, i.e., consumers' gasoline purchases are less responsive to price changes in the short term; consumers' demand for gasoline is more inelastic over the short term. But over longer periods, they can switch to more efficient cars, change their work arrangements to reduce driving needs, and otherwise substantially reduce their consumption of gasoline. The longer they have to adjust, the more they can reduce their gasoline consumption in response to price increases, i.e., consumers' gasoline purchases are more responsive to price changes in the long term; consumers' demand for gasoline is more elastic over the long term.

As we stated above, there are other types of elasticity. **Income Elasticity of demand** measures the effect of changes in (consumer) income on changes in the quantity demanded of a product. All elasticities (not just price elasticity of demand) may be computed using the arc method.

Income Elasticity = Percentage change in **quantity demanded**
    of Demand   Percentage change in **income**

A positive income elasticity indicates a **normal good**, which means that as consumer income increases, the quantity demanded of the normal good also increases. A negative number indicates an **inferior good**, so as income increases, the quantity demanded of the inferior good will decrease. For example, if incomes increase and the quantity demanded of new cars also increases, new cars are a normal good. However, incomes increase and the quantity demanded of used cars decreases, used cars are an inferior good.

Cross-elasticity of demand measures the change in the *quantity demanded of* a good to a change in the *price* of another good, and is used to determine if two different goods are **substitutes** (butter and margarine), which would result in a direct relationship (positive number), or **complements** (chips and salsa), which would result in an inverse relationship (negative number). If the coefficient is zero, the products are **unrelated**.

Cross-Elasticity = <u>*Percentage change in the* **quantity demanded** *for product* **X**</u>
of Demand   *Percentage change in the* **price** *of product* **Y**

> For example, if the price of butter increases by 10% and the quantity demanded of margarine increases by 12%, .12 / .10 = 1.2, then their cross-elasticity of demand is positive and they are *substitutes*. However, if the price of chips increases by 10% and the quantity demanded of salsa decreases by 12%, -.12 / .1= -1.2, then their cross-elasticity of demand is negative and they are *complements*.

Lecture 1.03 – Microeconomics: Supply Curve

Supply

Remember that the sUPply curve, including the letters UP, slopes up

A supply curve shows the *direct relationship* between the price of a product or service and the quantity that a group of producers and/or sellers are willing to supply at a particular time (i.e., the quantity supplied). For instance, as the price of a product increases (e.g., from 10 to 20), the quantity supplied by sellers increases (e.g., from 30 to 50).

Important tip!!! Economists are very specific about the usage of the terms "supply" vs. "quantity supplied." The term "supply" refers to the supply curve that can be plotted on a graph with quantity supplied on the x-axis (horizontal) and price on the y-axis (vertical). The supply curve may also be thought of as a schedule listing multiple combinations of prices and quantities supplied (e.g., those for points C and D in the graph). Thus, economists would not say that higher prices increase "supply." Instead, economists would say that at higher prices, "quantity supplied" is higher. As prices increase, one moves along the supply curve to find higher quantities supplied.

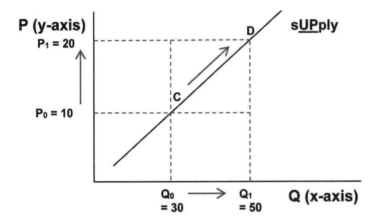

Just as in the case of demand, the **supply curve shifts** if there are changes in relevant factors other than a change in price. Economists use a variety of terms to describe supply curve shifts:

- **Changes in the supply curve where quantity supplied becomes larger for each and every price** are described as "the supply curve shifted outward" (not upward), "the supply curve shifted to the right," or "supply increased."

- **Changes in the supply curve where quantity supplied becomes smaller for each and every price** are described as "the supply curve shifted inward" (not downward), "the supply curve shifted to the left," or "supply decreased."

Below we show a supply curve shift to the right from S_0 to S_1. Note that at a price of 20, sellers supply 70 instead of 50 units. Alternatively, for a quantity of 50, sellers charge a (lower) price of 10 instead of 20.

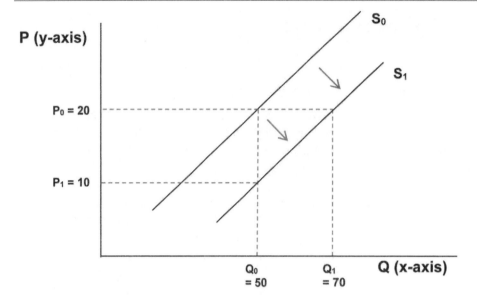

Some factors exhibit a **direct relationship** with the supply curve, meaning that increases in that factor cause the supply curve to shift outward (or supply to increase). Examples are:
- **Number of producers –** More producers normally increase the quantity supplied of a product at a given price. Entry by foreign suppliers into the U.S. auto market increases the supply of cars in the U.S.
- **Government subsidies –** Additional funding permits producers to purchase more inputs and, thus, increase quantity supplied at any given price.
- **Price expectations -** If producers expect higher prices, producers will increase their quantity supplied at any given price.
- **Technological advances –** Technological advances generally reduce production costs; hence, producers generally will increase their quantity supplied at any given price with an increase in technological advances.

Other factors exhibit an **inverse relationship** with the supply curve, meaning that increases in that factor cause the supply curve to *shift inward* (or supply to decrease). Examples are:
- **Increases in production costs (e.g., production taxes) –** If producers' costs increase, producers will decrease their quantity supplied at a given price.
- **Prices of other products –** If producers may produce both product A and B, and producing A becomes more profitable, producers will decrease their quantity supplied of B at any given price.

Price Elasticity of Supply

A measure of how sensitive quantity supplied of a good or service is to a change in price or cost. Tells us how a change in prices will affect the quantity supplied by firms.

> **Price Elasticity of Supply (Es)** = $\dfrac{\text{Percentage change in } \textbf{Quantity Supplied}}{\text{Percentage change in } \textbf{Price}}$
> *(Elasticity of Supply)*

Owners of factors of production (labor, natural resources, capital, and entrepreneurship) aim to shift those factors to their most productive uses. These efforts are reflected in **economic rents** or

surpluses, which are the excess of the payments for these factors when used most productively over their best alternative use, which is known as the opportunity cost.

Opportunity cost is also known as the benefit given up from not using the resource for another purpose (the foregone benefit from alternatives NOT selected). For example, if a worker accepts a job paying $60,000 instead of another offering $50,000, the worker would have received an economic rent of $10,000 from accepting the higher paying job, and faced an opportunity cost of $50,000 by doing so.

For suppliers themselves, **economic profit** refers to the excess of the profits they are receiving over the **normal profit rate** in the economy. Economic profits usually result in more suppliers entering the market, and economic losses will usually result in suppliers exiting the market.

Market Equilibrium

Generally speaking, prices, quantities supplied, and quantities demanded adjust to an equilibrium level, as long as governments do not interfere, where the demand and supply curves cross, so that there is adequate supply to satisfy buyers and adequate demand to allow suppliers to sell their output. Point E (with a price of 15 and a quantity of 40) in the graph below identifies such an equilibrium point. At the equilibrium price: *quantity demanded = quantity supplied*, so all the goods offered for sale will be sold.

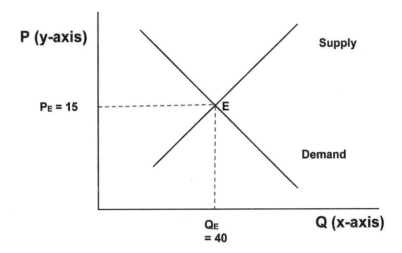

Some Government Actions that Affect Equilibrium

If governments impose a **price ceiling** (e.g., setting the maximum legal price at which a product or service may be sold at $7) below equilibrium (i.e., $15), the quantity demanded (i.e., 56) will exceed quantity supplied (i.e., 24), resulting in *shortages of goods* (i.e., 56 – 24 = 32 is the number of units that consumers would like to purchase at that price but are unable to; the lower line in the graph below represents the price ceiling and helps identify the various quantities).

For example, some cities set maximum rents that result in apartment shortages.

If governments impose a **price floor** (e.g., setting the minimum legal price at which a product or service may be sold at $17) above equilibrium, the quantity supplied (i.e., 52) will exceed quantity demanded (i.e., 28), resulting in unpurchased *surpluses of goods or services* (i.e., 52 – 28 = 24 is the number of units that suppliers would like to sell at that price but are unable to; the upper line in the graph below represents the price floor and helps identify the various quantities).

For example, a minimum wage for unskilled workers results in higher unemployment rates for unskilled workers.

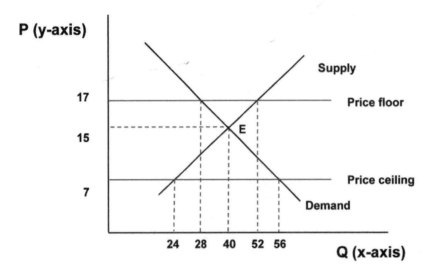

Shifts in demand and supply lead to somewhat predictable changes from an initial combination of equilibrium price and equilibrium quantity to a new combination:

Comparing an Initial and a New Equilibrium Resulting from an Increase in Demand

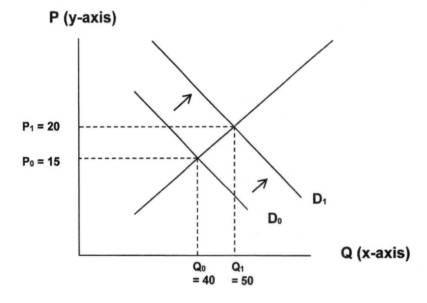

Comparing an Initial and a New Equilibrium Resulting from an Increase in Supply

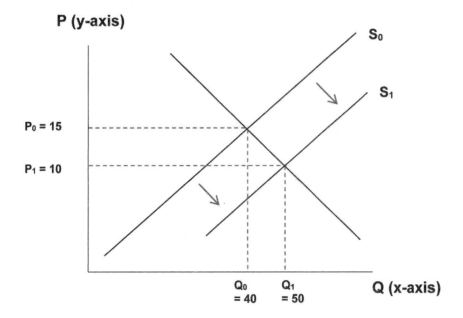

Below we summarize the changes in equilibrium price and quantity resulting from various shifts in supply and demand curves:

Demand	Supply	Equilibrium Price	Quantity Purchased
Increase	No change	Increase	Increase
Decrease	No change	Decrease	Decrease
No change	Increase	Decrease	Increase
No change	Decrease	Increase	Decrease
Increase	Increase	**Uncertain**	Increase
Decrease	Decrease	**Uncertain**	Decrease
Increase	Decrease	Increase	**Uncertain**
Decrease	Increase	Decrease	**Uncertain**

Lecture 1.04 – Microeconomics – Class Questions

1. The demand curve for a product reflects which of the following?
   a. The impact of prices on the amount of product offered.
   b. The willingness of producers to offer a product at alternative prices.
   c. The impact that price has on the amount of a product purchased.
   d. The impact that price has on the purchase amount of two related products.

2. Which of the following characteristics would indicate that an item sold would have a high price elasticity of demand?

   a. The item has many similar substitutes.
   b. The cost of the item is low compared to the total budget of the purchasers.
   c. The item is considered a necessity.
   d. Changes in the price of the item are regulated by governmental agency.

3. A city ordinance that freezes rent prices may cause

   a. The demand curve for rental space to fall.
   b. The supply curve for rental space to rise.
   c. Demand for rental space to exceed supply.
   d. Supply of rental space to exceed demand.

4. In which of the following situations would there be inelastic demand?

   a. A 5 percent price increase results in a 3 percent decrease in the quantity demanded.
   b. A 4 percent price increase results in a 6 percent decrease in the quantity demanded.
   c. A 4 percent price increase results in a 4 percent decrease in the quantity demanded.
   d. A 3 percent price decrease results in a 5 percent increase in the quantity demanded.

5. If in the market for widgets demand increases,

   a. Price will fall.
   b. Quantity demanded and price will both increase.
   c. Quantity demanded will increase and price will fall.
   d. Quantity demanded for complement goods will fall.

6. If in the market for widgets, demand increases and supply decreases, based on that information, what would economic theory predict?

   a. Price will decrease, and quantity will fall
   b. Price will increase, and change in quantity is indeterminate
   c. Price will be indeterminate, and quantity will increase
   d. Price will be indeterminate, and quantity will decrease

Class Solutions

1. (c) The demand curve presents the relationship between prices and quantities demanded of a product (i.e., amount of a product purchased). Answer (a) is incorrect because the influence of price on the amount of a product offered is a description of the supply curve, not the demand curve. Answer (b) is incorrect because willingness of producers to offer a product at alternative prices is a description of the supply curve, not the demand curve. Answer (d) is incorrect because the impact that price has on the purchase amount of two related products describes cross elasticity, not the demand curve.

2. (a) A high price elasticity indicates that an increase in price will result in a decrease in demand for the item. If there are similar substitutes for an item, an increase in the price of the item will cause many consumers to switch to one of the substitutes. Answer (b) is incorrect because an entity with a budget of $1,000,000 will not likely expend much effort to find substitutes for an item that has increased in price if its total cost is only $50, for example, but might be inclined to do so if the total cost of the time was $250,000. Answer (c) is incorrect because a high price elasticity indicates that an increase in price will result in a decrease in demand for the item. When an item is considered a necessity, purchasers will have no alternative and will continue to purchase the item despite an increase in price. This, of course, will likely only be temporary as, in the long term, a higher price may attract other suppliers into the market and may cause purchasers to seek substitutes. Answer (d) is incorrect because whether changes in prices are regulated by a governmental agency or determined by a supplier's management would not affect the impact a change in prices will have on demand and, therefore, does not affect elasticity.

3. (c) In periods of rising prices, a city ordinance to freeze rents would cause rents to remain the same while other prices are rising, reducing the relative cost of rent. As the relative price of an item decreases, the demand for it increases. Answer (a) is incorrect because as the relative price of an item decreases, the demand for it increases, moving the item along its demand curve, but not shifting the demand curve itself. Answer (b) is incorrect because as the relative price of an item decreases, the supply will also decrease, moving the item along its supply curve, but not shifting the supply curve itself. Answer (d) is incorrect because as the relative price of an item decreases, the demand for it increases and the supply decreases. As a result, demand will exceed supply, not the opposite.

4. (a) Elasticity refers to the change in demand that results from a change in prices. Elasticity is indicated when an increase in demand is proportionate to a decrease in price, or vice versa. An item is inelastic if the increase in demand is proportionately lower than a decrease in price, or vice versa, such as indicated by a 3% decrease in demand associated with a 5% increase in price.

5. (b) An increase in demand when the supply curve does not change results in a movement along the supply curve and higher quantity supplied (and demanded) and price. Answers (a) and (c) are incorrect because price would rise. Answer (d) is incorrect because, by definition, quantity demanded for complement goods would rise.

6. (b) Not knowing which of the effects is stronger, both higher demand and lower supply would push prices higher. Since higher demand would push quantity higher and lower supply would push quantity lower, the overall impact on quantity is indeterminate. Answer (a) is incorrect because the effect on quantity is indeterminate. Answer (c) and (d) are incorrect because price would rise.

Lecture 1.05 – Consumers

Microeconomic theory assumes that consumers, whether buying for their own personal, family, or household use, seek to maximize their *satisfaction* (which economists commonly refer to as **utility**).

Although measuring satisfaction is difficult, microeconomics generally assumes that people have some sense of the relative utility of different ways to spend their money, and that they spend money on one thing rather than another such that the **marginal utility** of spending money on the product or service chosen will be greater than from the alternatives they didn't choose.

According to the **law of diminishing marginal utility**, the more a consumer consumes of a particular product, the less satisfying will be the next unit of that product. The twentieth chocolate chip cookie doesn't taste nearly as good as the first one. *A consumer maximizes total satisfaction when the last dollar spent on each product generates the same amount of marginal utility* (i.e., if the marginal utility per dollar is greater from product A than from product B, the consumer will increase consumption of product A, reducing its marginal utility per dollar, and decrease consumption of product B, until marginal utility per dollar is equal for both products A and B, and ultimately across all products).

Microeconomics illustrates the allocation of consumers' resources between two products plotting an **indifference curve (IC)** that represents the combination of quantities of each product that yield a certain total utility. Curves representing more total utility will, of course, involve increasing quantities of the two products, so curves plotting various total utility amounts will never cross. In a simplified model with two goods (e.g., sports events and dinners), the choice that maximizes a consumer's utility is found at the intersection between the consumer's budget constraint (which is determined by what the consumer plans to spend and the relative price of the two goods) and the indifference curve with the highest level of utility the consumer may attain.

Sports events

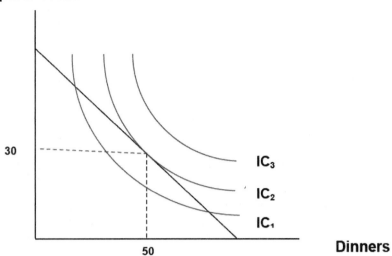

Consumers do not, of course, have unlimited amounts of money to spend. The available income of a consumer after subtracting mandatory payment of taxes (or adding receipt of government benefits, if applicable) is known as **personal disposable income.** Consumers have only two choices with each dollar of personal disposable income: they can either spend (consume) it or save it. The **marginal propensity to Consume (MPC)** is the percentage of the next dollar of income that the consumer would be expected to spend (change in consumption / change in income), and the **marginal propensity to Save (MPS)** is the percentage of the next dollar that the consumer would be expected to save (change in savings / change in income). Since these are the only choices, the two calculations must add up to 100%, MPS + MPC = 1.

$$\textbf{MPS} = \frac{\textit{Change in Savings}}{\textit{Change in Disposable income}} \qquad \textbf{MPC} = \frac{\textit{Change in Consumption (spending)}}{\textit{Change in Disposable income}}$$

Lecture 1.06 – Production Costs

Over short periods of time and limited ranges of production, firms have costs that include both fixed and variable components:

- **Fixed costs (FC)** – Costs that won't change even when there is a change in the level of production. *Average fixed costs* (AFC) are total fixed costs divided by the number of units produced. An example of a fixed cost is rent paid on the production facility.
- **Variable costs (VC)** – Costs that rise as production rises. *Average variable costs* (AVC) are total variable costs divided by the number of units produced. An example is materials used in the manufacture of the product. The boundary between fixed and variable costs of course depends on the length of period under consideration. Over a period that is short enough, one might consider the payments to hourly workers as a variable cost (i.e., the number of hours are readily adjusted) and the payment to salaried workers as a fixed cost (i.e., most companies will not change the number of salaried workers in the very short term).
- **Total costs (TC)** – The sum of fixed and variable costs (TC = FC + VC). *Average total costs* (ATC) are total costs divided by the number of units produced.
- **Marginal cost (MC)** – The increase in cost that results from producing one extra unit. Only variable costs are relevant, since fixed costs won't increase in such circumstances. Any set of production arrangements will be most ideal for a given production level, thus marginal cost falls until some level is attained (e.g., different parts of a large factory may be too far apart from one another if production is small) and then rise after some level is attained (e.g., a factory of a given size will eventually become overcrowded if more and more workers are there). Note that for the first unit, MC = VC = AVC.
- **Marginal Revenue (MR)** - The change in total revenue (TR) associated with the sale of one more unit of output.
- **Marginal Revenue Product** - The increase in total revenue received by the addition of one additional unit of an input or resource (e.g., one more worker).

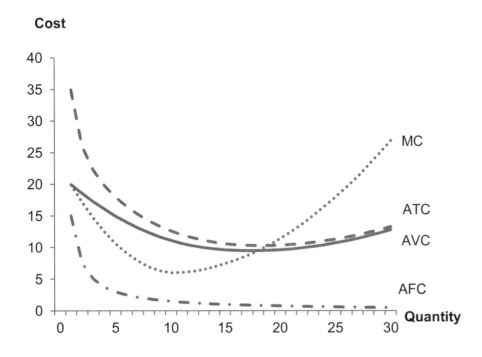

To maximize profits, managers would choose levels of production (output or quantity) such that their company's marginal revenue equals their marginal cost. If the marginal revenue of producing one extra unit exceeds its marginal cost, it is profitable to increase production. Facing a downward sloping demand curve, to increase their sales, firms must accept lower prices (and marginal revenues). Once the marginal revenue equals marginal cost, managers will have attained the level of production that maximizes profits in the short term. Increasing production further would result in marginal revenues falling short of marginal costs.

For example, a company operating below capacity can sell units at a profit for any price in excess of VC. Once capacity is reached, however, the production of one additional unit will also increase total fixed costs and the increase in revenue from the sale of a single unit would be lower than the increase in TC.

In the following graph, MR = MC for a quantity of 50. The total cost (TC) is $1,200 (= ATC × Q = $24 × 50). The firm would set the price at the maximum possible level given the demand curve (= 30), not at the marginal revenue (of about 12). Total revenue (TR) is $1,500 (= P × Q = $30 × 50). Profit is $300 (= TR – TC = $1,500 – $1,200). Note that the profit maximizing quantity does not involve the minimum level of ATC (i.e., where MC crosses ATC), but (in this graph a slightly) higher level (= 24).

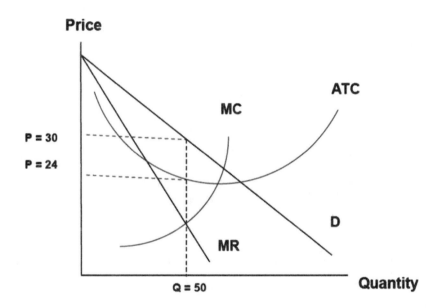

In economic analysis, over periods of time that are long enough, all costs are *variable*, since firms may change how much they use of any input (hire more or fewer hourly or salaried workers, expand factories, build additional factories, etc.). In the long run, i.e., even if a firm may adjust its level of usage of all inputs (e.g., expand or redesign factories, or build new ones), it may find that increases in production may reduce, have no effect on, or increase their per unit (or average) costs. Note that in the long run, by definition there are no fixed costs and thus variable cost equals total cost.

Returns to scale are the increases in units produced (output) that result from increases in production costs (i.e., costs of inputs).

> ***Returns to scale*** = <u>*Percentage increase in* **output**</u>
> *Percentage increase in* **input**

At lower levels of production (and of use of inputs), many firms face returns to scale greater than 1, or **increasing returns to scale**. Alternatively, these firms may be described as facing **economies of scale**, or increased efficiencies from producing more units of a product. This may result from spreading fixed costs over larger numbers of units, being able to save on transaction and transportation costs by buying in larger quantities, having employees specialize in different tasks and improve their abilities, or automatic procedures that are performed repetitively. Thus, in the long run, firms that increase their size by some amount may experience increasing returns, operate more efficiently, and lower their average costs.

However, ever larger levels of production (and of use of inputs) may eventually result in returns to scale smaller than 1, or **decreasing returns to scale.** These firms may be described as facing **diseconomies of scale**, or increased inefficiencies. This may result from increasing volumes of inventory stored, making retrieval more difficult; increasing the number of employees working, making effective supervision more difficult; or hiring lower skilled workers, resulting in more errors and a lower product acceptance rate.

Between increasing and decreasing returns to scale (and economies and diseconomies of scale), firms may operate in ranges of levels of production (and of use of inputs) where they face constant returns to scale. Over this range, increasing production would not affect their average costs.

Firms should not increase production beyond levels at which marginal revenue from output exceeds marginal costs from inputs.

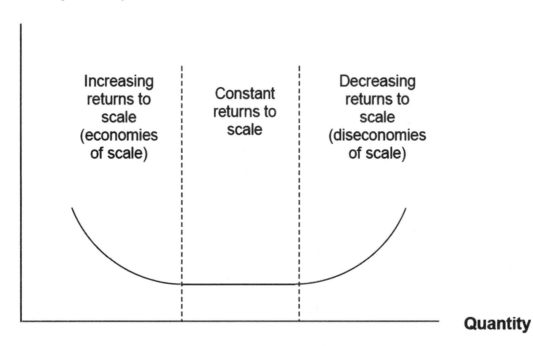

**Average Cost
(or Cost per unit)**

Increasing returns to scale (economies of scale) | Constant returns to scale | Decreasing returns to scale (diseconomies of scale)

Quantity

- **Increasing returns to scale**—Output increases by a greater proportion > 1.0
- **Constant returns to scale**—Output increases in same proportion = 1.0
- **Decreasing returns to scale**—Output increases by a smaller proportion < 1.0

Using some mathematical examples:

- **Increasing returns to scale**– Range of output for which increases in the use of inputs (e.g., from 20 to 30 and 40, both increases of 10 units) yield more than proportionate increases in output (i.e., from 100 to 200 and 320, or increases of 100 and 120). Alternatively, this concept means that increasing output (e.g., from 100 to 200 and 320), involves falling per unit costs (i.e., respectively 0.2, 0.15, and 0.125)

- **Constant returns to scale** Range of output for which increases in the use of inputs (e.g., from 50 to 60 and 70, both increases of 10 units) yield proportionate increases in output (from 550 to 660 and 770, or increases of 110). Alternatively, this concept means that increasing output (e.g., from 550 to 660 and 770) involves constant per unit costs (i.e., all 0.091).

- **Decreasing returns to scale** Range of output for which increases in the use of inputs (e.g., from 100 to 110 and 120, both increases of 10 units) yield less than proportionate increases in output (i.e., from 1,100 to 1,190 and 1,270, or increases of 90 and 80). Alternatively, this concept means that increasing output (e.g., from 1,100 to 1,190 and 1,270) involves rising per unit costs (i.e., respectively 0.091, 0.092, and 0.094).

Lecture 1.07 – Market Structure & Industry Analysis

Economics defines an industry as a group of firms that produce products or services that consumers would identify as similar enough to be considered substitutes. To better understand how firms and industries may operate, economists have developed several key models (i.e., simplifications of reality) of market structures that illustrate varying levels of competition. Ranging from most to least competitive, these models are perfect competition, monopolistic competition, oligopoly (or oligopolistic competition), and pure monopoly.

Perfect (or Pure) Competition

While few, if any, industries or markets may actually be perfectly competitive, having a model of perfect competition is useful in terms of assessing how close or far various industries may come to being perfectly competitive. Perfect competition would involve a situation with large numbers of sellers, where each individual seller is too small to affect the overall market price, easy entry and exit of suppliers (no barriers to entry/exit), a homogeneous (standardized or identical) product, and an absence of non-price competition (such as advertising and perceived quality differences).

Some commodities markets (wheat, soybeans, corn, etc.) are commonly mentioned as coming closest to being perfectly competitive. In a perfectly competitive market, an individual firm effectively faces a horizontal demand curve and prices are perfectly elastic: The firm can sell as many goods as it can produce at the equilibrium price but no goods at a higher price. In other words, the firm is a *price taker*. Thus, for the individual firm, the equilibrium market price is its marginal revenue curve for all production levels. The individual firm faces an incentive to expand quantity produced until its marginal costs rise to equal the equilibrium market price (which is the firm's marginal revenue curve).

While each individual firm alone has no effect on the overall market price and the demand curve for each individual firm is horizontal, the *market demand curve* is downward sloping. Therefore, quantity demanded increases if entry of more suppliers lowers prices and quantity demanded decreases if exit by some suppliers raises prices. If the equilibrium market price is high enough that individual firms earn economic profits, large numbers of new suppliers will enter the market, lowering prices until firms earn only normal profits (i.e., an economic profit of zero). If the equilibrium market price is so low that individual firms incur economic losses, large numbers of the most marginal (i.e., least efficient) suppliers will exit the market, lifting prices until the remaining firms earn normal profits.

To recap, an industry would be *perfectly competitive* if it met the following conditions:
- It includes a large number of sellers, each of which is too small to affect the overall market price.
- All firms sell a homogeneous (i.e., largely identical) product (e.g., wheat, soybeans, corn, etc.).
- There is no non-price competition (e.g., no advertising).
- Firms may enter or exit the market very easily (i.e., there are no significant barriers to entry, ceilings or floors).
- Each individual firm faces a demand curve that is perfectly elastic (horizontal).

Pure Monopoly

In this model, there is only one firm that sells a product or service for which there are no close substitutes. Monopolies may exist as a result of public policy or of "technical" conditions. Common examples of monopolies resulting from public policy include the local monopolies that cable companies operate in most areas or the national monopolies that each drug manufacturer has for each given product for which it has a **patent**, which ultimately is a *barrier to entry*.

For markets where there is no relevant range of output, where decreasing returns to scale set in, **natural monopolies** may exist as economies of scale would permit the largest firm to underprice, and eliminate, all others. Companies with lower costs may seek to engage in **predatory pricing**, charging temporarily low prices to drive their competitors out of existence, only to increase their prices as monopolists once they have eliminated their competitors. Unless restricted by regulation, a pure monopoly would have great pricing power and, producing only to the level where marginal revenue equals marginal costs, would result in economic profits (earnings higher than normal profits), with substantially higher prices and lower output than under more competitive market structures in both the short and long runs.

Various laws have been passed to reduce anticompetitive market practices, including:
- **The Sherman Act** (1890) prohibited price fixing, boycotts, market division, and restricted resale agreements among suppliers.
- **The Clayton Act** (1914) prohibited stock mergers that reduce competition, price discrimination, and common directorships among competing firms.
- **The Robinson-Patman Act** (1936) prohibited discounts to large purchasers not based on cost differentials.
- **The Celler-Kefauver Act** (1950) prohibits acquisition of the assets of a competitor if it would reduce competition.

To recap, an industry would be a *pure monopoly* if it met the following conditions:
- There is only one producer.
- No close substitutes are available.
- There is blocked entry (patent or Government franchise-public utility).
- The firm's Demand curve is substantially downward sloping (almost vertical).

Monopolistic Competition

In this model, large numbers of firms produce heterogeneous products and engage in a great deal of non-price competition. Entry and exit are relatively easy, but not as easy as under perfect competition. The products offered by different firms are close substitutes, but not identical. Examples might include mom-and-pop restaurants, groceries, hair dressers, etc. Firms' efforts to differentiate their products in the minds of their customers give firms some control over prices (i.e., individual firms' demand curves and the marginal revenue curves are not completely horizontal as in perfect competition, but are slightly or somewhat downward slopping). Thus, as firms produce to the point where marginal revenue equals marginal costs, this model yields prices that are somewhat higher and quantities that are somewhat lower than under perfect competition. In this model, however, easy entry and exit generally tends to eliminate large economic profits. Thus, prices are generally substantially lower and quantities substantially higher than in pure monopoly situations. Again, products and services under monopolistic competition tend to be priced somewhat higher than in a perfectly competitive market, but substantially lower than in a pure monopoly.

To recap, an industry would be *monopolistically competitive* if it met the following conditions:
- It includes a large number of sellers.
- Firms sell heterogeneous products.
- There is lots of non-price competition (advertising, products with slightly differing features, actual quality differences).
- It is relatively easy to enter and exit the market.
- Each individual firm faces a demand curve that is slightly or somewhat downward sloping.

Some customers may be willing to pay higher prices than others. **Price discrimination** works most effectively when consumers are split into distinct segments. For example, consumers buying prestige shampoo for humans generally are willing to pay more than consumers buying shampoo for horses—even if the formula is the same; with different packaging, the producer may charge more to purchasers intending to use the shampoo on humans. A seller may contrive segmentation where none naturally exists, with coupons or early bird sales. For instance, a seller may give significant discounts to the first 100 shoppers on the day after the Thanksgiving holidays or small discounts to buyers with coupons placed in strategically chosen periodicals.

Oligopoly (or Oligopolistic Competition)

In this type of market structure, significant barriers to entry ensure that there are only a small number of (typically large) firms. Barriers to entry may result from a variety of reasons: Developing new products or factories may be very costly or involve substantial lags from development to sales (e.g., automobiles and aerospace) or setting up the infrastructure to service large numbers of customers may be costly (e.g., car dealerships). In some cases, government licensing effectively creates oligopolies (e.g., cell companies, etc.). In oligopolistic competition, products may be homogeneous (such as a given grade of oil) or heterogeneous (such as the airline manufacturing market). In oligopolistic markets, since there are few competitors, the actions by one firm are likely to affect the decisions of other firms (**game theory**), and the market as a whole.

Because the actions of rivals cannot be easily predicted in such a strategic setting, there is not a single model that describes well all markets with few firms. In some cases, a company's decision to gain market share by lowering its prices may result in other companies matching its pricing (i.e., there would be a **price war** and market shares might not change appreciably). Thus, oligopolistic firms often attempt to engage in non-price competition (by product differentiation or providing high levels of service). In other oligopolistic markets, a small number of smaller firms simply base their pricing on that of a larger firm that acts as a pricing leader.

Governments seek to regulate oligopolistic competition variously, for instance, by forbidding formal quantity agreements among competitors, known as **cartels** and price fixing (or collusive pricing). A concentration ratio is a measure of the total output of an industry by a certain number of firms in that industry, such as the 4 or 8 largest. The Herfindahl index (concentration ratio) is a measure of the size of firms within an industry. These measures indicate the degree to which an industry is oligopolistic. Under oligopolistic competition, products and services tend to be priced substantially higher than under monopolistic competition, since barriers to entry cause economic profits to remain, but pricing is typically somewhat lower than under pure monopoly.

To recap, an industry would be *an Oligopoly* if it met the following conditions:
- A small number of large sellers
- Barriers to entry (cost or patents)
- Non-price competition exists.
- Rival actions are observed.
- The firm's Demand curve is Kinked.

Industry Analysis

To analyze their industry, firms may use **competitor analysis** to understand and predict the behavior of a major competitor. The two components of competitor analysis are collecting information and using that information to understand, predict and respond to that competitor. Firms must also analyze their **target market,** which involves determining who their customers are and why they are purchasing their products.

Strategic planning involves organizations' efforts to identify their long-term goals and to determine how best to reach those goals. To develop **business strategies**, managers commonly engage in formal analyses of their *strengths, weaknesses, opportunities, and threats* (i.e., **SWOT** analyses).

Formal strategic planning typically involves several steps. A typical first step involves creating (or updating) an organization's **mission statement**, which outlines the long-term purposes of an organization. The purposes of different organizations vary across the different types of organizations, ranging, for instance, from for-profit, family, mutual or cooperative, government, or charitable organizations (e.g., delivering profits to owners, delivering a quality product to consumers, serving unmet needs of specific groups, etc.). Some organizations create a values statement first, from which the mission statement flows.

After the organization has a mission statement, it may set its **goals and objectives**. The boundary between goals and objectives is definitional and different organizations may use different terms but, in general, goals are expressed in general terms (e.g., deliver good returns to investors) and objectives (often several objectives per goal) set specific targets (e.g., increase ROE from 15% to 20% within 5 years).

Next, organizations determine what **actions** should be taken to meet their goals and objectives and establish mechanisms to collect data to be able to engage in **assessment** of whether the goals and objectives were met. Once data has been collected, organizations review whether their actions were successful and restart the cycle, perhaps revising strategic plans, but specifically using the data and assessment results to develop new action plans.

To successfully implement their strategies, firms must ensure that formal strategies are not simply developed by an ad hoc committee and then not implemented, but rather that management is on board with the development and implementation of its business strategies. **Business strategies** are commonly classified as product differentiation or cost leadership strategies.

- **Product differentiation strategies** involve developing a range of slightly different products that are more attractive to one's target markets or simply to ensure that they differ substantially from competitors' offerings. This strategy will (1) make the firm's sales less responsive to changes in the prices charged by other competitors, (2) allow the firm to charge different prices (i.e., some higher) for different products, and (3) ultimately allow the firm to charge higher prices than otherwise (and potentially higher than those of one's competitors). Products may differ in many ways:

- o *Physical differences* – individual features, quality, appearance
- o *Perceived differences* – image, brand name, advertising
- o *Customer support differences* – return policies, technical support

- **Cost leadership strategies** concentrate on *cutting the costs* of producing, selling, and distributing a firm's range of products. These strategies include:
  - o *Process reengineering* – In-depth redesigns of firms' existing processes to improve performance.
  - o *Lean manufacturing* – Identifying and removing the misuse of resources in the firms' existing production processes.
  - o *Supply chain management* – Sharing relevant information in the chain of sales that ranges from the final consumer to the various levels of suppliers, independently of whether each step took place within one's firm or not. For example, all steps of the chain, from retailers to wholesalers to suppliers and supplier's suppliers, might be able to operate with leaner inventories overall if each party shared more readily its plans and forecasts.

Lecture 1.08 – Market Structure – Class Questions

7. Which of the following is an assumption in a perfectly competitive financial market?

   a. No single trader or traders can have a significant impact on market prices.
   b. Some traders can impact market prices more than others.
   c. Trading prices vary based on supply only.
   d. Information about borrowing/lending activities is only available to those willing to pay market prices.

8. Which of the following are true about monopolistic competition?

   a. Prices are lower, and quantities higher than under perfect competition.
   b. There are few producers and large barriers to entry.
   c. Firms in these markets sell products that are close substitutes to one another, but that are not identical.
   d. Prices are higher, and quantities lower than under pure monopoly.

9. Predatory pricing

   a. Involves efforts by one (or more) companies to eliminate competitors by charging prices lower than their competitors' costs of production.
   b. Hurts consumers in the short term.
   c. Benefits consumers in the long term.
   d. Is practiced commonly by firms in monopolistically competitive markets.

10. What is strategic planning?

   a. It establishes the general direction of the organization.
   b. It establishes the resources that the plan will require.
   c. It establishes the budget for the organization.
   d. It consists of decisions to use parts of the organization's resources in specified ways.

Class Solutions

7. (a) In perfectly competitive markets, individual participants are price takers, i.e., their individual actions do not affect prices. Answer (b) is incorrect because individual actions do not affect prices. Answer (c) is incorrect because trading prices will vary based on fluctuations in both supply and demand. Answer (d) is incorrect because in a perfectly competitive market, it is assumed that all information is immediately available to all participants.

8. (c) Under monopolistic competition many firms sell slightly different versions of similar products. Answer (a) is incorrect because under monopolistic competition, prices are higher and quantity lower than under perfect competition. Answer (b) is incorrect because under monopolistic competition, there are many firms. Answer (d) is incorrect because under monopolistic competition, prices are lower and quantity higher than under pure monopoly.

9. (a) Answer (b) is incorrect because consumers benefit from lower prices in the short term. Answer (c) is incorrect because consumers may suffer from higher prices in the long term. Answer (d) is incorrect because predatory pricing can be afforded only by oligopolistic firms (potential pure monopolists), not by monopolistically competitive firms.

10. (a) A strategic plan begins with the establishment of a mission statement, based on which an entity establishes objectives. Those objectives are then translated into goals, an action plan is developed to enable the achievement of the goals, and performance measures are developed to enable the entity to determine if progress is being made toward achieving them. Strategic planning is a process that an organization uses to identify its long-term goals and determines the best approach to achieve those goals. The strategic planning process is used to establish the general direction of the organization. Strategic planning does not determine the resources that the plan will require directly, but rather allocates existing resources to achieve the long-term goals. Budgeting is more detailed than strategic planning.

Lecture 1.09 – Macroeconomics

Macroeconomics is the study of the economy as a whole. Key concerns in macroeconomics include unemployment, inflation, and long-term economic growth. Other subsidiary concerns in macroeconomics include lending growth, interest rates, exchange rates, the trade balance, and government budget deficits and debts. Macroeconomics studies the roles of households (consumers), (nonfinancial) businesses, governments, the financial sector, and foreign economies in causing and/or alleviating undesired fluctuations in domestic economic conditions. ***Economic systems*** may generally be classified as one of three broad categories:

- **Capitalism,** also known as *free enterprise*, refers to a system where private parties (i.e., non-government ones) own most of the means of production and make most economic decisions (i.e., what and how much to produce, at what prices, and given their incomes and available prices, what and how much to consume).

- **Communism (or socialism)** refers to a system where *government entities own* most of the means of production and make most economic decisions.

- **Mixed economies** refers to the "in between" systems where both private parties and governments own substantial fractions of the means of production and make substantial fractions of economic decisions. Historically, virtually all countries, including the United States, have combined some elements of private and government ownership of the means of production and private and government economic decision making. Governments may, for instance, influence economic decision making through taxes (including tariffs on trade) that favor or disfavor certain activities, through their spending of tax revenues, and through regulatory policies that encourage or discourage various activities.

Some of the most important *measures and indicators of economic conditions* (i.e., benchmarks to measure economic activity) are gross domestic product (GDP, also known as nominal GDP), real GDP, gross national product (GNP), inflation, and aggregate supply and demand.

Gross Domestic Product (GDP)

The total dollar value, at current (or nominal) market prices, of all the "final" goods and services produced within **one country's borders** (regardless of the citizenship of the individual residents or the country of headquarters of the companies involved) during a period of time (typically a year). The word "final" refers to the fact that GDP aims to avoid double counting of inputs used in the production of other products. For instance, if a farmer reports sales of flour to a baker, and a baker uses that flour to make bread, and reports sales of bread to "final" consumers, the original sale of flour is not considered a final sale (to a consumer). Thus, the production of that flour is included in GDP in as much as it is included in the price of bread, but not simply by adding total sales of flour plus total sales of bread).

GDP may be computed using either of two theoretically-equivalent approaches:

- *The income approach* sums all income earned in the production of final goods and services, such as wages, interest, rents, business profits, plus adjustments for indirect taxes and economic depreciation (expenditures to replace physical equipment that wears out).

- *The expenditure approach* sums all expenditures to purchase final goods and services by households (personal consumption expenditures), businesses (gross private investment, e.g., machinery), the government, and the foreign sector (exports), minus adjustments for expenditures produced abroad (imports).

Real GDP

Real GDP is the total dollar value of all the final goods and services produced expressed using a price level that is constant (chained) over time. Nominal GDP is adjusted to yield Real GDP by removing the effects of increases in prices (i.e., inflation) from the sum of total purchases of goods and services (i.e., to focus on the changes in units sold, not on the changes in prices).

Real GDP (often simply referred to as GDP, economic production, or output) is the most commonly used and most comprehensive measure of economic production. Comparing economic size or levels of development across countries, economists commonly compare respectively total GDP for a country or GDP per capita. Assessing an individual country's progress, economists commonly focus on annual rates of percentage change in real GDP.

Economists use a variety of terms and concepts that imply that there is a "sort of" speed limit for economic growth that economies may sustainably attain, but should be careful to not to exceed. Thus, aside from the "actual" nominal and real GDP, the Congressional Budget Office (CBO) also computes **potential GDP** (in nominal and real versions), that helps to estimate the degree to which the economy is either underutilizing resources or "overheating." If, for instance, actual real GDP falls short of potential real GDP, resources will be underused (unemployment rates will be higher). If actual real GDP exceeds potential real GDP, the economy will be overheating (resulting in unsustainably low unemployment rates, boom conditions in various markets, and eventually price inflation). Concepts similar to potential GDP are the "natural" or **"non-accelerating-inflation" rate of unemployment (NAIRU),** where if the actual unemployment rate falls below NAIRU, boom conditions follow in the short term and problems such as higher inflation eventually follow.

A key problem in macroeconomic management is that the negative consequences of exceeding these speeds limits take place with **long and variable lags**, i.e., it may take several years before there is clear evidence of a problem. Economists "joke" that macroeconomic policymaking is similar to driving a car being able to use only one's rearview mirrors.

Gross National Product (GNP)

Gross National Product (GNP) is the total dollar value of all goods and services produced by a country's **residents** (including companies headquartered there) regardless of whether they were produced within or outside that country's borders. While both GNP and GDP are computed routinely, the U.S. government emphasized GNP until 1991, when it switched to emphasize GDP, to match common practice in most other countries. GNP differs from GDP in that GNP includes, for instance, earnings of U.S. companies abroad, and excludes earnings of foreign companies within the U.S.

Inflation

Inflation is commonly defined as the percentage rate of increase in the price level of goods and services. Rising inflation means that individuals can purchase less either if they are on fixed incomes or with their past savings. Stating that inflation is higher is equivalent to stating that money is losing its purchasing power at a higher rate. From the point of view of financial statements, inflation tends to affect most accounting measures that take place over extended periods of time (e.g., assets and depreciation entered using historic or book values) and affects relatively fewer accounting measures that compare factors that take place within the last time period. For example, higher inflation may affect all of revenues (prices), costs (wages and interest), and resulting earnings more simultaneously.

Protecting oneself against inflation effectively is difficult. The price of some assets (e.g., commodities, **precious metals** such as gold, and real estate) tend to outpace overall consumer inflation (i.e., provided a hedge) during some periods when inflation is climbing or expected to climb. However, those same assets may fall in price when the risk of inflation subdues. Thus, while precious metals may provide protection over short periods of climbing inflation, over the long term, common stocks, for instance, have delivered far higher returns. Companies' costs and sales and workers' wages often increase in line with inflation for many (growing) sectors of the economy, but fail to do so for other sectors with worse long-term prospects. While some parties include inflation adjustments in contracts (e.g., **cost of living adjustment clauses**), such clauses remain relatively rare in the U.S. Also, while such clauses may benefit one party, they may be costly and ultimately shift the risk to a counterparty. The U.S. government started to sell Treasury Inflation-indexed Securities (commonly abbreviated as TIPS since the securities once included the word "protected" instead of "indexed") in 1997. As an example of how protecting against inflation is costly, these securities provide larger payouts if the CPI increases, but if inflation turns out to be low, as in the early 2010's, buyers may receive negative nominal returns.

Inflation is most commonly reported on an annual or year-on-year basis (e.g., comparing the price level in a given month, say April of 1995, to the price level in the same month in the previous year, i.e., April of 1994). **Hyperinflation** is similar to inflation, except that the value of the currency is decreased at a much faster rate, so prices increase much more rapidly.

Deflation is a term describing a general decline in the price level (i.e., not a decline in the prices of just a few goods) or a negative inflation rate. Periods of weak economic growth are sometimes (like the 1930's in the U.S., Japan in recent decades, and part of the recent U.S. financial crisis) accompanied by bouts of very low inflation or outright deflation, and by low nominal interest rates. Many economists argue that deflation can damage the economy as businesses may not want to take loans when they are uncertain about how well the economy will perform (i.e., will sales justify the loan?) and about whether the purchasing power of the principal of their loan will actually have increased. The solution for deflation (that is most commonly cited and that is most theoretically accepted) is *to increase the money supply.* However, the experience of Japan since the mid-1990's shows that ending long periods of deflation may be easier in theory than in practice.

There are three common measures of price inflation:

- **The Consumer price index (CPI)** compares the price of a fixed basket of goods and services that a typical urban consumer might purchase in an earlier base period (e.g., 100 in 1982-84) and the price of the same basket of goods and services at later times. The CPI is commonly used to convert "nominal" figures that are not readily comparable across years into "real" figures that use the same level of prices and are therefore more comparable. Consider, for instance, one worker who earned (and for simplicity spent) $40,000 in 2002 when the CPI was 180 and the same worker who earned (and spent) $50,000 in 2012 when the CPI was 230. Converting the $40,000 from 2002 into 2012 dollars (or prices), one finds that the income in 2002 purchased the equivalent of $51,111 in 2012 (= $40,000 × 230 / 180); so, in this example the workers' real income actually fell by 2.2% during this period.

- **The Producer price index (PPI)** compares the price of a fixed basket of goods, inputs, and materials purchased by producers at the wholesale level, instead of focusing on the prices paid at the retail level by consumers.

- **The GDP deflator** is the most comprehensive measure of price levels, including prices paid by all parties included in GDP instead of only consumers. The GDP deflator is the index used to convert nominal GDP into real GDP.

Aggregate Demand and Supply

Just as there are demand and supply curves for individual products, some economists find it helpful to use aggregate demand and supply curves for the overall levels of prices and production of goods and services of an entire economy. An **Aggregate Demand Curve** seeks to represent the relationship between (1) total expenditures by consumers, businesses, government, and the foreign sector and (2) the price level, at a given point of time.

The *aggregate demand curve* may slope downward for several reasons:

- **Interest rate effect** – Higher inflation rates increase nominal interest rates and may decrease consumer borrowing, reducing the quantity demanded (negative shift in the demand curve) of items whose purchase is typically financed, such as houses and automobiles.

- **Wealth effect** – Higher inflation rates reduce the value of most fixed income investments (such as conventional bonds). Having less wealth, individuals may consume less.

- **International purchasing power effect** – Domestic inflation makes domestic goods and services more expensive relative to foreign goods and services, increasing the quantity demanded of foreign products and decreasing the quantity demanded (negative shift in the demand curve) of domestic goods and services.

An **Aggregate Supply Curve** seeks to represent the relationship between (1) total goods and services produced (production, output, or quantity) and (2) the price level, at a given point of time. Economists don't often agree on the precise shape of the supply curve, but for the purposes of the CPA exam, we will simply assume that it is generally upward sloping, as shown in the two examples below.

Just like in the market for a single product, the aggregate demand and aggregate supply curves may also shift. A "first-pass" simplified macroeconomic model focuses on shifts in the aggregate demand, increasing or decreasing depending, for instance, on consumer, business, and foreign sector confidence about the future, and countercyclical policy by the government. The standard assumption is that looser fiscal policy (i.e., larger government budget deficits) and looser monetary policy (i.e., lower interest rates) increase aggregate demand. It is also assumed that the opposite is true with tighter fiscal policy and tighter monetary policy decreasing aggregate demand. We review fiscal and monetary policy and their commonly expected effects in more detail further below.

We may use the aggregate supply, aggregate demand framework to illustrate two possible causes of inflation.

Demand-Pull Inflation (i.e., the demand curve shifted upward)

When aggregate spending increases, the **demand** curve moves to the **right**, causing the market equilibrium to occur at higher price levels (see graph below). Excess demand bids up the cost of labor and other resources. Excess demand may be a result, for instance, of improved expectations by consumers or businesses, of the foreign sector, or from government fiscal and monetary policy that turned out to be too loose.

Notice that, according to this simplified model, the equilibrium point occurs at higher levels of both prices AND quantity. Economists have historically found that in the short term (i.e., less than a few years), there is a trade-off between inflation and unemployment. We often observe that when economies are growing quickly and unemployment rates fall particularly low (e.g., below NAIRU), wages, company costs, and consumer inflation rates rise more quickly. Conversely, when economies are not growing as fast and unemployment rates are higher (above NAIRU), wages, company costs, and consumer inflation rates rise less quickly, if at all. This short-term tradeoff between inflation and unemployment is known as the short-term **Phillips Curve**. However, this tradeoff holds only in the short term. In the long term (i.e., after a few years), unemployment rates rise back to NAIRU. Thus, in a graph (not shown here) where inflation is in the y-axis and unemployment in the x-axis, the long-term Phillips Curve is said to be vertical: policies that seek to reduce unemployment below NAIRU may seem to succeed in the short term, but do not yield sustainable reductions in unemployment, but increases in inflation.

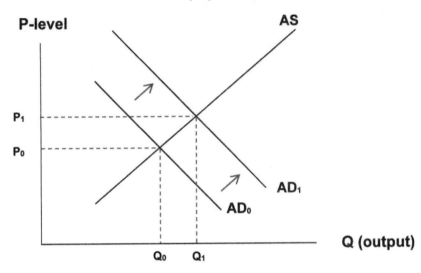

Cost-Push Inflation (i.e., the supply curve shifted inward)

If producers (or suppliers) within one country face increases in the costs of using some inputs (e.g., commodities such as oil), the **aggregate supply** curve would shift to the **left**, causing the market equilibrium to occur at a higher price level and at a lower quantity. Since the prices of many production inputs are set in international markets, individual countries may experience changes in those input costs that are not directly, or strictly, related to economic conditions within that country. Many observers argue that such a "**negative supply shock**" played a key role in the **stagflation** that affected the U.S. during the 1970's. Stagflation is a term that combines the words "stagnation" and "inflation," but it is generally used to describe periods of high inflation and high unemployment.

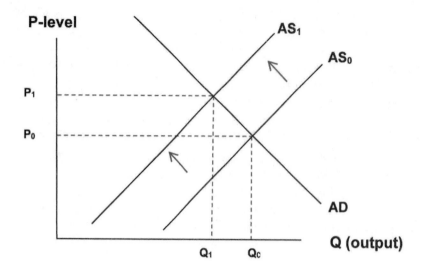

Lecture 1.10 – Multiplier Effect

If an economy is producing below its potential, increases in spending by consumers, businesses, the government, or the foreign sector may cause increases in output that exceeds the increase in spending. Any initial increase in spending may act with what is called a **multiplier effect** mobilizing otherwise idle or unemployed resources, as the first round of increased spending becomes income to previously underutilized suppliers, who in turn will spend more, increasing the income of other suppliers, etc.

In a simplified macroeconomic model, the size of the multiplier effect depends on the percentage of increased income that consumers are likely to spend, the **marginal propensity to consume (MPC),** and the related percentage of increased income that they will save, the **marginal propensity to save (MPS).**

In a simplified macroeconomic model, the *increase in output (equilibrium GDP)* that results from an injection of new spending may be computed as follows:

$$\text{Increase in output (equilibrium GDP)} = \frac{\text{Change in spending}}{\text{Marginal Propensity to Save (MPS)}}$$

For example, if those making up the economy overall are likely to consume/spend 75% of increased income and save the other 25%, then a change in spending of $300 will raise GDP by $1,200:

$300 / 25\% = \$1,200$

Lecture 1.11 – Macroeconomics – Class Questions

11. The main concerns of macroeconomics are:

    a. Unemployment, economic growth, and inflation
    b. The trade balance, foreign investment, and exchange rates
    c. The national debt and the budget balance
    d. Lending growth, interest rates, and asset prices (e.g., the stock and housing markets)

12. Gross domestic product includes which of the following measures?

    a. The size of a population that must share a given output within one year.
    b. The negative externalities of the production process of a nation within one year.
    c. The total monetary value of all final goods and services produced within a nation in one year.
    d. The total monetary value of goods and services including barter transactions within a nation in one year.

13. The following information is available for economic activity for year 1:

	In billions
Financial transactions	$60
Second-hand sales	50
Consumption by households	40
Investment by businesses	30
Government purchases of goods and services	20
Net exports	10

What amount is the gross domestic product for year 1?
    a. $210 billion
    b. $160 billion
    c. $100 billion
    d. $90 billion

14. If a CPA's client expected a high inflation rate in the future, the CPA would suggest to the client which of the following types of investments?

    a. Precious metals.
    b. Treasury bonds.
    c. Corporate bonds.
    d. Common stock.

Class Solutions

11. (a) Answers (b), (c) and (d) are incorrect because while those are concerns of macroeconomics, they are only concerns in as much as they affect unemployment, economic growth, and inflation.

12. (c) Gross domestic product (GDP) is defined as the total monetary value of all final goods and services produced within a nation in one year. Answer (a) is incorrect because GDP does not count population. Answer (b) is incorrect because GDP does not measure whether the output helps (positive externalities) or harms anyone (negative externalities). Answer (d) is incorrect because GDP does not include barter transactions.

13. (c) Gross domestic product (GDP) is defined as the total monetary value of all final goods and services produced within a nation in one year. It does not include financial transactions, which do not represent outputs. Nor does it include second-hand sales, which would have been included when the goods were originally produced. It does include consumption by households of $40 billion, investment by businesses of $30 billion, government purchases of $20 billion, and net exports of $10 billion for a total of $100 billion.

14. (a) When high inflation is anticipated, precious metals will likely fluctuate in price proportionately to other goods and commodities and, as a result, an investment will be neither benefited nor hurt. Answers (b) and (c) are incorrect because bonds generally bear interest at a fixed rate. As a result, in periods of high inflation, the fixed amount of interest will be able to purchase fewer goods and bond investors will be hurt. Answer (d) is incorrect because although common stock may be a better investment in the long run, in the short run, business is often adversely affected by inflation due to the increase in costs that may not be immediately matched by an increase in revenues. As a result, an investment in common stock may decrease in periods of inflation.

Lecture 1.12 – Business Cycles

Business cycles are fluctuations in economic production (output) typically lasting several years. Some business cycles have been shorter (barely a couple of years) and others longer (over one decade). Some business cycles are deep, involving large fluctuations (like the recession surrounding the financial crisis of 2008) and others relatively shallower (like the recession in 2001 following the dot.com bust). By convention, each business cycle includes one recession (or contraction) and one expansion. Each recession begins at the peak (or maximum level of output) from the previous expansion and ends at its trough (or minimum level of output for the recession). Each expansion begins at the trough of the previous recession and ends at the next peak.

The early stages of expansions are called recoveries. Recoveries are commonly described as having become full expansions when the previous peak is passed. Over the long term, nearly all measures of economic activity and personal well-being have grown or improved enormously in virtually every capitalist economy. However, growth has not taken place at a steady pace, but typically alternates between longer periods of strong growth and shorter periods of decline.

Terms used in connection with the business cycle include:

- **Expansion –** Typically extended period (i.e., several years) of increased economic production. The early stages of many expansions (i.e., recoveries) during the second half of the twentieth century were marked by fast declines in unemployment rates. However, declines in unemployment have grown increasingly slower (i.e., so-called **jobless recoveries**) following each of the last three recessions (i.e., those of 1990-1991, 2001, and 2007-2009). The final stages of many expansions during the twentieth century were marked by booming economic conditions, including GDP above potential and higher rates of inflation. Increased spending will cause a positive shift in the demand curve to the right (higher equilibrium GDP). Technological advances will also cause a positive shift in the supply curve, also resulting in a higher equilibrium GDP.

- **Recession (or Contraction) –** Typically briefer periods (i.e., several months or only a few years) of decreased economic production. Formally, the business cycle dating committee of the National Bureau of Economic Research (NBER, technically a non-profit) determines the beginning and end of recessions and expansions based on a variety of parameters. As a rule of thumb, economists describe recessions as periods of at least two consecutive quarters of negative growth in real GDP. During the twentieth century, **many recessions followed efforts by the Federal Reserve (see section below on monetary policy) to restrain higher inflation rates through increases in interest rates**. The declines in economic production during recessions are accompanied by declines in employment and increases in unemployment rates (Okun's law provides a commonly-mentioned rule of thumb relating declines in GDP and increases in unemployment). At the end of recessions, GDP is well below potential. Periods of decreased aggregate spending will shift the demand curve to the left and result in a lower equilibrium GDP. Trade wars cause a negative shift in the supply curve and also cause a decline in GDP.

- **Depression –** A recession that is either particularly deep or long lasting. There is no formal agreement as to the boundary between recession and depression. For perspective, the Great Depression of 1929-1933 involved declines in real GDP of 27% and increases in unemployment rates from 3.2% to 25.2%. Since unemployment rates had declined only to 9.9% by 1941, the Great Depression is often dated as having spanned 1929-1941. In contrast, the recent Great Recession was the deepest recession since World War II and involved declines in real GDP of 4.7% and increases in unemployment rates from 4.7% to 10.1%.

- **Recovery –** The early stages of an expansion, commonly thought to become a full expansion when the peak from the previous expansion is passed.

Output

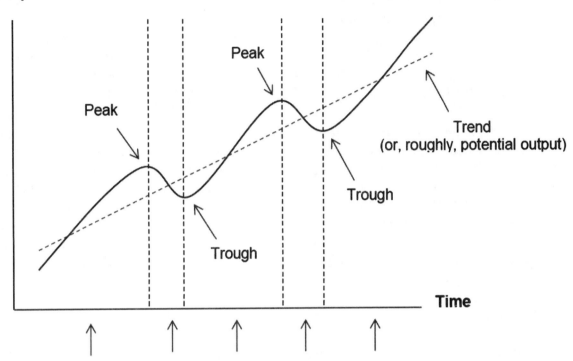

Economists track many indicators to gauge, evaluate, and predict current and future economic conditions. These indicators may be classified into three broad categories:

- **Leading Indicators –** seek to predict whether expansions (or recessions) are likely to end within the next few months. Economists have experimented with many indicators for these purposes, but their effectiveness, of course, varies across business cycles. Some commonly-used leading indicators include changes in **stock market prices**, average hours worked per week, **new orders for durable goods**, average initial claims for unemployment insurance, building permits, and new private **housing starts**.

- **Coincident Indicators –** normally move up and down simultaneously (coincide) with economic expansions and recessions. Examples include **industrial production** and manufacturing and trade sales.

- **Lagging indicators –** only move up and down months after economic conditions change. Examples include the **average prime rate** for bank loans, the **average duration of unemployment,** and the **unemployment rate**.

Increases in economic growth do not necessarily result mechanically in increases in job growth in the short term. For instance, if businesses are afraid that growth is temporary, they may rely on overtime from existing employees rather than hiring new workers. However, in the long term, subject to long and variable lags, economic growth does tend to result in job growth. In a sense, sustained declines in the unemployment rates serve as one of the most important lagging indicators of economic recovery.

Economists commonly identify three or four **types of unemployment:**

- **Frictional unemployment –** affects workers who are unemployed as a result of the normal turnover of workers between jobs or of new entrants into the work force. Some of these workers may leave their employers voluntarily searching for something better. In other cases, employers may have discontinued employment, but the employees find new work relatively quickly. In a mobile society and given unavoidable "imperfections in the labor market," or "search costs" (i.e., the time needed to find and compare alternative jobs and to decide that it is not worth waiting for something else better), market economies unavoidably always have some level of this type of unemployment, even in "full" employment.

- **Structural unemployment –** affects workers who lose their jobs as a result of changes in the demands for goods and services (e.g., manufacturers of horse buggies when automobiles took off) or of technological advances that reduce the need for their current skills (e.g., car mechanics unused to electronics in automobiles). Addressing this type of unemployment normally requires retraining. The problem underlying this type of unemployment is not deficient aggregate demand, but the speed with which workers may be retrained to meet new demands and technologies.

- **Cyclical unemployment –** involves job losses resulting from the fluctuations in the business cycle. This type of unemployment is the key concern during recessions and decreases during expansions.

Note: The "*Full*-employment," "natural," or "non-accelerating-inflation" rate of unemployment (NAIRU) rates, are the rates below which unemployment may not fall sustainably without causing boom conditions that eventually may result in higher rates of inflation. If we identify only the three types of unemployment above, NAIRU would largely be the sum of *frictional and structural* unemployment.

- **Institutional unemployment –** Some economists identify this type of unemployment as that affecting workers who cannot find employment as a result of government restrictions on the economy, e.g., wage floors for younger workers, restrictions on the ability of small businesses to launch, etc. Since injections of aggregate demand may not help these workers and result in inflation, this type of unemployment would also be part of NAIRU. Differences in NAIRU across countries often result from different institutional frameworks and, thus, from different levels of institutional unemployment.

Lecture 1.13 – Interest Rates & Government Involvement in the Economy

Interest Rates

Interest rates refer to the prices that various borrowers (households, businesses, governments, even financial institutions) pay in exchange for "funds" (i.e., loans and bonds), and the prices that lenders (or depositors) receive in exchange for forgoing the use of their funds for various periods of time (ranging from long periods as in mortgages and certificates of deposit to potentially "zero" time, as in checking and savings accounts). Interest rates are determined by the demand and supply of funds. Businesses, for instance, may demand funds (loans) if they expect the return on their projects to exceed the interest rate they pay. Governments and households (e.g., students and younger home buyers) are, of course, also large demanders of funds (borrowers).

The supply of funds is affected by past and current saving by households (e.g., older ones) and many firms, but also by government monetary policy. Increases in the demand for loans (whether by households, businesses, or governments) put upward pressure on interest rates.

Types of interest rates include:

- **Nominal interest rates** – are those regularly quoted by financial institutions. Setting interest rates, financial institutions and markets will include "premiums" to protect themselves against expected problems, such as inflation, loan defaults ("credit risk"), etc. Of course, actual levels of inflation and loan defaults often vary from those expected when interest rates are originally set.

- **Real interest rates** – are adjusted for inflation. Calculations of real interest rates often seek to incorporate the rate of inflation that is expected in the future. In practice, such expectations typically largely mimic recent historical experience.

- **Risk-free interest rates** – are those that would be charged to borrowers if lenders had an absolute certainty of being repaid (i.e., no credit risk). Financial markets largely treat the rates paid on conventional United States Treasury securities (or Treasurys, i.e., it is not spelled Treasuries) as indicators of risk-free interest rates. The U.S. Treasury issues securities through a large range of maturities (from 4 weeks to 30 years) in both a conventional format (where the buyer bears inflation risk) and in an inflation-indexed format (i.e., TIPS, where buyers are compensated for deviations in the CPI). Interest rates on conventional U.S. Treasurys are indicators of risk-free rates plus an inflation premium. Interest rates on TIPS are indicators of risk-free rates. The difference between conventional and TIPS Treasurys for a given maturity are indicators of expected inflation over that maturity (even though there are also, typically small, liquidity premiums involved). For instance, if 10-year conventional Treasurys yield 2.0% and the 10-year TIPS yield -0.5%, then the expected inflation rate (plus the difference in liquidity premiums) over the next ten years would be 2.5%.

- **Federal funds rate (Discount rate)** – are those that commercial banks charge and pay one another for short-term loans of reserves (i.e., unlent cash, also called "federal funds") at the Federal Reserve System (the U.S. central bank, commonly called the "Fed"). In recent decades, the Fed has conducted monetary policy largely through "open market operations," i.e., setting a target rate for the federal funds rate and buying and selling short-term U.S. Treasurys (bills) to ensure that the actual (effective) rate in the federal funds market matched its target. Below, in the section on monetary policy, we explain the details further.

- **Prime rate** – The rate banks charge their most creditworthy business customers on short-term loans. Throughout the last two decades, most banks have routinely set their prime rates at a 3% premium over the federal funds rate.

Government Involvement in the Economy

While the proper role and extent of government involvement is likely to be debated indefinitely, governments are very likely to continue to regularly intervene in many aspects of the economy for the foreseeable future through **fiscal policy, monetary policy,** and **regulatory policy**.

Fiscal Policy

Fiscal Policy involves governments setting, applying, and changing levels of taxes, subsidies, and government spending. Many economists argue that, if (1) economic production (GDP) is below potential, (2) the financial sector is failing to lend funds adequately, and (3) unemployment rates are too high, then governments may successfully use **deficit spending** as **expansionary fiscal** policy to increase aggregate demand and, thus, output. Deficit spending involves increasing spending levels without increasing tax revenues by an equivalent amount, or lowering tax revenues without decreasing spending by an equivalent amount.

The (federal) **deficit** is the amount by which (federal) government expenditures (or spending or outlays) exceed (federal tax) revenues (or inlays) within a period of time (typically, reported for one year, or one month). The U.S. government finances its deficits through the sale of U.S. Treasurys (called bills, notes, and bonds depending on their maturity). The (federal or national) **debt** is the total amount of outstanding U.S. Treasurys or the sum of past deficits (subject to some adjustments as some government agencies hold securities issued by other branches of government).

Conversely, if (1) economic production is above potential and (2) there are concerns about boom economic conditions and current or upcoming rates of inflation that are too high, then governments may run budget surpluses as **contractionary fiscal** policy (increase taxes) to reduce aggregate demand and, thus, inflation. Historically far rarer, (federal) surpluses involve revenues exceeding expenditures.

Types of taxes include income and payroll taxes (like those for social security and Medicare) and international trade tariffs (all of the above chiefly used by the federal government), sales (consumption or excise) taxes (chiefly used by state governments), and property taxes (chiefly used by local governments). Current income taxes use "progressive" tax rates that are higher for those with higher incomes and zero or, even negative, for those with lower incomes. Some economists argue that income taxes reduce incentives for individuals to work and, conversely, that switching to consumption taxes would increase incentives for individuals to save.

Monetary Policy

Monetary Policy involves efforts by the central bank of the U.S., the Federal Reserve System (or "Fed") to manage credit conditions, interest rates, and the money supply. Like other elements of macroeconomic policy, the key goals of monetary policy include (1) maximizing economic growth, (2) minimizing unemployment rates, (3) minimizing inflation rates, and (4) minimizing economic and financial fluctuations, i.e., ensuring financial stability, minimizing boom-bust cycles, avoiding financial crises, and minimizing failures of financial institutions. The Fed has several tools at its disposal to carry out **expansionary monetary policy** (e.g., to reduce unemployment rates) and **contractionary monetary policy** (e.g., to reduce inflation rates). Some of these tools include:

- **Reserve requirements (ratio)** – The Fed may affect the total amount of lending in the economy (e.g., tighten/loosen credit conditions) by changing (i.e., increasing/decreasing) the percentage of customer's deposits that the Fed requires banks to hold in reserve (i.e., not to be loaned out). In recent decades, the Fed has rarely changed reserve requirements, i.e., it has effectively not used them as a tool of monetary policy.

- **Discount rate** – The Fed may affect the total amount of lending in the economy (e.g., tighten/loosen credit conditions) by changing (i.e., increasing/decreasing) the interest rate (called the discount rate) that it charges banks for short-term emergency loans. Except in, fortunately, still relatively rare crisis conditions, few banks request these types of loans to avoid the stigma of informing the Fed (their regulator in many cases) that they need "emergency" help. Thus, in recent decades, the discount rate has largely not been a key tool of monetary policy.

- **Open-market operations** – In recent decades, the Fed has conducted monetary policy largely through "open market operations," i.e., setting a target rate for the federal funds rate and buying and selling short-term U.S. Treasurys (bills) to ensure that the actual (effective) rate in the federal funds market matched its target. When the Fed is concerned about high unemployment rates, it can engage in expansionary monetary policy by lowering its target for the federal funds rate, buying government securities on the open market, thereby increasing the amount of reserves available for banks to lend (the money supply).

When the Fed is concerned about boom conditions or current or expected high inflation rates, it can engage in contractionary monetary policy by increasing its target for the federal funds rate, or selling government securities on the open market, or both, thereby decreasing the amount of reserves available for banks to lend (the money supply).

Until the financial crisis, the federal funds rate was routinely substantially above 0%. Under such conditions, many observers interpreted monetary policy as largely involving changes in interest rates. At that time, increasing (reducing) interest rates (i.e., akin to the *price* of credit) would typically make credit conditions tighter (looser), i.e., reduce (increase) the *quantity* (or the rate of increase) of money (and eventually lending).

During the years following the financial crisis of 2008, the federal funds rate was almost zero (the Fed could technically have insisted on banks formally charging one another negative interest rates, but it did not). Thus, when, for instance in 2013, the Fed engaged in open market operations to buy Treasurys, and increase the *quantity* of money, the Fed did not formally affect the federal funds rate (a *price*), i.e., the federal funds rate remained at almost zero and did not formally become negative in nominal terms. Since Fed open market operations then did not formally affect the level of the federal funds rate (i.e., a *price*), but only affected the *quantity* of money, these types of policies are widely known as **quantitative easing**.

Another difference between Fed open market operations before and after the financial crisis is that before the crisis, the Fed bought almost exclusively Treasurys and now the Fed buys large amounts of real estate-related securities (albeit issued by Fannie Mae and Freddie Mac, institutions currently managed by the federal government).

Monetary policy may impact economic conditions because looser (or tighter) credit conditions may affect the decisions of individual economic agents (e.g., households and businesses). Looser credit conditions (e.g., lower interest rates and more readily available credit) tend to stimulate consumer and business spending (and thus aggregate demand). Tighter credit conditions (e.g., higher interest rates and less readily available credit) tend to discourage consumer and business spending, of course. Because monetary policy is beset with long and variable lags that may be several years long, achieving the many goals of monetary policy sustainably is not easy in practice.

Economists use a variety of measures to track credit conditions, including interest rates, lending volumes, surveys of underwriting standards, and monetary aggregates such as the **monetary base, M1,** and **M2**. While the theoretical relationship between money, output, and prices (subject to lags) still stands, (1) far deeper financial markets, (2) the large role of the U.S. dollar abroad, (3) regulatory changes, and (4) technological innovations have jointly reduced the relevance of short-term changes in monetary aggregates in predicting the short-term impacts of monetary policy.

Regulatory Policy

Governments may further influence economic activity through regulations affecting environmental issues, labor issues (e.g., immigration and minimum wage laws), occupational health and safety, energy policy, healthcare, bank capital, lending practices, etc. On one hand, governments may choose to channel resources from disfavored sectors to favored sectors. On the other hand, governments could seek to reduce the likelihood of financial crises, for instance, by requiring banks to develop thicker capital cushions over time, or by adjusting minimum permissible mortgage downpayments if other housing bubbles surfaced in the future.

Economic Theories

There are several theories and schools of thought in macroeconomics that seek to explain recurring business cycles and whether, how, and how much governments contribute to alleviating or worsening business cycles. Some theories focus on the **private sector** (changing consumer and business confidence, and periodic unbridled lending excess by the financial sector) as chief contributors to economic and financial instability. Other theories focus on **government actions**, and their poor timing and incentives, as chief contributors to economic and financial instability. Few practicing macroeconomists openly embrace one of the following labels, but the labels remain useful for identifying the overall background behind various policy proposals.

- **Classical economic theory** (no government intervention) argues that, in the absence of government-induced distortions (e.g., price and wage controls, restrictions on banks' note issuance and lending, and restrictions on banks' geographic expansion, like branching restrictions), economies would be largely self-stabilizing, with only relatively small fluctuations in unemployment and inflation rates. This theory **does not support government intervention**, like fiscal policy or monetary policy, to manage macroeconomic conditions.

- **Keynesian theory** (fiscal policy – lower taxes and more government spending) argues that prices and wages in the economy do not adjust quickly enough on their own. Thus, economies would not self-stabilize quickly enough and governments must use ***Fiscal Policy*** to manage macroeconomic conditions, for instance, increasing budget deficits (lower taxes or more government spending) during recessions and running surpluses (higher taxes or less government spending) during expansions or, at least, during periods of high inflation.

- **Monetarist theory** (monetary policy – open market operations) argues that to minimize fluctuations in both unemployment and inflation rates, central banks (e.g., the Fed) should target rates of growth in money (and thus lending) that are stable over time. This theory focuses on **stable Monetary growth**, not on stable interest rates; so, the Fed would (1) allow interest rates to climb if banks and borrowers wanted to lend and borrow more than the long-term average growth rate of money (and lending) and (2) allow interest rates to fall if banks and borrowers wanted to lend and borrow less than the long-term average. This theory argues that efforts by the Fed to occasionally increase monetary growth by more than the long-term average are more likely to add instability (i.e., worse boom-bust cycles and inflation) than to succeed in minimizing instability.

- **Supply-side theory** (reduce taxes) argues that government policy should focus less on managing short-term fluctuations in the aggregate demand curve, and more on removing impediments to economic production (saving, investment, work, innovation), thereby shifting the aggregate supply curve outward over the long term. This theory underpins investigating what government laws and regulations may be counterproductive and updating or removing them. The most well-known application of this theory is the **Laffer Curve**. This curve points out that if tax rates are high enough, increasing tax rates further will not yield more revenue (e.g., in an extreme example, workers will work less if the tax rate is 100% than if it is 50%). Under such conditions, **lowering tax rates** may actually increase tax revenues. An example of an application of this theory took place during the Kennedy administration, as maximum income tax rates were lowered from 90% to 70%.

- **New Keynesian theory** represents the closest to whatever consensus there is today in macroeconomic thinking by combining some elements of Keynesian and monetarist theories. The theory argues that the relationships between monetary aggregates and economic conditions have been too loose to rely strictly on a constant (i.e., very, very stable) rate of monetary growth to minimize fluctuations in unemployment and inflation rates. The theory argues that policymakers should use both *Fiscal and Monetary* **Policy** to manage macroeconomic conditions, loosening (or tightening) both in response to higher rates of unemployment (or inflation).

- **Austrian theory** provides some insights as to how monetary policy may lead to dislocations in the allocation of resources, play a role in the formation of bubbles, and contribute to boom-bust cycles (i.e., make the economy less stable). For instance, excessively low interest rates at one point may push businesses to initiate more long-term oriented projects (e.g., factories and housing developments) that, once finished, may turn out to have overestimated actual consumer demand. The resulting oversupply in one sector (e.g., housing) may result in higher unemployment in that sector and, as excess inventories may take long to be worked out, recovery may be slow.

Lecture 1.14 – Business Cycles – Class Questions

15. Which of the following economic terms describes a general decline in prices for goods and services and in the level of interest rates?

    a. Expansion
    b. Inflation.
    c. Deflation.
    d. Recession.

16. Which of the following actions is the acknowledged preventive measure for a period of deflation?

    a. Increasing interest rates.
    b. Increasing the money supply.
    c. Decreasing interest rates.
    d. Decreasing the money supply.

17. An economy is at the peak of the business cycle. Which of the following policy packages is the most effective way to dampen the economy and prevent inflation?

    a. Increase government spending, reduce taxes, increase money supply, and reduce interest rates.
    b. Reduce government spending, increase taxes, increase money supply, and increase interest rates.
    c. Reduce government spending, increase taxes, reduce money supply, and increase interest rates.
    d. Reduce government spending, reduce taxes, reduce money supply, and reduce interest rates.

18. Which of the following strategies would the Federal Reserve most likely pursue under an expansionary policy?

    a. Purchase federal securities and lower the discount rate.
    b. Reduce the reserve requirement while raising the discount rate.
    c. Raise the reserve requirement and lower the discount rate.
    d. Raise the reserve requirement and raise the discount rate.

19. In standard macroeconomic theory, to address unemployment the Congress should

    a. Reduce taxes, increase government expenditures, and thus run deficits.
    b. Reduce taxes, reduce government expenditures, and run balanced budgets.
    c. Increase taxes, increase government expenditures, and run balanced budgets.
    d. Reduce taxes, maintain government expenditures, and run budget surpluses.

20. The full-employment gross domestic product is $1.3 trillion, and the actual gross domestic product is $1.2 trillion. The marginal propensity to consume is 0.8. When inflation is ignored, what increase in government expenditures is necessary to produce full employment?

    a. $100 billion
    b. $80 billion
    c. $20 billion
    d. $10 billion

21. Which of the following types of unemployment typically results from technological advances?

    a. Cyclical.
    b. Frictional.
    c. Structural.
    d. Short-term.

Class Solutions

15. (c) Deflation represents a decrease in the price level of an economy, which would cause declines in prices and interest rates. Answer (a) is incorrect because expansion refers to an increase in output, not prices. Answer (b) is incorrect because inflation is the opposite of deflation. Answer (d) is incorrect because recession refers to a decrease in output, not prices.

16. (b) Deflation can be avoided when there is an increase in the demand for goods, causing an increase in prices. Increasing the money supply will provide consumers with more disposable income, with which they will buy more goods and prices will increase, avoiding deflation. Answer (a) is incorrect because increasing interest rates will make it costlier to borrow, decreasing the disposable income available to consumers. Answer (c) is incorrect because decreasing interest rates may make it less costly to borrow, but will not make more money available to lend and, in fact, by reducing the return to lenders, may reduce the amount available. Answer (d) is incorrect because decreasing the money supply would have the opposite effect of increasing the money supply.

17. (c) The economy will be slowed and inflation prevented through the use of contractionary fiscal and monetary policies, which would include decreasing, not increasing, government spending; increasing, not reducing, taxes; reducing, not increasing, the money supply; and increasing, rather than reducing, interest rates.

18. (a) Expansionary policies would involve purchasing federal securities, which increases the money supply, lowering the discount rate, which makes borrowing less expensive, and reducing the reserve requirement, which increases the amounts that banks and other lending institutions will be able to lend.

19. (a) Standard macroeconomic advice during periods of high unemployment calls for an increase in aggregate expenditures, achieved through lower taxes (higher private consumption) or higher government expenditures, which result in deficits. Answers (b), (c) and (d) are incorrect because standard macroeconomic advice accepts government deficits during periods of high unemployment.

20. (c) When the marginal propensity to consume (MPC) is 0.8, 80% of the next dollar spent will come from consumption. In order to increase spending by $100 billion, $80 billion will come from consumer spending and $20 billion will come from another source, such as government expenditures.

21. (c) Structural unemployment results when there is both a demand for and supply of labor, but the supply and demand does not match, as would be the case when there are changes in technology and the work force is not adequately trained. Answer (a) is incorrect because cyclical unemployment results from changes in aggregate demand. Answer (b) is incorrect because frictional unemployment refers to the normal turnover of workers between jobs. Answer (d) is incorrect because the effects may be short-term or long-term.

Lecture 1.15 – International Trade & Economic Globalization

International Trade Theory

International trade theory, and the overwhelming majority of the evidence on international trade, show that trade among individuals and firms across borders is mutually beneficial, i.e., over time trade tends to increase the average standards of living for all countries involved. Trade across countries, like that among individuals within a country, increases overall production (and consumption) as the different parties specialize in producing more of the products and services that, as a result of differences in resources, climate, and specific skills, each party can produce more of. Economists differentiate between two types of trade-related advantages:

- **Absolute advantage –** A country being able to produce a good at a lower cost than another country.

  > For example, companies and/or farmers in Germany may be able to produce one small car, paying workers $12,000, and one ton of sugar, paying workers $300. Companies and/or farmers in Haiti (having access to worse factories, equipment, transportation systems, irrigation, etc., and fewer well-trained employees) may be able to produce one small car, paying workers $36,000, and one ton of sugar, paying workers $400. In this example, Germany would have an absolute advantage in the production of both products, i.e., costs are lower in Germany. Note that the comparison does not focus on hourly wages, but on costs of producing a certain amount of output. Having more equipment, German workers may require fewer hours to produce the same output.

- **Comparative advantage –** A country being able to produce a good at a lower relative cost than another country (the *opportunity costs, the amounts of the other good given up,* are less).

  > In our example, if Germans want to consume 40 more tons of sugar by shifting German labor away from car production, their production (and consumption) of cars falls by 1 car (= 40 × 300 / 12,000). In contrast, if Haitians reduced their production of cars by 1, they could increase production of sugar by 90 tons (= 36,000 × 1 / 400). If instead of reducing German car production by 1, (1) Germans increased car production by 1 and reduced sugar production by 40, (2) Haitians reduced their car production by 1 and increased sugar production by 90, and (3) Germans sold the extra car to Haiti, if Haitians shipped an amount of sugar higher than 40 tons and lower than 90 tons (i.e., between the relative costs in each country), then both countries would be able to consume more sugar and thus have increased their material standard of living (for simplicity, we designed this example such that consumption of cars did not change in either country).

International trade theory shows that even if one country had an absolute advantage in the production of all goods (like Germany in our example), for every pair of countries and every pair of goods, one country will have a comparative advantage in the production of one good (e.g., Germany in cars) and the other country will have a comparative advantage in the production of the other good (Haiti in sugar), such that both countries will be better off if each specializes in what they are better at (relative to the other) and they trade with one another.

Obstacles to International Trade

While all countries on average theoretically benefit from international trade, large fractions of goods and services are not traded across international borders. There are many barriers to international trade; some are "natural" and some are the result of government policy.

Examples of **natural barriers** to international trade include **transportation and information costs**. While a simple mathematical calculation (as the one shown above) might imply that China has a comparative advantage on warm dumplings and the U.S. on hot French fries, we do not observe massive shipments of dumplings and French fries in either direction daily. Simply, transportation costs may overwhelm the cost reductions promised by trade. In this extreme example, the costs of ensuring that French fries are delivered warm to China are prohibitive. As a result of transportation costs, many personal services (haircuts, restaurant food, etc.) are produced and consumed domestically, with little international trade. However, as transportation costs continue to fall (container ships, etc.), in recent decades, larger and larger fractions of economic production are involved in international trade.

Since economic conditions are constantly changing in every country, the relative costs of many products across many countries are always changing. While there are theoretical benefits from international trade, most firms find it easier to keep track of relative costs in a relatively smaller number of markets, and in particular those that are closer by. Economists use the term "information costs" to describe the fact that individuals and firms routinely forgo many possible gains from trade.

In recent decades, improvements in communication technology have also greatly reduced information costs and increased the scope for international trade. In a recent (if domestic) example, fishermen off the coast of India started receiving far better prices on their fish by using cell phones from the sea to check the prices available for various fish in various ports, instead of routinely selling all their fish in one single port. Improvements in information technology also play a role in the growth of international trade in services (call centers, technical support, accounting and legal services, etc.).

Many **governments** have historically established additional barriers to international trade. Historically, the most common type of trade barrier had been **tariffs** (taxes on imported goods). Domestic industries that are losing market share to foreign competitors (e.g., textiles, furniture, some food products in the U.S.) often advocate trade restrictions. Below we summarize some effects of trade restrictions.

- **Domestic Producers of protected goods** – Positive. The demand curve they face shifts to the right as the availability of substitute goods has been reduced. They sell more goods at higher prices. Managements and unions typically sought the restrictions as both parties benefit from higher sales and prices, with some of the gains passed on to owners, managers, and workers (in the form of higher wages and more job security than they would have otherwise).

- **Domestic Users** – Negative. The supply curve they face shifts to the left, forcing them to pay higher prices and being able to buy fewer goods.

- **Domestic Producers of exported goods** – Negative. The demand curve they face shifts to the left, as their consumers are made worse off overall by the higher prices they pay on protected goods. Since these negative impacts are diffused across many industries and the positive impacts of protection are concentrated on the protected industries, often each individual protected industry can lobby effectively for its protection without major opposition from all the other industries that are hurt only by a small amount (per industry).

- **Foreign Producers encountering protection elsewhere** – Negative. The demand curve they face shifts to the left, resulting in lower sales and prices.
- **Foreign Users of protected goods** – Positive. The supply curve shifts to the right, as their producers will have to do more selling in their own market. They buy more goods at lower prices.

Learning from the negative effects of **trade wars** during the interwar period and the Great Depression, throughout the second half of the twentieth century, many governments have moved to reduce many trade barriers and to coordinate some aspects of their economic policies. The **World Trade Organization (WTO)** is an international organization that (1) provides a forum to continue to negotiate greater liberalization of international trade policies, (2) provides a forum to resolve international trade disputes, and thus (3) seeks to help prevent trade wars and the growth of other trade barriers. Under the **North American Free Trade Agreement (NAFTA),** the *U.S., Mexico, and Canada* impose far lower trade restrictions on one another than on other countries.

Following the financial crisis, the **G-20** is the main forum that the governments of the leading countries of the world use to discuss global economic and financial stability. As its name implies, it brings together 20 leading economies, but for the first time includes both higher income (or industrialized or developed) countries and lower income (or emerging or developing) countries.

The **European Union (EU)** provides another example of international efforts to remove international barriers to trade. In its current format, the EU includes 28 European countries. The EU is commonly defined as an "**economic union**," providing for the free circulation of goods, services, firms, capital, residents, and labor. Combining some characteristics of a confederation and a federation, EU countries have many laws in common. 17 EU countries also share a single currency (the euro) and, thus, form a "**monetary union,**" known as the euro area or **Eurozone**. The European Central Bank (ECB) sets monetary policy for the Eurozone. The 19 Eurozone countries are Austria, Belgium, Cyprus, Estonia, Finland, France, Germany, Greece, Ireland, Italy, Latvia, Lithuania, Luxembourg, Malta, the Netherlands, Portugal, Slovakia, Slovenia, and Spain.

One example of governments' efforts to reduce trade barriers is that since World War II, many have increasingly reduced their reliance on tariffs as a means of trade protection. However, just as they moved away from tariffs, many countries continue to experiment and switch to other less transparent means of protection, such as import quotas; embargoes; foreign-exchange controls; subsidies; and technical, health, and safety requirements. Import **quotas** place limits on the quantity of a good that may be imported during a period. *Embargoes* are total bans on importing either a number of goods or nearly all goods from a country (e.g., the U.S. may place an embargo on armaments from specific countries, or on nearly all goods from Cuba).

In an example of how protection efforts can become blurred and complex, during the 1980's, the U.S. auto industry realized that the U.S. government was formally restricted by its international agreements from imposing tougher explicit restrictions on Japanese competitors. Thus, the U.S. auto industry pushed the U.S. government to push the Japanese government to push the Japanese auto industry to self-impose "voluntary" quotas, called "**voluntary export restraints" (VER).** One key result of these policies was Japanese companies switching from producing in Japan to sell in the U.S., to setting up factories in the U.S. to sell in the U.S.

Many governments also attempt to manipulate trade through **foreign-exchange controls.** These policies may restrict the types of domestic parties that may use foreign currencies, their amounts, and their uses. Governments may use these policies to favor some industries over others (e.g., encourage high tech imports over luxury goods, or vice versa, favor government-owned companies over domestic citizens traveling or studying abroad, etc.). Some countries operate multiple exchange rates, requiring more or less favored domestic parties to use the various rates for different purposes.

Dumping involves a manufacturer being found to have exported a product to one country at a price that was unjustifiably low and harmed the domestic producers of that country. In practice, World Trade Organization (WTO) and U.S. regulations to determine whether firms priced their products below their costs of production are difficult to maneuver for all parties (e.g., the calculations may take into account not only the exporters' costs of production but also those of their domestic competitors).

Companies operating in different countries (with different currencies) may engage in **dual-pricing** strategies, for instance, charging customers in new markets lower prices to introduce them to their products, or charging customers in countries with more elastic demand curves lower prices (even though that may open them to accusations of dumping).

Many governments also use **export subsidies** to encourage the production and export of specific products. Subsidies may take many forms, some more or less overt, ranging from outright payments to favored tax treatment, or access to subsidized lending. Under WTO rules, if a WTO panel finds that one country is in breach of international trade rules (e.g., by having illegal export subsidies) and the country refuses to correct the situation, the countries bringing the complaint may impose **countervailing duties** (i.e., tariffs) for an equivalent amount on products from the offending country.

Balance of Payments (BoP)

The Balance of Payments summarizes a country's transactions with other countries during a period of time. Its two key components are the current account and the capital account.

The Current Account focuses on the flow of goods and services. It also includes flows of government grants, net interest and dividends, and net unilateral transfers during a specific period of time.
- **The Balance of Trade** is the difference between *goods* exported and goods imported, excluding services. If exports are higher, a *trade surplus* exists. If imports are higher, a *trade deficit* exists.
- **The Balance of Goods and Services** is the same comparison, but with both *goods & services* included. However, in common parlance, observers often refer to the more comprehensive term of "deficits in the balance of goods and services" simply as "trade deficits."
- **Net Interest & Dividends** are interest and dividends received within a country from investments outside the country minus the interest and dividends paid to residents outside the country for investments within the country.
- **Net Unilateral Transfers** include foreign aid, payments to relatives and pension payments. They affect the deficit or surplus depending on whether the transfer is in or out of the country.

The Capital Account focuses on the flow of investments in fixed and financial assets during a specific period of time. The capital is largely a reverse image of the current account. If a country experiences a deficit on its balance of goods and services, i.e., foreigners sold more into the country than they bought from it, then those foreigners hold more of the country's assets (whether simply domestic currency or, exchanging that currency for something else, other assets such as stocks, bonds, land, etc.). Thus, the country with a current account deficit (more imports than exports) will have a matching capital account surplus (an increase in foreigners' holdings of the country's assets).

The International Monetary Fund (IMF) is another international organization that seeks to aid in the coordination of countries' economic policies. During crises, some countries may find that they may obtain funding to cover their short-term deficits in their balance of payments from private parties (e.g., banks granting loans to governments or individuals buying government bonds) at only very high interest rates, or that they may not obtain private funding at all. At those times, the IMF may not only be the only party willing to provide **funding at relatively low interest rates**, but also maybe the only party willing to provide funding at all. In exchange for short-term help during a crisis, the IMF typically requires countries to reduce their budget deficits and debts and engage in other supply-side "**structural reforms**" over the long term (privatization, deregulation, opening of closed sectors to competition from small businesses and foreign companies, etc.).

Foreign Exchange Rates

The exchange rates between countries' currencies are very important to any company that faces foreign competitors regardless of whether the company is an exporter facing competitors abroad or the company faces imports from foreign competitors domestically. When a foreign country's currency weakens, products from companies from that country become cheaper for purchasers in the U.S., providing those foreign companies' products an advantage. Fluctuations in currencies' exchange rates are ultimately based on relative changes in the supplies and demands of those currencies. However, the importance and speed with which various factors affect exchange rates is only poorly understood. In the last few decades, we have learned that, for instance, the purchasing powers of two currencies may drift apart considerably (20%-40%) for extended periods of time (one or two decades) before the two currencies' purchasing powers converge again. For instance, one might expect that if one country's inflation rate is 40% higher than another's, its exchange rate will fall by 40%, but, in practice, the exchange rate may only fall by 20% for an extended period of time. Companies considering decisions regarding short-term international trade and long-term international investments face these types of (nominal and real) exchange rate risks. **Repatriation** is the process of converting a foreign currency into your own country's currency ($U.S.), at the current exchange rate.

Exchange rates may be expressed by dividing by either currency, e.g., if €1 (i.e., 1 euro) buys $1.25, the exchange rate may be expressed as €1 = $1.25, or $1 = €0.80. In a table listing multiple exchange rates for one currency, it is customary to express all exchange rates on the same basis, e.g., how many units of the various foreign currencies does it take to buy $1. It is also customary to choose the "direction" of the exchange rates that ensures that most exchange rates are greater than 1 (i.e., $1 = 80 yen, instead of $0.0125 = 1 yen).

Commonly cited exchange rates between currencies include:
- **The Spot rate** is the exchange rate at which a financial party (a financial institution, a currency dealer, etc.) will exchange two currencies at this time, i.e., "on the spot."
- **The Forward rate** is the exchange rate at which a financial party will exchange two currencies at a specific future date (called the settlement date), e.g., three months later.

In forward markets, one currency is at a premium (discount) if its forward rate is higher (lower) than the spot rate (both rates expressed per the foreign currency), i.e., if it is expected to appreciate (depreciate). For instance, according to the spot rate, 1 Kuwaiti dinar may equal $3.57, and according to the 3-month forward rate, 1 Kuwaiti dinar may equal $3.53. In this case, there is a discount since the Kuwaiti dinar will be worth less in the future (i.e., it will buy fewer dollars). The size of the forward premium (or discount) is expressed in annual terms as follows:

$$\frac{\text{Forward rate} - \text{Spot rate}}{\text{Spot rate}} \times \frac{\text{Months in a year}}{\text{Months in the forward period}}$$

$$\frac{3.53 - 3.57}{3.57} \times \frac{12}{3} = -4.5\%$$

Some commonly cited *factors affecting foreign exchange rates* include:

- **Inflation –** Currencies from countries with higher inflation rates tend to depreciate (fall in value) relative to others. Because holding one unit of the currency with higher inflation purchases fewer goods and services, demand for those currencies falls.

- **Interest rates –** Currencies from countries with higher (inflation-adjusted, or real) interest rates appreciate (rise in value) relative to others. Since individuals and firms may shift some of their funds to those countries, demand for those currencies rise.

- **Balance of payments –** Currencies from countries that are net exporters (i.e., that have surpluses of goods and services) appreciate. Since net importers (i.e., the countries with other currencies) ultimately use the currencies of the net exporters to pay for their goods, demand for those currencies rise.

- **Government intervention –** In the long term, central banks' policies (interest rates and resulting inflation rates) are the key determinants of the exchange rates of their countries' currencies. In the short term, however, many central banks seek to manage their currencies, i.e., prevent short-term fluctuations away from long-term underlying trends, through the buying and selling of their holdings of foreign currencies. For example, official reserves are often held in the form of short-term securities from the leading countries in the world, e.g., the U.S., and each individual country's main trade partners.

- **Long-term economic stability –** Currencies from countries that are generally perceived to be more stable tend to endure fewer short-term fluctuations, i.e., currency markets will respond faster and more strongly to changes in factors that affect exchange rates in countries with worse long-term records in stability. For instance, short-term increases in inflation or budget deficits in Switzerland are less likely to cause the Swiss franc to depreciate than similar changes might have on the currencies of other countries. Under the **safe haven** effect, during international crises, international investors tend to buy more of the currencies of countries traditionally perceived to be more stable (e.g., the dollar, the Swiss franc, etc.).

Countries use a variety of **exchange rate systems** to manage the value of their currencies relative to those of other countries:

- Under **floating exchange rates,** a country's central bank never (or rarely) buys and sells foreign currencies (i.e., intervenes in foreign exchange markets) to influence the exchange rate of its currency relative to those of the other countries. Instead, the currency's exchange rates are set by the supply and demand of the currency by private parties (for travel, international trade, and international investment) as well as by the actions of other foreign central banks. Relatively few countries have ever used pure versions of floating exchange rates.

- Under **fixed exchange rates,** a country's central bank stands ready to buy and sell foreign currencies as needed constantly to maintain its exchange rate "fixed" relative to the currency of a key trading partner (e.g., dollar, the euro, the British pound). If a country simultaneously (1) permits its individuals and firms to buy and sell foreign currency somewhat freely and (2) wants to maintain a fixed exchange rate, then the country's central bank effectively forgoes control of its own monetary policy, largely having to match the monetary policy of the country against which it fixed its currency. The central banks of countries that pursue separate monetary policies (for instance, by having higher inflation rates) eventually run out of official reserves, and abandon their fixed exchange rates. Many countries attempt to fix their exchange rates, but find that they have to periodically "reset" the value of their "fixed exchange rate." A monetary union (like the euro) is an extreme form of fixed exchange rates. However, historically, monetary unions may break apart.

- **Managed exchange rates** fall somewhere in between floating and fixed exchange rates. Under these systems, a country's central bank may buy and sell foreign currencies to minimize short-term fluctuations in exchange rates away from long-term underlying trends, and/or target a broad band within which the currency may fluctuate (e.g., plus or minus 15% of some value of an exchange rate against the currency of a key country (or occasionally a basket of currencies). There are a variety of types of managed exchanged rates, and terms, ranging from formal "pegs" (closer to pure fixed exchange rates) to "dirty" floats (closer to pure floating rates).

Companies with operations in more than one country bear various types of **foreign exchange (or currency) risk**:

- A company with operations in countries with different currencies will likely have assets and liabilities in more than one currency. Creating financial statements (e.g., balance sheets) that cover the whole company will require using exchange rates to convert the value of the assets and liabilities from one country's currency into the currency used where the company is headquartered. Changes in those values resulting from changes in exchange rates involve **translation (accounting) risk** and are entered as gains or losses on the balance sheet as other comprehensive income (OCI). Companies may seek to manage their translation risk by **matching assets and liabilities** in each market where they operate. For instance, a company operating a plant (or a distribution network) in a foreign country might finance those operations in the local currency (i.e., through loans with local banks or by issuing bonds in that country's currency).

- A company with operations in countries with different currencies will likely have streams of future revenues and costs in more than one currency. Thus, forecasting future earnings, expressed in the currency used where the company is headquartered, will involve one additional type of risk that is known as **transaction risk**. Companies may seek to manage their transaction risk, similarly, by **matching** as many **revenues and costs** as possible in each market where they operate. For instance, a Japanese company selling cars in the U.S. would reduce the volatility of its earnings if its dollar-denominated revenues were matched by dollar-denominated labor costs, i.e., by producing some of those cars in the U.S. Short of matching revenues and costs by currency, companies also use derivatives, or *hedging contracts* to manage these risks.
    - **Options** permit, but do not require, holders to buy or sell commodities (e.g., a specific type of wheat) or instruments (a stock, bond, or currency), at a given price

until some date (under an American option) or at some date (under a European option).

- **CALL** Options permit the holder to BUY a security at a fixed price.
- **PUT** Options permit the holder to SELL a security at a fixed price.

o **Forwards** are specifically-negotiated contracts in which two parties agree to exchange (one party buys and the other sells) some quantity of a commodity or instrument (e.g., currency) at a pre-set price on a future date. Forwards differ from options in that they do not just permit the exchange, but require both parties to participate.

o **Futures** are standardized versions of forward contracts that are traded (bought and sold) in exchange markets (like the Chicago Board of Trade or the Chicago Mercantile Exchange). Future contracts have standardized sizes (e.g., $1 million) and dates (e.g., the end of a quarter).

o **Currency swaps** contracts under which one party A agrees to make payments in one currency to another party B (e.g., twelve monthly payments of 10 million pesos) and the other party B agrees to make payments to party A in the other currency (e.g., twelve monthly payments of $1 million) independently of how spot rates change during that period of time.

o **Money market hedges** involve turning transaction risk (which may result in either gains or losses) into a loan. This strategy involves the cost of certain interest payments, but removes the possibility that currencies may change unfavorably. In our example above, a U.S. company expecting 12 monthly payments of 10 million pesos could take a loan whose repayment schedule was 12 monthly payments of 10 million pesos (or twelve separate loans with single payments each one month apart) and convert the peso proceeds from the loan(s) into dollars today using the spot rate.

Asset-liability matching, derivative products, and other techniques may be used to hedge or manage a variety of business risks. For instance,

- Financial institutions bear **interest rate risk**, or the risk that changes in economy-wide interest rate levels may affect their earnings adversely. Typically, banks have assets with longer maturities (including for instance some long-term mortgage loans) and liabilities with shorter maturities (including for instance relatively few long-term bonds and few CDs with maturities much longer than one year). As a result, increases in interest rates may leave banks with assets that reprice slowly (i.e., they continue to pay the low interest rates they started charging in previous years) and liabilities that reprice quickly (i.e., they will pay higher rates on most liabilities quickly). Again, financial institutions may manage this risk (1) by seeking to reduce the amount of assets with long maturities and to increase the amount of liabilities with long maturities. They may also (2) reduce the amount of fixed-rate long-term assets and increase the amount of variable-rate long-term assets. Financial institutions may also (3) use interest rate derivatives (including swaps), albeit the fees for interest rate derivatives grow larger and larger the further out one seeks to be protected.

- Financial institutions, as well as other companies, bear **credit risk**, or the risk that the parties that one has lent to, or who owe payments, may fail to pay. Standard techniques to deal with credit risk include (1) diversifying one's customers, (2) selling future streams of payments, i.e., turning from being a lender who "originates to hold" and earns profits from interest payments to being a lender who "originates to distribute" and earns profits from origination fees, (3) implementing internal control mechanisms to ensure that credit standards are appropriately tight, (4) requiring greater guarantees from borrowers (e.g., requiring larger downpayments or other forms of collateral, and (5) using derivatives, such as credit default swaps (CDS). Companies, and other investors, holding bonds issued by third companies may purchase CDS that are essentially insurance products that protect against defaults on bonds in exchange for premiums. (Sophisticated) investors holding bonds (or debts) owed by companies for which CDS are not available may still purchase portfolios of CDS to protect themselves if not exactly against the default by their particular borrower, at least against the threat of an economy-wide surge in defaults (since defaults, to a large extent, do typically take place in waves when there are economy-wide problems).

- Financial institutions, as well as other companies, bear **liquidity risk**, or the risk that while they may be solvent on a long-term basis (i.e., their long-term revenues outweigh their long-term costs), during a crisis situation, their short-term obligations might outweigh their access to liquid funds, forcing them to sell long-term assets at "**fire sale prices**" or at depressed prices, effectively making them insolvent in the short term and, hence, indefinitely. Companies may manage their liquidity risk (1) by matching more the maturities of their assets and liabilities such that, as liabilities come due, some assets can be liquidated at full prices. Companies may also seek to (2) maintain a large cushion of liquid assets (cash and short-securities) albeit at the cost of foregoing returns on those assets. Companies may also (3) maintain a variety of long-term lines of credit with a variety of providers. Of course, the greater the number of lines, the more secure that they are, and the longer they extend into the future, the higher the fees they will involve.

- Financial institutions, as well as other companies, bear price or **market risk**, or the risk that sales of their products or the value of some of their assets may decline. To manage this risk, companies may (1) shift their financing sources from debt to equity, since equity can accommodate more easily temporary declines in the value of their assets. Companies may also seek to (2) diversify their income streams and the assets they hold, albeit greater diversification may be accompanied by losses in managerial focus. (Sophisticated) companies may (3) use hedging strategies such as purchasing instruments whose value will increase should the company, its competitors, or the economy as a whole experience difficulty. At the simplest level, "shorting" the S&P 500 stock index provides some protection against short-term, market risk.

- Companies also bear **country risk** when investing overseas, which affects profits and the value of assets, as they have very little control over the political and financial risks associated with investing in a foreign country.

Globalization

Economists use the term globalization to describe how the economies of nearly all individual countries in the world are developing increasingly deeper connections in their markets for goods, services, labor, capital, and technologies. Globalization plays a role in many deeply transformative processes that have been ongoing for several decades now:

- **Increased foreign direct investment (FDI).** Many companies from developed countries operate in multiple other countries, both developed and developing, operating factories, research facilities; call, service and technical support centers; and distribution networks. Growing levels of FDI have contributed to the growing importance of intra-company international trade and to growing levels of international transfers of technology and knowhow.

  Economic theory had traditionally expected that richer countries, having lower growth prospects, would have excess savings (i.e., be net savers). Poorer countries, having higher growth prospects, would have saving deficits (i.e., be net borrowers). Thus, richer countries would finance projects in poorer countries whether the financing took place as foreign direct or indirect investment, or through loans.

However, following the East Asian financial crisis of 1997-98, a large number of developing countries have engaged in policies that promote internal saving and the accumulation of international reserves (largely assets from developed countries like the U.S.). Independently of the precise causes and contrary to the traditional expectations of economic theory, over the last few decades many poorer countries have become net savers (and lenders) to richer countries, many of which became net borrowers. Much of the flow of funds into developed countries did not go to financing business investment but residential real estate and consumption. Along with traditional official reserves (i.e., government securities), poorer countries' position as net savers has also surfaced in the form of growing numbers of companies from developing countries that, like traditional multinationals from richer countries, are now expanding their operations both in other developing countries and in developed countries.

- **Increased foreign indirect, or portfolio, investment**. Seeking diversification in their portfolios, international investors have been shifting growing fractions of their savings into financial (or portfolio) assets (i.e., stock and bonds) denominated in the currencies of other countries. This shift undoubtedly helps individual savers, and may help improve how well international savings flow to the countries with the most promising projects, but it also results in a greater interconnectedness among all financial markets, such that the share of foreign owners in any individual market that might flee during international crises has increased. The traditional tendency of most investors to have a large fraction of their portfolio in assets denominated in their own currency is described as **home bias**.

- **Falling natural and artificial barriers to international trade** (transportation, information, and communication costs, and tariffs) have resulted in many forms of greater interconnectedness across countries, including growing levels of international trade, growing levels of international business and tourism travel, and growing levels of immigrant populations worldwide including both skilled workers (expatriates) and less-skilled workers (e.g., Latin Americans in the U.S., Middle Easterners and Africans in Europe, South and East Asians in the Persian Gulf, etc.).

- **Increased modernization of developing countries**. Companies from developed countries may once have operated in developing countries primarily to extract natural resources and to benefit from their lower labor costs. However, growing fractions of the developing world have long not fit neatly into a classification of the world into rich and poor countries. Many countries once considered developing have levels of human development, education, standards of living, and income that far exceed those of countries that have long been considered developed. Examples of such countries and regions that have "graduated" from their developing status include South Korea, Taiwan, Hong Kong, Singapore, and others. Many other developing countries have large and growing middle classes (e.g., Brazil, Russia, India, China, and Mexico).

Operating across multiple countries, managers and employees benefit from being aware about how many societal norms, customs, values, and accepted behaviors may differ widely across countries. If not prepared properly, these differences may derail negotiations, management-labor relations, marketing research and efforts, product launches, and ultimately negatively affects revenues and earnings. However, many societal norms might be merging. Societal norms that were once common only among developed countries are spreading throughout the rest of the world, including increased democratization, greater government transparency, greater openness of more business sectors to competition from the private, domestic, and foreign sectors, etc. Simultaneously, and perhaps paradoxically, there is both a homogenization of consumer tastes (i.e., some brand names are recognizable worldwide) and greater consumer choice (products from more countries, once thought exotic, are available in more places). Along with greater incomes, some of the ills common in developed countries are also fast spreading among developing countries (e.g., growing occurrence of health conditions associated with more sedentary lifestyles, such as obesity, diabetes, heart conditions, etc.).

Despite having labor costs that are higher per hour worked, companies in developed countries have long been able to compete with companies in developing countries. Companies and workers in developed countries may compete with those in developing countries ultimately because the relevant comparison does not revolve around costs per hour worked, but costs per unit produced. As we showed above in the example regarding comparative advantage, taking into account the amount of equipment (machinery, transportation infrastructure, etc.) and education and labor skills, workers in developed countries (Germany in our example) may actually be more productive than those in developing countries (Haiti in our example). Expressed differently, the labor costs per unit produced (for one car) may be lower for many products in a developed country than in developing countries, even if workers in developed countries earn higher wages per hour. In less theoretical terms, **reasons that companies in developed countries are able to compete with those in developing ones include:**

- Greater ability to develop, maintain, and use advanced machinery and technology to enhance the productivity of their more educated and skilled workforces.
- Using more sophisticated process management techniques like just-in-time and continuous improvement.
- Continually searching for ways to add value and move higher up the value-added ladder through research, innovation, and development for current and new goods and services.
- Emphasizing product quality and quality control in manufacturing and distribution processes.
- Emphasizing customer service and support through local distribution networks.
- Leveraging the financial resources traditionally only available to companies in developed countries to adopt global strategies such as, for instance, reaching consumers in both developed and developing markets with products that are appropriately targeted in each market, and producing in both developed and developing countries, shifting tasks as appropriate across markets to those that involve more or less value added and that may be performed by more or less skilled workforces.

Companies operating across countries may routinely buy inputs in several countries, ship them to other countries where they are combined, ship them to yet other countries where final products are assembled, and ship them yet again to be sold in other countries. While a company may view the flow of inputs across countries as an integral process, the tax (and international trade tariff) laws of each country may require **prices** to be assigned to those inputs when the subsidiary of a company in one country ships or **transfers** them to another subsidiary of the same company in another country. The practices that companies follow to assign such prices are called **transfer pricing.**

Transfer prices are relevant for tax calculations as companies may be taxed in each country based on the difference between what they paid for inputs and the transfer prices they assigned to those inputs upon shipping them to other company subsidiaries abroad. Determining some transfer prices is straightforward, as in the case of standardized basic inputs that are commonly bought and sold (e.g., a certain type of wheat). Many other inputs, however, are not standardized as they may be specific parts of final products for which there are no independent markets (e.g., the undercarriage for a specific model of a car from a particular brand). Companies and tax authorities may disagree on companies' transfer pricing practices, as tax authorities may suspect companies of increasing the transfer prices of inputs shipped from lower tax jurisdictions to high tax jurisdictions, thereby increasing the share of profits taxed at low rates and decreasing the share taxed at high rates.

Lecture 1.16 – International Trade – Class Questions

22. A country's currency conversion value has recently changed from 1.5 to the U.S. dollar to 1.7 to the U.S. dollar. Which of the following statements about the country is correct?

    a. Its exports are less expensive for the United States.
    b. Its currency has appreciated.
    c. Its imports of U.S. goods are more affordable.
    d. Its purchases of the U.S. dollar will cost less.

23. Which of the following Federal Reserve policies would increase money supply?

    a. Change the multiplier effect
    b. Increase reserve requirements
    c. Reduce the discount rate
    d. Sell more U.S. Treasury bonds

24. The difference between Monetarists and New Keynesians is that

    a. New Keynesians favor a more active role for the government in macroeconomic policy.
    b. Monetarists argue that prices and wages are very flexible.
    c. New Keynesians worry more that loose monetary policy may lead to financial bubbles.
    d. Monetarists argue that interest rates should not rise and fall with the business cycle.

25. The Laffer curve

    a. Shows that all reductions in tax rates result in higher tax revenues.
    b. Shows that reductions in very high tax rates may result in higher tax revenues.
    c. Shows that increases in tax rates do not affect tax revenues.
    d. Shows that changes in tax rates have larger impacts on the poor than on the rich.

26. Which of the following is true about international trade and investment?

    a. Companies always benefit from setting up factories in countries with the lowest wages, independently of other considerations such as transportation costs, labor productivity, or how secure property rights may be.
    b. Many companies are shifting lower-value-added tasks to countries with lower wages.
    c. Companies operating across countries each match their assets and liabilities across countries and currencies.
    d. Companies operating across countries each match their flows of revenues and costs across countries and currencies.

Class Solutions

22. (a) When a currency's exchange rate increases in relation to the U.S. dollar, holders of U.S. dollars will be able to buy more of the foreign currency with the same amount of dollars. If the price of goods, denominated in the foreign currency, does not change, it will require fewer dollars to buy them, making the exports from that country relatively less expensive. Answer (b) is incorrect because when a currency appreciates, its exchange rate would decrease as U.S. dollars would buy fewer units of the foreign currency. Answer (c) is incorrect because it will require more units of the foreign currency to buy U.S. dollars, making U.S. goods relatively more expensive. Answer (d) is incorrect because it will require more units of the foreign currency to buy U.S. dollars, making U.S. goods relatively more expensive.

23. (c) Reducing the discount rate reduces the cost of borrowing and encourages banks to borrow, which makes funds available for lending to businesses and consumers, increasing the money supply. Answer (a) is incorrect because the multiplier effect is the impact on the economy that results from the fact that when money is spent, the party receiving it will spend it again, and so on. It is not within the control of the Federal Reserve. Answer (b) is incorrect because increasing reserve requirements reduces the amount that banks will be able to lend, reducing the money supply. Answer (d) is incorrect because when the Federal Reserve increases sales of U.S. Treasury bonds, money that might have been used to lend to businesses and consumers is, instead, used to buy Treasurys and, as a result, the money supply is reduced.

24. (a) New Keynesians favor a more active role for the government in both monetary and fiscal policy than monetarists who simply advocate stable growth in the money supply. Answer (b) is incorrect because monetarists recognize that prices and wages may fail to be flexible. Answer (c) is incorrect because New Keynesians tend to worry less about the long-term effects of excessively-loose monetary policy. Answer (d) is incorrect because monetarists argue for stable monetary growth, which permits interest rates to rise during expansions (along with loan demand) and fall during recessions (along with loan demand).

25. (b) Reductions in very high tax rates may result in substantially more of the economic activity being taxed, and thus in more tax revenue. Answer (a) is incorrect because reductions in already low tax rates may result in lower tax revenues. Answer (c) is incorrect because increases in tax rates may sometimes increase tax revenues, and sometimes decrease them. Answer (d) is incorrect because the Laffer curve does not address whether changes in tax rates affect the rich and poor differently.

26. (b) Many companies are shifting lower-value-added tasks to developing countries with lower wages, while higher-value-added tasks remain in developed countries. Answer (a) is incorrect because countries with low wages and insecure property rights are not necessarily attracting much investment. Answers (c) and (d) are incorrect because while matching assets and liabilities and flows of revenues and expenses by currency may reduce exchange rate risk, achieving that goal is (1) not necessarily easy and (2) is only one goal among many.

Lecture 1.17 – Economics – Class Question – DRS

Durable, Inc., is an auto parts manufacturer with many experienced employees. Durable has three product lines: contract parts, high-performance parts, and bargain parts.

Major automobile manufacturers contract parts for Durable to supply parts for their production lines and dealerships. Durable competes with in-house shops as well as other independent contractors for these contracts and basically is a price taker in this market. The contract product line is made of parts patented by the automobile manufacturers. Durable makes these products to the manufacturers' specifications. The manufacturers sell these parts under their own labels. While the manufacturers guarantee these parts to their customers, a system of serial numbers allows these parts to be traced to the manufacturing plant and Durable is liable to manufacturers if failures exceed maximums set by the contracts.

Durable also supplies parts to which it holds the patents to distributors for independent garages to install and retailers to sell to consumers to install in their own vehicles. Durable has a high-performance line and a bargain line in the retail market. In the retail market, Durable has more influence on these prices than in the contract work for automobile manufacturers. The high-performance parts are guaranteed for a longer life and retail for more than the contract parts. The bargain parts are guaranteed for a shorter life and retail for less than the contract parts. The margins on the retail market sales are higher than the sales of the contract product line, but demand is significantly smaller. There are few sellers in the retail auto parts market and these rivals are aware of each other's actions.

Durable's Michigan plant concentrates on steel parts. Durable's Tennessee plant concentrates on parts that are mostly fiber, such as filters. Durable's Utah plant concentrates on parts that are mostly rubber, such as hoses and gaskets. The vast majority of Durable's sales occur within the United States.

Durable is planning to acquire 100% of Flexible Manufacturing, LLC. Flexible was founded six years ago by young materials scientists to take advantage of the high-performance aspects of silicone. Flexible makes silicone parts for plumbing applications and appliances, such as washing machines and heat pumps. Flexible's products are made to both metric and Imperial sizes and ship worldwide. While a little more expensive, these parts are considerably more durable than comparable rubber parts. Durable plans to retain Flexible's existing product lines and to use Flexible's expertise in developing silicone auto parts. Neither the automobile manufacturers nor Durable's rivals currently manufacture, or have announced plans to manufacture, silicone auto parts. The acquisition will involve both cash and stock paid to Flexible's members along with stock options for Flexible's key technicians and sales staff. As envisioned, the acquisition will be 5% cash and 95% Durable's common stock.

Based on the previous year's audit file and preliminary discussions with Durable's management, an intern developed the following draft analysis of Durable's operating environment in preparation for interim work on the annual audit.

Amend the draft as appropriate. Any information contained in an item is unique to that item and is not to be incorporated when answering other items.

To revise the document, click on each segment of underlined text below and select the needed correction, if any, from the list provided. If the underlined text is already correct in the context of the document, select "original text." If none of the statements are appropriate in the context of the document, select "delete text."

To: Adrian Cutt, Audit Team Leader
From: Ben Paste, Staff
Re: Preliminary Analysis of Durable's Operating Environment
Date: June 25, Year 2

1. Average credit card debt held by U.S. consumers increased 4% from a year ago. This probably will have no significant effect on the economy as a whole and no effect on Durable's bargain product line sales.

2. The national average duration of employment increased 4 weeks from a year ago. This probably will have no significant effect on the economy as a whole and no effect on Durable's high-performance product line sales.

3. Nationwide, there is a 10% increase in residential building permits over the previous year. This probably will have no significant effect on the economy as a whole and no effect on Durable's contract sales.

4. Reliable, a competitor in the retail auto parts sales market responsible for about 9% of market revenues, is undergoing liquidation due to management embezzlement uncovered in January. This probably will have no significant effect on the economy as a whole and no effect on Durable's retail market sales.

5. Viewership of "Carz @ Home," a cable TV show for the non-mechanically inclined car owner, has risen 25% in the past year. This show illustrates simple maintenance and enhancement tasks and encourages novices to work on their vehicles. This probably will have no significant effect on the economy as a whole and no effect on Durable's retail market sales units.

6. One significant business reason for the acquisition of Flexible Manufacturing is gaining the means to manage hypercompetition.

7. Another significant business reason for the acquisition of Flexible Manufacturing is to take advantage of increased efficiencies in communication.

Items for Analysis

This probably will have no significant effect on the economy as a whole and no effect on Durable's bargain product line sales.

Average credit card debt held by U.S. consumers increased 4% from a year ago.

1. Choose an option below:

   - [Original text] This probably will have no significant effect on the economy as a whole and no effect on Durable's bargain product line sales.

   - [Delete text.]

   - This probably will have no significant effect on the economy as a whole and decrease Durable's bargain product line sales.

   - This probably will have no significant effect on the economy as a whole and increase Durable's bargain product line sales.

- This probably will have a contracting effect on the economy as a whole and no effect on Durable's bargain product line sales.
- This probably will have a contracting effect on the economy as a whole and decrease Durable's bargain product line sales.
- This probably will have a contracting effect on the economy as a whole and increase Durable's bargain product line sales.
- This probably will have an expansive effect on the economy as a whole and no effect on Durable's bargain product line sales.
- This probably will have an expansive effect on the economy as a whole and decrease Durable's bargain product line sales.
- This probably will have an expansive effect on the economy as a whole and increase Durable's bargain product line sales.

This probably will have no significant effect on the economy as a whole and no effect on Durable's high-performance product line sales.

The national average duration of employment increased 4 weeks from a year ago.

2. Choose an option below:

- [Original text] This probably will have no significant effect on the economy as a whole and no effect on Durable's high-performance product line sales.
- [Delete text.]
- This probably will have no significant effect on the economy as a whole and decrease Durable's high-performance product line sales.
- This probably will have no significant effect on the economy as a whole and increase Durable's high-performance product line sales.
- This probably will have a contracting effect on the economy as a whole and no effect on Durable's high-performance product line sales.
- This probably will have a contracting effect on the economy as a whole and decrease Durable's high-performance product line sales.
- This probably will have a contracting effect on the economy as a whole and increase Durable's high-performance product line sales.
- This probably will have an expansive effect on the economy as a whole and no effect on Durable's high-performance product line sales.
- This probably will have an expansive effect on the economy as a whole and decrease Durable's high-performance product line sales.
- This probably will have an expansive effect on the economy as a whole and increase Durable's high-performance product line sales.

This probably will have no significant effect on the economy as a whole and no effect on Durable's contract sales.

Nationwide, there is a 10% increase in residential building permits over the previous year.

3. Choose an option below:

- [Original text] This probably will have no significant effect on the economy as a whole and no effect on Durable's contract sales.
- [Delete text.]

- This probably will have no significant effect on the economy as a whole and decrease Durable's contract sales.
- This probably will have no significant effect on the economy as a whole and increase Durable's contract sales.
- This probably will have a contracting effect on the economy as a whole and no effect on Durable's contract sales.
- This probably will have a contracting effect on the economy as a whole and decrease Durable's contract sales.
- This probably will have a contracting effect on the economy as a whole and increase Durable's contract sales.
- This probably will have an expansive effect on the economy as a whole and no effect on Durable's contract sales.
- This probably will have an expansive effect on the economy as a whole and decrease Durable's contract sales.
- This probably will have an expansive effect on the economy as a whole and increase Durable's contract sales.

This probably will have no significant effect on the economy as a whole and no effect on Durable's retail market sales.

Reliable, a competitor in the retail auto parts sales market responsible for about 9% of market revenues, is undergoing liquidation due to management embezzlement uncovered in January.

4. Choose an option below:

- [Original text] This probably will have no significant effect on the economy as a whole and no effect on Durable's retail market sales.
- [Delete text.]
- This probably will have no significant effect on the economy as a whole and decrease Durable's retail market sales.
- This probably will have no significant effect on the economy as a whole and increase Durable's retail market sales.
- This probably will have a contracting effect on the economy as a whole and no effect on Durable's retail market sales.
- This probably will have a contracting effect on the economy as a whole and decrease Durable's retail market sales.
- This probably will have a contracting effect on the economy as a whole and increase Durable's retail market sales.
- This probably will have an expansive effect on the economy as a whole and no effect on Durable's retail market sales.
- This probably will have an expansive effect on the economy as a whole and decrease Durable's retail market sales.
- This probably will have an expansive effect on the economy as a whole and increase Durable's retail market sales.

This probably will have no significant effect on the economy as a whole and no effect on Durable's retail market sales units.

Viewership of "Carz @ Home" a cable TV show for the non-mechanically inclined car owner has risen 25% in the past year. This show illustrates simple maintenance and enhancement tasks and encourages novices to work on their vehicles.

5. Choose an option below:

- [Original text] This probably will have no significant effect on the economy as a whole and no effect on Durable's retail market sales units.
- [Delete text.]
- This probably will have no significant effect on the economy as a whole and decrease Durable's retail market sales units.
- This probably will have no significant effect on the economy as a whole and increase Durable's retail market sales units.
- This probably will have a contracting effect on the economy as a whole and no effect on Durable's retail market sales units.
- This probably will have a contracting effect on the economy as a whole and decrease Durable's retail market sales units.
- This probably will have a contracting effect on the economy as a whole and increase Durable's retail market sales units.
- This probably will have an expansive effect on the economy as a whole and no effect on Durable's retail market sales units.
- This probably will have an expansive effect on the economy as a whole and decrease Durable's retail market sales units.
- This probably will have an expansive effect on the economy as a whole and increase Durable's retail market sales units.

One significant business reason for the acquisition of Flexible Manufacturing is gaining the means to manage hypercompetition.

One significant business reason for the acquisition of Flexible Manufacturing is....

6. Choose an option below:

- [Original text] One significant business reason for the acquisition of Flexible Manufacturing is gaining the means to manage hypercompetition.
- [Delete text.]
- One significant business reason for the acquisition of Flexible Manufacturing is gaining the means for mass customization.
- One significant business reason for the acquisition of Flexible Manufacturing is to increase technological innovation.
- One significant business reason for the acquisition of Flexible Manufacturing is to increase workforce diversity.
- One significant business reason for the acquisition of Flexible Manufacturing is to increase equity financing.
- One significant business reason for the acquisition of Flexible Manufacturing is to increase debt financing.

Another significant business reason for the acquisition of Flexible Manufacturing is to take advantage of increased efficiencies in communication.

7. Choose an option below:

    - [Original text] Another significant business reason for the acquisition of Flexible Manufacturing is to take advantage of increased efficiencies in communication.

    - [Delete text.]

    - Another significant business reason for the acquisition of Flexible Manufacturing is to appeal to customers with a heighted environmental awareness.

    - Another significant business reason for the acquisition of Flexible Manufacturing is to diversify the markets that Durable serves.

    - Another significant business reason for the acquisition of Flexible Manufacturing is to enhance quality measures.

    - Another significant business reason for the acquisition of Flexible Manufacturing is to decrease equity financing.

Document Review Simulation Solution 1

To: Adrian Cutt, Audit Team Leader
From: Ben Paste, Staff
Re: Preliminary Analysis of Durable's Operating Environment
Date: June 25, Year 2

1. Average credit card debt held by U.S. consumers increased 4% from a year ago. This probably will have a contracting effect on the economy as a whole and increase Durable's bargain product line sales.

2. The national average duration of employment increased 4 weeks from a year ago. This probably will have an expansive effect on the economy as a whole on the economy as a whole and increase Durable's high-performance product line sales.

3. Nationwide, there is a 10% increase in residential building permits over the previous year. This probably will have an expansive effect on the economy as a whole on the economy as a whole and increase Durable's contract sales.

4. Reliable, a competitor in the retail auto parts sales market responsible for about 9% of market revenues, is undergoing liquidation due to management embezzlement uncovered in January. This probably will have no significant effect on the economy as a whole and increase Durable's retail market sales.

5. Viewership of "Carz @ Home," a cable TV show for the non-mechanically inclined car owner, has risen 25% in the past year. This show illustrates simple maintenance and enhancement tasks and encourages novices to work on their vehicles. This probably will have no significant effect on the economy as a whole and increase Durable's retail market sales units.

6. One significant business reason for the acquisition of Flexible Manufacturing is to increase technological innovation.

7. Another significant business reason for the acquisition of Flexible Manufacturing is to diversify the markets that Durable serves.

Explanations

1. **This probably will have a contracting effect on the economy as a whole and increase Durable's bargain product line sales.**

    As debt levels rise, consumers tend to rein in purchases; this tends to have a contracting effect on the economy as a whole. Durable's bargain parts may be considered inferior goods, as opposed to normal goods. During a recession, many consumers experience lower income. Consumers experiencing lower income will purchase more inferior goods than when experiencing growing income. In other words, consumers will purchase more "bargain parts" as opposed to the higher-priced high-performance or "genuine factory" parts. [other answers] As debt levels rise, consumers tend to rein in purchases; this tends to have a contracting effect on the economy as opposed to an expansive or no effect. An expansion would tend to decrease Durable's bargain product line sales. Stability in the economy as a whole would tend to result in Durable's bargain product line sales remaining constant.

    This probably will have an expansive effect on the economy as a whole and increase Durable's high-performance product line sales.

    The average duration of employment, in weeks, is a common trailing indicator of business cycle changes. An increase in this duration signifies a recovery or expansion in the economy as a whole. Durable's high-performance parts may be considered normal goods; during a recovery, more people will be experiencing growing income. Consumers with increased income spend more on normal goods (Durable's high-performance parts). [other answers] A decrease in this duration signifies a contraction in the economy as a whole; sales of normal goods generally contract during such a period. No change in this duration signifies a stable economy; sales of normal goods generally remain constant during such a period.

3. **This probably will have an expansive effect on the economy as a whole and increase Durable's contract sales.**

    An increase in housing permits indicates that residential construction soon will increase, fueling demand for household furnishings as well as construction materials. This generally heralds an expansive period (rather than a recessionary or stable period) as the ripple effect works its way through the economy as a whole. Auto manufacturers will want to have inventory ready for when people not building homes, but feeling more confident about the economy, are ready to buy new vehicles. Thus, Durable's contract sales likely would increase, rather than decrease or remain stable.

4. **This probably will have no significant effect on the economy as a whole and increase Durable's retail market sales.**

    The liquidation of one competitor in the retail auto parts market probably will not have a significant impact on the economy as a whole. Durable's sales may increase as the sudden absence of one competitor in the retail auto parts market is an opportunity for Durable to gain market share. [other answers] The retail auto parts market does not exert sufficient influence over wider markets to inflate expectations in the economy as a whole before the embezzlement is uncovered or for the embezzlement discovery to undermine confidence in the economy as a whole. It is unlikely that Durable's sales would decrease due to embezzlement at a competitor. While it is possible that embezzlement at a competitor would have no effect on Durable's retail market sales, it is more likely that Durable's sales would increase.

5. **This probably will have no significant effect on the economy as a whole and increase Durable's retail market sales units.**

    The increase of do-it-yourselfers (DIYs) in the retail auto parts market probably will not have a significant impact on the economy as a whole. The increase of DIYs will increase the quantity demanded at the retailers where Durable's retail market lines are sold. [other answers] The retail auto parts market does not exert sufficient influence over ancillary markets for this event to undermine or boost confidence. The increased sales of parts to DIYs will be offset by reduced sales to garages and dealerships. The mechanics who formerly would have been hired to repair and maintain vehicles are unlikely to suffer so much unemployment that it would start a downward spiral in other employment fields. Further, any reduction in hours is dissipated, unlike a factory closing that potentially could shut down a town. The increase of DIYs would not decrease the quantity demanded of Durable's retail market products. While it is possible that the increase of DIYs would have no effect on Durable's retail market sales quantity, it is more likely that Durable's sales quantity would increase.

6. **One significant business reason for the acquisition of Flexible Manufacturing is to increase technological innovation.**

    Flexible has experience with a material that Durable does not currently use. Durable plans to use that expertise to develop new products for its current markets and diversify the company. [other answers] The scenario does not indicate that the industry is undergoing hypercompetition. There is no mention that Flexible customizes product from a set of standard components, adapted to each consumer's specifications, as is the case with mass customization. Age diversity is implied by this acquisition; there is no indication that any other type of diversity in the workforce will increase when these two entities combine. Given the scenario, there is a better response available than workforce diversity. Also, if the goal was simply increased workforce diversity, Durable could accomplish this goal merely by changing its employment practices. Increased equity financing is the means by which the acquisition of Flexible will be accomplished, but not the reason for the acquisition. As envisioned, the acquisition will be 5% cash and 95% common stock; no debt financing is mentioned.

7. **Another significant business reason for the acquisition of Flexible Manufacturing is to diversify the markets that Durable serves.**

    Flexible currently serves the plumbing and appliance markets, not auto manufacturers or auto parts consumers; Durable acquires a presence in these markets when it purchases Flexible. [other answers] There is no indication that Flexible is any better at communications than Durable. There is no indication that Flexible has any particular environmental credentials. There is no indication that Flexible is any better at quality control than Durable. As envisioned, the acquisition will be 5% cash and 95% common stock; this would increase equity financing, not reduce it.

Lecture 1.18 – Economics – Written Communication TBS

Written Communication 1

The President of XYZ Community Bank, Phillip Rodriguez, has been approached by the bank's regulators who are concerned about XYZ's preparedness for increases in interest rates in coming years. Write a memorandum explaining why interest rates might increase in coming years and how XYZ could manage this interest rate risk.

REMINDER: Your response will be graded for both technical content and writing skills. Technical content will be evaluated for information that is helpful to the intended reader and clearly relevant to the issue. Writing skills will be evaluated for development, organization, and the appropriate expression of ideas in professional correspondence. Use a standard business memo or letter format with a clear beginning, middle, and end. Do not convey information in the form of a table, bullet point list, or other abbreviated presentation.

To: Mr. Phillip Rodriguez, President
     XYZ Community Bank
From: CPA Candidate

Written Communication Solution 1

To: Mr. Phillip Rodriguez, President
     XYZ Community Bank
From: CPA Candidate

Thank you for your inquiry about why interest rates might increase in the coming years and how your company, XYZ, could manage this interest rate risk.

Interest rates may increase in coming years as the economy recovers and as the Federal Reserve attempts to prevent inflation rates from rising. XYZ Community Bank may manage its interest rate risk by reducing the mismatch between the maturities of its assets and liabilities. Historically, interest rates have fluctuated considerably, and XYZ's loans have had far longer maturities than its deposits.

As the economy continues to recover, businesses are likely to increase their demands for loans, and the Federal Reserve will discontinue its expansionary monetary policy.

XYZ has large fractions of its assets in loans with long maturities and the overwhelming majority of its liabilities in deposits with very short maturities. Thus, when interest rates rise, XYZ's long-term assets will reprice slowly, while nearly all liabilities will reprice quickly. XYZ will then face strong pressures on its earnings. To manage this interest rate risk, XYZ should replace long-term loans with shorter-term loans.

As the economy recovers, interest rates are likely to increase. Since XYZ's loans have far longer maturities than its deposits, as interest rates rise the institution will suffer pressure on its earnings. XYZ should manage this interest rate risk by reducing the mismatch between the maturities of its assets and liabilities. If you need any additional information or have questions, don't hesitate to contact me.

Sincerely,

CPA Candidate

_____

Written Communication 2

The President of DEF Consulting Inc., Clint Westwood, has received an inquiry from a client interested in understanding better how governments may manage the business cycle. The client has expressed concerns that news media and experts often offer conflicting views. Write a memorandum explaining the key tools of macroeconomic management and how views on the subject may differ across various schools of economic thought.

REMINDER: Your response will be graded for both technical content and writing skills. Technical content will be evaluated for information that is helpful to the intended reader and clearly relevant to the issue. Writing skills will be evaluated for development, organization, and the appropriate expression of ideas in professional correspondence. Use a standard business memo or letter format with a clear beginning, middle, and end. Do not convey information in the form of a table, bullet point list, or other abbreviated presentation.

To: Mr. Clint Westwood, President
    DEF Consulting
From: CPA Candidate

Written Communication Solution 2

To: Mr. Clint Westwood, President
    DEF Consulting Inc.
From: CPA Candidate

Thank you for your question regarding the key tools of macroeconomic management and how views on the subject may differ across various schools of economic thought.

Throughout the last two centuries, economies have experienced business cycles. Governments manage business cycles through fiscal policy and monetary policy. Schools of economic thought disagree on whether governments alleviate or aggravate business cycles.

As you requested, this memorandum explains the tools of macroeconomics and how views differ. Macroeconomics manages unemployment and inflation. Fiscal policy is controlled by Congress and involves changing taxes and government spending. Monetary policy has been delegated to the Fed and involves changing interest rates.

To address unemployment, policymakers may cut taxes, increase government spending, or lower interest rates. To address inflation, policymakers may increase taxes, reduce government spending, or raise interest rates.

While the basics are well understood, applying macroeconomics is difficult. Macroeconomic goals conflict with one another. Further, many macroeconomic tools operate with lags. Policymakers cannot know whether they reduced or increased interest rates by the right amount or at the right time.

Some schools of thought (e.g., Keynesians) advocate more activist roles for the government. Other schools of thought (e.g., monetarists) argue that overactive policymakers may actually contribute to the business cycle.

Governments use fiscal policy and monetary policy to manage the business cycle. However, schools of thought disagree on whether governments alleviate or aggravate business cycles. If you need any additional information or have questions, don't hesitate to contact me.

Sincerely,

CPA Candidate

Written Communication 3

The Chief Financial Officer of PRC Corp., Xiao Guo, is considering whether to expand PRC in the United States. In the past, the company has manufactured solely in its home country and relied on other companies to distribute its product abroad. Write a memorandum describing whether and why other companies from developing countries might also be considering changing strategies, and how such a strategy might help the company manage currency risk.

REMINDER: Your response will be graded for both technical content and writing skills. Technical content will be evaluated for information that is helpful to the intended reader and clearly relevant to the issue. Writing skills will be evaluated for development, organization, and the appropriate expression of ideas in professional correspondence. Use a standard business memo or letter format with a clear beginning, middle, and end. Do not convey information in the form of a table, bullet point list, or other abbreviated presentation.

To: Mr. Xiao Guo, CFO
     PRC Corp.
From: CPA Candidate

Written Communication Solution 3

To: Mr. Xiao Guo, CFO
    PRC Corp
From: CPA Candidate

Thank you for your question regarding how your company can manage currency risk.

Many companies from developing countries are expanding into developed countries. These expansions help companies improve their level of service to customers and to manage currency risk.

As you requested, this memorandum describes why companies from developing countries are changing their strategies and how the new strategies help manage currency risk. Historically, few companies from developing countries operated outside their home countries. Traditionally, developed countries invested in developing countries. However, in recent years, growing numbers of companies from developing countries are expanding their operations in developed countries. These expansions initially involve developing distribution networks, but eventually lead to operating production plants.

Companies bear currency risk if they have revenues and costs in different currencies. Companies manage their currency risk, for instance, by matching revenues in one currency with costs in the same currency. For instance, a foreign company with revenues from the U.S. bears less currency risk if it operates its own distribution network in the U.S. or if it manufactured more in the U.S.

Many companies from developing countries are expanding into developed countries. Having operations in their export markets helps these companies manage their currency risks. If you need any additional information or have questions, don't hesitate to contact me.

Sincerely,

CPA Candidate

Section 2 – Corporate Governance, Internal Control & Enterprise Risk Management

Table of Contents

EXAM NOTE: *Please refer to the AICPA BEC Blueprint in the Introduction of this book to find a listing of the representative tasks (and their associated skill levels—i.e., Remembering and Understanding, Application, and Analysis) that the candidate should be able to perform based on the knowledge obtained in this section.*

Corporate Governance, Internal Control & Enterprise Risk Management

Lecture 2.01 – Corporate Governance: Board of Directors

Corporate Governance Overview

Corporations have many stakeholders, including stockholders, who may be the most obvious, but also including customers, suppliers, employees, regulators, and the communities that are affected by the entity's operations or activities. It is the role of corporate governance to make certain that the objectives of the entity are met while the legitimate needs and concerns of all stakeholders are being addressed.

Corporate governance consists of the systems that are applied to control and to direct a corporation. Those responsible for governance will depend largely on the size and nature of the entity. In a small organization, governance may be the responsibility of owner-managers. In larger organizations, however, the responsibility for governance is disbursed among a variety of individuals in a somewhat more structured environment.

In the case of most publicly-held companies, for example, stockholders, the owners of the entity, are not directly involved in its operations. They, instead, elect a board of directors who in turn are responsible for strategic planning as well as for the selection and oversight of the entity's management. The board of directors will use various forms of **compensation** to incentivize managers to perform their responsibilities to the best of their abilities. The board will also use various means of **monitoring management** to make certain that its decisions are consistent with achieving the entity's objectives.

There have been numerous studies on corporate governance and it is an area that is subject to a significant amount of legislation, including the Sarbanes-Oxley Act (SOX). In many respects, SOX is an attempt to legislate principles that were included in 2 significant earlier reports related to corporate governance. These include the 1992 Cadbury Report and the Principles of Corporate Governance, originally published by the Organization for Economic Co-Operation and Development (OECD) in 1998 and re-written in 2004.

The Cadbury report suggested a voluntary code for corporate governance. Companies listed on the London stock exchange are required to comply or explain the extent to which they do comply, the areas where they do not, and the reasons for any noncompliance. Some of the principles of the Cadbury report include:
- There should be a clear division of responsibility at the top, primarily that the position of chairman of the board be separated from that of Chief Executive, or there should be a strong independent element on the board.
- The majority of the Board members should be outside directors.
- Remuneration of Board members should be determined by non-executive directors.
- The Board should select an audit committee that includes at least 3 non-executive directors.

The Organization for Economic Co-Operation and Development (OECD), an international organization, developed the OECD Principles of Corporate Governance. It developed principles in 6 key areas:

- **Effective Corporate Governance Framework** – "The corporate governance framework should promote transparent and efficient markets, be consistent with the rule of law and clearly articulate the division of responsibilities among different supervisory, regulatory and enforcement agencies."
- **Shareholder Rights and Ownership Functions** – "The corporate governance framework should protect and facilitate the exercise of shareholders' rights."
- **Equitable Treatment of Shareholders** – "The corporate governance framework should ensure the equitable treatment of all shareholders, including minority and foreign shareholders. All shareholders should have the opportunity to obtain effective redress for violation of their rights."
- **Stakeholders' Role in Corporate Governance** – "The corporate governance framework should recognize the rights of stakeholders established by law or through mutual agreements and encourage either active co-operation between corporations and stakeholders in creating wealth, jobs, and the sustainability of financially sound enterprises."
- **Disclosure and Transparency** – "The corporate governance framework should ensure that timely and accurate disclosure is made on all material matters regarding the corporation, including the financial situation, performance, ownership, and governance of the company."
- **Board Responsibilities** – "The corporate governance framework should ensure the strategic guidance of the company, effective monitoring of management by the board, and the board's accountability to the company and the shareholders."

Board of Directors

A Board of Directors (BOD) gets its responsibilities and authority from an authority outside of itself. Upon formation, a corporation will file **articles of incorporation** (corporate Charter when approved), with the secretary of state and create bylaws. The articles will include such information as the name of the company, its address at the time of filing, and its purpose, the name of the registered agent of the corporation, name and address of each incorporator and the number of authorized shares of stock and types of stock. The **bylaws** (internal rules of the corporation), generally indicate the minimum and maximum number of directors, how they are to be selected and compensated, how often they are to meet, and the nature of their responsibilities. The typical **duties of a board of directors** include:

- The board members have a **fiduciary duty** to:
  - ***Act loyally*** and in the best interest of the corporation and shareholders, which includes not putting their interests above the company's and acting without personal economic conflict.
  - ***Act with a Duty of Care*** and be diligent when making company decisions.
  - ***Act with Due Diligence,*** which means using reasonable care when entering into agreements or transactions with another party.
- Determining or revising the entity's mission and amending its bylaws
- Strategic planning and the development of broad objectives and policies
- Selection and oversight of the chief executive
- Securing the availability of financial resources
- Budget approval, and approval of major operating and financial proposals

- Accounting to stakeholders, including making certain that reliable financial information is reported by the entity
- Providing advice to management and determining its compensation
- Establishing dividend policies
- Reacquiring treasury stock

The New York Stock Exchange (NYSE) and the National Association of Securities Dealers Automated Quotations (NASDAQ) have established **requirements related to the boards of directors of listed companies**. These include:
- The majority of directors are required to be independent and information must be provided to investor's regarding director independence.
- A director is *not independent if* they were recently an employee or affiliate of the entity, a former partner or employee of the external auditor, or if a family member was recently an officer of the entity (5 years for NYSE, 3 years for NASDAQ); if the director or a family member received more than $120,000 from the corporation, excluding director fees, for any 12-month period within the last 3 years; or if the director is an executive of another entity that receives significant amounts of revenue from the entity.
- Non-management directors are required to meet on a regularly scheduled basis.
- The directors must adopt and publish a code of conduct that is applicable to all parties within the entity, including directors, officers, and employees, disclosing any waivers to directors or officers.
- The entity must maintain an independent audit committee.
- The entity must identify relationships that automatically indicate that a director is not independent.

A director has some protection against liability when decisions do not provide the anticipated results. The **business judgment rule** was established as a result of case law and it requires a director to fulfill a **fiduciary duty** to the entity by acting in good faith, being loyal, and applying due care. When they do so, the courts will not review their business decisions regardless of the outcome. In general, directors will not be liable for their decisions unless they are guilty of fraud.

For example, if directors reasonably rely on information showing that dividends may be declared and declare such dividends when, in fact, the corporation was insolvent, the directors will not be held liable for the illegal dividends. (The shareholders will have to repay the dividends if the corporation was insolvent when the dividends were declared.)

Boards of directors will **establish various committees** in order to disburse the board's responsibilities. Johnson & Johnson, a U.S. publicly-held company, for example, has 6 committees that are part of its board, including:
- Audit
- Compensation & Benefits
- Nominating & Corporate Governance
- Finance
- Regulatory, Compliance & Government Affairs
- Science, Technology & Sustainability

Pepsi's board, on the other hand, has 3 committees:
- Nominating and Corporate Governance
- Audit
- Compensation

In some cases, committees are required to be made up of independent, or **outside directors**. These are directors who have no involvement with the entity other than in their capacity as a director. An **inside director**, on the other hand, has some significant involvement in the entity, often as a member of management, in addition to being a director. Some entities will apply the term **executive director** exclusively to the chief executive officer (CEO), while others will apply it to any director who is also an executive, or officer, of the corporation.

There are **three committees** that a publicly-held company is required to maintain. These are the nominating committee, the audit committee, and the compensation committee.

The **nominating committee** is responsible for the overall corporate governance of an organization. The primary duty of the nominating committee is to determine who is suitable for service on the board of directors. It is charged with developing and suggesting governance principles and policies to the board, overseeing CEO succession, enhancing the quality of nominees to the board, and making certain of the integrity of the nominating process.

The Wall Street Reform and Consumer Protection Act, referred to as **Dodd-Frank**, requires an entity to disclose whether or not the chair of the board of directors is also the chief executive officer. The entity is also required to indicate the reasons why they are, or are not, the same individual.

The **audit committee** has a variety of responsibilities. Under Sarbanes-Oxley Act (**SOX**) Title IV, the audit committee is required to be made up of independent directors and at least one member of the audit committee is required to be a financial expert or, if there is none on the audit committee, the *reasons* the audit committee does not include at least one. A **financial expert** has:
- An understanding of GAAP and financial statements
- Experience preparing or auditing comparable financial statements and experience in applying financial statement or audit knowledge to the accounting for estimates, accruals, and reserves
- Experience with internal accounting controls
- An understanding of the functions of the audit committee
  - Need not be a CPA

Under SOX Title III, the audit committee is responsible for overseeing the financial reporting process. It is to make certain that reliable information that is useful to stakeholders is available on a timely basis. The audit committee is responsible for the appointment, compensation, and oversight of the entity's auditors, who are to report directly to the audit committee.

In addition, the audit committee has several responsibilities related to the entity's **internal controls** under section 404 Title IV of SOX. It is required to oversee the establishment of appropriate controls, including programs for the prevention and detection of fraud. It is responsible for maintaining a code of ethics for senior financial officers and making it publicly available (SOX Title IV) and is also required to establish procedures for **dealing** with complaints about accounting, internal control, or audit matters, and to facilitate a process for employees to anonymously and confidentially express concerns about accounting related issues (**whistleblowers**).

Section 906 of SOX requires the CEO and CFO to certify that the reports filed with the SEC (10Q, 10K) comply with relevant securities laws and also fairly present the financial condition and results of operations of the company. If they are found criminally liable for certifying false and defective financial statements, they could be imprisoned for 10 to 20 years and fined from $1 million to $5 million.

The **compensation committee**, made up of independent directors, is responsible for establishing compensation policies for directors and executives of the corporation. It is charged with making certain that their policies are both appropriate and supportable and that they are consistent with the mission and objectives of the entity.

Because of the significance of the compensation committee, it has been subjected to various forms of regulation. The SEC, the NYSE, and the NASDAQ all require the compensation committee to assume certain **responsibilities** that include:
- Developing a compensation approach or philosophy
- Establishing compensation for the CEO and other executive officers
- Use outside experts, as appropriate
- Receive and evaluate proposals regarding executive compensation put forth by shareholders

Although the **Dodd-Frank Act** was designed to regulate the financial services industry, there are 4 significant provisions that directly relate to the *compensation committee* of the board of directors.
- **Say-on-Pay** – Stockholders are required to be allowed to determine, by vote, if they approve of the compensation of executive officers; whether the vote on compensation should occur every 1, 2, or 3 years; and, in the event of a merger, whether or not they approve any compensation related to a "Golden Parachute." The votes on executive compensation and "Golden Parachute" compensation are not, however, binding on the board of directors.
- **Independence** – Committee members and advisers are required to adhere to a higher standard in determining whether or not they are sufficiently independent to serve on, or advice to, the compensation committee. The bill also calls for enhanced disclosure regarding the use of compensation consultants and any conflicts of interest.
- **Disclosure** – The bill requires enhanced disclosure relating executive compensation to the entity's financial performance. Disclosure includes the relationship of the median employee compensation, excluding that of the CEO, to the total annual compensation of the CEO.
- **Claw backs** – The bill requires an entity that is required to restate its financial statements to establish policies for the recoupment of compensation (SOX Title III).

Executive Oversight

One of the most significant responsibilities of the board of directors is the oversight of management. The board meets this responsibility through its management compensation policies and through monitoring of management.

Management compensation policies require the board to find a balance between different forms of compensation that may, on one hand, motivate management to strive to perform at the utmost level or may, on the other, cause management to find ways to maximize their own compensation at the detriment of, or at least without considering benefit to, the entity.
- If the compensation package includes too high a proportion of fixed compensation and too low a proportion of incentive compensation, management will not have incentives to take risks that may be appropriate and necessary for the achievement of the entity's objectives.
- If the opposite is true, it may provide management with the incentive to take risks that are not consistent with the entity's risk appetite. As a result, the combination of fixed and incentive compensation should be carefully evaluated.

Fixed compensation generally consists of the officer's salary and perquisites (perks). Perks may include such items as a company automobile or access to a company plane or limousine, health and life insurance, and retirement benefits.

Incentive compensation can be provided in a wide variety of forms. Some of the most common include:

- *Bonuses* – In most cases, bonuses are based on some version of accounting profit. While this rewards management for good entity performance, it is often easy to manipulate profits in the short run by deferring or accelerating expenses or revenues, through capitalization and depreciation policies, and various other means.
- *Share based compensation* – This includes such items as stock options, shared appreciation rights, restricted shares, and performance shares.
  - *Stock options* give the officer the ability to buy shares at a fixed price for a specific period of time. Although this clearly ties compensation to performance, it may cause management to focus too heavily on short-term stock price rather than long-term objectives. In addition, a decline in price may make it appear that the option will never be "in the money" (where the stock price exceeds the option price), negating any incentive.
  - *Shared appreciation rights* operate similarly to stock options with the same advantages and disadvantages. The additional advantage to officers is that it provides them with cash payments resulting from increases in the stock price rather than the opportunity to buy shares at a potential bargain.
  - *Restricted shares* are shares of stock that may not be disposed of for a specified period of time. This provides the advantage that the officer does not have to pay for shares and gives management an incentive to strive to increase the stock price, at least during the period of restriction. Clearly, the longer the restriction, the greater the potential for benefit to the entity.
  - *Performance shares* are shares that are issued to management if specific performance objectives are met. These are potentially very effective to encourage management to concentrate on the meeting of specific performance objectives.

Lecture 2.02 – Corporate Governance: Internal Audit Function

There are various ways in which the board of directors can **monitor management**. One of the most common, and often the most effective, is through the use of internal auditors. When internal auditors report directly to the audit committee of the board of directors, they are more likely to be effective in helping the board monitor the performance of management, largely because the audit committee is made up exclusively of independent directors.

According to requirements of the NYSE, "Listed companies must maintain an **internal audit function** to provide management and the audit committee with ongoing assessments of the company's risk management process and system of internal control." Many large companies will have a chief auditing executive (CAE) who will report to the audit committee and who will be responsible for the internal audit function within the entity.

The Institute of Internal Auditors (IIA), an international professional association that many internal auditors belong to, has developed an International Professional Practices Framework (IPPF) that consists of three components:
1. The definition of internal auditing
2. The code of ethics
3. International Standards for the Professional Practice of Internal Auditing (ISPPIA)

1. The IIA provides the following *definition of internal auditing*:

> "Internal auditing is an independent, objective assurance and consulting activity designed to add value and improve an organization's operations. It helps an organization accomplish its objectives by bringing a systematic, disciplined approach to evaluate and improve the effectiveness of risk management, control, and government processes."

2. The IIA's *code of ethics* identifies the principles that internal auditors are expected to uphold and the rules of conduct that they are expected to follow.
- Principles
  - Integrity
  - Objectivity
  - Confidentiality
  - Competency
- Rules
  - Integrity
    - Honesty, diligence, and responsibility
    - Observation of the law, including providing disclosures expected by the law and the profession
    - Not knowingly engaging in illegal acts or acts discreditable to the profession or the organization
    - Respect for, and contribution to, ethical objectives of the organization
  - Objectivity
    - Not participating in activities or relationships that may impair objectivity or be in conflict with the organization's interests
    - Not accepting anything that might impair professional judgment

- Disclosing all material relevant facts that are known
  - o Confidentiality
    - Exercising prudence in use and protection of information acquired through performance of responsibilities
    - Not using information for personal gain, in a manner contrary to the law, or detrimental to the appropriate objectives of the organization
  - o Competency
    - Engaging only in services for which they are qualified
    - Performing internal audit services in accordance with ISPPIA
    - Continually improving proficiency and quality of service

3. **ISPPIA** are designated as attribute standards and performance standards.
   - **Attribute Standards** fall into 4 categories
     - o Purpose, Authority, and Responsibility
       - Recognition of the Definition of Internal Auditing, the Code of Ethics, and the Standards in the Internal Audit Charter
     - o Independence and Objectivity
       - Organizational Independence
       - Direct Interaction with the Board
       - Individual Objectivity
     - o Proficiency and Due Professional Care
       - Proficiency
       - Due Professional Care
       - Continuing Professional Education
     - o Quality Assurance and Improvement Program
       - Requirements of the Quality Assurance and Improvement Program
       - Internal Assessments
       - External Assessments
       - Reporting on the Quality Assurance and Improvement Program
       - Use of "Conforms with the International Standards for the Professional Practice of Internal Auditing"
       - Disclosure of Nonconformance
   - **Performance Standards** fall into 7 categories
     - o Managing the Internal Audit Activity
       - Planning
       - Communication and Approval
       - Resource Management
       - Policies and Procedures
       - Coordination
       - Reporting to Senior Management and the Board
       - External Service Provider and Organizational Responsibility for Internal Auditing
     - o Nature of Work
       - Governance
       - Risk Management
       - Control
     - o Engagement Planning
       - Planning Considerations
       - Engagement Objectives
       - Engagement Scope

- Engagement Resource Allocation
- Engagement Work Program
  - o Performing the Engagement
    - Identifying Information
    - Analysis and Evaluation
    - Documenting Information
    - Engagement Supervision
  - o Communicating Results
    - Criteria for Communicating
    - Quality of Communications
    - Errors and Omissions
    - Use of "Conducted in Conformance with the International Standards for the Professional Practice of Internal Auditing"
    - Engagement Disclosure of Nonconformance
    - Disseminating Results
    - Overall Opinions
  - o Monitoring Progress
  - o Communicating the Acceptance of Risks

External Auditors

In addition to internal auditors, **external auditors** are potentially effective in contributing to the monitoring of management. SOX requires the external auditor to be a public accounting firm that is registered with the Public Company Accounting Oversight Board (PCAOB) and establishes very strict rules as to the independence of the external auditors, including a prohibition against the performance of many nonaudit services, a requirement that any nonattest services performed by the auditor be preapproved by the audit committee, and audit partner rotation.

As part of their monitoring role, the independent external auditor is required **to communicate** with the *auditing committee* regarding:

- Critical accounting policies and practices being used.
- Alternative treatments, acceptable under GAAP, that have been discussed with management, including implications of such treatment and the public accounting firm's preference.
- Any additional written communications with management, including any management letter or schedule of unadjusted differences.

In addition to performing an audit of the entity's financial statements, the external auditor has responsibilities in relation to the entity's **internal control**. Section 404 of Title IV of SOX, "Management Assessment of Internal Controls," requires management to provide, with each annual report, a report on internal control indicating management's responsibility for establishing and maintaining adequate controls and assessing the effectiveness of controls as of the end of the most recent fiscal period. The registered independent accounting firm is required to attest to (Opinion), and report on, management's assessment. This is the result of an examination of internal control that is **integrated** with the audit of the financial statements.

Under SOX a CEO or CFO who misrepresents financial information may be both imprisoned and fined. The penalties could range from $1 million and 10 years to $5 million and 20 years in prison.

Generally accepted auditing standards (GAAS) require the external auditor to **communicate with those *charged with governance*** regarding certain matters. These include:
- The auditor's responsibility to form and express an opinion on the financial statements, which does not relieve those charged with governance of any responsibilities
- The planned scope and timing of the audit
- The auditor's view about qualitative aspects of the entity's accounting practices, including policies, estimates, and disclosures
  - Why, if applicable, a practice acceptable under GAAP is not appropriate under the circumstances
  - Determining that those responsible for governance are informed about the process used in formulating estimates and the auditor's conclusions about their reasonableness.
- Significant difficulties, disagreements with management, and other findings or issues, if any.
- Uncorrected mistakes, along with their effects, accumulated by the auditor as well as the effect of uncorrected misstates from prior periods.

In some cases, all of those charged with governance are also involved in management. When that is not the case, the auditor is required to communicate additional matters to those charged with governance.
- Material corrected mistakes brought to management's attention
- Significant findings or issues discussed with management
- Auditor views on matters that were the subject of management consultation with other accountants
- Written representations requested by the auditor

Other Monitoring Devices

There are several other means by which management is monitored:
- The company will be scrutinized by various members of the investment community, including **investment banks** and **securities analysts**, who use information about the company to make their decisions or recommendations as to the purchase or sale of its securities.
- **Creditors** and **credit agencies** make similar analyses and monitor compliance with debt covenants, although they largely depend on management and external auditors for the information on which they base their decisions.
- **Attorneys** also monitor management when they are involved in securities filings, legal conflicts, or are engaged to advise management.

The **Securities and Exchange Commission** (SEC) is one of the more significant agencies responsible for monitoring management and enforcing the U.S. securities laws. In addition to its various components, which were initially established to protect investors, there have been several forms of legislation that have expanded the SEC's monitoring responsibilities. These include the SOX and the Dodd-Frank Act.

The SEC was originally created by the Securities and Exchange Act of 1934 as the result of a major fraud scheme perpetrated by the publicly-held company Kreuger and Toll. The SEC includes several components that are relevant to the monitoring of corporate governance. These include:
- The primary function of the **Division of Corporation Finance** is to provide interpretive guidance in regard to the Securities Act of 1933, the Securities and Exchange Act of 1934, the Trust Indenture Act of 1939, and the Sarbanes-Oxley Act of 2002. It also, however,

reviews filings made under the 1933 Act to evaluate compliance with disclosure and accounting requirements.

- The role of the **Division of Enforcement** is to investigate possible securities law violations. It recommends when the SEC should take action in a federal court, take action before an administrative law judge, or negotiate a settlement.
- The **Office of the Chief Accountant** is the component of the SEC that is responsible for the transparency and relevancy of financial reporting, for improving the professional performance of auditors of public companies, and for ensuring the fair presentation and credibility of financial statements used for investment decisions. It does so by establishing and enforcing accounting and auditing policy. Its three major groups are Accounting, Professional Practice, and International Affairs.

Other means of indirectly monitoring management performance include activities of the ***Internal Revenue Service*** (IRS), through the scrutiny of tax filings; ***shareholder actions***, which may involve replacing board members or filing class action lawsuits; and the potential for ***corporate takeovers***, which a corporation may make itself susceptible to as a result of ineffective management.

In 2012, the **JOBS** (Jumpstart Our Business Startups) **Act** was passed to encourage small business, specifically by making it easier for small business to participate in the capital markets (easier to go public, which in turn will create more jobs). It did so by extending the amount of time that certain new public companies will have to comply with certain requirements of the SOX. The entities are exempted from some provisions and compliance with others was extended by periods of 2 to 5 years.

The **JOBS Act** also:

- Increases the number of shareholders a company could have before being required to register its stock (1934 Act).
- Exempts certain small offerings from registration with the SEC (Reg A).
- Provides an exemption from some of the regulatory and disclosure requirements to certain companies with less than $1 billion in revenues before going public, or 5 years from the date they go public, referred to as emerging growth companies (EGC).
- Allows for general solicitation and advertising in certain types of private placements (Reg D, 506).
- Raises the limit for exemptions under Regulation A from $5 million to $50 million (Reg A).
- Raises the number of allowed shareholders of community banks from 500 to 2,000 (1934 Act).
- Prohibits crowdfunding of investment funds, which is the use of small amounts of money from a large number of investors to fund a venture.
- Exempt from the rules requiring shareholder vote on executive compensation.
- Not required to have audits of internal control (SOX 404).

Lecture 2.03 – Corporate Governance – Class Questions

1. In order to comply with a director's duty of loyalty to a corporation, what action(s) should a director take when presented with a corporate opportunity?

   a. Reject the opportunity and not offer it to the corporation
   b. Accept the opportunity and not offer it to the corporation
   c. Accept the opportunity and disclose the acceptance to the corporation
   d. Offer the opportunity to the corporation and accept it if the corporation rejects it

2. Which of the following positions best describes the nature of the Board of Directors of ABC Co's relationship to the company?

   a. Agent
   b. Executive
   c. Fiduciary
   d. Representative

3. In a large public corporation, evaluating internal control procedures should be the responsibility of

   a. Accounting management staff who report to the CFO
   b. Internal audit staff who report to the board of directors
   c. Operations management staff who report to the Chief operations officer
   d. Security management staff who report to the chief facilities officer

4. Which of the following is necessary to be an audit committee financial expert according to the criteria specified in the Sarbanes-Oxley Act of 2002?

   a. A limited understanding of Generally Accepted Auditing Standards (GAAS)
   b. Education and experience as a certified financial planner
   c. Experience with internal accounting controls
   d. Experience in the preparation of tax returns

5. According to the Sarbanes-Oxley Act of 2002, a CEO or CFO who misrepresents the company's finances may be penalized by being

   a. Fined, but not imprisoned
   b. Imprisoned, but not fined
   c. Removed from the corporate office and fined
   d. Fined and imprisoned

6. According to the SOX act of 2002, which of the following statements is correct regarding an issuer's audit committee financial expert?

   a. The issuer's current outside CPA firms audit partner must be the audit committee financial expert.
   b. If an issuer does not have an audit committee financial expert, the issuer must disclose the reason why the role is not filled.
   c. The issuer must fill the role with an individual who has experience in the issuer's industry.
   d. The audit committee financial expert must be the issuer's audit committee chairperson to enhance internal control.

Class Solutions

1. (d) A director must act in the best interest of the corporation. All opportunities should be first offered to the corporation. If the corporation doesn't wish to pursue the opportunity, then the board member may consider pursuing the opportunity for their own benefit.

2. (c) The Board of Directors of a corporation has a fiduciary duty to that entity, meaning that it must act in the best interests of the corporation in all business dealings and not in a director's self-interest. Answer (a) is incorrect because a director is not an agent of the corporation, which is a party with authority to bind the corporation and who also owes a fiduciary duty to the corporation. Answer (b) is incorrect because an executive is a member of senior management, but not necessarily a member of the Board of Directors. Answer (d) is incorrect because a representative, like an agent, is a party that is authorized to speak on behalf of the corporation and, in certain circumstances to bind the corporation, not a role of the Board of Directors.

3. (b) Since internal control affects the entire organization, including management, its evaluation should be at the highest level. As a result, it is generally performed by a group of internal auditors that is independent and reports directly to the Board of Directors. Answer (a) is incorrect because internal controls affect the accounting management staff, as well as the CFO, and it would not be appropriate for either to be responsible for evaluating internal control. Answer (c) is incorrect because internal controls affect the operations management staff, as well as the chief operations officer, and it would not be appropriate for either to be responsible for evaluating internal control. Answer (d) is incorrect because internal controls affect the security management staff, as well as the chief facilities officer, and it would not be appropriate for either to be responsible for evaluating internal control.

4. (c) According to SOX, the Audit committee financial expert per SOX should understand GAAP, financial statements, and have experience with internal accounting controls. Answer (a) is incorrect because a limited understanding of GAAS is not sufficient. Answer (b) is incorrect because there is no requirement that the individual be knowledgeable about financial planning. Answer (d) is incorrect because there is no requirement that the individual have experience preparing tax returns.

5. (d) Under SOX, a CEO or CFO who misrepresents financial information may be both imprisoned and fined. The penalties could range from $1 million and 10 years to $5 million and 20 years in prison.

6. (b) SOX requires every issuer to have a financial expert on the audit committee. If there is no financial expert on the audit committee, this fact and the reasons are required to be disclosed. Answer (a) is incorrect because the outside CPA firm's audit partner may not serve on the audit committee as it would impair the firm's independence. Answer (c) is incorrect because although the financial expert may benefit from experience in the issuer's industry, SOX does not specify that as a requirement. Answer (d) is incorrect because although the financial expert may be best suited to chair the audit committee, that is not required by SOX.

Lecture 2.04 – Internal Controls

PCAOB Integrated Audit

AS 2201 (previously AS 5) requires the auditor to examine the design and operating effectiveness of internal control over financial reporting (ICFR) in order to provide a sufficient basis for an opinion on its effectiveness in preventing or detecting material misstatements of the financial statements. The results may be expressed in either separate reports or one combined report on the financial statements and the internal control over financial reporting. The financial statement audit portion of the integrated audit is similar to any other financial statement audit, but its "integrated" nature means that auditors rely much more on internal control and less on substantive procedures.

COSO's Internal Control Framework

The most commonly used framework to benchmark internal controls in the U.S. is *Internal Control – Integrated Framework* developed by the Committee of Sponsoring Organizations of the Treadway Commission (COSO). COSO describes internal control as *"a process, effected by the entity's board of directors, management, and other personnel designed to provide reasonable assurance regarding the achievement of objectives relating to operations, reporting, and compliance."*

- Operational objectives relate to the effectiveness and efficiency of operations and incorporate the achievement of financial performance goals and the safeguarding of assets.
- Reporting objectives relate to the reliability, timeliness, and transparency of financial and nonfinancial reporting for both internal and external uses.
- Compliance objectives relate to complying with applicable laws and regulations.

Since internal control is a process that is affected by people, it can only provide reasonable assurance, as opposed to absolute assurance, that the entity's objectives will be met.

The COSO Board added the **17 Internal Control Principles** because they are presumed essential in assessing that the five components (CRIME) are present and functioning properly. Here are the 17 listed by internal control component (**CRIME**):

CONTROL *E*NVIRONMENT

1. Demonstrates commitment to integrity and ethical values
2. Exercises oversight responsibility
3. Establishes structure, authority, and responsibility
4. Demonstrates commitment to competence
5. Enforces accountability

RISK ASSESSMENT

6. Specifies suitable objectives
7. Identifies and analyzes risk
8. Assesses fraud risk
9. Identifies and analyzes significant change

CONTROL ACTIVITIES

    10. Selects and develops control activities

    11. Selects and develops general controls over technology

    12. Deploys through policies and procedures

INFORMATION & COMMUNICATION

    13. Uses relevant information

    14. Communicates internally

    15. Communicates externally

MONITORING

    16. Conducts ongoing and/or separate evaluations

    17. Evaluates and communicates deficiencies

Under COSO (The Committee of Sponsoring Organizations of the Treadway Commission) internal control includes the following **five components** which contain the 17 COSO Internal Control Principles mentioned above (**CRIME**):

The Control **E**nvironment

The control environment is the combination of standards, processes, and structures that enable internal control to be effective throughout the organization. Setting the tone of an organization by influencing the control consciousness of people, the control environment is the foundation of internal control. The control environment encompasses 5 principles.

    a. Commitment to integrity and ethical values demonstrated through

        o The tone at the top established through the directives, actions, and behavior of management and governance

        o Standards of conduct understood by all members of the organization and others with which it interacts and against which behavior and performance is evaluated

        o Timely and consistent identification of and response to deviations from standards

        o COSO indicates that the control environment, or tone at the top, is the most significant internal control component when it comes to sending a message throughout the organization as to the entity's attitude about ethical behavior. It further indicates that this can best be demonstrated through the exemplary behavior of the leadership.

    b. Governance's independence from management and oversight of internal control demonstrated through:

        o Identification and acceptance of oversight responsibilities

        o Inclusion of members with appropriate levels of skill and expertise to effectively oversee management with sufficient numbers independent of management and objective

        o Involvement in and oversight of internal control

    c. Management's establishment of an appropriate hierarchy and structure to achieve entity objectives demonstrated through:

        o Establishment of reporting lines considering all structures of the entity

        o Assignment of, and limitations on, authorities and responsibilities

d. Commitment to attracting, developing, and retaining individuals who are competent and in accord with entity objectives demonstrated through:

- o Setting expectations requiring appropriate levels of competence
- o Evaluating competence and addressing deficiencies
- o Providing mentoring and training to attract, develop, and retain competent personnel and business relationships
- o Establishing contingency and succession plans

e. Individuals are held accountable for their control responsibilities, demonstrated through:

- o Establishment of mechanisms that hold individuals accountable for performance of internal control responsibilities including performance measures, incentives, and rewards, which are to be evaluated for relevance on an ongoing basis
- o Evaluation and moderation of pressures associated with performance
- o Evaluation of performance including rewards or remedial action, as appropriate

Factors of the control environment include (**CHOPPER**):

- o *Commitment to Competence* – Employees must possess the skills and knowledge essential to performing their jobs, especially those responsible for performing important control functions.
- o *Human resource policies and procedures* – Effective policies and practices for hiring, training, evaluating, counseling, promoting, and compensating employees are vital to the environment.
- o *Organizational structure* – Provides a basis for planning, directing and controlling operations.
- o *Philosophy and Operating style of Management* – The manner in which management runs the organization can have a significant effect on the control environment. Unethical management can lead to unethical employees.
- o *Participation of the Board of directors or audit committee* – Both groups play a key role in establishing IC.
- o *Ethical and Integrity values* – Management should encourage appropriate behavior and lead by example. Values are established through a code of conduct, official policies, and by example. This includes codes of conduct, the attestation process, whistle-blower processes, investigation and resolution, training and reinforcement both internally and with third parties.
- o *Responsibility and Authority Assignment* – Communicated through documents such as job descriptions and organizational charts; personnel need a clear understanding of their responsibilities and the rules and regulations that govern their actions.

Risk Assessment

Risk assessment refers to an entity's recognition of the fact that events may occur that pose risks to the achievement of the entity's objectives and the process that is established to identify and evaluate those risks. Risk assessment encompasses 4 principles.

a. Objectives are sufficiently clear to allow for identification and evaluation of risks to their achievement, demonstrated through:

- o Consideration of operational objectives, internal and external reporting objectives, and compliance objectives
- o Reflects management's choices in relation to operational objectives, and internal reporting objectives

b. Risks are identified and analyzed to determine appropriate management, demonstrated through:

- o Consideration of internal entity level risks, such as related to infrastructure, management structure, personnel, access to assets, and technology; and external entity level risks, such as related to the economy, the environment, regulation, foreign operations, and the social and technological environment.
- o Consideration of risks at the transaction level.
- o Consideration of factors such as likelihood of occurrence and its effect if it does; the speed with which the effect will be incurred upon occurrence of the event representing the risk; and the length of time the effect will last after occurrence of the event.
- o Consideration as to whether the appropriate response is accepting the risk by taking no preventive action; avoiding the risk by changing the objective or discontinuing the activity that creates the risk; sharing the risk by entering into a relationship, such as a joint venture, or participating in hedging activities; or reducing the risk through a variety of decisions, including the establishment of control activities.

c. Risk assessment includes a consideration of the possibility of fraud, demonstrated through:

- o Consideration of the nature of fraud, including the types of fraud that may be perpetrated against the entity.
- o Assessment of the characteristics of fraud, including incentives or pressures that may be inherent in the entity's activities; opportunities to commit or conceal fraud; and attitudes and rationalizations that may allow management or others to commit fraud.

d. The potential impact of changes within the entity on the effectiveness of internal control is identified and assessed, as demonstrated through:

- o Identification and assessment of changes in the external environment.
- o Identification and assessment of changes in the business model or the entity's leadership.

An entity's risk assessment for financial reporting purposes is its identification, analysis, and management of risks (risk response) relevant to the preparation of financial statements that are fairly presented in conformity with GAAP. Risk assessment includes risks that may affect an entity's ability to properly record, process, summarize, and report financial data. Risk assessment, for example, may address how the entity considers the possibility of unrecorded transactions or identifies and analyzes significant estimates recorded in the financial statements.

- o Risks relevant to financial reporting include *external and internal* **factors** such as the following:
  - ▪ Changes in operating environment (competition)
  - ▪ New personnel
  - ▪ New or revamped information systems (internal factor)
  - ▪ Rapid growth
  - ▪ New technology
  - ▪ New lines of business, products or activities
  - ▪ Corporate restructurings
  - ▪ Foreign operations
  - ▪ Accounting pronouncements

Control Activities

Control activities are the actions established by policies and procedures that help ensure that management's directives are carried out   Control activities encompass 3 principles.

    a. Selection and development of control activities contribute to reducing risks to the achievement of the entity's objectives, as demonstrated through:

- o Integration with the entity's risk assessment and consideration of entity specific factors, including the various levels within the entity requiring control activities.
- o Identification of those processes and activities that require control activities.
- o Inclusion of a range of types of control activities, including manual and automated controls, preventive and detective controls, and appropriate segregation of duties.

    b. General controls over technology are developed to support the achievement of the entity's objectives, as demonstrated through:

- o Management's understanding of the relationship between internal processes, automated controls, and general controls over technology.
- o The establishment of relevant control activities regarding technology infrastructure; security management; and acquisition, development, and maintenance.

    c. Policies identify expectations and procedures convert policies into actions, as demonstrated through:

- o The incorporation of control activities into daily processes, designating responsibility and establishing accountability.
- o Tasks are performed in a timely manner, using competent personnel, with corrective action taken as appropriate.
- o The regular reassessment of control activities to verify their continued relevance.

Types of control activities include:

- **P**erformance reviews – actual vs. budget, P/Y, financial to non-financial
- **I**nformation processing – (IT) General vs. Application controls
- Application controls include Input, Processing and Output controls
- **P**hysical controls – Access to assets
- **S**egregation of duties includes assigning different people the responsibilities of **authorizing** transactions, **recording** transactions, maintaining **custody** of assets, and performing **comparisons**. It is intended to reduce the opportunities to allow any person to be in a position to both *perpetrate and conceal errors or irregularities* in the normal course of their duties (**ARCCS**).
    - o **A**uthorization of transactions
    - o **R**ecording (posting) of transactions
    - o **C**ustody of assets
    - o **C**omparisons

Information and Communication

Information and communication refers to the processes by which management obtains or generates and uses information and how it is disseminated throughout the entity and to appropriate business relationships. Information and communication encompass 3 principles.

    a. The functioning of all components of internal control is supported by relevant, quality information obtained or generated by the entity, as demonstrated through:

- o   Identification of information requirements and the internal and external sources from which it is derived.
- o   The transformation of data into information through processing throughout which quality is maintained.
- o   Consideration of the cost of obtaining and disseminating information, weighed against the benefits.

b.   The functioning of all components of internal control is supported by the internal communication of objectives and responsibilities, as demonstrated through:

- o   Establishment of processes to communicate objectives and responsibilities to all appropriate personnel.
- o   Communication between management and governance.
- o   The provision of mechanisms, such as whistle-blower hotlines, that establish alternate channels of communication, allowing anonymous or confidential communication as needed.
- o   Consideration of factors such as the nature and timing of information and its intended audience in establishing methods of communication.

c.   External parties are informed as to matters affecting the effectiveness of appropriate components of internal control, as demonstrated through:

- o   The establishment of channels and processes for communicating with external parties to provide relevant and timely information and obtain relevant and timely information from others.
- o   The communication with governance of relevant information obtained from external parties.
- o   The establishment of alternative communication channels and the selection of relevant methods of communication.

Managers must have access to timely, reliable, and relevant information in order to make effective decisions. Information systems should be implemented to capture information and process, summarize and report the information on an accurate and timely basis. Proper communication involves providing employees with an understanding of their roles and responsibilities. Open communication channels are essential to the proper functioning of internal control.

- **Info system** consists of the methods and records used to identify, record, measure, process, summarize, present, disclose and report co.'s transactions and to maintain accountability for the related accounts.
- **Communication** involves establishing individual duties and responsibilities relating to internal control and making them known to involved personnel.

Monitoring Activities

Monitoring refers to the processes the entity uses to determine if all components of internal control, including the principles within each component, are in place and are functioning in the manner intended. Monitoring activities encompass 2 principles.

a.   Evaluations are conducted on an ongoing basis, on a separate periodic basis, or both to determine if controls are in place and are functioning effectively.

b.   Internal control deficiencies are communicated to parties responsible for corrective action on a timely basis.

To assess the quality of internal control performance (are controls working?), controls are monitored by performing *ongoing evaluations* of activities (e.g., reviewing customer complaints when they come in) or by *separate evaluations* (e.g., periodic audits). Information systems can have embedded modules that look for unusual or suspicious transactions or relationships. Two main categories of monitoring activities include "ongoing evaluations" and "separate evaluations."

In 2009, COSO issued *Guidance on Monitoring Internal Control Systems* that elaborates on the monitoring component of internal control. Individuals who monitor controls within an organization are referred to as evaluators. **Evaluators** should be both *competent and objective.*

Internal control systems *fail* because the controls are not designed or implemented properly; the environment changes or their operation has changed. Within a corporation, internal control should be evaluated by the internal audit staff who report to the board of directors.

Monitoring may be considered as consisting of the following **sequence of activities**:
- Control baseline – development of an understanding of how the system of internal control was designed and implemented.
- Change identification – use of ongoing and separate evaluations to identify and address changes in the effectiveness of I/C to initiate changes to controls.
- Change management – determination of when changes to I/C are needed and the types of changes that are likely to be effective.
- Control revalidation/update – development of a new baseline understanding of the revised system.

Limitations of Internal Control (inherent – COCO)
Internal control may not be effective because:
- Collusion
- Override by management
- Competence – errors or mistakes, poor human judgment
- Cost/benefit constraints
- Obsolescence – change in Co's operations or size

The mnemonic **CRIME** reminds management that it would be a crime not to consider all of the internal control elements when designing the system.

Lecture 2.05 – Fraud Risk Management Program

Fraud is any illegal act characterized by deceit, concealment or violation of trust. It is generally considered to be intentional, and deals with the integrity of the perpetrator, as opposed to errors, which are considered unintentional and deal with the competency of the perpetrator.

Typically, it can be divided into asset misappropriation (theft) or misstatement of financial statements. Members of upper management generally are more likely than non-management employees to misstate financial statements. Non-management employees generally are more likely than upper management to steal assets and then take steps to conceal the theft.

By its very nature, fraud involves some sort of deceit. An entity is vulnerable to severe long-term impact from fraud without active measures to deter, detect and minimize it. Basically, an ounce of fraud prevention is worth a pound of cure.

When an entity uncovers something that looks like fraud, it typically engages a certified fraud examiner (CFE) to investigate and assist in documenting it for prosecution and recovery, if any. Well-managed entities over a minimal size (often consulting with a CFE or CPA) develop a fraud risk management program (FRMP) long before a probable fraud event occurs.

Purpose

Reasons for a fraud risk management program span the spectrum from legal duty to entity survival.

- A FRMP helps the board of directors satisfy
  - Duty of care to stakeholders.
  - Statutory/regulatory requirements (Sarbanes-Oxley, SEC, PCAOB standards, etc.)
- A FRMP helps support stakeholder confidence (impact of fraud on profitability and available funding). Shareholders are unwilling to invest to support a fraudster; they invest to receive financial returns.
- A FRMP helps entity survival
  - Greater profitability
  - Intact or enhanced image
  - Improved efficiency & increased ability to meet commitments and obtain financing
- A FRMP helps to prevent, detect, and deter fraud.
- A FRMP helps enhance employee morale (makes it easier to attract and retain well-qualified talent)
  - Reduced stress
  - Greater job satisfaction and security
- Most fraud is **not** found by external auditors
  - Internal measures often find fraud while it still is relatively small, increasing the likelihood of recovery or, at least, reducing the size of the loss.
  - Internal measures often are cheaper to implement than paying an external audit firm for essentially the same results.
- The Association of Certified Fraud Examiners (ACFE) report an annual audit and a code of conduct present in about 80 percent of fraud cases. Clearly, these are insufficient alone.

Small entities are particularly vulnerable to fraud, as they tend not to have anti-fraud controls.

Fraud Discovery

According to the Association of Certified Fraud Examiners Report to the Nations on Occupational Fraud & Abuse (Using one's occupation for personal gain):

- Tips and whistle-blowers uncover about 40 percent of fraud. Management review and internal auditors each uncover about 15 percent of fraud. Accidents uncover over 5 percent of fraud. External auditors uncover **less** than 5 percent of fraud.
- Fraud losses are estimated at 5 percent of revenues.
- Typical losses are $140,000 per case and typical cases have an 18-month duration
  - ○ Fraud has the highest impact on small entities.
  - ○ The importance of the position of the perpetrator generally bears a direct relationship to the size of the loss.
- "Red flags" are present in over 80 percent of cases:
  - ○ Living beyond means or personal financial difficulties
  - ○ Unusually close relationships with vendors or customers
  - ○ Excessive control issues

Occupational fraud is the use of one's occupation for personal gain through the deliberate misuse or misapplication of the organization's resources or assets. Types of Occupational Fraud and Abuse include misappropriations of assets, corruption and financial statement Fraud.

Five Steps in a Fraud Risk Management Program (FRMP)

1. Establish governance policies
2. Conduct a comprehensive risk assessment
3. Plan and execute preventive and detective control processes
4. Perform timely and confidential investigations
5. Monitor and assess the program (periodically, on an ongoing basis, or both periodically and on an ongoing basis) reporting the results and improving the processes

An effective FRMP will deter, but not eliminate, fraud. An effective FRMP:

- Initiates a visible and rigorous fraud governance process
- Promotes a transparent and sound anti-fraud culture
- Entails a thorough periodic fraud risk assessment
- Plans, executes, and maintains preventive and detective fraud control processes
- Responds quickly to fraud allegations, including loss recovery actions and proceedings against perpetrators

Five Fraud Risk Management Principles (CRIME) under COSO

1. Control **E**nvironment: The organization establishes and communicates a Fraud Risk Management Program that demonstrates the expectations of the board of directors and senior management (Tone at the Top) and their commitment to high integrity and ethical values regarding management fraud risk (CHOPPER).
2. **R**isk Assessment: The organization performs comprehensive fraud risk assessments to identify specific fraud schemes and risks, assess their likelihood and significance, evaluate existing fraud control activities, and implement actions to mitigate residual fraud risks.
3. **C**ontrol Activities: The organization selects, develops, and deploys preventive and detective fraud control activities to mitigate the risk of fraud events occurring or not being detected in a timely manner.

4. *I*nformation & Communication: The organization establishes a communication process to obtain information about potential fraud and deploys a coordinated approach to investigation and corrective action to address fraud appropriately and in a timely manner.

5. *M*onitoring Activities: The organization selects, develops, and performs ongoing evaluations to ascertain whether each of the five principles of fraud risk management is present and functioning and communications FRMP deficiencies in a timely manner to parties responsible for taking corrective action, including senior management and the board of directors.

Roles of Key Parties in Managing Fraud Risk (outlined by ACFE)

- **Those Charged with Governance (ideally, the Audit Committee)**
  - Consider the risk of management override of controls.
  - Monitor fraud risks throughout the entity (using internal auditor or other personnel).
  - Meet privately with appropriate individuals (e.g., internal auditor, external auditors).
  - Consider reputation risk when reviewing work of management, internal auditors, and external auditors.
  - Remain cognizant of the external auditor's responsibilities pertaining to fraud.
  - Seek counsel when responding to allegations of fraud.

- **Board of Directors (BOD)**
  - Understand fraud risks (both generally and those affecting the entity).
  - Establish and communicate an appropriate level of risk tolerance for the entity.
  - Maintain oversight of the fraud risk assessment.
  - Monitor management's reports on fraud risks, policies, and control activities.
  - Ensure that management provides effective fraud risk management documentation to encourage ethical behavior.
  - Retain outside experts as appropriate.
  - Remain cognizant of the external auditor's responsibilities pertaining to fraud.

- **Management (CEO, CFO, COO, etc.)**
  - Design, implement, maintain and document the fraud risk management program.
  - Maintain documentation of antifraud controls.
  - Evaluate design and operating effectiveness of antifraud controls.
  - Report to the BOD on actions that have been taken to manage fraud risks and the effectiveness of the fraud risk management program.
  - Educate the entity on areas of potential compliance violations.
  - Enforce the entity's Code of Ethics.

- **Internal Auditors**
  - Report to those Charged with Governance
  - Provide assurance to the BOD and management regarding existing controls' appropriateness given the risk tolerance established by the BOD.
  - Evaluate the design and operation of antifraud controls for comprehensiveness and adequacy, especially regarding management override risks.
  - Support the audit committee in performing detective activities around the risk of management override of controls
  - Consider fraud risks when developing audit plans.
  - Support management's education of the entity regarding areas of potential fraud and compliance violations.

- **Employees (in all functions and at all levels)**
  - Have a basic awareness of fraud and "red flags."
  - Comprehend policies and procedures (e.g., fraud policy, code of conduct, whistleblower policy, internal controls specific to position, etc.).
  - Contribute to a strong control environment.
  - Report suspicions or incidences of fraud and corruption.
  - Cooperate with audits and investigations.

Typical Shortcomings

A fraud risk assessment (part of an entity's broader risk assessment process) considers the ways that fraud and misconduct can occur by and against the entity. The ACFE finds that fraud risk assessment failures typically are due to one or more of the following:

- Assessment consists of an identification of risk factors, but omits an identification of schemes and scenarios.
- Lack of follow up after identification of fraud risks and linkage to mitigating controls.
- Potential perpetrators are not identified (which can lead to insufficient consideration of management override).
- Inadequate consideration of collusive fraud and management override of controls.
- Lack of appropriate involvement in assessment by internal auditors and other appropriate personnel.
- Lack of appropriate monitoring by the audit committee.

While a FRMP cannot guarantee the absence of fraud, it can deter fraud and minimize fraud loss much less expensively than other measures. Entities cannot rely complacently on an annual audit and a code of ethics to prevent fraud.

Lecture 2.06 – Controls over Business Processes

When designing an internal control structure, a systematic process should be applied that will provide assurance that all types of transactions and activities are considered, that risks associated with each type are considered, and that the systems have those elements that are conducive to more effective controls.

The foundation of the system will be developed around those repetitive transactions that affect the entity on a regular basis. This includes processes for cash receipts, cash disbursements, sales, purchases, payroll, and, depending on the industry in which the entity operates and the nature of its operations, may include various other core systems. For each system, the process will include:

- **Initiation** – At what point is a transaction initiated? In a sales transaction, for example, some transactions may be initiated when a customer contacts the entity, such as by arriving at a retail outlet, contacting the company by phone, or placing an order over the Internet. In others, sales personnel or other representatives of the entity call upon potential customers seeking orders.

- **Authorization** – What must occur before the entity is willing to commit resources to fulfilling its performance obligations in the transaction? In a sales transaction, for example, the credit department may need to determine that the customer is within its credit limit and is current on its account before a sale may be approved.

- **Execution** – What procedures will entity personnel perform, and what forms will be completed, as the entity meets its performance obligations associated with the transaction? In a sales transaction, for example, the entity will identify and isolate the products sold, ship the merchandise, verify receipt, and prepare an invoice. Execution includes all procedures involved from the time a transaction is initiated until the time the entity's role in it has been fulfilled.

- **Verification** – What safeguards are built into the system to make certain that errors are not made and fraud is not committed? In a sales transaction, for example, this may involve completing a pre-numbered sales order when an order is received and having someone in accounting verify that all forms within a sequence are accounted for (Completeness). Verification occurs throughout the process.

A well-designed system for a business process will include forms that are designed to require the process to be completed properly; make certain that all appropriate parties, and only appropriate parties, receive copies that have the information needed to fulfill their role in the process; and provide for the **segregation of incompatible duties**. Incompatible functions, which should be kept separate, are (**ARCC**):
- **A**uthorization of transactions
- **R**ecording of the transactions
- **C**ustody of resources associated with those transactions
- **C**omparison and reconciliations of physical resources to recorded information

Segregation of duties is generally accomplished by having different parties or departments responsible for different aspects of a transaction. This is not necessarily achievable in a small business environment, in which there may be limited numbers of individuals among whom to allocate responsibilities. It is also challenging in an environment that is heavily **technology oriented**, in which the duties of authorization, reporting, and custody are segregated with authorization associated with inputs, reporting associated with operations, and custody associated with output and the librarian function. Segregation can often be accomplished by limiting physical access to various components of the system to those who need access and by the use of firewalls and passwords to limit access from within the system. This will be discussed in more detail in the Information Technology section of this book.

Controlling Changes to Processes

Entities are always evolving. In some cases, change may be pervasive as entities re-evaluate their missions, get involved in new types of transactions, expand into new geographical areas, establish relationships with new customers or suppliers, and get involved in activities that were performed by others within the entity's supply chain. Change also occurs as systems become obsolete or as resources become available to enhance systems.

In order to make certain that change does not have any adverse effects, management will need to develop a process for controlling change. The basic **change control processes components** will include:

- **Change Requests** - Identifying when change is needed or desired. This may result from change requests from parties within the existing system; from the failure of some aspect of the system, including a piece of equipment reaching the end of its useful life; experimentation to determine if processes can be made more efficient or effective; or a wide variety of other reasons.

- **Change Analysis** - Evaluating the change. Various factors will be considered in determining whether or not a change is justified. The analysis basically involves comparing the costs to the benefits. Costs to be considered will include both economic costs as well as those associated with a potential disruption in the system, the need for training, and the likelihood of mistakes (especially when the process is new).

- **Change Decisions** - Deciding on the change. Based on the evaluation, management will determine if a change is justified and if the benefits outweigh the costs.

- **Planning and Implementing the Change**. This involves developing a plan that not only includes the new processes or components, but also indicates all aspects of the existing process and all personnel within the entity that will be affected, may require the design or modification of forms or development of new management reports, and will involve the training of those who are part of the system. Care must be taken to avoid scope creep (the incremental *ad hoc* expansion of a change) during implementation.

- **Monitoring and Tracking the Change**. Once a change is made, it will be monitored with two objectives in mind. First, management will want to make certain that the change is being properly executed. In addition, management will want to determine if the change is having the intended effects.

Reporting on Internal Control

An accountant may be required to report on internal control. Section 404 of SOX (Title IV) requires each annual report to contain a report on internal control in which management acknowledges its responsibility for establishing and maintaining internal control relevant to financial reporting and includes an assessment by management as to the effectiveness of internal control relevant to financial reporting as of the end of the most recent fiscal period. The registered accounting firm that audits the entity's financial statements is also required to attest to the assessment made by management.

Management's **report on internal control over financial reporting** (ICFR) should include:

- Management's acknowledgment of its responsibility for internal control over financial reporting (ICFR).
- Management's assessment of ICFR as of the end of the most recent period.
- An identification of the framework used to evaluate ICFR.
- An indication that the auditor has issued an attestation report on management's assessment.

The **auditor's report** attesting to management's assessment will include:

- A title indicating that the auditor is independent
- An indication of management's responsibility for ICFR and for assessing its effectiveness
- Identification of management's report on ICFR
- An indication that the auditor's responsibility is the expression of an opinion on ICFR based on the audit
- A definition of ICFR
- A statement that the audit was conducted in accordance with PCAOB standards and that those standards require the auditor to plan and perform the audit to obtain reasonable assurance about the effectiveness of ICFR
- A statement describing that an audit consists of understanding internal control, assessing risk, testing and evaluating controls, and performing other procedures the auditor considers necessary
- A statement that the auditor believes that the audit provides a reasonable basis for the opinion
- An indication of the limitations on internal control
- The auditor's opinion as to the effectiveness of ICFR as of the end of the most recent period
- The signature of the firm and the city and state from which the report was issued

Lecture 2.07 – Internal Controls – Class Questions

7. Which of the following is not a component of an entity's internal control?

    a. Control risk.
    b. Control activities.
    c. Monitoring.
    d. Control environment.

8. According to COSO, the use of ongoing and separate evaluations to identify and address changes in internal control effectiveness can best be accomplished in which of the following stages of the monitoring-for-change continuum?

    a. Control baseline
    b. Change identification
    c. Change management
    d. Control revalidation/update

9. According to COSO, which of the following is the most effective method to transmit a message of ethical behavior throughout an organization?

    a. Demonstrating appropriate behavior by example
    b. Strengthening internal audit's ability to deter and report improper behavior
    c. Removing pressures to meet unrealistic targets, particularly for short-term results
    d. Specifying the competence levels for every job in an organization and translating those levels to requisite knowledge and skills

10. Within the COSO Internal Control—Integrated Framework, which of the following components is designed to ensure that internal controls continue to operate effectively?

    a. Control environment
    b. Risk assessment
    c. Information and communication
    d. Monitoring

11. According to COSO, an effective approach to monitoring internal control involves each of the following steps, except

    a. Establishing a foundation for monitoring
    b. Increasing the reliability of financial reporting and compliance with applicable laws and regulations
    c. Designing and executing monitoring procedures that are prioritized based on risks to achieve organizational objectives
    d. Assessing and reporting the results, including following up on corrective action where necessary

12. Management of a company has a lack of segregation of duties within the application environment, with programmers having access to development and production. The programmers have the ability to implement application code changes into production without monitoring or a quality assurance function. This is considered a deficiency in which of the following areas?

    a. Change control
    b. Management override
    c. Data integrity
    d. Computer operations

Class Solutions

7. (a) The five components of internal control are (CRIME) the control environment (d), risk assessment, control activities (b), information and communication, and monitoring (c). Control risk is the risk that internal control will not prevent a misstatement due to error or fraud or detect and correct it on a timely basis. It is not a component of internal control.

8. (b) Monitoring internal control for changes involves a multi-step process that begins with an understanding of the control baseline, the basic design of the system; identifying areas of ineffectiveness that may require change; making decisions as to the extent and nature of changes, if any; and developing an understanding of the revised system. The stage at which changes in effectiveness are identified and addressed is the change identification stage.

9. (a) COSO indicates that the control environment, or tone at the top, is the most significant internal control component when it comes to sending a message throughout the organization as to the entity's attitude about ethical behavior. It further indicates that this can best be demonstrated through the exemplary behavior of the leadership. Answer (b) is incorrect because internal audit, a form of monitoring, enhances the effectiveness of internal control and facilitates the reporting of improper behavior but does not send a message throughout the entity as to the ethical perspective. Answer (c) is incorrect because removing pressures to meet unrealistic targets reduces or eliminates one of the reasons that fraud may be committed but does not send a message throughout the entity about ethical behavior. Answer (d) is incorrect because specifying competence levels for every job provides assurance that management's directives are less likely to be violated due to error but does not send a message throughout the entity about ethical behavior.

10. (d) Monitoring ensures that internal control continues to operate effectively by evaluating its effectiveness on an ongoing basis, using separate evaluations, or both to identify when it is not. Answer (a) is incorrect because the control environment, also referred to as the tone at the top, sets the tone of the organization and indicates its attitude about ethical behavior but does not make certain that controls continue to operate effectively. Answer (b) is incorrect because risk assessment is the process by which the entity identifies the ways in which it is at risk of not achieving its objectives so that controls can be designed and implemented, as appropriate. Answer (c) is incorrect because information and communication is the means by which the entity obtains and develops information from internal and external sources and disseminates that information. It can create tools that make monitoring more efficient or effective but does not ensure the continued effectiveness as controls.

11. (b) Monitoring of internal control involves first establishing a foundation for monitoring by identifying how controls are designed and what they are intended to accomplish. Procedures can then be designed to monitor the controls to determine if they have been put into operation, whether or not they are being followed, and whether or not they are effective. The results can then be assessed to determine whether remedial action is appropriate and whether it be in the form of modifying or enhancing controls or enforcing existing controls. Increasing the reliability of financial reporting would involve developing controls, not monitoring.

12. (a) The ability of inappropriate individuals to implement code changes into production without monitoring or a quality control function indicates a deficiency in change control, the controls designed to prevent unauthorized changes to the system. Answer (b) is incorrect because management override would be indicated if management was making unauthorized changes to the system. Answer (c) is incorrect because a deficiency in data integrity occurs when data is not properly protected or when it is not carefully reviewed when input or processed. Answer (d) is incorrect because a deficiency in computer operations occurs when operators are applying the incorrect programs, using inappropriate equipment, or are using equipment inappropriately.

Lecture 2.08 – Enterprise Risk Management (ERM)

The business and economic environment is often unpredictable with significant technology evolution, rapidly shifting customer behavior, global influences, and fierce competition—all factors that stress strategic planning and the need to maximize operational capabilities to survive and thrive. All this creates uncertainty, which provides both risk and opportunity, and management must determine how to balance those risks and opportunities in alignment with the objectives of the entity. As you can imagine, this can be an extremely daunting task without an organized ERM approach to help keep up with the pace of change facing entities today.

To respond to the need for this organized approach, COSO developed an ERM **framework** in 2004 and updated it in 2017 to complement the internal control framework previously discussed. COSO's ERM framework is designed to be applied by all types and sizes of entities *to strategically identify events that may affect the entity and to manage those risks in accordance with the entity's risk appetite, to provide reasonable assurance of achieving the entity's objectives*. As updated in 2017, due to the increasing complexity of business risks, the accelerated rate of emerging new risks, and the demand for better risk reporting, the framework, retitled *Enterprise Risk Management—Integrating with Strategy & Performance,* dives deeper to redefine risk in relation to strategy and performance and focuses on the need to embed ERM proactively throughout the entity.

Benefits

COSO touts several benefits to implementing its ERM framework:
- Promotes identification and *management of entity-wide risks*.
- *Increases identification of opportunities* by examining the pros and cons of possibilities.
- *Reduces costs* of negative surprises and *maximizes positive outcomes*.
- Manages performance risks to *reduce disruption and increase opportunity*.
- Prioritizes and *maximizes allocation of resources*.
- Enhances entity *resilience*—the ability to anticipate and respond to change.

Components & Principles Overview

COSO's new ERM framework has *5 components* **(COPe RR)** and *20* different associated *principles* as outlined below.

Governance & Culture
1. Exercises board risk oversight
2. Establishes operating structures
3. Defines desired culture
4. Demonstrates commitment to core values
5. Attracts, develops, and retains capable individuals

Strategy & Objective Setting
6. Analyzes business context
7. Defines risk appetite
8. Evaluates alternative strategies
9. Formulates business objectives

Performance

10. Identifies risks
11. Assesses severity of risks
12. Prioritizes risks
13. Implements risk responses
14. Develops portfolio view

Review & Revision

15. Assesses substantial change
16. Reviews risk and performance
17. Pursues improvement in ERM

Information, Communication & Reporting

18. Leverages information systems
19. Communicates risk information
20. Reports on risk, culture, and performance

Governance & Culture

The first of the five components of the COSO ERM Framework is *Governance and Culture*. It sets the overall tone for the organization, addressing such issues as mission, vision, and core values. Governance encompasses the establishment of oversight responsibilities for ERM and the entity's tone. Culture refers to the ethical mindset, standards of acceptable behavior, and understanding the entity's risk.

Principle 1: Exercises Board Risk Oversight

"The board of directors provides oversight of the strategy and carries out governance responsibilities to support management in achieving strategy and business objectives."

The board's oversight role supports the creation of value in an entity and prevents its decline. The framework catalogs risk oversight responsibilities for boards. These responsibilities include overseeing governance and culture; strategy and objective-setting; performance; information, communications and reporting; and the reevaluation and improvement of practices to enrich entity performance. The board's risk oversight role includes, but is not limited to:
- Cultivating investor and stakeholder relations
- Authorizing management pay and incentives
- Reevaluating, questioning, and agreeing with management on:
  - Suggested strategy and target risk appetite
  - Coordination of strategy and business objectives with the entity's mission, vision, and values
  - Major decisions including mergers, acquisitions, capital allocations, funding, and dividend-related decisions
  - Reactions to substantial fluctuations in entity performance or the risk portfolio
  - Treatment of instances of deviation from values

Management is responsible for managing risks to the entity. To evaluate management's performance, a board generally would determine the answers to the following questions, among others. The answers may illustrate the entity's actual mindset for risk taking as opposed to what appears in documentation.

- Can all levels of management—not just senior management—articulate how risk is considered in the selection of strategy or business decisions?
- Can all levels of management clearly articulate the entity's target risk appetite and how it might influence a specific decision?
- How does the culture promote or retard responsible risk taking?
- How does management monitor the risk culture and how it changes? What changes have occurred?
- As changes occur, how does management ensure a suitable and prompt response?

Principle 2: Establishes operating structures

"The organization establishes operating structures in the pursuit of strategy and business objectives."

Principle 3: Defines desired culture

"The organization defines the desired behaviors that characterize the entity's desired culture."

Principle 4: Demonstrates commitment to core values

"The organization demonstrates a commitment to the entity's' core values."

Principle 5: Attracts, develops, and retains capable individuals

"The organization is committed to building human capital in alignment with the strategy and business objectives."

Principles 2 through 5 represent the *internal environment*, which sets the tone for the organization. It establishes a basis for the analysis of risk, incorporating management's philosophy, the entity's risk appetite, and the values that are important to the entity, such as *integrity and ethical values.*

The internal environment is exhibited in a variety of ways, both formal and informal. Some of the more formal components will include the entity's mission statement and its code of conduct. These should be evident in all aspects of the entity and should be incorporated into the entity's culture. A well-designed **mission statement** may address some or all of the following:
- The moral or ethical position of the entity and its desired public image
- The key strategic influence for the entity's operations
- A description of the entity's products or services, target market, and geographical domain
- Expectations in relation to growth and profitability

The informal aspect of the internal environment is probably the most important. It is comprised of the actual behavior of members of management and others who might be seen as influential within the organization. Whenever the behavior of such individuals is in conflict with the entity's mission statement or core values, or its formal policies and procedures, individuals both inside the organization and outside of it will assign more significance to the behavior.

One significant aspect of management and executive behavior is the relationship established with employees. Management should exhibit a willingness to tolerate mistakes, listen, and learn.

Strategy & Objective Setting

The second component of the COSO ERM Framework is *Strategy & Objective Setting*. It represents the entity's process for strategic planning. The entity determines its risk appetite, aligns it with its strategy, and develops business objectives to execute the strategy. This process serves as a basis for recognizing, evaluating, and responding to risk.

Principle 6: Analyzes Business Context

"The organization considers potential effects of business context on risk profile."

Business context refers to the environment in which the business operates. ERM involves considering a full range of potential events, enabling management to identify and take advantage of opportunities. Also see principle 10.

Principle 7: Defines Risk Appetite

"The organization defines risk appetite in the context of creating, preserving, and realizing value."

It is important for management to consider what level of risk is acceptable when evaluating alternatives, establishing goals, and developing policies, procedures, and other mechanisms to manage risks. For example, an entity should consider its risk appetite when determining its policy regarding the amount of information that must be obtained about a potential customer and how much must be verified independently before extending credit in order to avoid selling to someone who is not likely to pay.

Principle 8: Evaluates Alternative Strategies

"The organization evaluates alternative strategies and potential impact on risk profile."

Strategy is about developing a plan of action to achieve the entity's objectives. In evaluating alternative strategies, the entity must first align potential business strategies with the entity's mission, vision, and core values, and then determine the impact of those strategies with respect to the entity's risk profile (i.e. risk appetite). COSO's ERM framework provides 3 types of risks to consider in this process:
- **Risks *to* a chosen strategy** and the performance of that strategy—These are factors an entity should address when choosing a strategy, such as customer demand, supply, competition, and technology infrastructure.
- **Risks that the strategy chosen will *not align* with the mission, vision, and values**— Even if a strategy is successful, a misaligned strategy increases the risk that the entity will not achieve its mission and vision, or its values will be compromised. While some entities have been reluctant to truly embrace their mission, vision, and values, they have been shown to be extremely important to risk management and resilience in times of change.
- **Risks *of, or from*, the chosen strategy**—Every choice has some downsides. The risks of the strategy that is chosen should be considered and aligned with the risk appetite of the entity. The board and management should determine how the strategy will steer the entity in setting objectives and whether resources will be allocated efficiently.

Note: It's important to realize that ERM is as much about *understanding* all the risks as it is about managing them to enhance the performance of the entity.

Principle 9: Formulates Business Objectives

"The organization considers risk while establishing the business objectives at various levels that align and support strategy."

While an entity's mission describes what it would like to accomplish, it does not set out a specific plan for accomplishing the mission. Management translates the mission into goals or objectives that support the mission and take into account the entity's risk appetite. The *department manager* would be the best person to devise and execute the risk procedures for a particular department, as they are the most able to identify risky events within that department.

There are four types of business objectives to establish:

- Setting objectives begins at the top with **strategic objectives**, which establish a unifying theme for the entity and direct actions and decisions. While strategic objectives set the direction for the entity, objectives related to *operations, reporting, and compliance* provide the mechanisms for meeting those objectives. To be most effective, objectives should be set at each level and, when appropriate, in each of the three categories. A division manager, for example, should know what outputs their division is expected to provide, to whom, to what specifications, and on what timetable so that the manager can make the decisions that will accomplish those objectives.

- The strategic objectives may relate to the quality and other characteristics of the outputs and how the division will be operated. In order to achieve the strategic objective as to quality, the division manager will need the appropriate raw materials, qualified laborers, and the equipment or other resources necessary to convert those inputs into the desired outputs. **Operational objectives**, as a result, may be set to address the acquisition of raw materials, the screening and assignment of laborers, the acquisition and maintenance of equipment and support, and the process for completing the outputs.

- **Reporting objectives** would be established to determine how the division is progressing toward meeting the operational objectives and, ultimately, the strategic objectives. The manager will need to devise a means of determining if the needs of the customer are being met. This may involve obtaining feedback from a subsequent department as to the quality and amount of output that is being transferred. It may involve obtaining feedback from the work force as to the quality of the raw materials that are being provided or from supervision regarding the efficiency of the labor. Achievement of reporting objectives may require sophisticated reports that provide a large amount of information manipulated in a variety of ways. The most effective information is often limited in scope to one or very few parameters, does not require a great deal of effort to accumulate and report on a timely basis, and can be simply understood.

- **Compliance objectives** make certain that the division operates within appropriate guidelines, including both regulatory requirements and internal company policies. This includes making certain that employees are not working against the better interests of the employing entity. At the same time, they must be designed so that an employee does not violate requirements externally imposed in a misguided attempt to help the entity.

*Pe*rformance

The third component of COSO's ERM Framework is *Performance*. It represents the process of actually identifying, evaluating, and responding to risks. The risks should be prioritized by severity with regard to the entity's risk appetite. The entity then chooses the appropriate responses, while keeping an overall view of the amount of risk assumed. Results are reported to the appropriate stakeholders.

Principle 10: Identifies Risks

"The organization identifies risk that impacts the performance of strategy and business objectives."

The occurrence or nonoccurrence of certain events (i.e., risks) will determine whether or not the entity will achieve its objectives. Thus, risk identification involves determining what those events may be and how to distinguish between those events that representing opportunities, which should be encouraged and exploited, and those representing threats, which should be dealt with in accordance with the entity's risk appetite.

- **Opportunities must be exploited** in order to gain a competitive advantage, sustain one, or prevent a competitor from obtaining one. As such, opportunities should be considered in developing the strategic and other objectives of the entity. A plan might be established, and resources might be set aside, to take advantage of an opportunity in case it arises. Of course, the amount of effort going into the design of the plan and the resources set aside to take advantage of the opportunity will be a function of the likelihood that the event will occur, which is analogous to risk assessment, and the benefit that will be derived from it, which will be a factor in determining the appropriate response.
- Likewise, **risks must be prepared for** so that the entity does not lose a competitive advantage or allow a competitor to gain one. As a result, adverse events are considered in the entity's risk management process. The entity will consider the likelihood that an event will occur, the magnitude of the effect of the event, and the amount the effect will be influenced by actions of the entity in determining an appropriate response.

Event identification is primarily the identification and monitoring of the sources of information that pertain to areas of risk for the entity. Since resources are limited, the entity must be discreet in deciding which sources of information will be monitored. One approach, an aspect of risk assessment, is to determine the resources that are critical to achieving the objectives of the entity. The entity might then be able to identify the types of events that would affect that resource and might be able to seek out sources of information that would help the entity estimate the likelihood of the event and alert the entity of its occurrence, or imminent occurrence, on a timely basis. There are various techniques for identifying relevant events for ERM:

- **Event inventories** are detailed lists of the types of events the entity may be subject to due to the industry it is in, its geographic location, or other characteristics of its operations.
- **Internal analysis**, often done as part of routine business planning, may consist of discussions at meetings, or formal processes that are conducted on a routine basis. They utilize information that is developed internally as well as that obtained from external sources including customers, suppliers, and business relationships, as well as from the news, governmental reports, and other general sources.
- **Escalation or threshold triggers**, which involves the establishment of benchmarks or other criteria against which experiences can be compared to identify those that may require attention. These may be routine, such as reports on delinquent accounts receivable that will trigger collection procedures or monitoring devices that warn of factory temperatures exceeding certain limits.
- **Facilitated workshops or interviews** may be conducted for the specific purpose of learning of event indicators. They may involve staff, outside consultants, or experts in various fields. An auditor, for example, is required to conduct a brainstorming session with key staff to identify fraud risk factors. This enables the auditor to use the combined knowledge and experience of all participants to identify signs of fraud. Similarly, a meeting with factory staff may be useful in identifying signs of an unsafe condition, thereby preventing an undesirable event in the form of an accident.
- **Process flow analysis** involves the consideration of all components of a process including its inputs, tasks, responsibilities, and outputs. The factors affecting each aspect of the process can be considered to identify events that may be relevant, such as a potential scarcity of a resource used as a raw material in the process.

- **Leading event indicators** involves identifying data that is indicative of a pending event, such as an increase in consumer spending, which may correlate with possible increases in future interest rates.
- **Loss event data methodologies** are collections of information regarding past losses that may have been incurred by the entity or others to identify causes or trends. In anticipating allocating a new contract among different manufacturing plants, analyzing returned goods may identify that certain plants are delivering defective parts and the company can avoid a loss by not awarding the contract inappropriately. *Black swan analysis* involves evaluating the occurrence of events that had a negative effect and were unanticipated or viewed as highly unlikely.

ERM also identifies categories of events, including:
- *Internal* factors such as infrastructure, personnel, processes, and technology
- *External* factors such as economy, natural environment, politics, social factors, and technology

Three broad approaches might be employed to identify events that may have an adverse effect on an entity. These approaches are not mutually exclusive and an entity should apply all in its risk assessment at all levels of the organization. These three approaches can be described as a balance sheet approach, a process approach, and an event identification approach.

- Under the **balance sheet approach**, the entity should identify the resources within its control and determine which ones might be vulnerable and the degree of vulnerability. Most any assets might be misappropriated, for example, but the likelihood of misappropriation and the damage the entity would sustain upon misappropriation will be important factors in evaluating risk.

    o   *Assets essential to the achievement of the entity's objectives*, such as raw materials; exclusive information, formulae, or processes; and customer lists, for example, might be so essential to the entity that they will require protection regardless of their cost or the likelihood of their misappropriation. Other assets might not be essential to the entity but might be used by employees or general consumers in their everyday lives. These might include cash, supplies, and other assets like certain inventories. The risk evaluation must take into account that these assets are particularly susceptible to misappropriation or other misuse.

    o   When applying the balance sheet approach, it is important to consider *assets owned by the entity, its intellectual property, and its human resources*. It is also important to consider all of the individuals who are in position to create events that will affect the entity. This might include employees with access to, or custody of, assets. As discussed earlier, threats may come from internal sources, including employees, officers, and directors. They may also come from external sources, including competitors and potential competitors, customers, and con artists.

- The **process approach** involves evaluating the processes that are used to achieve the entity's objectives. At the entity level, this might include the process for establishing objectives and allocating resources. All processes, at all levels, should be considered. This will include the process for determining when a raw material or supply should be purchased, the process for providing a service or manufacturing a component of inventory, the process for obtaining supplies, and the process for recording a transaction. The evaluation of risk under this approach includes the consideration of various possibilities.

For each possibility, the entity must consider the likelihood that the possibility will become a reality and its consequences. Examples might include the risk that a process will not be performed, that it will not be performed on a timely basis, or that it will not be performed correctly. Consequences may range from being negligible to very significant. Neglecting to perform a process properly may result in defective inventory, a work stoppage, or product liability.

- The **event identification approach** incorporates many of the principles already discussed. One of the most difficult aspects of this approach is limiting the number of areas in which sources for information are sought. This might be accomplished when viewing the entity from the standpoint of competition. In *Contemporary Strategy Analysis*, Robert Grant discusses Michael Porter's Five Forces of Competition. These include customers, suppliers, competitors, potential entrants into the market, and substitutes. The entity should seek to identify events that might affect any of these five forces.

  o In the case of *customers*, increases or decreases in the *demand* for their products or services may affect the demand for the entity's products or services. *Economic events* may make it easier or more difficult for customers to pay for the entity's products or services on a timely basis. *Changes in customers' needs* may make certain features of the entity's products or services more or less valuable to customers. Other types of events may create *new customers*, such as a change in an industry's manufacturing process that makes the entity's products or services valuable to entities that had no previous use for them.

  o When an entity is evaluating *events that may affect suppliers*, it must consider all of its suppliers, including *suppliers of human resources, financial resources, and physical resources*. Events including changes in school enrollments or *graduation rates, failing or emerging industries*, and *shifts in population* may affect the supply of human resources. *Economic and social events*, as well as events affecting other entities seeking the same human resources, may affect the compensation and benefits required to attract or retain the appropriate human resources.

  o *Economic events may affect the availability and the cost of capital.* The entity's access to financial resources will also be affected by the availability of investment alternatives. The availability of physical resources may be affected by events related to weather or other natural phenomena. In addition, increases or decreases in the *demand* for the goods and services of an entity's suppliers will affect the cost and availability of those goods and services to the entity.

  o *Events that affect competitors* also affect the entity. Innovations that result in changes to their processes may provide them with a competitive advantage or eliminate one held by the entity. When operating in a finite market, events that create an advantage to competitors generally result in a disadvantage to the entity. As competitors devote more resources to marketing, they may improve their access to customers and reduce the entity's market share. More resources devoted to recruiting may increase access to human resources, decreasing those available to the entity. When events affect competitors' sales volumes, it affects their demand for raw materials, which will affect the price and availability of those raw materials to the entity.

o *Events that change the cost of entry into the market* will encourage or discourage potential competitors. Events might include those related to the *cost of capital, access to customers or suppliers, or the ability to emulate or improve processes.* Obviously, events that lower the cost of entry into the market will increase competition, while events that increase it may decrease competition and, at a minimum, will slow down increases in it.

o *Substitutes* affect the entity in two ways. They are in competition for the attention of suppliers as well as for the attention of customers. Substitutes include those who might use the same resources that are used by the entity. *Events that increase or decrease their need for common resources* will affect the price and availability of those resources to the entity. In addition, the extent to which events will cause customers to see other products or services as substitutes for those of the entity will increase or decrease *demand* for the entity's products or services.

Principle 11: Assesses Severity of Risks

"The organization assesses the severity of risks."

Management must evaluate the extent of potential effects of identified events on the ability of the entity to achieve its objectives. The likelihood of the occurrence of each identified risk is measured as well as the potential effect on the entity if the event were to occur. Here's three approaches used to quantify risk:

- **Benchmarking**, which compares expected outcomes to common measures.
- **Probabilistic models**, which develop expected values using probabilities of possible outcomes (quantifying risk).
- **Nonprobabilistic models**, which use subjective assumptions to measure possible outcomes (qualitative, but not quantitative).

Principles 12. Prioritizes Risks

"The organization prioritizes risks as a basis for selecting responses to risks."

Once management has identified and assessed the severity of the risks that may affect the entity's ability to achieve its objectives, it can decide how to prioritize the risks so that management can effectively assess capital needs and allocate capital where it is most needed or will be most productive.

Principle 13. Risk Response

"The organization identifies and selects risk responses."

When deciding on an appropriate risk response, the entity must consider inherent risk and residual risk.

- **Inherent risk** is the risk to the entity *if no action is taken*.
- **Residual risk** is the risk to the entity that would remain *if action were taken* and controls are taken into account.

The *reduction in risk*—basically the difference between an event's inherent risk and its residual risk—*can be compared to the cost of taking action to determine if action is appropriate*. This type of analysis is also useful in deciding among alternative actions when more than one risk response is available.

Among the **alternative responses to risks** are the decisions to *avoid* a risk, *mitigate* the risk, *share* the risk, or simply *accept* the risk. For example, if there is not sufficient verifiable information about a potential customer, the company can avoid risk by not extending credit, reduce it by limiting the amount of credit extended, share it by entering into an agreement with a third party, such as a bonding company or a guarantor, or accept it by extending credit.

- **Acceptance** of a risk indicates that the entity would take no action and simply allow the event to occur. This would be appropriate when the entity believes that inherent risk is already at an acceptable level or that the cost of taking action would exceed the reduction in risk that would result from the action anticipated.

- If the inherent risk is above an acceptable level, an entity might next seek to share that risk. **Sharing** the risk might involve the use of insurance or fidelity bonds, entering into an arrangement with another entity to share the risk, or outsourcing an activity. Outsourcing may be considered an example of sharing risk or avoiding it. In addition, the risks being "avoided" by the outsourcing entity are taken into account and incorporated in the cost of the product or service being outsourced.

- An entity that cannot find a cost-efficient manner of sharing the risk may decide to reduce it. **Reducing** the risk may require a change in the internal environment or may be accomplished through control activities, which can often reduce risk to an acceptable level. An entity may reduce the risk of inventory misappropriation, for example, by keeping it in a more secure location. It may also minimize losses through early detection. This could be accomplished if the entity maintains a perpetual inventory system and conducts regular and frequent counts. Such a system may be costly, and the costs should be compared to the anticipated reduction in risk to determine whether such control activities would be cost effective.

- When risk cannot be reduced to an acceptable level, **avoidance** may be the best alternative. This may require an entity to change an internal process, eliminate a line of business or product, stop using a particular raw material or buying from a specific supplier, or discontinue selling to a particular customer. An entity may determine that it does not have the ability to monitor receivables efficiently and the cost of reducing losses to an acceptable level would be prohibitive. As a result, the entity may decide to make all sales for cash, checks, and debit or credit cards and discontinue accepting sales on open account.

Principle 14. Risk Portfolio

"The organization develops and evaluates a portfolio view of risk."

ERM is designed to help management evaluate the interrelated impacts of decisions and deal with multiple risks. One risk may combine with other risks or offset other risks. Management must be careful when developing policies and procedures that are designed to affect one issue as, due to the integrated nature of business, it increases a different risk. For example, if we decide not to sell to the customer on credit, we also risk losing the customer to a competitor and adversely affecting the enthusiasm of the sales person who worked to bring the customer in.

Review & Revision

The fourth component of the COSO ERM Framework is Review & Revision. It represents the process of evaluating how well ERM components perform over time and refining the components as conditions change, as necessary.

Principle 15: Assesses substantial change

"The organization identifies and assesses changes that may substantially affect strategy and business objectives."

Principle 16: Reviews risk and performance

"The organization reviews entity performance and considers risk."

Principle 17: Pursues improvement in ERM

"The organization pursues improvement of enterprise risk management."

Risk assessment is an ongoing process, not a "one-time" activity. The entire ERM system must be monitored so that changes can be made on a timely basis. Monitoring may be through ongoing management activities or as part of a separate evaluation of the entity's ERM process.

Information, Communication & Reporting

The last of the five COSO ERM Framework components is *Information, Communication & Reporting.* It represents the ongoing exchange of internal and external information up and down as well as across the entity.

Principle 18: Leverages information and technology

"The organization leverages the entity's information and technology systems to support enterprise risk management."

Principle 19: Communicates risk information

"The organization uses communication channels to support enterprise risk management."

Principle 20: Reports on risk, culture, and performance

"The organization reports on risk, culture, and performance at multiple levels and across the entity."

People must have relevant information to carry out their responsibilities. As a result, the entity must have a means of identifying what information is pertinent from all of its internal and external sources.

Relevant information may be financial or nonfinancial and may be quantitative or qualitative in nature. It may also be formal or informal, such as that derived from conversations with customers or suppliers. It can potentially come from such a wide range of sources that it becomes very important for an entity to determine what sources are reliable as well as what information is relevant.

Once identified, relevant information must be captured, processed, and communicated to those who can benefit from it. It must be put into a form that is usable and must be provided on a timely basis so that decisions can be made to prevent losses.

Communication must include parties to whom it is relevant. It is most effective when lines of communication move in all directions within and around an organization. There should be communication at all levels, including upward and downward communication. Likewise, relevant information should be communicated with customers or suppliers to enhance the entity's ability to meet the needs of customers and have its needs met by suppliers.

Inherent Limitations of ERM

Applying ERM may enhance an entity's opportunity to be successful, but it does not ensure it. Regardless of how well a system is designed, implemented, and operated, there are certain *inherent limitations on ERM:*

- The future, by its nature, cannot be predicted with certainty.
- Some events are beyond management's control and, due to the need to allocate scarce resources, the entity will not necessarily be able to pursue all objectives to the extent desired.
- No system process, regardless of how well designed and managed, will necessarily always accomplish what it is intended to accomplish (i.e., there is no absolute assurance).

As is true of most systems, ERM can provide reasonable, but not absolute assurance that objectives will be met. Some of the reasons that this is the case include:

- Decisions made in designing, implementing, and operating a system are often largely depending on human **judgment**, which is not perfect.
- Systems can suffer **breakdowns** due to changes in personnel, technology, or the failure of any component of the system.
- Systems can be overcome by dishonest individuals through **collusion**, which negates effective segregation of duties.
- Decisions in design, implementation, and monitoring always require an analysis of **costs versus benefits** because entities do not have unlimited resources.
- Effective controls are often subject to **management override**.

Lecture 2.09 – Enterprise Risk Management – Class Questions

13. Which of the following activities would the COSO Enterprise Risk Management framework consider part of the governance and culture component?

    a. Demonstrating commitment to core values
    b. Formulating business objectives
    c. Defining risk appetite
    d. Leveraging information and technology

14. A manufacturing firm identified that it would have difficulty sourcing raw materials locally, so it decided to relocate its production facilities. According to COSO, this decision represents which of the following responses to the risk?

    a. Risk reduction
    b. Prospect theory
    c. Risk sharing
    d. Risk acceptance

15. Each of the following is a limitation of enterprise risk management (ERM), except:

    a. ERM deals with risk, which relates to the future and is inherently uncertain.
    b. ERM operates at different levels with respect to different objectives.
    c. ERM can provide absolute assurance with respect to objective categories.
    d. ERM is as effective as the people responsible for its functioning.

16. According to COSO, under which of the following components of enterprise risk management does the practice of prioritizing risks fall?

    a. Information, Communication & Reporting
    b. Strategy & Objective Setting
    c. Performance
    d. Review & Revision

Class Solutions

13. (a) Demonstrating commitment to core values is a principle that COSO classifies under the Governance & Culture component. Answer (b) is incorrect because formulating business objectives is a principle that COSO classifies under the Strategy & Objective Setting component. Answer (c) is incorrect because defining the risk appetite is a principle that COSO classifies under the Strategy & Objective Setting component. Answer (d) is incorrect because Leveraging information and technology is a principle that COSO classifies under the Information, Communication & Reporting component.

14. (a) By moving its production facility, the entity improves its access to raw materials. This reduces the risk that raw materials will not be obtainable, which would represent a risk to the achievement of the entity's objective. Answer (b) is incorrect because prospect theory is not an ERM component. Answer (c) is incorrect because risk sharing would involve taking action, such as entering into a joint venture, so that other entities share losses if the risk materializes. Answer (d) is incorrect because risk acceptance would involve taking no action to mitigate the risk.

15. (c) ERM cannot provide absolute assurance with respect to objective categories since it deals with future actions which are inherently uncertain and is dependent on people who may commit errors or may not share in the entity's ethical values. It is instead designed to provide reasonable, not absolute assurance, as to the achievement of the entity's objectives.

16. (c) According to COSO's enterprise risk management framework, the prioritization of risk is a practice that occurs within the Performance component. Answer (a) is incorrect because Information, Communication & Reporting relates to how the entity obtains and develops information and how it is disseminated. Answer (b) is incorrect because the Strategy & Objective Setting component represents the entity's process for strategic planning, where the entity determines its risk appetite, aligns it with its strategy, and develops business objectives to execute the strategy. Answer (d) is incorrect because Review & Revision represents the process of evaluating how well ERM components perform over time and refining the components as conditions change.

Lecture 2.10 – Dodd-Frank Act

Following the housing and financial crises that resulted in the recession of 2007-2009, there were many calls for financial reform. These calls resulted in the wide-ranging Dodd-Frank Wall Street Reform and Consumer Protection Act of 2010, referred to as "Dodd-Frank."

Dodd-Frank was passed to promote the *financial stability* of the U.S., *improve the accountability and transparency* of the financial system, end *"too big to fail," end bailouts* (GM, Chrysler, Citigroup, and Bank of America), and to protect consumers from *abusive financial services practices*. It affects many aspects of the financial system and many financial regulatory agencies (i.e., regulators), sets up new regulatory agencies, and calls for regulators to adopt over 240 new rules and regulations. There are 16 titles within the Act.

Title I – Financial Stability

This title creates the Financial Stability Oversight Council (FSOC). The council is tasked with identifying risks to U.S. financial stability, promoting market discipline by eliminating the expectation of a government bailout, and responding to emerging threats to financial stability. It is responsible for monitoring the financial system, collecting information, and making recommendations to other agencies and is subject to audit by the U.S. Comptroller General.

The Council is authorized to require registration with and oversight by the Federal Reserve of nonbank financial entities if their financial distress or other factors could make them a threat to U.S. financial stability (systemically important financial institutions, SIFIs). The Council may also require bank holding companies with total assets of at least *$50 billion* and nonbank financial entities required to register to *submit certified reports* indicating their financial condition, systems for managing risks, transactions with subsidiary depository institutions, the extent to which adverse conditions may affect U.S. financial stability (stress tests), and companies' plans for orderly shutdown should they become insolvent (living wills).

This title also creates the Office of Financial Research (OFR) to support the Council in fulfilling its purpose. It consists of a data center, responsible for data collection, and a research and analysis center. The OFR can also issue a subpoena when necessary.

Title II – Orderly Liquidation Authority

This title gives the Secretary of the Treasury the authority to liquidate financial companies that pose a significant threat to U.S. financial stability. It will identify financial companies as candidates for receivership, appointing the Federal Deposit Insurance Corporation (FDIC) as receiver. The companies may voluntarily go into receivership or will be evaluated by the FDIC and a determination will be made. Federal authority over liquidations of depository institutions (by the FDIC and NCUA) and brokerage firms (by the SIPC) already existed before Dodd-Frank. Dodd-Frank adds authority over SIFIs, which may include any financial institution individually identified by FSOC (including potentially any of insurance companies, investment banks, private equity firms, etc.).
- The Securities Investor Protection Corporation (SIPC) continues to oversee liquidations of covered brokers or dealers.
- For most depository institutions (commercial banks and thrifts) and, newly, SIFIs, the Federal Deposit Insurance Corporation (FDIC) will oversee liquidations. For credit unions, the National Credit Union Administration (NCUA) continues to oversee liquidations.

This title also requires that various studies be performed related to:
- Protections for secured investors
- The liquidation process for financial institutions

Title III – Transfer of Powers to the Comptroller of the Currency (i.e., the OCC), the Corporation (i.e., the FDIC), and the Board of Governors (i.e., the Federal Reserve)

The objectives of this title are indicated as:
- Providing safe and sound operation of the U.S. banking system;
- Preserving and protecting the dual system of Federal and State chartered depository institutions;
- Ensuring fair and appropriate supervision of each depository institution; and
- Streamlining and rationalizing the supervision of depository institutions and their holding companies

It eliminates the Office of Thrift Supervision (OTS). (Thrifts are depository institutions, commonly referred to as (1) savings and loans or (2) savings banks, with federal or state charters that historically emphasized lending for housing or charitable purposes, but that, in recent decades became largely similar to commercial banks - except for some remaining emphasis on residential mortgage lending). Dodd-Frank transferred the three sets of functions of the OTS as follows. (1) Thrifts with federal charters will be regulated by the Office of the Comptroller of the Currency (OCC, which was already the regulator of federally-chartered commercial banks, i.e., national banks. (2) Thrifts with state charters will have the FDIC as their federal regulator (along with their state regulators). The FDIC was already the federal regulator of state-chartered commercial banks. (3) Savings and loan (i.e., thrift) holding companies will be regulated by the Federal Reserve (like bank holding companies).

This title also includes reforms to the Federal Deposit Insurance Act, including:
- Giving the FDIC the authority to suspend the declaration or payment of dividends
- Changing the reserve ratio requirements for depository institutions
- Making indefinite the increase in the amount insured (the cap or ceiling) from $100,000 to **$250,000.** (The cap had been increased, on a temporary basis, earlier during the financial crisis). Per 2006 law (still in force), the cap is to be updated every five years to keep up with inflation (but only in $10,000 increments).

Other matters in this title include:
- Requiring each agency to establish an Office of Minority and Women Inclusion, responsible for diversity in management, employment, and business activities.
- Dodd-Frank provided for unlimited deposit insurance for noninterest bearing transaction accounts (i.e., for businesses) during the years 2011-2012. Since that period has ended, noninterest bearing transaction accounts are insured only up to the $250,000 cap.

Title IV – Regulation of Advisers to Hedge Funds and Others (referred to as the Private Fund Investment Advisers Registration Act of 2010)

This title requires investment advisers to hedge funds and private equity funds with more than *$150 million in assets* to register with the Securities and Exchange Commission (SEC). Hedge funds with under $150 million in assets, venture capital funds, and family offices remain exempt from registration.

This title requires the SEC to study the appropriate criteria for an **accredited investor** and amends the current standard by requiring a minimum net worth at the time of investment of **$1 million** *excluding the value of the person's primary residence*.

Title V – Insurance (referred to as the Federal Insurance Office Act of 2010)

This title establishes the Federal Insurance Office to monitor all aspects of the insurance industry, excluding health insurance, long-term care insurance, and crop insurance. Responsibilities include:

- Identifying issues or gaps in regulation that could contribute to a systemic crisis in the industry;
- Monitoring whether traditionally underserved market segments have access to affordable insurance products (minorities and low-income consumers); and
- Recommending that the Financial Stability Oversight Council designate an insurer as subject to registration as a nonbank financial entity.

Title VI – Improvements to Regulation of Bank and Savings Association Holding Companies and Depository Institutions (referred to as the Bank and Savings Association Holding Company and Depository Institution Regulatory Improvement Act of 2010)

This title requires financial holding companies to be well capitalized and well managed. It also enhances limitations on bank transactions with affiliates. It adds derivatives to the instruments to be considered when evaluating adherence to lending limits.

The title also includes what is referred to as the **Volcker Rule**, named for Paul Volcker, former Chairman of the Federal Reserve, intended to prevent depository institutions from making risky investments with depositor funds. It increases regulation of the transactions of banking entities. It prohibits proprietary trading and the acquisition or holding, unless immaterial, of an ownership interest in a hedge fund or private equity fund. It limits investments by a banking entity in hedge funds and private equity funds:

- Banking entities must not exceed **3%** of the total of the ownership interests in hedge funds and private equity funds.
- The total of all investments in hedge and private equity funds may not exceed 3% of the entity's Tier 1 equity.

It regulates a banking entity's transactions prohibiting an asset purchase or sale transaction with an executive officer, director, or principal shareholder other than on market terms and the transaction must be pre-approved when it exceeds 10% of the capital stock and surplus of the depository institution.

Title VII – Wall Street Transparency and Accountability

This title regulates trading involving swaps, including credit default swaps and credit derivatives, requiring those that are currently traded over-the-counter (OTC) to be cleared through exchanges or clearinghouses that are registered with the SEC. The clearing organization is required to submit the swap to the SEC, which will determine whether or not clearing is required. The SEC will consider whether or not to exempt depository institutions, farm credit system institutions, and credit unions with total assets of $10 billion or less.

The title defines swaps broadly to include options, many forward contracts, and other transactions not formerly considered derivatives.

Companies using swaps OTC could only net them in their balance sheet by counterparty. Using swaps through clearinghouses, companies will be able to net them by clearinghouse; i.e., companies will likely be able to net far more swaps.

The title also prohibits any federal assistance to a swap entity unless its involvement in swaps is limited to hedging activities or acting as a swaps entity for certain permissible swaps, which excludes credit default swaps.

Title VIII – Payment, Clearing, and Settlement Supervision

The objectives of this title are to mitigate systemic risks in the U.S. financial system and promote financial stability by authorizing the Board of Governors of the FDIC to establish uniform standards for management of risk and conduct of payment, clearing, and settlement activities by financial institutions when they are systemically important (SIFIs).

It also gives the Board of governors an enhanced role in the supervision of the standards and in strengthening the liquidity of financial market utilities that are systemically important.

Title IX – Investor Protections and Improvements to the Regulation of Securities

This title, which includes 10 subtitles, requires various studies to enable revisions to the authority and structure of certain participants in the financial markets and the relationships among them, including the SEC and credit rating agencies and the relationship between customers and broker-dealers or investment advisers.

The **10 subtitles** are:

- *Increasing Investor Protection* – Establishes the Office of the Investor Advocate and authorizes the SEC to require a *fiduciary duty* by broker-dealers to customers (i.e., for recommendations to be in the customers' best interests).

- *Increasing Regulatory Enforcement and Remedies* – Created a *"whistleblower bounty program"* which allows someone who provides information which leads to a successful SEC enforcement to receive 10% to 30% of the monetary sanctions over $1 million.

- *Improvements to the Regulation of Credit Rating Agencies* – Requires the SEC to establish an Office of Credit Ratings to oversee nationally recognized statistical rating organizations (NRSRO) and enhances the regulation of NRSROs, including a requirement to establish, maintain, enforce, and document effective internal control and report on it annually. It also prohibits linking the compensation of the compliance officer to the financial results of the NRSRO.

- *Improvements to the Securitization Process* – In securitizations, a securitizer (e.g., an investment bank) buys many individual assets (e.g., mortgages) from various individual lenders (e.g., commercial banks). The securitizer next sells securities to investors that are backed by the payments resulting from the "pool" of assets (hence the term asset-backed securities (ABS). Dodd-Frank requires lenders to retain an economic interest of at least *5% (skin in the game)* for assets they sell to securitizers, unless the assets meet safe harbor provisions (e.g., qualified residential mortgages, QRM). Mortgages meeting the standards of government-sponsored securitizers (Fannie Mae and Freddie Mae) will qualify as QRMs. When the safe harbor provisions are not met, the rules for determining how much of securitized assets to continue to include in companies' balance sheets are complex.

- *Accountability and Executive Compensation* – Requires a nonbinding shareholder vote every 3 years to approve executive compensation (say on pay) and every 6 years to affirm that a vote every 3 years is frequent enough. It requires that members of the compensation committee be independent directors and it also requires the entity provide shareholders information about the relationship of executive compensation and:
    - Entity performance

        ○   Average compensation of nonexecutive employees

Companies larger than $1 billion in assets receive incentives to make managerial compensation less sensitive to short-term performance, using longer performance periods, and delaying some compensation until after those periods.

Financial institutions larger than $50 billion in assets are required to defer at least 50% of annual incentive-based compensation for at least 3 years.

Disclosure of security hedging activities of employees and directors is required. Although it is not binding, shareholders are also entitled to vote to disapprove any "golden parachute" arrangement.

In addition, stock exchanges are required to establish "**claw back**" provisions requiring the recovery of *executive compensation* when an entity has an accounting restatement.

- *Improvements to the* Management *of the Securities and Exchange Commission* – Gives employees a way to report problems with the SEC.

- *Strengthening* Corporate *Governance* – Authorizes the SEC to allow shareholders to make nominations to the board of directors by proxy. Also requires disclosure of reasons for the Chairman and CEO being the same individual if that is the case. Companies **must** alternately disclose why, if the Chairman and CEO are **different** individuals, the reasons why.

- *Municipal Securities* – Creates a guarantee of trust with municipal advisors (a municipal advisor provides investment advice to state and local governments) who must also register with the SEC.

- *Public Company Accounting Oversight Board, Portfolio Margining, and Other Matters* – Allows the SEC to authorize rules, as necessary with respect to securities for borrowing.

- Securities and Exchange Commission Match Funding – Changes the way the SEC is funded.

Title X – Bureau of Consumer Financial Protection

This title creates the Bureau of Consumer Financial Protection (more commonly known as the *Consumer Financial Protection Board, CFPB*) regulate financial products and services sold to the consumer (e.g., credit counseling, check-cashing, etc.) and oversees, among other things, fair lending. The Bureau is an independent unit located inside and financed by the Federal Reserve.

Title XI – Federal Reserve System Provisions

Requires the GAO to audit the Fed and requires the Fed to regulate institutions they oversee through the development of prudent standards regarding such matters as liquidity and risk management. It also requires that off-balance sheet financing be taken into consideration when evaluating compliance with capital requirements.

Title XII – Improving Access to Mainstream Financial Institutions

This title indicates its objective "is to encourage initiatives for financial products and services that are appropriate and accessible for millions of Americans who are not fully incorporated into the financial mainstream." Through grants, cooperative agreements, and other arrangements, the Secretary of the Treasury is to promote programs:

- Enabling low to moderate income individuals to establish accounts in federally insured depository institutions;
- Providing low cost small loans to consumers; and
- Providing financial literacy and education opportunities.

Title XIII – Pay it Back Act

This title was designed to recapture any unspent funds that were committed as part of a stimulus package and use them for deficit reduction. It reduces funds available for TARP (Troubled Asset Relief Program) from $700 billion to $475 billion and requires that proceeds from the sale of securities issued by Government-Sponsored Enterprises that became owned by the Treasury be used for deficit reduction.

Title XIV – Mortgage Reform and Anti-Predatory Lending Act

This title creates standards related to residential mortgage loan organizations, mortgages, high-cost mortgages, mortgage servicing, and appraisal services that are overseen by the Bureau of Consumer Financial Protection.

Title XV – Miscellaneous Provisions

This title requires the SEC to pass rules requiring issuers of securities to provide disclosures as to (1) whether they use "conflict minerals" (e.g., gold, cassiterite (tin ore), etc.), (2) whether the minerals were imported from the Democratic Republic of Congo or adjoining countries, and (3) their due diligence about the chain of custody of those materials.

Title XVI – Section 1256 Contracts

This title excludes securities futures contracts and swap forms of derivatives from section 1256 contracts for purposes of calculating capital gains and losses.

Lecture 2.11 – Dodd Frank Act – Class Questions

17. Which of the following is not one of the sections of the Dodd-Frank Act (Wall Street Reform and Consumer Protection Act of 2010)?

  a.   Orderly Liquidation Authority.
  b.   Crowdfunding.
  c.   Wall Street Transparency and Accountability.
  d.   Financial Stability

18. Under Title IX of The Wall Street Reform and Consumer Protection (Dodd-Frank) Act of 2010 – Investor Protections and Improvements to the Regulation of Securities, stockholders are entitled to vote:

  I.   Every 3 years to approve executive compensation
  II.   Every 6 years to re-elect members to the board of directors
  III. On a non-binding basis to disapprove "golden parachute" arrangements

  a.   I, II, and III.
  b.   I only.
  c.   I and II only.
  d.   I and III only.

Class Solutions

17. (b) Financial Stability, Orderly Liquidation Authority, and Wall Street Transparency are among the 16 titles of the Dodd-Frank Act. Crowdfunding is a title of the JOBS Act of 2012.

18. (d) Title IX of the Dodd-Frank Act gives authorizes stockholders to vote to approve executive compensation every 3 years and to vote every 6 years to determine if voting to approve compensation every 3 years is frequent enough. It also authorizes them to vote to disapprove a "golden parachute" arrangement, although the vote is not binding. It does not address elections to the board of directors.

Lecture 2.12 – Corporate Governance, I/C & ERM – Written Communication TBS

Written Communication 1

Following are selected tasks from the job description of a staff accountant at Purft, Inc.:
- Endorsement, coding, and recording of checks received for deposit
- Reconciliation of the accounts receivable sub-ledger to the general ledger
- Reconciliation of the accounts payable sub-ledger to the general ledger
- Reconciliation of investment and borrowing sub-ledgers to the general ledger
- Mailing of checks to vendors
- Recording of fixed asset transactions, including updates to the asset master file

You have been asked to prepare a memorandum discussing the internal control issues relating to the selected tasks from the job description.

REMINDER: Your response will be graded for both technical content and writing skills. Technical content will be evaluated for information that is helpful to the intended reader and clearly relevant to the issue. Writing skills will be evaluated for development, organization, and the appropriate expression of ideas in professional correspondence. Use a standard business memo or letter format with a clear beginning, middle, and end. Do not convey information in the form of a table, bullet point list, or other abbreviated presentation.

To: Purft, Inc.
Re: Internal control issues related to the staff accountant

Written Communication Solution 1

To: Management of Purft, Inc.
RE: Internal control issues related to staff accountant

We have reviewed the job description of one of your staff accountants and would like to bring some areas of concern to your attention. When one employee is involved in many aspects of a single transaction, it gives that employee the opportunity to both commit fraud and to hide it. As a result, it is desirable, when possible, to segregate the following duties so that no two or more of them are performed by the same individual. These are the authorization of transactions, custody of assets, recordkeeping, and reconciliations, such as of physical assets to recorded amounts.

It seems as if your staff accountant is responsible for a few incompatible duties. Although it does not appear that this individual has responsibility for authorizing transactions, the staff accountant's responsibilities include custody of assets, recording of related transactions, and reconciliations.

Endorsing and coding checks received for deposit gives this employee custody of those checks, as does the responsibility for mailing checks to vendors. The job description indicates that the staff accountant also records checks received for deposit and records fixed asset transactions. This gives the employee recording responsibilities and custody in relation to the same assets.

In addition, this employee performs reconciliations of the accounts receivable sub-ledger to the general ledger. This combination of responsibilities might allow the employee to misappropriate a check received, record the amount as if deposited, and hide it by improperly completing the reconciliation of the sub-ledger to the general ledger.

Other reconciliations performed by this employee include a reconciliation of the accounts payable sub-ledger to the general ledger, which gives the employee the opportunity to misappropriate a check intended for mailing and to hide it by improperly completing that reconciliation.

If possible, these responsibilities should be divided among different employees so that no employee has incompatible responsibilities. Recognizing that this may not be possible, carefully monitoring the activities of this staff accountant, including the review of all work, is highly recommended.

If you need any additional information or have questions, don't hesitate to contact me.

Sincerely,

CPA Candidate

Written Communication 2

You have a new client, Ms. Amy Pemberton, who is in the process of forming a new company and has asked your assistance in developing a system of internal control. She would like to start off on a very positive note and is very concerned about promoting ethical behavior within her company.

She has been reading about COSO's integrated framework and is curious as to what she should do to make certain that she establishes the appropriate control environment. She would like you to describe the control environment component of internal control and the five principles that relate to it.

REMINDER: Your response will be graded for both technical content and writing skills. Technical content will be evaluated for information that is helpful to the intended reader and clearly relevant to the issue. Writing skills will be evaluated for development, organization, and the appropriate expression of ideas in professional correspondence. Use a standard business memo or letter format with a clear beginning, middle, and end. Do not convey information in the form of a table, bullet point list, or other abbreviated presentation.

To: Ms. Amy Pemberton
Re: The control environment and its underlying principles

Written Communication Solution 2

To: Ms. Amy Pemberton
RE: The control environment and its underlying principles

It is our pleasure to provide you with assistance in establishing a system of internal control for your new business. We believe that an effective system of internal control is essential to the achievement of an entity's objectives and understand that the control environment can set a tone that will have a significant impact on the effectiveness of internal control.

The control environment consists of the standards, processes, and structures that you set up to provide the basis for carrying out internal controls throughout the organization. You, as board chair, along with the remainder of your board and your senior management establish the tone through your directives and your actions, informing members of your organization and those with whom you do business of the importance you place on internal control and your expectations for standards of conduct to be maintained.

There are five principles associated with the control environment. The first indicates that the organization should demonstrate a commitment to integrity and ethical values. This can be accomplished through your behavior and that of others in leadership, the establishment of standards of conduct. Those standards will be much more effective if the performance of individuals within the organization is measured against those standards and if any deviations are dealt with in a meaningful way on a timely basis.

The second principle indicates that you and your fellow board members should demonstrate your independence from management and that you should exercise oversight in the development and performance of internal control. Your board should include members with the expertise appropriate for accepting responsibility for the oversight of internal control, for asking probing questions of management, and taking appropriate actions. Oversight responsibility for internal control includes providing guidance to management in its design, implementation, and conduct.

The third principle indicates that management, subject to the oversight of the board, should establish lines of authority and responsibility by creating structures, and reporting lines, considering all of the organization's lines of business, operating units, legal entities, geographical presence, and business relationships. Individuals within the organization should clearly understand their responsibilities, the extent of their authority, who they report to and who reports to them, and the criteria against which their performance will be evaluated.

The fourth principle indicates that there should be a commitment to attract, develop, and retain competent individuals within the organization to enable the achievement of objectives. This commitment can be demonstrated by establishing expectations that require competence, evaluating competence, and responding to deficiencies. This can be enhanced if the organization provides mentoring and training. In addition, your board and management should establish contingency plans to make certain that significant responsibilities do not go unattended.

The final principle indicates that the organization should hold individuals accountable for their responsibilities, including their roles in the achievement of the entity's objectives. Accountability can be incorporated into the structure of the system and expectations can be established against which performance can be measured. Incentives and rewards are effective tools for enhancing accountability, but they must be evaluated regularly to make certain they remain relevant.

Management and the board should also consider evaluating objectives to determine if they are realistic or if their achievement may create undue pressure.

If you need any additional information or have questions, don't hesitate to contact me.

Sincerely,

CPA Candidate

Written Communication 3

In your role as CFO, you are part of the team that regularly evaluates internal control. In its risk assessment, your team has identified a concern that your work force may not be adequately prepared for anticipated changes in technology. The change will affect the manufacture of a specific part that is a device used along with the company's main product. The team has asked you to identify the alternative ways in which the entity could respond to this risk and to prepare a memo to the team explaining the choices and indicating your recommendations as it relates to Enterprise Risk Management (ERM).

REMINDER: Your response will be graded for both technical content and writing skills. Technical content will be evaluated for information that is helpful to the intended reader and clearly relevant to the issue. Writing skills will be evaluated for development, organization, and the appropriate expression of ideas in professional correspondence. Use a standard business memo or letter format with a clear beginning, middle, and end. Do not convey information in the form of a table, bullet point list, or other abbreviated presentation.

To: Internal control evaluation team
Re: Alternative responses to risks of an untrained work force

Written Communication Solution 3

To: Internal control evaluation team
Re: Alternative responses to risks of an untrained work force

Our team has determined that anticipated changes in technology may make our work force obsolete and has asked me to evaluate our alternative responses to this risk. We can choose among four alternatives. We may accept the risk, reject the risk, share the risk, or we could mitigate the risk.

Accepting the risk means taking no action in response. This will mean that, if the anticipated changes to technology do render our work force obsolete, we will experience a period of significant inefficiency at best and will likely be producing units that will not conform to specification. Since we have a competent staff with a positive attitude, I am confident that our staff will learn relatively quickly and the period will not be extended. Despite that, I see this as an unfavorable alternative.

Rejecting the risk would mean discontinuing those activities that are affected by the change in technology, under the assumption that the risk is too great to endure. Since the parts that are affected by the change in technology are not essential to our business, this is a viable alternative. Those parts, however, do provide both income and cash flows to the entity and may stimulate the sales of other products. I do not think this is a good alternative either.

Sharing the risk both allows us to continue providing our entire product line to our customers while reducing our company's exposure to the risk. We could, for example, outsource our production of those parts to a subcontractor. It will become their responsibility to respond to the change in technology, something they may be well prepared to do. In addition, with the increase in volume our business will provide, they may hire those of our employees who become redundant. I consider this a pretty good alternative.

Finally, we could mitigate, or reduce the risk, by establishing procedures that will help us prepare for the changes. We could, for example, institute training for our employees, creating incentives to learn the technology quickly and effectively. In addition, this approach reinforces our commitment to competence and gives a message to our employees that we provide job security. I consider this our best alternative.

If you need any additional information or have questions, don't hesitate to contact me.

Sincerely,

CPA Candidate

Section 3 – Financial Management & Capital Budgeting

Table of Contents

EXAM NOTE: *Please refer to the AICPA BEC Blueprint in the Introduction of this book to find a listing of the representative tasks (and their associated skill levels—i.e., Remembering and Understanding, Application, and Analysis) that the candidate should be able to perform based on the knowledge obtained in this section.*

Financial Management & Capital Budgeting

Lecture 3.01 – Managing Working Capital

Financial Management involves five main functions:

- The **financing function** of raising the capital necessary to fund a business.

- The **capital budgeting function** of choosing the best long-term projects to which to dedicate the firm's resources, based on the projects' expected risks and returns.

- The **financial management function** of managing the business's internal cash flows and capital structure (the mix of debt and equity) minimizing financing costs and ensuring obligations can be paid when due.

- The **corporate governance function** of making sure that managerial behavior is ethical (toward all parties) and in the interests of the business's owners.

- The **risk-management function** of identifying and managing the business's various kinds of risk.

Businesses use several financial measures to determine the efficiency with which they use working capital (or liquidity). Managing working capital involves ensuring that the business has the net short-term financial assets necessary to meet the firm's short-term financial obligations. Key elements of managing working capital are managing inventories and receivables.
- **Working Capital =** Current Assets (CA) – Current Liabilities (CL)
- **Current Ratio =** CA/CL
- **Quick (or Acid test) Ratio =** Quick assets / CL
- **Quick assets =** Cash + Marketable securities + Accounts receivable

The **Cash Conversion Cycle (CCC = 2-4)** combines the three calculations below and measures the number of days from when a business pays for its inputs to when the business collects cash from the resulting sales of finished goods. Businesses seek to shorten the CCC to minimize their need for financing. The CCC is also referred to as the *net operating cycle."* Shortening the CCC improves profitability because larger CCCs require businesses to use more financing.
- CCC = ICP + RCP – PDP

The **Inventory Conversion Period (ICP = 1-3)** is the average number of days required to convert inventory to sales (assume 365 days in a year unless told otherwise).
- ICP = Average inventory / COGS per day (or sometimes: Sales per day)
- Average inventory = (Beginning inventory + Ending inventory) / 2

The **Accounts Receivable Collection Period (RCP, or average collection period = 3-4)** is the average number of days required to collect accounts receivable.
- RCP = Average accounts receivable / Average credit sales per day
- Also assume 365 days per year unless told otherwise.

The **Accounts Payable Deferral Period (PDP = 1-2)** is the average number of days between buying inventory (including materials and labor for a manufacturing entity) and paying for that inventory.
- PDP = Average payables / Purchases per day (or COGS/365)

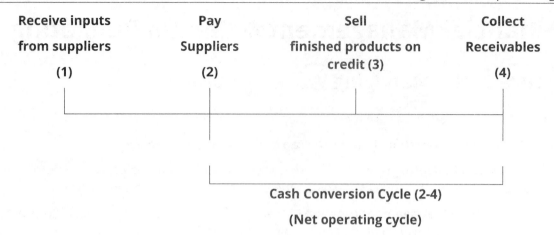

Lecture 3.02 – Managing Working Capital – Class Questions

1. When dealing with cash management, the time period from when goods are paid for and the accounts receivables are collected is called?

    a.   Accounts Receivable collection period
    b.   Inventory Conversion period
    c.   Accounts Payable deferral period
    d.   Cash conversion cycle

2. Roger's Appliance Warehouse has an inventory conversion period of 60 days, an accounts receivable collection period of 25 days and an accounts payable deferral period of 29 days. How long is their Cash Conversion Cycle?

    a.   54 days
    b.   56 days
    c.   64 days
    d.   85 days

3. Each of the following periods is included when computing a firm's target cash conversion cycle, except the

    a.   Inventory conversion period.
    b.   Payables deferral period.
    c.   Average collection period.
    d.   Cash discount period.

Class Solutions

1. (d) The cash conversion cycle is the time period from when raw materials are paid for and the receivables from the sales are collected. The Accounts Receivable Collection Period (RCP, or average collection period) is the average number of days required to collect accounts receivable. The Inventory Conversion Period (ICP) is the average number of days required to convert inventory to sales. The Accounts Payable Deferral Period (PDP) is the average number of days between buying inventory (including materials and labor for a manufacturing entity) and paying for that inventory.

2. (b) The cash conversion cycle measures the number of days from when a business pays for its inputs, to when the business collects cash from the resulting sales of finished goods. It is the calculation of the inventory conversion period + the accounts receivable collection period – the accounts payable deferral period. In this situation, the calculation is 60 + 25 – 29 = 56 days.

3. (d) The cash conversion cycle is the period from when inventory is paid for until the cash is collected from its sale. This would be equal to the inventory conversion period, which is the period from the date of acquisition to the date it is ready for sale, minus the payable deferral period, which makes the starting point the date of payment instead of acquisition. This is added to the average collection period, the time it takes to convert the inventory into a cash receipt. The cash discount period affects the average collection period but is not a factor that is considered separately.

Lecture 3.03 – Managing Cash

Businesses keep cash balances for several purposes:

- **Operations** – Funds to pay for ordinary expenses.

- **Compensating balances** – Banks may require businesses to maintain minimum checking account balances as an alternative (non-cash) form of compensation for bank services and loans.

- **Trade discounts** – Quick payment of bills may result in early payment discounts.

- **Speculative balances** to take advantage of unexpected business opportunities.

- **Precautionary balances** that may be needed in emergencies.

Float refers to the time it takes for checks to be mailed, processed, and cleared. Managing cash involves *maximizing* float on payments to others and *minimizing* float on receipts from others.

- **Pay by Draft (3-party instrument)** – Customers pay by check for slower processing.

- **Zero-balance accounts** – Banks offering these accounts notify their customers each day of checks presented for payment and transfer only the funds needed to cover them.

- **Concentration banking** – Customers pay local branches instead of main offices, so the business gets funds more quickly, reducing float. However, periodic wire transfers from local branches to main offices can be costly.

- **Lock-box system** – Customers send payments directly to the bank to speed up deposits and increase internal control over cash.

- **Electronic funds transfers** – Customers pay electronically for fastest processing. For example, using your debit card at the store. Using electronic funds transfers eliminates float from both payments and receipts.

Lecture 3.04 – Managing Marketable Securities

To maximize their earnings, businesses may choose to use various short-term investments instead of cash (or zero-interest business checking accounts). Choosing among these investments, the most important considerations are *liquidity and risk (safety)*. Some examples include:

- **Treasury bills** (T-bills) are short-term obligations of the U.S. government with original maturities under 1 year. T-bills use a zero-coupon format, under which holders do not receive coupon payments, but instead receive "interest" by buying the securities at a discount from the value that will be paid at maturity. T-bills are one of the largest and most liquid securities markets in the world, so buyers bear virtually no risk of capital losses even if they sell before maturity.

- **Treasury notes** are U.S. government obligations with original maturities between 1 and 10 years. Treasury notes pay coupons (interest payments) semi-annually.

- **Treasury bonds** are the same as notes but with original maturities over 10 years.

- **Treasury Inflation-Indexed Securities (TIPS)** are treasury notes and bonds that pay a fixed real rate of interest by adjusting the principal semi-annually for inflation. These securities retained TIPS as their acronym when the word "protected" was substituted with the word "indexed."

- **Federal agency securities** are offerings that may or may not be backed by the full faith and credit of the U.S. government. They do not trade as actively as Treasury securities but pay slightly higher rates.

- **Certificates of deposit** (CDs) are time deposits at banks with limited government insurance. Interest yields are typically higher on CDs than on U.S. government securities, since, for amounts lower than the FDIC limit, they are not as liquid and, for amounts higher than the FDIC limit, they are not as safe.

- **Commercial paper** is promissory notes issued by corporations with lives up to 9 months.

- **Bankers' acceptances** are drafts drawn on banks that are payable at a specific future due date (not on demand, as checks would be), usually 30-90 days after being drawn. They are usually generated to pay for goods across international borders, and trade in secondary markets at a discount prior to their due dates.

- **Money market mutual funds** invest in instruments with short maturities (i.e., under one year), and generally maintain a stable value for investors. During the financial crisis, the Federal Reserve provided temporary insurance for these products.

- **Short-term bond mutual funds** invest in instruments with maturities of under 5 years, generating higher returns than money market mutual funds, but with the potential for fluctuations in value.

- Individual **stocks and bonds** offer substantially higher potential returns, but also greater risk (of losses of up to the whole amount invested).

Lecture 3.05 – Managing Receivables

Managing accounts receivable (receivables or A/R) includes setting up and updating credit approval mechanisms and monitoring the resulting receivables. Businesses' credit policies include four key elements:

- **Credit period:** the time buyers are given to make payments (typically 30 days for business buyers).
  - *Seasonal dating* is a procedure for inducing customers to buy early by not requiring payment until the selling season begins.

- **Discounts:** Price reductions for paying early (such as a 2% discount for paying within 10 days).

- **Credit criteria:** Financial strength requirements for customers to be granted credit.

- **Collection policies:** Methods employed to collect on receivables that are behind schedule.

To generate immediate cash, a business may do the following with its receivables (A/R financing):

- **Pledging** – The business obtains a loan offering receivables as collateral.

- **Assignment of A/R** – A lending agreement whereby the borrower assigns an A/R for cash, but must pay interest and usually a service charge on the advance.

- **Factoring w/o recourse** – The business may sell receivables to a financing company, which accepts the risk of non-collection, and charges a percentage fee for accepting that risk (based on an estimate of the uncollectible rate) as well as an interest rate based on the funds advanced prior to the date collection of the receivables is due.

  Factoring receivables generally improves companies' A/R turnover ratio.

  Accounts Receivable (A/R) turnover = $\dfrac{Net\ credit\ sales}{Average\ A/R}$

  - **Average accounts receivable =** (Beginning A/R + Ending A/R) / 2
  - Remember to use net *credit* sales and **not** net sales.

  Number of days of sales in average receivables = $\dfrac{360}{A/R\ turnover}$

Lecture 3.06 – Inventory Management

Budgeting for inventory purchase decisions involves determining when to place orders (or start production) to replace inventory, and how much to purchase (or produce). Managing inventories requires weighing many potentially conflicting factors. Higher costs of carrying inventories would push businesses to reduce inventories to the extent possible. Higher costs of placing small orders would likely push businesses to make fewer but larger orders, which would likely increase their inventories. Longer lead times in the delivery of inventories would push businesses to carry larger inventories to avoid running out of products to sell. Higher sales are also typically associated with higher inventory needs.

Materials Requirements Planning (**MRP**) is a computerized system that uses demand forecasts to manage the production of finished goods and the required inventory levels for various raw materials.

Deciding when to order involves calculating the **reorder point**. To do so, the business determines the quantity used per day and the lead time needed for orders to be filled. For example, if the company uses 25 units per day, and an order normally takes 10 days to fill, then an order should be placed, at the latest, when the inventory consists of 25 × 10 = 250 units. Of course, the time it takes to fill an order may vary somewhat, so businesses often use the maximum lead time rather than normal lead time to determine when to place orders. The difference between the two inventory levels is known as the **safety stock**. If, in the above case, the maximum lead time is 15 days, then an order might be placed when there are 25 × 15 = 375 units remaining, and the safety stock is 375 – 250 = 125 units.

Reorder point

Average daily demand
× average lead time
= reorder point without a safety stock
+ safety stock
= reorder point with a safety stock

Businesses may decide the appropriate quantity to order based on a calculation called the **economic order quantity** (EOQ). The formula (which is obtained using calculus) takes into account the Annual Usage of inventory (A), costs involved in Placing orders (P), and Storage costs for carrying inventory (S):

$$EOQ = \sqrt{\frac{2 \times A \times P}{S}}$$

     A = Annual Usage of inventory
     P = Cost of Placing an order
     S = Cost of Storing or carrying an individual unit of inventory for one period, obsolescence cost

If the annual usage of the product is 100 units, it costs $4 to process each order, and $8 to store each unit of inventory for a year, then:

$$EOQ = \sqrt{\frac{2 \times 100 \times 4}{8}} = \sqrt{100} = 10 \ units$$

Some companies follow a **just-in-time (JIT)** philosophy to manage their inventories. To keep their inventories low, these businesses order as little as possible and order as close to the time when inventories are needed as possible. JIT may be used effectively when (1) the costs of storing (non-value-adding operations) inventory are high, (2) lead times are low, (3) needs for safety stock are low because of having good relationships with suppliers who are very reliable, and (4) costs per purchase order are also low. Under JIT, goods are produced on demand rather than based on long-range forecasts of sales.

In a mature JIT system, units are in process for a relatively short period of time due to the efficiency of the system and the higher speed of manufacturing. As a result, traditional accounting approaches for keeping track of costs in work-in-process are not effective and many companies adopt a *backflush costing* approach.

In a backflush costing approach, costs assigned to jobs will not be tracked in as much detail as in traditional costing systems. Under a **backflush approach** (Delayed or Endpoint costing)**:**
- All manufacturing costs are charged directly to cost of goods sold since little or no inventory is expected to remain at any point in time.
- At the end of an accounting period, the company determines if there are inventories.
- When inventories exist on a reporting date, costs are allocated from cost of goods sold into the appropriate inventory accounts, such as finished goods using standard costs.

Businesses use a wide variety of techniques to manage and assess (audit) their inventories. For instance, traditional "physical inventories" involve counting all actual inventories on a specific date (often requiring production to stop temporarily). In contrast, "cycle counting" focuses on counting small subsets of inventory in specific locations.

Inventory Turnover Ratio　　=　　　　　$\dfrac{COGS}{Average\ Inventory}$

- o　Remember to use cost of goods sold and **not** sales.

Number of days of supply in average inventory　=　$\dfrac{360}{Inventory\ Turnover}$

Lecture 3.07 – Cash & Inventory Management – Class Questions

4. Which of the following effects would a lockbox most likely provide for receivables management?

    a. Minimized collection float.
    b. Maximized collection float.
    c. Minimized disbursement float.
    d. Maximized disbursement float.

5. In computing the reorder point for an item of inventory, which of the following is used?

    I. Cost
    II. Usage per day
    III. Lead Time

    a. I and II
    b. II and III
    c. I and III
    d. I, II, and III

6. To determine the inventory reorder point, calculations normally include the

    a. Ordering cost.
    b. Carrying cost.
    c. Average daily usage.
    d. Economic order quantity.

7. Asher Industries sells 45,000 Smart Phones in its California establishment, evenly throughout the year. Their desired safety stock is 1,250 units, their average cost of processing a purchase order is $24 and the cost of carrying one unit in inventory for one year is $6. What is Asher Industries' economic order quantity?

    a. 150
    b. 424
    c. 600
    d. 608

Class Solutions

4. (a) Collection float is the lapse between the time money is collected and when it can be spent. When customers send payments directly to a lockbox, the bank receives the money earlier, making it accessible to the company sooner, reducing collection float. Disbursement float refers to the time period between the issuing of a check and when the entity's bank account is reduced, not affected by using a lockbox for collections.

5. (b) The reorder point is the quantity of inventory that will be on hand when the company places its next order. To make certain it does not run out of stock, the reorder point is calculated by multiplying daily demand (II) by the lead time, or the number of days it takes to receive an order (III). The cost of the inventory is not considered.

6. (c) The reorder point is the quantity of inventory that will be on hand when the company places its next order. To make certain it does not run out of stock, the reorder point is calculated by multiplying daily demand, or average daily usage, by the lead time, or the number of days it takes to receive an order. Answer (a) is incorrect because ordering cost is a factor in determining the economic order quantity but not the reorder point. Answer (b) is incorrect because carrying cost is a factor in determining the economic order quantity but not the reorder point. Answer (d) is incorrect because economic order quantity is the amount that should be ordered whenever the entity purchases inventory to minimize the total of ordering and carrying costs.

7. (c) The formula for EOQ takes into account the Annual Usage of inventory (A), costs involved in Placing orders (P), and Storage costs for carrying inventory (S). Notice that safety stock is used to calculate the reorder point, but not the EOQ.

$$EOQ = \sqrt{\frac{2 \times A \times P}{S}}$$

> **A** = Annual Usage of inventory
> **P** = Cost of Placing an order
> **S** = Cost of Storing or carrying an individual unit of inventory for one period, obsolescence cost

If the annual usage of the product is 24,000 units, it costs $24 to process each order, and $6 to store each unit of inventory for a year, then:

$$EOQ = \sqrt{\frac{2 \times 45,000 \times 24}{6}} = \sqrt{360,000} = 600 \; units$$

Lecture 3.08 – Present Value: Time Value of Money

Determining the value of a financial instrument that represents a stream of future cash inflows or outflows, such as the exact selling price of a bond, requires using present value concepts. Money that is received at a future date is less valuable than money received immediately, and present value concepts measure future cash flows in terms of the equivalent present dollars. Present value is defined as the current measure of an estimated future cash inflow or outflow, discounted at an interest rate for the number of periods between today and the date of the estimated cash flow. Many decisions require adjustments related to the time value of money:

- The **Present Value of an Amount (lump sum)** is used to examine a single cash flow that will occur at a future date and determine its equivalent value today. Alternatively, it is the amount you need to invest today, for a certain number of years, at a specific interest rate, to get some amount back in the future.

- The **Present Value of an Ordinary Annuity** refers to the value today of repeated cash flows on a systematic basis, with amounts being paid at the *end* of each period (it may also be known as an **annuity in arrears**). Bond interest payments are commonly made at the end of each period and use these factors.

- The **Present Value of an Annuity Due (Now)** refers to the value today of repeated cash flows on a systematic basis, with amounts being paid at the *beginning* of each period (it may also be known as an **annuity in advance** or special annuity). Rent payments are commonly made at the beginning of each period and use these factors.

- **Future Values (compound interest)** look at cash flows and project them to some future date. Future values can be computed using the three variations applicable to present values. The future value factor is the amount that would accumulate at a future point in time if $1 were invested now. As a result, the future value factor is equal to 1 divided by the present value factor.

> For example, an investment of $10,000 in two years at 10% would result in the principal multiplied by the future value factor. In this case the $10,000 × 1/0.8265 = $12,100.

Present and Future Value Tables*

Future Value (Amount) of $1

(n) Periods	6%	8%	10%	12%	15%
1	1.060	1.080	1.100	1.120	1.150
2	1.124	1.166	1.210	1.254	1.323
3	1.191	1.260	1.331	1.405	1.521
4	1.262	1.360	1.464	1.574	1.749
5	1.338	1.469	1.611	1.762	2.011
10	1.791	2.159	2.594	3.106	4.046
15	2.397	3.172	4.177	5.474	8.137
20	3.207	4.661	6.728	9.646	16.367
30	5.743	10.063	17.449	29.960	66.212
40	10.286	21.725	45.259	93.051	267.864

Present Value of $1

(n) Periods	6%	8%	10%	12%	15%
1	0.943	0.926	0.909	0.893	0.870
2	0.890	0.857	0.826	0.797	0.756
3	0.840	0.794	0.751	0.712	0.658
4	0.792	0.735	0.683	0.636	0.572
5	0.747	0.681	0.621	0.567	0.497
10	0.558	0.463	0.386	0.322	0.247
15	0.417	0.315	0.239	0.183	0.123
20	0.312	0.215	0.149	0.104	0.061
30	0.174	0.099	0.057	0.334	0.015
40	0.097	0.046	0.022	0.011	0.004

Future Value (Amount) of an Ordinary Annuity of $1

(n) Periods	6%	8%	10%	12%	15%
1	1.000	1.000	1.000	1.000	1.000
2	2.060	2.080	2.100	2.120	2.150
3	3.184	3.246	3.310	3.374	3.473
4	4.375	4.506	4.641	4.779	4.993
5	5.637	5.867	6.105	6.353	6.742
10	13.180	14.486	15.937	17.549	20.304
15	23.276	27.152	31.772	37.280	47.580
20	36.786	45.762	57.275	72.052	102.444
30	79.058	113.283	164.494	241.333	434.745
40	154.762	259.056	442.592	767.091	1779.090

Present Value of an Ordinary Annuity of $1

(n) Periods	6%	8%	10%	12%	15%
1	0.943	0.926	0.909	0.893	0.870
2	1.833	1.783	1.736	1.690	1.626
3	2.673	2.577	2.487	2.402	2.283
4	3.465	3.312	3.170	3.037	2.855
5	4.212	3.993	3.791	3.605	3.352
10	7.360	6.710	6.144	5.650	5.019
15	9.712	8.559	7.606	6.811	5.847
20	11.470	9.818	8.514	7.469	6.259
30	13.765	11.258	9.427	8.055	6.566
40	15.046	11.924	9.779	8.243	6.642

Present Value of an Annuity Due of $1

(n) Periods	6%	8%	10%	12%	15%
1	1.000	1.000	1.000	1.000	1.000
2	1.943	1.926	1.909	1.893	1.870
3	2.833	2.783	2.736	2.690	2.626
4	3.673	3.577	3.487	3.402	3.855
5	4.465	4.312	4.170	4.037	3.855
10	7.802	7.247	6.759	6.328	5.772
15	10.295	9.244	8.367	7.628	6.724
20	12.158	10.604	9.365	8.366	7.198
30	14.591	12.158	10.370	9.022	7.550
40	15.949	12.879	10.757	9.233	7.638

* All values rounded to the nearest thousandth of a percent.

Actual factors for $1 are typically provided in tables to be multiplied by the cash flows in exam problems.

Converting from an Ordinary Annuity to an Annuity Due - The difference between an ordinary annuity and an annuity due is just the first payment. To convert from an ordinary annuity to an annuity due, you need to add the $1 and 1 year. For example, if you want to figure out the factor for an annuity due for 3 years at 6%, start with an ordinary annuity for 2 years at 6% (1.833) and add the value of $1. So, an annuity due now for 3 years at 6% = 2.833.

Another approach would be to multiply the present value of an ordinary annuity factor by 1 plus the interest rate. For example, the present value of an ordinary annuity at 6% for 2 years = 1.833 × 1.06 = 1.943 (present value of an annuity due for 2 years).

Lecture 3.09 – Capital Budgeting

Businesses use **capital budgeting** techniques to make long-term investment decisions. For instance, businesses use discounted cash flow techniques to determine the present value (today) of future cash returns from various possible competing investments or projects. While all capital budgeting methods are based on uncertain predictions of future income or cash flows, capital budgeting may be used to help select the most profitable or best investment alternative based on the, unavoidably limited, information available. The CPA exam likes to test *4 techniques*:

- Payback period
- Internal (time adjusted) rate of return (IRR)
- Accounting rate of return
- Net present value (NPV)

Maturity matching (or the self-liquidating approach) to financing assets involves matching asset and liability maturities.

Capital Budgeting Techniques

$$\textbf{Payback period} = \frac{\textit{Initial investment}}{\textit{After Tax Annual Net Cash Inflows}} = \# \; years$$

$$\textbf{IRR: } \textit{PV Factor} = \frac{\textit{Investment}}{\textit{Annual Cash Flows}}$$

$$\textbf{Accounting Rate of Return} = \frac{\textit{Accounting Income}}{\textit{Avg. Investment}} = ROI$$

$$\textbf{NPV} = \begin{array}{l} \textit{PV Cash inflows} \\ \underline{- \; \textit{PV Cash outflows}} \\ \textit{Net PV} \qquad \textit{If + good} \\ \qquad\qquad\quad \textit{If − bad} \end{array}$$

Payback Period

Payback Period is the length of time it takes for an initial cash outlay for the investment to be recovered in cash. Net cash flows are not the same as income, since depreciation is not subtracted in the determination of net cash flows. If the net cash flows are the same each year, then the payback period equals the initial investment divided by the annual net cash inflow. If cash flow is uneven, start with the initial investment, and then subtract each year's cash inflow until the entire investment has been recovered.

Some *disadvantages* of the payback period are that it does not take into account either the project's total profitability or the time value of money. The **discounted payback method** uses the present value of each individual annual net cash flow.

Payback period = Initial investment / After tax net cash inflows

Internal Rate of Return (IRR)

The Internal Rate of Return (IRR) is the discount rate at which the net present value is zero. Alternatively, the IRR is the rate of interest that equates the present value of cash outflows (commonly referred to, simply, as the project's initial costs) and the present value of cash inflows. It can be used to compare alternative investments. It is also known as the *time-adjusted rate of return* from an investment.

IRR: PV factor = Investment/annual cash flows

If a business has the funds in hand to launch all the projects that managers were potentially considering (e.g., if the firm has outside holdings of cash or marketable securities), capital budgeting may lead the business to conclude that not all projects should be launched. The business could compare the calculated internal rate of return on each project to pre-specified **hurdle rates** that the business sets as its minimum acceptable rates of return. Businesses may set several hurdle rates based on market rates of return for projects with similar risk. Accept projects only if the IRR is greater than the hurdle rate, otherwise reject the project. Businesses commonly use the weighted-average cost of capital (WACC, see below) as the hurdle rate against which they compare projects' IRRs to decide whether to undertake those projects.

Some *advantages* of using IRRs are:
- They take into account the time value of money.
- Hurdle rates may take into account rates of return on investments with similar risk.
- Many practitioners and audiences find IRRs to be more readily understandable than net present values.

Some *disadvantages* of IRRs are:
- Under different assumptions, some cash flow patterns may actually yield multiple IRRs.
- Some cash flow patterns may not have an IRR for which the project's NPV equates to zero.

Accounting Rate of Return (ARR)

The Accounting Rate of Return (ARR) computes an approximate rate of return that does not take into account the time value of money and does not use actual cash flows. ARR is calculated dividing accounting income by the investment. Accounting income is net of all expenses, *including depreciation and income taxes.* The investment usually refers to the initial investment, but occasionally the exam requires the use of the average book value of the investment each year. In the first year, average book value is the initial investment reduced by one-half year of depreciation.

> For example, if an asset costs $1,000, has a 5-year life, no salvage value, and straight-line depreciation is used, depreciation in the first year will be $1,000/5, or $200. The book value at the beginning of the year would be the cost of $1,000. At the end of the year, book value would be $1,000 - $200, or $800. As a result, average book value in the first year is ($1,000 + $800) × ½ = $900.

ARR = Accounting income / Average (or initial) investment

Since ARRs have the *advantage* of being easy to compute and understand, they are often used to rate managerial performance (simple and intuitive).

Some *disadvantages* of ARRs are:
- ARRs do not take into account the time value of money.
- ARRs do not take into account differences in risk across investments (no project risk).
- Using different depreciation methods yields different ARRs.

Net Present Value (NPV)

Net Present Value (NPV) is the excess of the present value of the cash inflows over the present value of the outflows (typically the investment today). The time value discount rate used is known as the *hurdle rate* of return or cost of capital, and represents the minimum rate of return the company is willing to accept on an investment. A project that earns the hurdle rate of return has an NPV = 0. NPV > 0 means the project earns more than the hurdle rate.

NPV = (Present value of future cash flows – Required investment)

NPVs are the most accepted approach to compare projects financially. Some *advantages* of NPVs are
- NPVs take into account the time value of money.
- NPVs may take into account risk, using higher discount rates for riskier projects.
- NPVs take into account total profitability.
- NPVs yield results in dollars, which may be readily interpreted as the changes in owners' wealth if a project is carried out.

Some *disadvantages* of NPVs are:
- NPVs require more involved computations (not simple and intuitive).
- Some audiences may understand NPVs less readily.
- NPVs do not take into account that managers may not actually follow the originally scheduled investments (or expenses).

Of course, IRRs and NPVs are ultimately different ways to express the same concept. If a project returns more (less) than its discount or hurdle rate, it has a positive (negative) NPV. Summarizing:

NPV	*IRR*
NPV > 0	IRR > Discount or hurdle rate
NPV = 0	IRR = Discount or hurdle rate
NPV < 0	IRR < Discount or hurdle rate

The **excess present value index (or profitability index)** is the ratio of the present value of cash inflows to the initial cost of a project. When businesses are faced with several potential projects with positive NPVs, but do not have the funds to carry out all of them, they may use this index to choose which projects to carry out first. If the ratio is > 1.0, then the NPV is positive. To calculate, divide the present value of the annual after-tax cash flows by the original cash invested in the project.

For example, assume a business is considering buying a machine, and has the following information:

Cost	$900
Useful life	5 years
Salvage value	NONE
Depreciation method	Straight-line
Annual depreciation	$180
Annual net cash flow	$250
Hurdle rate of return	10%

In addition, present value information is available for a 5-year ordinary annuity:

Rate	10%	11%	12%	13%
Factor	3.79	3.70	3.60	3.52

The **accounting rate of return** on the original investment is:

Income / Investment = ($250 - $180) / $900 = $70 / $900 = **7.78%**

The **payback period** is:

Investment / Annual cash flow = $900 / $250 = **3.6 years**

The **net present value** at the 10% hurdle rate of return is:

	Cash	PV Factor	Present Value
Inflows	250	3.79	948
Outflows	900	1.00	900
Net			**48**

The **internal rate of return** is the rate at which the present value of the annual cash inflows of $250 equals the investment of $900, and this occurs when the present value factor for the annuity is $900 / $250 = 3.6, at **12%**. Notice that the net present value at 12% is zero:

	Cash	PV Factor	Present Value
Inflows	250	3.60	900
Outflows	900	1.00	900
Net			-0-

Depreciation Tax Shield

When determining cash outflows and inflows for payback, NPV, and IRR analysis, the effect of depreciation expense on cash flows must be considered if the given information starts with net income, rather than cash inflows and outflows. (Presumably, income from all projects will be taxed at the same marginal rates.) While depreciation is not a cash expense, it affects the cash paid for taxes (i.e., it produces tax savings).

> For example, assume estimated annual net income before taxes from a project is $100,000; the estimated annual depreciation expense is $30,000; and the estimated marginal tax rate is 40%. The estimated annual taxes are 0.40 × $100,000 NI = $40,000. Thus, the estimated annual cash inflow is equal to net income before taxes with the non-cash expense of depreciation added back, less taxes: $100,000 NI + $30,000 dep. - $40,000 taxes = $90,000 inflow. Without the depreciation deduction, annual taxes would be 0.40 × ($100,000 + $30,000) = $52,000 taxes; thus, the cash inflow would be $100,000 NI + $30,000 dep. - $52,000 taxes = $78,000 inflow.

The $12,000 difference between the tax amounts with the depreciation deduction versus without the depreciation deduction is called the depreciation tax shield. In other words, the non-cash expense shields what would otherwise be taxable income, resulting in a reduced cash outflow for taxes. The depreciation tax shield can be simply calculated as the tax rate × depreciation (in our example, 0.40 × $30,000 dep. = $12,000.)

We meet this tax shield concept again when considering the debt/equity mix for a business. Interest expense is tax deductible, but dividends are not.

Mutually Exclusive, Dependent, or Independent

Projects may be classified by whether they are mutually exclusive, dependent, or independent.

- **Mutually exclusive**—the entity can implement only one of two or more projects. For instance, a company owns a restaurant with a kitchen not in compliance with the health code and an outdated, but operable, dining area. The entity can either sell the property or upgrade the kitchen and open the restaurant for business, but not both.

- **Dependent**—a dependent project's cash flows are influenced by another project. For instance, a company owns a restaurant with a kitchen not in compliance with the health code and an outdated, but operable, dining area. Redecorating the dining area of the restaurant is dependent on upgrading the kitchen to meet minimum health and safety standards since without an operable kitchen, the dining area will not have cash flows. In this situation, redecorating the dining area of the restaurant is a project dependent on updating the kitchen.

- **Independent**—the entity can implement an independent project regardless of the status of the other projects. For instance, assuming sufficient resources, opening restaurants in two different cities are independent projects.

In a sense, all projects are mutually exclusive as capital to be invested is limited. The NPV, IRR, and profitability index (a refinement of the NPV method) readily accommodate ranking mutually exclusive projects. When conflicts between NPV and IRR exist, the NPV ranking generally is more reliable as it does not assume that project earnings are reinvested at the same rate that the project earns.

Project Nature

Projects also may be classified by the nature of the projects. Entities may require less analysis for projects of some natures than for others. Low-analysis projects typically include mandated projects. High-analysis projects typically include development of a new product with unknown market demand. Categories include: maintenance-of-business replacements, cost reduction replacements, expansion of existing projects or markets, development of new projects or markets, mandated (such as by license, safety, or environment regulations) projects, strategic (providing differentiation from competitors, etc.), and other (mixed-purpose projects for which deciding on a category exceeds any benefit).

Forecasting

Businesses use forecasting techniques to develop projections of the environment in which they will operate in the future, including (1) economy-wide conditions such as interest rates, inflation, unemployment, economic growth, retail sales etc., (2) conditions in their sector of the economy such as sector-specific sales and prices, and (3) cash flows specific to the business, to specific subsidiaries, and to existing and proposed projects, etc.

Interpolation involves using available data to "fill in gaps" in data relevant to a business. For instance, if a business has reliable data that customers with credit scores in the 500-520 range have loan delinquency rates of 10% and customers with credit scores in the 540-560 range have loan delinquency rates of 8%, then interpolation might lead a business to forecast, project, assume, and/or conclude that customers with credit scores in the 520-540 range would have loan delinquency rates of about 9%.

Extrapolation involves using available data to make projections outside the range for which there is available data. Continuing with the earlier example, using the relationship between credit scores and loan delinquencies, a simple extrapolation would conclude that customers with credit scores in the 480-500 range would have delinquency rates of 11% and customers with credit scores in the 460-480 range would have delinquency rates of 12%.

In general, the results from interpolation are far more reliable than those for extrapolation. In addition, extrapolation becomes less reliable the further one moves from the range of actual data. However, the precise boundary between interpolation and extrapolation is often quite blurred. For instance, a company with retail outlets in many cities and data about both sales in each outlet and city characteristics might use forecasting techniques to project what sales might be in a retail outlet in a new city. This projection could be considered interpolation if the new city falls within the range of the characteristics of many cities where the business already operates. The projection could be considered extrapolation if the city is in a region, or country, where the business has little experience.

Univariate forecasting involves focusing on the past relationship between only one variable to be projected (e.g., delinquency rates) and actual (or projected) values for only one other variable (e.g., credit scores). **Multivariate forecasting** uses the past relationships between the variable to be projected (e.g., delinquency rates) and more than one other variable (e.g., credit scores, income, change in income, wealth, marital status, seasonal adjustments, etc.). Forecasting techniques typically employ variations of regression analysis techniques described elsewhere in this book.

While forecasting techniques may be more or less computationally sophisticated, ultimately, they involve determining past relationships among various variables and making projections based on the assumption that past relationships will continue and/or specific judgments of how some particular variables might behave in the future. As a consequence, forecasts (e.g., economy-wide ones) tend to be most accurate when economic conditions are most stable, and routinely miss turning points in business cycles, i.e., they commonly fail to predict recessions and often under predict the strength of recoveries. To a large extent, most forecasting techniques largely involve extrapolation assuming that ongoing **trends** will continue.

Some forecasting techniques seek to combine both the principles of **momentum**, i.e., that short-term trends will continue, and **mean reversion**, i.e., that deviations from long-term patterns will eventually be corrected. House prices provide an example of momentum and mean reversion in practice. Over short periods, if house prices are climbing (or falling) quickly, one may readily expect that pattern to continue. For instance, climbing prices may provide other potential buyers to also buy, pushing prices further up. Eventually, however, if prices become too high, younger families may find prices too high for their income, and/or lenders may find it too risky to engage in further lending, leading to a period of falling prices (a reversion of prices from high levels closer to their long-term means). While analysts may theoretically understand that momentum eventually runs out and that mean reversion takes place, existing forecasting techniques are very far from being able to determine when mean reversions will take place.

To address the common shortcomings in forecasts, some forecasters provide not only a "central" forecast (e.g., inflation will most likely be 2%), but also a range of possible values and probabilities for the various values (e.g., there might be a 10% probability of inflation below 0%, a 20% probability of inflation between 0% and 1%, a 40% probability of inflation between 1% and 3%. a 20% probability of inflation between 3% and 10%, and a 10% probability of inflation higher than 10%).

Risk Analysis

When applying capital budgeting techniques to evaluate whether or not to accept a project, one factor to consider is the risk associated with that project. Risk analysis involves identifying risks that might impair the ability of the entity to achieve the expected results from a particular project and estimating the probability that the risk will actually have an adverse effect and measuring the expected amount of the increase in cost, or reduction in return that will be experienced.

For example, the entity may be considering a project involving the acquisition of a piece of equipment that has a reputation for failing periodically. The entity will estimate the probability that the equipment will fail, estimate the additional cost that will be incurred as a result of the failure, and multiply the probability by the amount to estimate the expected value.

A company, for instance, may determine that there is a 25% probability that a machine's engine will fail, requiring an overhaul that is expected to cost $10,000. The expected cost of this **risk event** would be $10,000 × 25%, or $2,500.

Investment Life Cycle

When evaluating an investment's rate of return, all phases of the investment life cycle will be considered as will such factors as acquisition cost, the cost of managing the investment, cash flows, appreciation, depreciation, and costs of disposal.

When an entity makes an investment, the actions it takes over the period during which it is involved with the investment is considered the **investment life cycle**.

Pre-commitment Evaluation: An entity plans for the acquisition of an investment, including the evaluation as to whether or not the investment is likely to meet the entity's investing criteria. This includes the investment's cost, volatility, expected return, and whatever other factors the entity considers when comparing investments.

Acquisition of investment

Management: Manage the investment with an emphasis on growth, earnings, tax benefits, cash flows, or some other factor relevant to the entity. Some investments (such as ownership of a business, product line, or division) require ongoing decisions; others (such as a U.S. Treasury bond) are more passive.

Monitoring: Re-evaluate the investment to determine if there are diminishing returns, suggesting the investment either no longer meets the criteria or may no longer be the best alternative.

Disposal of investment

Product Life Cycle

A product's life cycle is from the time it is introduced to the time when it is withdrawn. Not all products make it to all phases. For instance, some go from introduction to decline.

Introduction
Few and intermittent sales.
- Limited production capacity
- Lack of appropriate retail outlets
- Consumer resistance to change to the established consumption patterns

Highest proportional promotional expenses: Small volume of sales to offset high promotion efforts to create demand.
- Informing potential and present consumers of the new and unknown product
- Inducing a trial of the product
- Screening distribution net-work

Highest product prices possible.
- Low volume to absorb fixed costs
- Technological problems not fully resolved
- Few or no competitors
- Sales to higher income groups/first adopters

Growth
Sales rise as consumers accept the product. The prices may remain high to recover some of the development costs. High profits encourage competitors to enter the market.

Sales accelerate.
- Consumer resistance fades
- Distribution network solidifies
- Production is optimized

High promotional expenses.
- Shift from informing consumer to brand identification
- Special offers to consumers or allowances to dealers

Product improvements.
- Competitors do not incur the same extent of research and development or promotional costs as the originator.
- Competitors or originator gain advantage by modifying products.
- Competitors or originator gain advantage by reducing prices.

Maturity

Sales accelerate at a declining rate.
- Market reaches saturation.
- Prices soften and become more uniform.
- Competition intensifies as each manufacturer tries to maintain production at a viable level.
  - The more capital-intensive the product is to produce, the more important it is to maintain high output to cover fixed costs at lower prices.
  - The Internet has lengthened the life cycle for many products.

Normal promotional expenses as competition squeezes margins. Manufacturers try to "milk the cash cow" for all it is worth.

Extension strategies: Substantial product modification can have the revised product re-enter the introduction phase to re-start the cycle.
- Development of new markets for existing product
- Development of new uses for existing product
- Development of more frequent use for existing product
- Development of wider range of products (more flavors, colors, etc.)
- Development of style change (slightly different product)

Decline

Sales decline rapidly.
- Prices fall
- Over capacity pushes manufacturers to cease production
- Conceivably, this could be a very profitable period for a producer with low fixed costs.

Little or no promotional expenses.

Lecture 3.10 – Capital Budgeting – Class Questions

8. Which of the following statements is correct regarding the payback method as a capital budgeting technique?

    a. The payback method considers the time value of money.
    b. An advantage of the payback method is that it indicates if an investment will be profitable.
    c. The payback method provides the years needed to recoup the investment in a project.
    d. Payback is calculated by dividing the annual cash inflows by the net investment.

Items 9 through 11 are based on the following:

Noah Co. is negotiating for the purchase of equipment that would cost $100,000, with the expectation that $20,000 per year could be saved in after-tax cash costs if the equipment were acquired. The equipment's estimated useful life is 10 years, with no residual value, and would be depreciated by the straight-line method. Noah's predetermined minimum desired rate of return is 12%. Present value of an annuity of 1 at 12% for 10 periods is 5.65. Present value of 1 due in 10 periods at 12% is .322.

9. The Net present value is:

    a. $ 5,760
    b. $ 6,440
    c. $12,200
    d. $13,000

10. The Payback period is:

    a. 4.0 years.
    b. 4.4 years.
    c. 4.5 years.
    d. 5.0 years.

11. The accrual accounting rate of return based on initial investment is:

    a. 30%
    b. 20%
    c. 12%
    d. 10%

Class Solutions

8. (c) The payback method is applied by dividing an initial investment amount by the undiscounted periodic cash inflows to determine the number of periods required to recover the investment. Answer (a) is incorrect because it does not consider the time value of money. Answer (b) is incorrect because it does not consider cash flows once the investment has been recovered and, as a result, does not consider an investment's profitability. Answer (d) is incorrect because the payback is not determined by dividing annual cash inflows by net investment, it is the other way around.

9. (d) Since the investment will result in after-tax cash savings of $20,000 per year for 10 years, the present value of the investment would be $20,000 × 5.65, or $113,000. At a cost of $100,000, the investment has a net present value of $13,000.

10. (d) The payback period is the length of time it will take to recover the investment. With an investment of $100,000 and an annual after-tax cash savings of $20,000, it will require $100,000/$20,000 = 5 years to recover the investment.

11. (d) The investment has a cost of $100,000 and a useful life of 10 years, indicating that depreciation is $10,000 per year. The after-tax cash savings of $20,000 would be reduced by depreciation of $10,000 to result in accrual net income of $10,000 per year. The accounting rate of return would be $10,000/$100,000 = 10%.

Lecture 3.11 – Short-Term Debt Management

Businesses may obtain short-term financing by purchasing goods on **Trade Credit.** For instance, *3/15, net 45* would mean a 3% discount if the balance due is paid within 15 days, otherwise the entire balance would be due within 45 days. If the business does not delay paying, the business does not pay the higher price, i.e., it does not pay the equivalent of interest. To calculate the *cost of NOT taking the discount:*

$$\textbf{\textit{Annual Financing Costs (AFC)}} = \frac{\textit{Discount \%}}{(100\% - \textit{Discount \%})} \times \frac{365 \text{ } (\textit{or } 360)}{(\textit{total pay period} - \textit{discount period})}$$

Compensating Balances are demand deposit balances (set as a percentage of loans) that lenders may require as a condition for receiving loans. Having to maintain compensating balances in practice increases the effective interest rate paid on the net part of the loan that borrowers get to use. To calculate the effective cost of the loan:

$$\textbf{\textit{Cost of the loan}} = \frac{\textit{Interest paid}}{\textit{Net funds available (or Principal} - \textit{Compensating Balance})}$$

Lecture 3.12 – Short-term Debt Management – Class Questions

12. A company has an outstanding one-year bank loan of $500,000 at a stated interest rate of 8%. The company is required to maintain a 20% compensating balance in its checking account. The company would maintain a zero balance in this account if the requirement did not exist. What is the effective interest rate of the loan?

    a.   8%
    b.   10%
    c.   20%
    d.   28%

13. One of your clients has been offered a discount if they pay for their purchases on a timely basis. They have been offered the following terms, 3/10 net 30. They are asking you what the cost of not taking the discount would cost them, assuming a 360-day year.

    a.   36.00%
    b.   45.73%
    c.   55.67%
    d.   65.00%

14. Amicable Wireless, Inc. offers credit terms of 2/10, net 30 for its customers. Sixty percent of Amicable's customers take the 2% discount and pay on day 10. The remainder of Amicable's customers pay on day 30. How many days' sales are in Amicable's accounts receivable?

    a.   6
    b.   12
    c.   18
    d.   20

Class Solutions

12. (b) Since the company is required to maintain a 20% compensating balance, or $100,000, the funds available for use are limited to $400,000 of the $500,000 borrowed. Interest, at 8% of $500,000, is $40,000 per year, which would be the equivalent of a 10% rate of interest on $400,000 (40/400).

13. (c) In order to figure out the cost of not taking the discount, we need to divide the discount percentage by 1 minus that percentage. Then multiply that by 360 days divided by the total pay period minus the discount period. The calculation would appear as follows:

$$\frac{3\%}{(100\% - 3\%)} \times \frac{360 \text{ days}}{(30 \text{ days} - 10 \text{ days})} = 55.67\%$$

14. (c) The number of days sales in accounts receivable represents the average time it takes to collect receivables. If 60% of customers pay on day 10 and 40% pay on day 30, the average is calculated as (60% × 10 days) + (40% × 30 days) or 6 days + 12 days = 18 days.

Lecture 3.13 – Long-Term Debt Management

Private Debt (variable interest) includes business obligations that may not be readily resold to (i.e., traded with) the general public. Private debt largely includes loans from banks, other financial institutions, or from syndicates of lenders. Most business loans have variable interest rates that are set at a premium over some base rate or **index**. Some businesses may also sell bonds to qualified (i.e., large or sophisticated) investors in "private placements" that may not be readily traded to other parties.

- The **Prime Rate** is the rate that each lender charges its most creditworthy customers. Since the mid-1990's, most banks have set their prime rates 3% above the federal funds rate. Other business customers may obtain loans at some premium above the prime rate (e.g., Prime plus 2%).

- The **London Interbank Offered Rate (LIBOR)** is also a common base rate for many business (and consumer) loans both abroad and in the U.S. LIBOR computes rates for many (short) maturities and currencies, including the U.S. dollar.

Public Debt (fixed interest) includes business obligations that may be readily resold (i.e., traded with) the general public in markets (e.g., exchanges) that the **Securities and Exchange Commission (SEC)** regulates. Public debt largely includes bonds that, typically large, corporations may issue directly to retail and institutional investors. Issuing bonds permits corporations to borrow from sources other than banks, paying interest rates that may be fixed and, depending on their credit history, may actually be lower than those that banks would charge.

- **Eurobonds** are bonds denominated in U.S. dollars that are sold abroad (i.e., despite their name, not only in Europe). Some countries have less stringent registration and disclosure requirements than those of the SEC.

Debt Covenants

To convince lenders, or investors, to lend, borrowers often agree to restrictions on their financial behavior or debt covenants.

Positive covenants stipulate what the *borrower must do* and might involve:
- Providing annual audited financial statements to the lender.
- Maintaining various financial ratios within preset parameters, e.g., a minimum ratio of current assets to current liabilities.
- Maintaining life insurance policies for officers or key employees of the company.

Negative covenants stipulate what the *borrower may not do* and might involve:
- Not borrowing additional sums during the time period from other lenders.
- Not selling various listed assets of the business.
- Not exceeding certain levels of dividend payments to shareholders.
- Not exceeding certain compensation limits for executives.

Secured and Unsecured Bonds

Debt obligations may be secured by certain collateral or may specifically be placed behind other forms of debt in the priority of repayment. For instance, larger firms sometimes float public debt offerings collateralized by the firms' accounts receivable. The creation of such asset-backed securities is sometimes called **securitization of assets**. In roughly declining order of safety (and increasing order of interest rate), there are:

- **Mortgage bonds** are secured by real estate owned by the borrower.

- **Collateral trust bonds** are secured by financial assets owned by the borrower.

- **Debentures** are unsecured bonds.

- **Subordinated Debentures** are unsecured bonds that, in a liquidation of the business, receive any repayments only after all other more senior creditors have been paid in full.

- **Income bonds** make interest payments only if the business has earnings in excess of some preset level.

Provisions Affecting the Repayment of Bonds

- **Term bonds:** the face value is repaid on a single maturity date.

- **Serial bonds:** a fraction of the face value is repaid on several dates (installments) throughout the life of the bond (e.g., every year for a 10-year bond).

- **Sinking funds:** Throughout the life of the bond, the borrower sets funds aside to cover the repayment of the face value of the bond.

- **Convertible bonds:** The bondholder may convert the bonds to the common stock of the company as repayment instead of holding them to maturity.

- **Redeemable bonds:** The bondholder may demand repayment in advance of the normal maturity date should certain events occur (such as the buyout of the company by another firm).

- **Callable bonds** – The borrower may repay the bondholders before the normal maturity date (force to redeem). As compensation for early redemptions, call provisions require borrowers to repay bondholders some premium over the face value of the bond.

Bond Interest Rates

- **Stated rate** – The fixed interest payment calculated from the face value of the bond. It is also known as the **coupon rate, face rate,** or **nominal rate.**

- **Current yield** – The fixed interest payment divided by the current selling price of the bond. When the bond is trading at a discount, the current yield will be higher than the stated rate, and when the bond is trading at a premium, the current yield will be lower than the stated rate. The current yield should be interpreted with some caution, since it reports the interest payment as a percentage of the current price, not taking into account the fact that the principal repayment of the bond will not be the current selling price, but the face value.

$$\frac{Annual\ interest\ paid}{Bond\ market\ price} = \textbf{\textit{Current Yield}}$$

- **Yield to maturity** – The interest rate at which the present value of the cash flows of interest and principal will equal the current selling price of a bond. For a bond selling at a discount, yield to maturity will be higher than the current yield, since it accounts for the "bonus" interest payments reflected in the discount. For a bond selling at a premium, yield to maturity will be lower than the current yield, since it reflects the loss of the premium when the face value is repaid. Yield to maturity is also known as the **effective rate** or **market rate**. The formula for calculating the **Effective Annual Interest** rate (**EAR**) is:

$$EAR = (1+r/m)^m - 1$$

   r = Stated interest rate

   m = compounding frequency

- The **yield curve** illustrates the relationship between short- and long-term interest rates. These relationships are important in determining whether to use long-term fixed or variable rate financing.

- The price of a bond depends on the economy-wide, risk-free interest rate and the credit risk involved in that bond. Bond rating agencies analyze bonds to assess their credit risk. *Some of the credit risk categories, as rated by Moody's investor service,* include:

Aaa	Aa	A	Baa	Ba	B	Caa	Ca	C

Lowest Risk   *Highest Risk*

(Investment grade)   *(Speculative grade, junk, or high yield)*

To calculate the **Present Value (PV) of the proceeds** for a bond, two amounts need to be PV'd.

- **PV of the Face Value** of the bonds (Face value × PV of a lump sum using the Effective interest rate)

- **PV of the interest payments** as an annuity (Face value × stated rate × time = interest × PV of an ordinary annuity at the effective interest rate)
    - The sum of these two amounts represents the PV of the bond.
    - If semi-annual interest is being paid, take the years × 2 and the interest rate/2
        - Ex. 5 yr bonds at 10% semi-annual. Use the PV table for 10 periods @ 5%.

Let's assume a Bond with a stated rate of interest of 8% and a market rate of 10% was issued. Because the stated rate of 8% is lower than the market rate (Yield/Effective rate) of 10%, the only reason someone would purchase this bond is if the bond effectively yields 10%. In order to do so, the issuer must sell the bond at a **DISCOUNT** (the actual cash proceeds must be precisely computed using present value factors and are only estimated in this journal entry).

Cash	900,000	
Discount	100,000	
Bonds Payable		1,000,000

The **discount must be amortized** over the life of the bond. Let's assume we are using straight-line amortization of $20,000 year (100/5yrs=20).

Interest expense	100,000 (10%)	
Discount		20,000
Cash		80,000 (8%)

Variations on Bond Interest

Zero-coupon bonds do not make coupon payments but only pay the face value on the date of maturity. A common example of zero-coupon bonds are short-term U.S. *Treasury Bills*. Zero-coupon bonds *sell at a discount*, with the return to be bondholders arising from the difference between the price at which the bond is bought and the face value paid at maturity.

Floating rate bonds do not have fixed coupon payments. Payments instead fluctuate with some general index of interest rates. In **reverse floaters,** payments actually increase when the general interested rate index goes down and payments decrease when the index goes up. These unusual bonds are one more tool through which businesses may hedge their interest-rate risks.

Registered bonds use a register in which the borrower has the names and addresses of bondholders, such that the borrower may send payments directly to the bondholders (i.e., not through a broker). In such cases, an actual bond certificate will usually not be issued.

Junk (high yield, or speculative grade) bonds are those issued by companies that credit rating agencies assess as more likely to default, and thus pay much higher interest rates. In the ratings of Moody's Investors Service, bonds with ratings lower than Baa are considered junk bonds. Some bonds are initially issued as investment-grade bonds but are subsequently downgraded to junk bonds.

Foreign bonds have interest and face value payments in another currency.

Lecture 3.14 – Advantages & Disadvantages of Debt Financing

Some of the *Advantages* of using debt to finance a business are:
- Interest is tax-deductible.
- With certain caveats, the obligation (i.e., interest and principal payments) is generally fixed (e.g., assuming that the debt was fixed-rate, that we are considering only nominal interest rates, and considering only the period until the maturity date of the debt).
- If current owners issue debt instead of new shares of stock, the current owners avoid giving up control to the new shareholders.
- If the business has excess earnings, those earnings will accrue to owners, not to debt holders.
- Debt is less costly than equity; so, the cost of capital will be lower.
- During inflationary periods, the debt is paid back with less valuable dollars.

Some of the *Disadvantages* of using debt to finance a business are:
- The business must make pre-determined interest and principal payments independently of its performance.
- While debt holders do not gain any formal control of the business (like new shareholders), by agreeing to the terms of loan and bond covenants, businesses effectively forgo some control (i.e., flexibility).
- High debt levels increase the risk that the business may fail, wipe out owners' claims, and, thus (despite their sometimes positive effects on returns on equity), high debt levels may reduce stock prices.

Leasing vs. Buying

Businesses may also finance their operations through leases rather than buying or borrowing to buy assets. From the lessee's point of view, there are generally two types of leases: Operating leases and Finance leases. With the issuance of ASC 842, the accounting for operating and finance leases have become more similar, i.e., they are both recognized on the balance sheet now, but most of the benefits of leasing versus buying remain unchanged:
- Capital that could be used to acquire an asset could be put to another use.
- Businesses unable to obtain credit to purchase an asset may be able to lease it instead.
- A loan may violate a debt covenant while an operating lease should not.
- Leases often do not involve down payments.
- A lease provides an additional source of capital with level payments, sometimes over a longer term.
- Leases are generally less expensive in that the lessee is not paying the entire amount of the asset's cost; thus, payments are generally lower than a loan, meaning lease payments may fit the cash flow budget better than loan payments to purchase the same asset.
- Terms in lease agreements are often less strict than in bond indentures.
- In bankruptcy, creditors have weaker rights over some assets financed by leases (e.g., real estate).
- Leases may transfer the tax benefits of debt financing to lessors, prompting lessors to reduce the cost of leases to lessees.
- Some leases provide maintenance services, making management of the asset easier and possibly less expensive.
- Leasing an asset vs. buying it provides a hedge against obsolescence; that is, a lease provides more flexibility, thus, reducing risk to the lessee.
- Disposal of the asset at the end of its useful life remains with the lessor.

Lecture 3.15 – Long-Term Debt – Class Questions

15. What would be the primary reason for a company to agree to a debt covenant limiting the percentage of its long-term debt?

    a. To cause the price of the company's stock to rise.
    b. To lower the company's bond rating.
    c. To reduce the risk for existing bondholders.
    d. To reduce the interest rate on the bonds being sold.

16. The benefits of debt financing over equity financing are likely to be highest in which of the following situations?

    a. High marginal tax rates and few noninterest tax benefits.
    b. Low marginal tax rates and few noninterest tax benefits.
    c. High marginal tax rates and many noninterest tax benefits.
    d. Low marginal tax rates and many noninterest tax benefits.

17. The capital structure of a firm includes bonds with a coupon rate of 12% and an effective interest rate is 14%. The corporate tax rate is 30%. What is the firm's net cost of debt?

    a. 8.4%
    b. 9.8%
    c. 12.0%
    d. 14.0%

Class Solutions

15. (d) A company with a lower debt to equity ratio is generally considered to entail a lower risk and, as a result, will generally enable the company to borrow at lower interest rates. By agreeing to a debt covenant limiting long-term debt, the company is providing assurance to lenders that the ratio will not get too high, keeping the cost of borrowing lower for the company. Answer (a) is incorrect because although limiting debt may cause stock prices to rise, that is not necessarily the case. Answer (b) is incorrect because limiting debt is more likely to increase a company's debt rating, allowing for borrowing at lower rates, than to decrease it. Answer (c) is incorrect because although limiting long-term debt does reduce risk for existing bondholders, the purpose of providing debt covenants limiting long-term debt is to reduce interest rates on subsequent borrowings.

16. (a) Since interest is tax deductible, the higher the tax rate, the greater the tax savings enjoyed by the debtor, whereas a lower rate reduces the benefit. In addition, when there are few noninterest tax benefits, the deduction for interest is relatively more valuable, whereas, when there are many noninterest tax benefits, the company may already be paying low taxes, reducing the advantage of debt financing.

17. (b) The coupon rate is the stated rate, but the actual interest rate is the effective rate of 14%. Since interest is tax deductible, this is reduced by the tax savings, which is 4.2% at a rate of 30%. As a result, the net cost of capital will be 14% - 4.2% = 9.8%.

Lecture 3.16 – Equity

Common Stock

Businesses are ultimately owned by their common shareholders (or stockholders). They control the business (i.e., they may appoint and remove management through elections to a board of directors) and have a claim to the residual (or leftover) assets and income after the claims by all creditors and preferred shareholders are satisfied. While most companies have only one class of common stock (class A), companies may have a second class of common stock (class B) with different rights to vote or to receive dividends. Common stock is generally issued at Par value, unless there is no par value, then Stated value is used.

Some *advantages* of common stock to the business are:

- Businesses have the flexibility that dividend payments to common shareholders are not fixed, i.e., they may be increased or decreased depending on performance.

- Businesses with more equity pose less risk to lenders, thus reducing businesses' borrowing costs.

- Many investors find common stock to be very attractive since it entitles them to businesses' future profit growth.

Some *disadvantages* of common stock to the business are:

- The costs of issuing common stock are larger than those for debt.

- Current owners dilute their ownership and control with each new issuance of stock.

- While tax law considers interest a tax-deductible cost, common dividends are not tax-deductible (out of retained earnings).

- Shareholders ultimately receive a much higher return than lenders if the business is successful, so relying more on common stock results in a higher cost of capital for the business.

Common stock trades in different markets:
- Primary market – new issues market (initial price offerings, IPOs)
- Secondary market – where already outstanding shares are resold
- Over-the-counter – market for unlisted securities

Preferred Stock

Preferred shareholders (or stockholders) must be paid a preset dividend before any dividends may be paid to common stockholders. In a liquidation, preferred stockholders must be paid in full before any payments are made to common stockholders, i.e., preferred have priority (or are "preferred") over common stockholders. Some possible features of *preferred stock* are:

- **Cumulative dividends:** Under this feature, if the business "skips" preferred dividends (**arrears**) for any period, the business must pay all previously skipped dividends before it may pay any dividends to common shareholders.

- **Redeemability:** Under this feature, stockholders may demand repayment of the face value at a specific date. In some cases, redemption is automatic. Such shares more closely resemble debt and are often presented before equity in the balance sheet.

- **Callability:** Under this feature, the business may force to repay the stockholders the face value of the stock and extinguish any future obligations (call features can typically be exercised only after a minimum number of years).

- **Convertibility:** Under this feature, preferred stockholders may convert their shares into common stock.

- **Participation:** Under this rare feature, preferred stockholders receive higher dividends when common dividends are increased.

- **Floating rate:** Under this feature, preferred dividends may vary, for instance, based on an interest or inflation index.

Some *advantages* of preferred stock are:

- The business has the flexibility of being able to skip preferred dividends (even if those dividends may have to be paid later when the business wants to pay common dividends).

- Businesses with more equity pose less risk to lenders, thus reducing businesses' borrowing costs.

- Issuing more preferred stock does not entail common stockholders giving up control over the business's decision making.

- If the business has more earnings, preferred stockholders rarely receive any of them.

Some *disadvantages* of preferred stock are:

- The costs of Issuing preferred stock are larger than those for debt and the dividend rates paid on preferred stock are higher than the interest rates paid on debt.

- While tax law considers interest a tax-deductible cost, preferred dividends are not tax-deductible.

- A business that has accumulated skipped dividends (arrears) over extended periods of time may encounter difficulties reducing that backlog and/or finding new sources of funding.

To make appropriate financing decisions, businesses take into account leverage and the cost of capital.

Leverage

The degree of **Operating leverage (DOL)** measures how the size of a business's *fixed costs* affects its performance when revenues change.

- Higher fixed costs (relative to total costs) mean there is greater risk of low (or negative) earnings should revenues (sales volumes) fall below expectations. The risk that profits may be lower than anticipated is commonly known as **Business Risk** and is measured by the degree of operating leverage (DOL).

    $$DOL = \frac{\% \text{ change in EBIT (Earnings before Interest and Taxes)}}{\% \text{ change in Sales volume}}$$

- Increases in revenues for businesses with high fixed costs (i.e., a high DOL) result in proportionately larger increases in return on equity. Having lower variable costs, increases in revenues result in proportionately larger increases in profits.

The degree of **financial leverage (DFL)** measures how much a business relies on *debt financing*. Using more debt can increase returns on equity, but also increases risks for stockholders. Because debt is generally cheaper than equity, businesses have an incentive to increase their reliance on debt. However, ever larger increases in debt increase leverage, risk, and ultimately the interest rate demanded by subsequent lenders. Of course, financial leverage is an extension of operating leverage that purely focuses on one type of fixed cost, the interest costs resulting from debt financing.

- Higher debt means higher interest and principal obligations for repayment, increasing risk if performance is not up to expectations.

- Debt financing costs less than equity financing and doesn't increase with greater performance, so overall profit potential and asset growth potential are greater.

$$DFL = \frac{\% \text{ change in Earnings per Share}}{\% \text{ change in EBIT}}$$

A leveraged buyout (LBO) is a method of financing the acquisition of all or a voting majority of the outstanding shares of a company. LBOs are financed primarily with debt secured by the assets of the target company.

Lecture 3.17 – Cost of Capital

A business's cost of capital is the average of the costs of its debt and equity (including preferred stock, common stock, and retained earnings), each weighted by its market value. These costs are expressed as percentages per annum.

The word *capital* can have different meanings in different contexts. In some contexts (e.g., bank regulation), capital is roughly equivalent to equity and excludes most liabilities (e.g., deposits and senior bonds). In the context of calculations of the cost of capital, project selection, etc., capital means all sources of funds, including both debt and equity.

The **Cost of Debt** financing is the after-tax cost of interest payments as measured by yields to maturity. It can be calculated in *two ways*:
- Yield to maturity × (1 – effective tax rate)
- (Interest expense – Tax deduction for interest) / Carrying value of debt

The **Cost of Preferred stock** financing is the stipulated dividend divided by the net issue price of the stock.
- Cost of Preferred stock = *Dividend/Net issue price*

The **Cost of *Existing* Common stock (equity)** financing represents the expected returns of common shareholders, and is difficult to estimate. Some techniques:

- The **Capital Asset Pricing Model (CAPM) (Security Market Line),** assumes that the expected return of a particular stock depends on its *volatility* relative to the overall stock market *(beta)* (describes relationship between risk and expected return).
  CAPM = (Beta × Excess of Normal Market Return over Risk Free Investments) + Return on Risk Free Investments.

  - The **Beta coefficient** of an individual stock is the correlation between changes in the stock's price and changes in the price of the overall market. If, for example, the market goes up 5% and the individual stock's price goes up 10%, the stock's beta coefficient is 2.0.

  - **CAPM** = Risk free rate + [(expected market rate – risk free rate) × Beta]

- The **Arbitrage Pricing Model** is a more detailed version of CAPM that uses separate excess returns and betas for various factors contributing to a stock performance.

- The **Bond Yield Plus** method is based on the historical relationship between equities and debt and, thus, simply adds 3% to 5% to the interest rate on the business's long-term debt.

- The **Dividend Yield plus Growth Rate** method adds the current dividend (as a percentage of the stock price) and the expected growth rate in earnings.

$$\frac{\text{Next expected dividend}}{\text{Current stock price}} + \text{expected growth in earnings} = \textbf{Dividend Yield Plus Growth Rate}$$

The **Cost of *New* Common stock** is a little higher than that of existing stock, since the business must recover the cost of issuing the new shares (selling or flotation costs).

$$\frac{\text{Next expected dividend}}{\text{(Current stock price} - \text{flotation costs)}} + \text{expected growth in earnings} = \textbf{Cost of new Common stock}$$

The **Weighted average cost of capital (WACC)** is a calculation of a firm's effective cost of capital taking into account the portion of its capital that was obtained as debt, preferred stock, and common stock. Businesses with capital structures that result in low WACCs have lower required rates of return, or hurdle rates, and are more likely to find projects that add to shareholder wealth. Therefore, businesses seek capital structures that minimize their WACC.

The optimal capital structure for a business involves a tradeoff between the fact that equity is typically higher cost than debt, and the fact that higher debt-to-asset ratios result in higher interest rates for an individual business. Thus, at very low debt-to-asset ratios, businesses may make their capital structure more optimal (reduce their WACC) by relying more on debt. However, at very high debt-to-asset ratios, businesses may make their capital structure more optimal (reduce their WACC) by relying less on debt. While conditions change, in general, determining the optimal capital structure for a business involves finding the debt-to-assets ratio that minimizes WACC.

> For example, if 40% of capital was obtained through long-term debt at an effective cost of 6%, 10% of capital was obtained by issuing preferred stock with an effective cost of 8%, and 50% of capital was obtained by issuing common stock expected to return 11% to shareholders, the weighted average cost of capital is:
>
> 40% × 6% + 10% × 8% + 50% × 11%
>
> = 2.4% + 0.8% + 5.5%
>
> = 8.7%

Lecture 3.18 – Cost of Capital – Class Questions

18. Bander Co. is determining how to finance some long-term projects. Bander has decided it prefers the benefits of no fixed charges, no fixed maturity date and an increase in the credit-worthiness of the company. Which of the following would best meet Bander's financing requirements?

    a. Bonds
    b. Common stock
    c. Long-term debt
    d. Short-term debt

19. Which of the following statements is correct regarding the weighted-average cost of capital (WACC)?

    a. One of a company's objectives is to minimize the WACC.
    b. A company with a high WACC is attractive to potential shareholders.
    c. An increase in the WACC increases the value of the company.
    d. WACC is always equal to the company's borrowing rate.

20. A company with a combined federal and state tax rate of 30% has the following capital structure:

Weight	Instrument	Cost of capital
40%	Bonds	10%
50%	Common stock	10%
10%	Preferred stock	20%

What is the weighted-average after-tax cost of capital for this company?

    a. 3.3%
    b. 7.7%
    c. 8.2%
    d. 9.8%

21. A company recently issued 9% preferred stock. The preferred stock sold for $40 a share with a par of $20. The cost of issuing the stock was $5 a share. What is the company's cost of preferred stock?

    a. 4.5%
    b. 5.1%
    c. 9.0%
    d. 10.3%

22. The stock of Fargo Co. is selling for $85. The next annual dividend is expected to be $4.25 and is expected to grow at a rate of 7%. The corporate tax rate is 30%. What percentage represents the firm's cost of common equity?

    a. 12.0%
    b. 8.4%
    c. 7.0%
    d. 5.0%

Class Solutions

18. (b) Generally all debt, including bonds, long-term debt, and short-term debt involves fixed charges and fixed maturity dates. In addition, the more debt financing a company has, the lower its credit worthiness. As a result, common stock would be the best alternative to meet the financing objectives.

19. (a) An objective of a company would be to minimize the weighted average cost of capital (WACC). By doing so, the company will be able to identify more projects with a return greater than the WACC, increasing shareholder wealth. Answer (b) is incorrect because a company with a low WACC, not a high one, will attract more investors. Answer (c) is incorrect because a decrease, rather than an increase in WACC increases the value of a company. Answer (d) is incorrect because WACC is not the company's borrowing rate but rather a weighted average that includes the borrowing rate and the rate on equity.

20. (d) The weighted average cost of capital is computed by weighing each rate base on the amount of debt or equity it applies to. Since bond interest is tax deductible, the applicable rate will be net of tax. At a tax rate of 30%, the net cost of 10% bond interest will be 7%. As a result, the weighted average rate would be (7% × 40%) + (10% × 50%) + (20% × 10%), or 2.8% + 5% + 2% = 9.8%.

21. (b) Preferred dividends pay an annual dividend based on the dividend rate applied to the par value. In this case, dividends will be 9% of the $20 par, or $1.80 per share. The proceeds from the sale of the shares would be $40 less the cost of issuance of $5, for a net amount of $35. As a result, the cost of the preferred stock to common shareholders is $1.80/$35, or 5.1% per year.

22. (a) The cost of common stock is measured as the dividend yield plus the growth rate. The dividend is $4.25 per share, which has a selling price of $85 per share for a yield of $4.25/$85, or 5%. This is added to the growth rate of 7% to give a cost of common stock of 12%.

Lecture 3.19 – Asset and Liability Valuation and Ratios

Approaches to Valuation

Businesses use valuations for many different purposes: to evaluate investments, capital budgeting, financial reporting, tax reporting, mergers and acquisitions, and litigation. The 3 major approaches to valuation are:

1. Using **Actual Prices for Identical Assets Traded in Liquid Markets**
   If an asset is actively traded in a liquid market, the most commonly recognized value for the asset is simply its market price.

2. Using the **Prices of Similar Assets Traded in Liquid Markets**
   To use this approach, one must carefully adjust for differences between the item being valued and the one that traded in a liquid market. These adjustments often require using financial models.

3. Using **Valuation Models**
   If neither the asset nor similar ones trade in liquid markets, businesses use valuation models to develop estimates of fair values for the asset. These models generally use assumptions about future conditions to estimate future cash flows and incomes. Since using different assumptions may yield widely different estimates, businesses must consider these assumptions carefully to ensure that they are broadly reasonable and in line with current and/or past market and economic conditions and experience.

Types of Mergers

- **Horizontal mergers** involve businesses that are in the *same market* (i.e., competitors).
- **Vertical mergers** involve businesses acquiring others in the *same supply chain* (i.e., a supplier or customer).
- **Conglomerate mergers** involve businesses acquiring others in *unrelated markets (i.e., not direct competitors, suppliers, or customers).*

Valuing potential merger targets, businesses may use:
- **Discounted cash flow analysis** to determine the present value of the cash flows expected from the acquisition of the company, discounted at the cost of equity capital.
- The **market multiple method** multiplies the current earnings of the company times a price-earnings ratio that is appropriate to that company (based on factors such as the typical ratio in that industry).

Key Ratios (Performance Measures)

Profitability Ratios

Gross Margin = Gross profit / Net sales

Operating Profit Margin = Operating profit / Net sales

Free Cash Flow = Net operating profit after taxes (NOPAT) + Depreciation + Amortization

        – Capital expenditures – Net increase in working capital

Residual income = Operating profit – Interest on investment
- **Interest on investment =** Invested capital × required rate of return

Economic Value Added: EVA = NOPAT – Cost of financing
- **Cost of financing =** (Total assets – Current Liabilities) × WACC

Economic Rate of return on Common stock (Total Return)
- (Dividends + change in price) / beginning price

Return on Investment (based on assets) = Net income / Total assets or Average invested capital

DuPont ROI analysis: ROI = Return on sales × Asset turnover
- **Return on sales =** Net income / Sales
- **Asset turnover** = Sales / Total assets

Return on Assets = Net income / Average total assets
- **Average total assets =** (Beginning total assets + Ending total assets) / 2

Return on Equity = Net income / Average common stockholders' equity
- **Common stockholders' equity =** Stockholders' equity – Preferred stock liquidation value

Used in isolation, different financial ratios have various advantages and disadvantages. For instance, businesses that set managerial and employee compensation based on ROIs focused on the short term may obtain results that maximize short-term ROIs by ignoring, and forgoing, projects that have short-term costs (and therefore less attractive short-term ROIs), but that overall, or long-term, would have positive net present values and, thus, add to shareholder wealth.

Asset Utilization Ratios

Receivable Turnover = Net credit sales / Average accounts receivable
- **Average accounts receivable =** (Beginning A/R + Ending A/R) / 2
- Remember to use net *credit* sales and **not** net sales.

Receivables Collection Period = Average accounts receivable / Average credit sales per day
- Use 365-day year unless told otherwise.

Inventory Turnover = Cost of goods sold / Average inventory
- Remember to use cost of goods sold and **not** sales.

Inventory Conversion Period = Average inventory / Average cost of goods sold per day

Total Asset Turnover = Sales / Average total assets

Fixed Asset Turnover = Sales / Average net fixed assets
- Remember that net fixed assets is after subtraction of accumulated depreciation.

Debt Utilization Ratios

Debt to Total Assets = Total liabilities / Total assets

Debt to Equity Ratio = Total debt / Total equity

Times Interest Earned Ratio = Earnings before interest and taxes (EBIT) / Interest expense

Liquidity Ratios

Current Ratio = Current assets / Current liabilities

Quick (or Acid Test) Ratio = Quick assets / Current liabilities
- **Quick assets =** Cash + Marketable securities + Accounts receivable

Market Ratios

Market Capitalization = Common stock price per share × Common stock shares outstanding

Market/Book Ratio can be calculated in two ways:
- Common stock price per share / Book value per share
- Market capitalization / Common stockholders' equity

Book Value per Share = Common stockholders' equity / Common stock shares outstanding

Price/Earnings (PE) Ratio = Common stock price per share / Earnings per share (EPS)

Many other ratios may be computed. Some ratios are, of course, more widely used than others. Other examples of less commonly used ratios include:

- The **Sales to Cash Flow Ratio**, which is generally interpreted to be a measure of financial strength.

- The **Investment Turnover Ratio** = sales / book value (or net worth)

It is important to understand the ratios and their *Purpose or Use*.

Ratio	Formula	Purpose or Use
Liquidity – Measures of the company's short-term ability to pay its maturing obligations.		
1. Working Capital	Current assets - Current liabilities	Measures the company's solvency
2. Current ratio	Current assets / Current liabilities	Measures short-term debt-paying ability
3. Quick or acid-test ratio	Cash, marketable securities, and receivables (net) / Current liabilities	Measures immediate short-term liquidity
4. Current cash debt coverage ratio	Net cash provided by operating activities / Average current liabilities	Measures a company's ability to pay off its current liabilities in a given year from its operations

Ratio	Formula	Purpose or Use

Activity – Measures how effectively the company uses its assets

Ratio	Formula	Purpose or Use
5. Receivables turnover	Net credit sales / Average trade receivables (net)	Measures liquidity of receivables
6. Inventory turnover	Cost of goods sold / Average inventory	Measures liquidity of inventory
7. Asset turnover	Net sales / Average total assets	Measures how efficiently assets are used to generate sales
8. Number of days' supply in average inventory	= 360 / Inventory Turnover **or** = Average (ending) inventory / Average daily cost of goods sold	Measures number of days required to sell inventory
9. Number of days' sales in average receivables	= 360 / Receivables Turnover	Measures number of days required to collect receivables

Profitability – Measures of the degree of success or failure of a given company or division for a given period of time.

Ratio	Formula	Purpose or Use
10. Profit margin on sales (Gross margin)	Net income / Net sales	Measures net income generated by each dollar of sales
11. Rate of return on assets	Net income / Average total assets	Measures overall profitability of assets
12. Rate of return on common stock equity (Return on equity)	Net income minus preferred dividends / Average common stockholders' equity	Measures profitability of owners' investment
13. Earnings per share	Net income minus preferred dividends / Weighted shares outstanding	Measures net income earned on each share of common stock
14. Price-earnings ratio	Market price of stock / Earnings per share	Measures the ratio of the market price per share to earnings per share
15. Payout ratio	Cash dividends / Net income	Measures percentage of earnings distributed in the form of cash dividends

Coverage – Measures of the degree of protection for long-term creditors and investors.

Ratio	Formula	Purpose or Use
16. Debt to equity	Total debt / Stockholders' equity	Shows creditors the corporation's ability to sustain losses
17. Debt to total assets	Total debt / Total assets	Measures the percentage of total assets provided by creditors
18. Times interest earned	Income before interest expense and taxes / Interest expense	Measures ability to meet interest payments as they come due
19. Cash debt coverage ratio	Net cash provided by operating activities / Average total liabilities	Measures a company's ability to repay its total liabilities in a given year from its operations
20. Book value per share	Common stockholders' equity / Outstanding shares	Measures the amount each share would receive if the company were liquidated at the amounts reported on the balance sheet

Lecture 3.20 – Ratio – Class Questions

23. Farrow Co. is applying for a loan in which the bank requires a quick ratio of at least 1. Farrow's quick ratio is 0.8. Which of the following actions would increase Farrow's quick ratio?

    a. Purchasing inventory through the issuance of a long-term note.
    b. Implementing stronger procedures to collect accounts receivable at a faster rate.
    c. Paying an existing account payable.
    d. Selling obsolete inventory at a loss.

24. The following information was taken from the income statement of Hadley Co.:

Beginning inventory	17,000
Purchases	56,000
Ending inventory	13,000

What is Hadley Co.'s inventory turnover?

    a. 3
    b. 4
    c. 5
    d. 6

25. At the end of its fiscal year, Krist, Inc. had the following account balances:

Cash	$ 5,000
Accounts receivable	10,000
Inventory	20,000
Accounts payable	15,000
Short-term note payable	5,000
Long-term note payable	35,000

What is Krist's quick (acid-test) ratio?

    a. 0.273
    b. 0.636
    c. 0.750
    d. 1.750

Class Solutions

23. (d) Selling inventory, regardless of whether it is sold at a profit or loss, decreases inventory, which does not affect the quick ratio, and increases cash or accounts receivable, which improves the quick ratio since liquid assets, the numerator, is increasing, without a corresponding increase in current liabilities, the denominator. Answer (a) is incorrect because purchasing inventory using a long-term note increases inventory and noncurrent liabilities, neither of which are used in computing the quick ratio. Answer (b) is incorrect because collecting accounts receivable at a quicker pace will increase one asset included in the quick ratio, cash, while decreasing another, accounts receivable, by the same amount. As a result, the quick ratio is not affected. Answer (c) is incorrect because by paying an existing account payable, cash and accounts payable are decreasing by the same amount. With a ratio below 1.0, decreasing the numerator and denominator by the same amount will decrease, not increase, the ratio.

24. (b) With beginning inventory of $17,000 and purchases of $56,000, cost of goods available for sale is $73,000. Subtracting ending inventory of $13,000 gives cost of sales of $60,000. Average inventory is the total of beginning plus ending inventory, divided by 2, so ($17,000 + $13,000)/2 = $15,000. Inventory turnover is cost of sales divided by average inventory, so $60,000/$15,000 = 4 times.

25. (c) The quick, or acid-test, ratio is equal to liquid assets, including cash of $5,000 and accounts receivable of $10,000, for a total of $15,000, divided by total current liabilities, including accounts payable of $15,000 and the short-term note payable of $5,000, for a total of $20,000; thus, the ratio is $15,000/$20,000 = .75.

Lecture 3.21 – Risk Management

Expected Returns

The total return of an investment includes cash distributions (interest, dividends, rents) and the change (growth) in the value of the asset (Total Return = Distribution Rate + Growth Rate). This model, known as the **Gordon Growth Model**, assumes that the reinvested assets will increase distributions by the amount of reinvestment, so that the growth in the assets will be the growth rate of future dividends. Eventually, all earnings are going to be distributed over the life of the company.

 For example, an investment of $100 that pays a dividend of $3 and grows in value to $107 at the end of the year has a total return of 10% (3% distribution + 7% growth). With $107 in assets, the company should be able to pay out a dividend of $107 × 3% = $3.21 next year, and add $107 × 7% = $7.49 to the value of the asset, increasing it to $114.49, on which an even higher 3% dividend can then be paid in the third year, and so on.

A group of investments (whether in similar types of assets or not) is known as a **portfolio**. The expected return on a portfolio is a weighted average of the expected return of the individual investments.

 For example, if a portfolio is invested 60% in Asset A, which is expected to return 10%, and 40% in Asset B, which is expected to return 5%, the expected return (ER) of the portfolio is:
(60% × 10%) + (40% × 5%)
= 6% + 2%
= 8%

Average Returns

Since investors cannot know the future, estimates of investments' expected returns (ER) are commonly simply the averages of historical (or past) rates of return. Average historical rates of return can be computed arithmetically (simple average) or geometrically (taking into account the effects of compounding):

- The *arithmetic (simple) average return rate* simply adds the returns for several periods and divides by the number of periods.

- The *geometric average return rate* is the single annual compound rate of return required to turn the initial value of an investor's investment into its final value over the number of periods intervening. Geometric averages are lower than arithmetic averages, except for the case when all single-period rates are identical.

For example, if an investment grew by 44% in one year and 0% in the next, then $100 would have grown to $144 in the first year and remained there in the second.
- Arithmetic average return = 22% (the average of 44% and 0%)
- Geometric average return = 20% (an investment of $100 earning a consistent 20% each year would grow to $120 after one year and $144 after two years).

Standard Deviation

A very common measure of investment risk is the **standard** deviation (SD, or the lower case Greek letter sigma, σ), which is a measure of the volatility of an investment. (The variance, σ^2, is simply the standard deviation squared, or multiplied times itself). To calculate SD, take the following steps:

1. Determine the arithmetic average return.
2. Calculate the difference from the average for each individual period.
3. Square those differences.
4. Determine the average of the squared values.
5. Calculate the square root of this average.

Since most investors are **risk averse**, investors demand higher expected returns from investments with a higher standard deviation (e.g., common stocks) and demand lower expected returns from investments with a lower standard deviation (e.g., bonds).

 As an example, assume an investment has returned 7%, 15%, and 8% in 3 different periods.

1. (7% + 15% + 8%) / 3 = 10% arithmetic average return.
2. –3%, +5%, -2% are the differences from the average in the 3 periods.
3. 9%, 25%, 4% are the squares of the differences.
4. (9% + 25% + 4%) / 3 = 12.67% average of the squared values.
5. Square root of 12.67% = 3.56% = the standard deviation (SD)

Notice that the SD of 3.56% is slightly higher than the average of the absolute values of the differences: (3% + 5% + 2%) / 3 = 3.33%. This result follows because the calculation of the SD gives disproportionate weight to bigger differences.

The **Coefficient of Variation** (CV) is another common measure of risk. Standard deviations (SDs) are somewhat related to the averages from which they are computed (e.g., SDs computed among values in the billions are typically going to be much larger than SDs computed among values in the thousands). The CV seeks to address this shortcoming in SDs and provide a measure of Relative Risk that is readily comparable across investments of different sizes (i.e., whether in the billions or thousands). To compute the CV (or relative risk) for an investment, one would divide the standard deviation (SD) of the investment's returns by the investment's average (or expected) return (ER). Depending on their degree of risk averseness, investors will weigh the expected returns (ER) and relative risks (CV) of their investment options, generally preferring some combination of higher ERs and lower CVs.

Portfolio Risk

Investors once largely assumed that portfolios consisting of individually riskier investments would be riskier, and that to reduce risk portfolios had to include safer investments. In 1951, Harry Markowitz revolutionized the investment field launching **Modern Portfolio Theory (MPT)** pointing out that the standard deviation of a portfolio of investments will generally be much smaller than the standard deviation of the individual investments, since the prices of various individual investments do not each move up and down at exactly the same time.

The measure of the degree to which various (i.e., typically more than two) investments move together may be captured by a **covariance matrix.** Since interpreting a covariance matrix is not straightforward, investors often focus on the **correlation coefficients** between pairs of investments (i.e., between only one investment and only one other investment at a time). We addressed correlation coefficients above, but repeat the key points here adapted for the case of portfolio theory.

- *Correlation coefficient = 1.00* When one investment goes up, the other always goes up. When one goes down, the other always goes down.

- *Correlation coefficient = 0* There is no identifiable relationship between the two investments, whether one goes up or down does not reliably predict whether the other goes up or down.

- *Correlation coefficient = -1.00* When one investment goes up, the other always goes down. When one goes down, the other always goes up.

Whenever the correlation coefficient between two investments is less than 1.00, the standard deviation of the portfolio will be lower than the average of the standard deviations of the individual investments. This result follows because the differences in the investments' price fluctuations somewhat offset each other.

By combining investments that have low covariances with each other, an investor can largely eliminate **unsystematic (unique) risk**, or the risk that pertains to one investment (e.g., a single company: Rio Tinto) or even to a group of similar investments (e.g., to mining stocks). What remains is the unavoidable or **systematic risk** that cannot be diversified away and that results from market-wide factors and economy-wide fluctuations in GDP, inflation, interest rates, etc. According to MPT, investors may expect some reward from bearing systematic risk in the form of the market's average (or expected) returns. In contrast, investors bearing unsystematic risks (i.e., portfolios that are not properly diversified) may expect only lower average (or expected) returns since they are bearing risks that may be avoided.

Investors may use the **mean-variance optimization** technique, combining the expected returns of various investments and their covariances with each other, to identify the specific portfolio that will, for any particular level of ("desired" or acceptable) volatility (or variance or risk), have the highest possible expected return (or, conversely, to identify the portfolio that will, for a particular expected return, have the lowest level of volatility). The portfolio with the highest average (or expected) return for a particular level of volatility is known as the most **efficient portfolio** for that level of variance. An **efficient frontier** plots the combinations of assets that yield the most efficient portfolios for various levels of risk (technically efficient frontiers exist in multi-dimensional space for multi-investment portfolios, but efficient frontiers are commonly shown for simplified two-asset portfolios (e.g., stocks vs. bonds) in graphs with "only" the standard two vertical and horizontal axes).

William Sharpe developed Beta as a standardized measure of investments' systematic risk. **Beta risk** measures how changes in the value of an individual investment compares with changes in the value of an overall or market-wide portfolio (commonly the S&P 500 stock index). Thus, Beta measures (or compares) the volatility of an individual investment relative to that of the portfolio (or the market) as a whole. A beta of 1 indicates that the investment moves up and down at approximately the overall rate for the portfolio (or market), a beta of 0.5 indicates that it moves up and down only half as much, and a beta of 2 indicates that it goes up and down twice as much as the overall portfolio. For instance, when the overall stock market goes up by 10%, a stock with a beta of 0.5 would be expected to go up only by 5%, and a stock with a beta of 2 would be expected to go up 20%. (Similarly, a 10% market drop will result in drops of 5% and 20%, respectively).

The **Capital Asset Pricing Model** (*CAPM*) for which Sharpe shared a Nobel Prize in Economics in 1990 (along with Harry Markowitz) suggests that investments with higher betas have higher expected returns to compensate for the extra volatility. The degree to which a portfolio does better or worse than the return predicted by its beta is known as **alpha**, and is considered to be a measure of the degree of success or failure of the individual portfolio manager. One implication of the CAPM is that the **asset allocation** of a portfolio (e.g., the percentage of a person's investments devoted to stocks vs. bonds) is overwhelmingly the most important factor in determining the returns an investor can expect.

Many academics conclude that markets generally reflect the combined knowledge of their participants, and that individual variations from an alpha of zero are largely a matter of luck. The conclusion that individuals cannot outperform market averages over long periods of time except by luck is known as the **Efficient Market Hypothesis** (*EMH*). This hypothesis led to the development of **index funds**, which buy all of the available investments in a particular category instead of trying to determine which ones will appreciate in value the most (for example, an S&P 500 stock index fund buys all 500 stocks in the Standard & Poor's market average). If unsystematic risk isn't rewarded reliably (and there are no particularly large costs for buying the smallest, least liquid stocks), buying less than all 500 would theoretically result in extra risk for no extra return. Also, since the strongest form of the EMH assumes that prices reflect the best judgment of the participants, the index fund should not invest equal amounts in each of the index components (e.g., not 0.2% each for the S&P 500), but hold stocks in proportion to the total market values of the different companies (i.e., more in Apple—a stock with a large total valuation—than in Disney—a stock with a smaller total valuation). (In practice, most analyses find that increasing the number of stocks in one's portfolio to 30 or 40 yields almost all the gains from reducing unsystematic risk. Of course, the 30-40 stocks would need to be chosen to be somewhat representative of the overall selection of 500 stocks. Buying 30-40 technology stocks would expose one to the unsystematic risks of the technology sector, and not to the systematic risk of the market as a whole).

More recently, there have been several challenges to both the CAPM and EMH. Beta has not proven to be a very good predictor of returns, and there is even some evidence that higher betas often result in lower expected returns. For example, initial public offerings (IPOs) generally represent relatively new and untested companies that are much more volatile than average, but they have consistently had worse-than-average subsequent performance in the market, combining high volatility and low returns. There is also some evidence that stocks with low prices in relation to earnings and assets (known as **value stocks**) do better than stocks with high relative prices (known as **growth stocks**), even though the latter are more volatile, and that stocks with a smaller total market capitalization do better than those with larger total market values, irrespective of volatility.

The EMH counterargument is that value stocks generally represent companies and industries that aren't growing quickly, and face more **business risk** (risk of outright bankruptcy or other failure), and that small companies are similarly far more likely to fail than large ones. Others believe these differences represent evidence of consistent bias by the participants in the market that may occasionally be exploited to gain higher-than-average returns by those who resist these biases (this view is studied by **Behavioral Finance Theory**).

Investors often use the term *market trend* to refer to the direction in which financial markets are moving. The terms ***bull market*** and ***bear market*** describe upward and downward movements in the market, respectively, and can be used to describe either the market as a whole or specific sectors and securities. A bear market normally refers to a period during which prices have fallen by more than 20% from their previous peak. A bull market normally refers to a period during which prices have risen by more than 20% from their previous trough (during the previous bear market). Multi-year periods of sustained price growth (even if they contain some bear markets) are commonly referred to as "secular bull markets" (e.g., that from the early 1980s to the late 1990s). Multi-year periods without sustained price growth (even if they contain some bull markets) are commonly referred to as "secular bear markets" (e.g., that from the mid-1960s to the early 1980s, and more recently from the late 1990s to the later 2000s).

Interest Rates and Risks

Through loans (and bonds) borrowers may use funds that they would otherwise not have and lenders forgo the use of those funds. In compensation, borrowers pay lenders interest. To provide funds to riskier projects (or borrowers), lenders (and investors) demand higher rates of return. Common risks that lenders (and investors) may consider include:

- **Credit (or default) risk:** The risk that borrowers will not abide by the terms of their contracts (e.g., fail to make some payments of interest or principal).
  - o **Sector risk:** The fraction of a borrower's credit risk associated with being in its industry.

- **Concentration of credit risk:** The credit risk resulting from lending to only a few borrowers or only to borrowers (even if a large number of them) in related industries. Lenders (and investors) may reduce this risk by diversifying their portfolios of loans (and bonds).

- **Market risk:** The risk that worsening economy-wide conditions will depress the value of all pre-existing assets (independently of whether credit risk worsens).

- **Interest rate risk:** The risk that rising interest rates will depress the resale value of pre-existing bonds (or loans).

The Yield Curve

The **yield curve** presents U.S. Treasury interest rates (yields) in the y-axis (vertical) and terms (or maturities, usually 3 months to 30 years) in the x-axis (horizontal). Most non-government bonds and loans are more or less loosely priced in reference to the yield curve, such that changes in the yield curve affect interest rates in almost all markets throughout the U.S. economy.

- **Normal yield curve:** Interest rates are higher for longer terms.
  According to the **liquidity preference theory**, interest rates would normally be higher for longer terms than for shorter terms since investors demand more compensation for long-term investments that are more subject to various risks (such as inflation or interest rate risk).

- **Inverted yield curve:** Interest rates are lower for longer terms.
  According to the **expectations theory**, long-term interest rates reflect future expected short-term interest rates. An inverted yield curve usually reflects investors' expectations of upcoming declines in economy-wide interest rates, usually because investors expect falling inflation rates and/or worsening economy-wide conditions (e.g., a recession).

- **Flat yield curve:** Interest rates are similar across terms. Of course, normal yield curves typically flatten before becoming inverted, and inverted yield curves typically flatten before returning to normal.

Moreover, according to the **market segmentation theory**, some participants in bond (and loan) markets may focus on lending at different terms. Thus, different changes in conditions for each set of participants (e.g., different levels of credit losses, capital, or regulatory differences) may result in interest rates, at least temporarily, changing in different directions for different terms. For instance, depository institutions focus more on short-term bonds and loans, while some institutional investors (e.g., life insurance companies and pension funds) focus more on longer-term bonds and loans.

In practice, yield curves may not always be "straight lines." **Changing expectations** about the future and the **relative liquidity** of bond (and loan) markets at various terms may even cause the yield curve to become temporarily "**humped**," i.e., with higher rates for intermediate terms than for short or long terms.

Note that the term "normal" does not mean to imply either "common" or "preferable." Normal simply means that shorter terms have lower rates. During periods of expansionary monetary policy, shorter terms are typically pushed lower, making the yield curve look "normal." In contrast, during periods when monetary policy is neutral, yield curves often look rather flat.

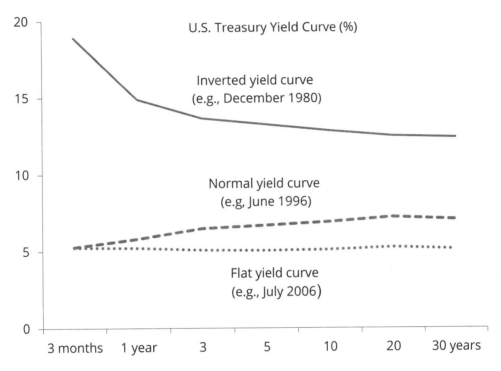

Predicting macroeconomic conditions and interest rates is inherently difficult. Thus, determining the ideal set of maturities and loan types (e.g., fixed vs. variable rates) for a firm to use is also difficult. For instance, a borrower using mostly long-term, fixed-rate debt would forgo the benefits of falling interest rates, should interest rates fall. A borrower using mostly short-term (and thus effectively variable rate) debt will experience more liquidity risk, may suffer more earnings volatility, and may, thus, be charged higher rates by lenders. Prudent financial policy would, thus, likely call for diversifying a firm's debt maturities and types.

Lecture 3.22 – Risk Management – Class Questions

26. A company is considering acquiring a derivative to hedge a risk associated with an investment it is currently holding. Which of the following coefficients of variation would indicate that the hedge will be effective?

    a. +0.91
    b. +0.19
    c. -0.19
    d. -0.91

27. Which of the following is a measure of the volatility of an investment?

    a. Expected return.
    b. Standard deviation.
    c. Graphical Evaluation and Review Technique (GERT).
    d. Coefficient of variation.

28. Which of the following is a risk taken by a lender that the value of the loan will decline as a result of a general economic decline?

    a. Market risk.
    b. Credit risk.
    c. Concentration of credit risk.
    d. Economy risk.

29. Which of the following is not a theory that describes the reasons for differences in the yields associated with interest rates?

    a. Expectations.
    b. Market segmentation.
    c. Behavioral finance theory.
    d. Liquidity preference.

Class Solutions

26. (d) In order for a hedge to be effective in offsetting a risk associated with an investment, it should respond to market conditions in the opposite way that the hedged investment acts. The closer a coefficient of variation is to 0, the less of a relationship there is between the two items. A coefficient of +1 indicates the two act in pretty much precisely the same manner and a coefficient of -1 indicates that they act in an opposite manner. A coefficient of -0.91 would indicate a strong inverse relationship and a potentially effective hedge.

27. (b) The standard deviation is a measure of the volatility of an investment and is the most common measure of investment risk. Answer (a) is incorrect because the expected return is the estimate of the return the company will receive, taking into account the probabilities of various possible outcomes occurring, each of which may provide a different return. It does not measure volatility. Answer (c) is incorrect because graphical evaluation and review technique (GERT) is a project management approach, not an investment measurement. Answer (d) is incorrect because the coefficient of variation measures the similarity in the way different investments will react to changes in market conditions. It does not measure volatility.

28. (a) Market risk is the risk that the value of a bond or loan will decline due to a decline in the aggregate value of all the assets in the economy. Answer (b) is incorrect because credit risk is the risk that the borrower will default on interest or principal payments. Answer (c) is incorrect because a concentration of credit risk is the risk associated with lending to a relatively small number of borrowers or borrowers with common characteristics. Answer (d) is incorrect because there is no risk assumed by lenders that is referred to as an economy risk.

29. (c) Liquidity preference, market segmentation, and expectations are three theories on the reason for differences in yields. Behavioral finance theory relates to the behavior of stocks, not interest rates.

Lecture 3.23 – Derivatives

Derivatives are financial instruments that derive their value from other underlying assets or prices (commodities, indices, stocks, exchange rates, interest rates, etc.).

- Derivatives are commonly settled through transfers of cash or other liquid assets, taking into account how the prices of the underlying asset evolved relative to the terms set in the original derivative contract.

- Derivatives are financial instruments that have the following **three** characteristics: (**NUNS**)
  - No net investment
  - An Underlying and a Notional amount
  - Net Settlement
    - There is an Underlying price to be used to settle the contract and a Notional amount to calculate the settlement. Little or no payment takes place at origination and the derivative can be settled in a net amount.

Common types of derivatives include:

- **Options** allow (but do not require) holders to *buy (call)* or *sell (put)* an underlying asset at a pre-specified price during a pre-specified period of time (American options) or at a specified date (European options).

- **Forwards** are negotiated contracts in which two parties agree to purchase and sell an underlying asset at a pre-specified price at a future date. The parties may tailor the contract for any amount or date.

- **Futures** are standardized versions of forwards for standardized amounts (e.g., X tons of grade Y steel) and dates (e.g., the last day of the quarter).

- **Swaps** are agreements by which two parties agree to swap certain streams of payments. In a **currency swap**, the parties may swap flows in two currencies, potentially removing exchange rate risk for both parties. In **interest rate swaps**, the parties may swap a fixed rate flow of payments and a variable rate flow of payments. **Swaptions** are contracts that give holders the option to enter into new swaps, or extend or terminate existing swaps.

Risks Associated with Derivatives

Derivatives may be used for two different purposes:

- **Speculation:** Businesses may use derivatives to raise revenues by shouldering other parties' risks, hoping that the losses feared by the counterparty do not materialize, e.g., issuer of credit default swaps (CDS) for subprime mortgages charge a premium to protect others against defaults. The issuer will make profits if the defaults do not take place.

- **Hedging:** Businesses may use derivatives to reduce their risks, e.g., an American company with costs in the U.S. but an expected future stream of revenues in Japanese Yen may use currency derivatives to lock in those future revenues as dollars using current exchange rates, thus eliminating its exchange rate risk.

Various business risks are associated with the use of derivatives.

- **Credit (or counterparty) risk:** the counterparty in a contract not honoring its obligations.

- **Market risk:** Adverse changes in economy-wide conditions will affect the fair value of the derivative. This risk is only applicable to derivatives used for speculation.

- **Legal risk:** Legislative or regulatory changes may alter or void the derivative's contracts.
- **Basis risk:** Changes in the value of the derivative may not match exactly changes in the value of the asset (or flows) that is being hedged. In this case, the derivative will fail to hedge risks completely.

Using Derivatives to Hedge

Three common uses of derivatives to hedge are:

- **Fair value hedges:** against changes in the value of an asset or liability that the firm has or expects to have.

- **Cash flow hedges:** against fluctuations in future cash flows.

- **Foreign currency hedges:** against the effects of fluctuations in the value of a foreign currency on the value of assets, liabilities, or cash flows.

According to the Accounting Standard Codification, derivatives must be reported at *fair value*. However, changes in the value of derivatives that qualify as hedges may be used to offset changes in the value of the hedged items. Unrealized gains and losses are reported as follows:

- **Fair value hedges:** For derivatives qualifying as fair value hedges, if the hedge is completely effective, changes in the value of the derivative and in the value of the item being hedged will offset one another perfectly, and neither change needs to be reported in earnings (the income statement). If the hedge is not completely effective, only the net effect of the changes in the value of the derivative and in the value of the item being hedged will be reported in earnings.

- **Cash flow hedges:** In contrast, for derivatives qualifying as cash flow hedges, the effective part of changes in the value of derivatives (i.e., the part offset by changes in the value of hedged items) is reported as "other comprehensive income" in the balance sheet section on stockholders' equity. The ineffective part of changes in the value of derivatives (i.e., that without an offset in changes in the value of hedged items) is reported in earnings (the income statement).

Valuing Derivatives

Derivatives that trade on public markets are reported at their quoted prices. For derivatives that do not trade on public markets, fair values are commonly estimated using various valuation models such as:
- **Black-Scholes:** used to estimate the value of stock options.
- **Monte Carlo simulations**
- **Binomial trees**
- **Zero-coupon method:** used to estimate the value of interest rate swaps.

The calculations used in these models are generally complex and require specialized knowledge or computer programs.

Next, we work through an example of using derivatives.

Assume your client is an oil distributor. On October 1, it purchased 1 million gallons of gasoline from its supplier (a refinery) paying $3.30 per gallon (a wholesale price). The client plans to sell oil to various airlines in early January, but is concerned that, in the meantime, the price of oil might drop considerably from the current selling price of $3.50 (a retail price). To protect from losses in the value of its inventory, the client sells a gasoline futures contract based on a wholesale gasoline price index per gallon (the underlying) times 1 million gallons (the notional amount), with a settlement date of January 2. Assume the price of the index drops $0.20 (or 20 cents) per gallon by the end of the year.

The purchase of the inventory by the distributor from the refinery is recorded as follows (assume immediate payment and entries in millions of dollars):

10/1	Inventory	3.30	
	Cash		3.30

When the futures contract is established, there is no entry, since no cash is involved. This is a **fair value hedge**, since the distributor is hedging against an existing asset.

As of the end of the year, the decline of $0.20 per gallon in the price of oil results in a loss on the inventory of $200,000. The futures contract, however, is now expected to result in a collection of $200,000 upon settlement. The entries are:

12/31	Loss on market decline in inventory	0.2	
	Inventory		0.2
	Receivable on derivative	0.2	
	Gain on fair value hedge		0.2

Both the loss on inventory and gain on the fair value hedge are included in the computation of net income, so there is no net income effect. This, of course, was the goal of the hedge.

Let's now go back to October 1 and consider the issues from the point of view of the airline that is planning on purchasing the gasoline in early January. The airline might enter into a mirror image of the very same contract to hedge against a price increase. However, for the airline, it would be a **cash flow hedge**, since, as yet, there is no asset (like the inventory), liability, or fixed commitment for the purchase.

On October 1, the airline enters into a derivative based on the gasoline index with the same notional amount of $1 million gallons. There is **no entry** on that date.

On December 31, the price decline of $0.20 per gallon in the index means that the airline expects to have to pay $200,000 on the settlement date. The entry is:

12/31	Other comprehensive income – loss on cash flow hedge	0.2	
	Payable on derivative		0.2

Note that the loss is **not** included in the calculation of net income. The reason why, is that the decline in gasoline is expected to reduce the cost of inventory in the next period; so, this loss will be offset by a reduction in the cost of sales in the next period. Since the offsetting event is not yet reflected in net income, neither can the hedge.

To summarize, when derivatives are used as speculation or fair value hedges, gains and losses are reported in net income (in the case of a fair value hedge, there will be offsetting amounts on the asset or commitment being hedged). When derivatives are used as cash flow hedges, gains and losses are reported in other comprehensive income (they are transferred to net income when the expected events occur, and offsetting amounts are reported in net income).

Derivatives Summary

Speculation (non-hedge)
- Acquired to take on risk, hoping for profit.
- Gain or loss in income from continuing operations **(I/S)**.

Fair value hedge
- Acquired to hedge against a recognized asset or liability or a firm purchase commitment.
- Gain or loss in income from continuing operations **(I/S)**.
- Should be offset by loss or gain on hedged item.

Cash flow hedge
- Acquired to hedge against a forecasted future transaction.
- Gain or loss in other comprehensive income (OCI) **(B/S)**.
- Nothing included in net income until forecasted activity occurs.

Foreign currency hedge against an investment in foreign operations
- Acquired to hedge against currency risk from a major investment in a company with a local currency (currency in which books are maintained) other than the U.S. dollar.
- Gain or loss in other comprehensive income (OCI) **(B/S)**.
- Offsets translation losses or gains from investment in foreign operations.

Lecture 3.24 – Derivatives – Class Questions

30. Which of the following is not a characteristic of a derivative?

    a. It can be settled in its net amount for cash or other liquid assets.
    b. It has an original maturity of three months or less.
    c. There is an underlying and a notional amount.
    d. There is either no initial payment or the initial payment is disproportionately lower than the cost of an investment that would react to the market similarly.

31. Rishard Corporation has a cash flow hedge that has increased in value by $60,000 during the year. The hedge is highly effective, and 95% of the change is expected to offset changes in future cash flows on the hedged transaction. How will Rishard report the $60,000 increase?

    a. $57,000 of the gain will be reported in other comprehensive income and the remainder will be disclosed in the footnotes.
    b. The entire amount will be reported in other comprehensive income.
    c. $57,000 of the gain will be reported in other comprehensive income and the remainder will be reported in income.
    d. $57,000 of the gain will be reported in income and the remainder will be reported in other comprehensive income.

32. A company is considering entering into an interest rate swap but is concerned that the counterparty may not perform. This is a description of:

    a. Performance risk.
    b. Legal risk.
    c. Market risk.
    d. Credit risk.

Class Solutions

30. (b) A financial instrument is a derivative if it will be settled in cash or liquid assets for its net amount, there is at least one underlying and notional amount, and there is either no initial cost or the initial cost is disproportionately low compared to other investments that would provide similar reactions to the market. There is no requirement that it have a maturity of 3 months or less.

31. (c) When a derivative is accounted for as a cash flow hedge, any gain or loss due to a change in the value of the hedge will be reported in other comprehensive income to the extent that the hedge is effective. With 95% effectiveness, $57,000 will be reported in OCI. The ineffective portion is recognized in income.

32. (d) Credit risk is the risk that the counterparty to a contract will fail to honor its obligations. Answer (a) is incorrect because there is no risk called performance risk associated with derivatives. Answer (b) is incorrect because legal risk is the risk that legal or regulatory action will invalidate the derivative. Answer (c) is incorrect because market risk, applicable to derivatives acquired for speculation purposes, is the risk that adverse changes will affect the fair value of the derivative.

Lecture 3.25 – Financial Management – Class Questions – DRS

Major Manufacturing will receive a windfall. Of this money, $3,500,000 is not earmarked for taxes, dividends, or an investment. Shareholders are not eager for an increase either in dividends or debt. Money not used for investment will be distributed to shareholders. Generally, the hurdle rate is 10%. As an S corporation, Major does not pay any income taxes.

Miles Stand, the CEO, asked the accounting staff to provide a table of the potential investments in Major's operations to Alice Abernathy so that she could compare the investments, rank each of them that exceeds the hurdle rate, and make a recommendation as to which investments or combination of investments, if any, are appropriate. Unfortunately, the accounting staff neglected to finish the chart for project D and Alice is unsure of how to complete it, so she needs you to look over the documents and help straighten out her memo.

Major has four manufacturing departments. Work in each department is finished at the fiscal year-end for extensive cleaning and repairs, so there is no work-in-process inventory at the fiscal year-end. Materials move through only one manufacturing department.

Amend the summary memo that Alice has drafted, as appropriate. Round the net present value to the nearest $1,000. Round the payback period to the closest year.

To revise the document, click on each segment of underlined text below and select the needed correction, if any, from the list provided. If the underlined text is already correct in the context of the document, select "original text." If the underlined text is extraneous, select "delete text."

To: Miles Stand, CEO
From: Alice Abernathy
Re: Analysis of Investment Opportunities
Date: January 7, 20X0

There are five potential projects (A, B, C, D and E) being considered. The accounting staff and I have prepared the following table for your comparison. I have compared the investments, ranked them, and provided a recommendation for each. Please let me if I can be of any further assistance.

		Investment (all first year)	Net present value at 10%	Internal rate of return	Payback period (in years)
A.	Machine shop	$1,600,000	$744,000	20%	4
B.	Replace press	1,000,000	988,000	30%	3
C.	Replace forklifts	800,000	179,000	15%	5
D.	Upgrade safety equipment	200,000	--	25%	--
E.	Solar electricity system	1,000,000	(601,000)	5%	15
	Total	$4,600,000			

Adjustments:

1. <u>The net present value of the safety equipment upgrade is $200,000.</u>

2. <u>The payback period of the safety equipment upgrade is non-existent, as this project will not recoup the expenditure.</u>

Recommendations:

3. <u>We should undertake the machine shop project. This project meets our internal rate of return criteria and there are sufficient funds to undertake it.</u>

4. <u>We should undertake the press replacement project. This project meets our internal rate of return criteria and there are sufficient funds to undertake it.</u>

5. <u>We should undertake the forklifts replacement project. This project meets our internal rate of return criteria and there are sufficient funds to undertake it.</u>

6. <u>We should undertake the safety equipment upgrade project. This project meets our internal rate of return criteria and there are sufficient funds to undertake it.</u>

7. <u>We should undertake the solar electricity system project. This project meets our internal rate of return criteria and there are sufficient funds to undertake it.</u>

Ranking of Projects:

8. <u>The project with the highest rank is project A, the machine shop project.</u>

9. <u>The project with the second-highest rank is project A, the machine shop project.</u>

10. <u>The project with the third-highest rank is project A, the machine shop project.</u>

11. <u>The project with the fourth-highest rank is project A, the machine shop project.</u>

12. <u>The project with the lowest rank is project A, the machine shop project.</u>

Items for Analysis

<u>The net present value of the safety equipment upgrade is $200,000.</u>

1. Choose an option below:

   - [Original text] The net present value of the safety equipment upgrade is $200,000.
   - [Delete text]
   - The net present value of the safety equipment upgrade is $0.
   - The net present value of the safety equipment upgrade is $50,000.
   - The net present value of the safety equipment upgrade is $100,000.
   - The net present value of the safety equipment upgrade is $150,000.

<u>The payback period of the safety equipment upgrade is non-existent, as this project will not recoup the expenditure.</u>

2. Choose an option below:

   - [Original text] The payback period of the safety equipment upgrade is non-existent, as this project will not recoup the expenditure.
   - [Delete text]
   - The payback period of the safety equipment upgrade is 1 year.
   - The payback period of the safety equipment upgrade is 2 years.
   - The payback period of the safety equipment upgrade is 4 years.

- The payback period of the safety equipment upgrade is 8 years.
- The payback period of the safety equipment upgrade is 10 years.

We should undertake the machine shop project. This project meets our internal rate of return criteria and there are sufficient funds to undertake it.

3. Choose an option below:

- [Original text] We should undertake the machine shop project. This project meets our internal rate of return criteria and there are sufficient funds to undertake it.
- [Delete text]
- We should undertake the machine shop project. This project does not meet our internal rate of return criteria.
- We should undertake the machine shop project. While this project meets our internal rate of return criteria, we have insufficient funds for this project with the other projects we will undertake.
- We should not undertake the machine shop project. This project meets our internal rate of return criteria and there are sufficient funds to undertake it.
- We should not undertake the machine shop project. This project does not meet our internal rate of return criteria.
- We should not undertake the machine shop project. While this project meets our internal rate of return criteria, we have insufficient funds for this project with the other projects we will undertake.

We should undertake the press replacement project. This project meets our internal rate of return criteria and there are sufficient funds to undertake it.

4. Choose an option below:

- [Original text] We should undertake the press replacement project. This project meets our internal rate of return criteria and there are sufficient funds to undertake it.
- [Delete text]
- We should undertake the press replacement project. This project does not meet our internal rate of return criteria.
- We should undertake the press replacement project. While this project meets our internal rate of return criteria, we have insufficient funds for this project with the other projects we will undertake.
- We should not undertake the press replacement project. This project meets our internal rate of return criteria and there are sufficient funds to undertake it.
- We should not undertake the press replacement project. This project does not meet our internal rate of return criteria.
- We should not undertake the press replacement project. While this project meets our internal rate of return criteria, we have insufficient funds for this project with the other projects we will undertake.

We should undertake the forklifts replacement project. This project meets our internal rate of return criteria and there are sufficient funds to undertake it.

5. Choose an option below:

- [Original text] We should undertake the forklifts replacement project. This project meets our internal rate of return criteria and there are sufficient funds to undertake it.

- [Delete text]
- We should undertake the forklifts replacement project. This project does not meet our internal rate of return criteria.
- We should undertake the forklifts replacement project. While this project meets our internal rate of return criteria, we have insufficient funds for this project with the other projects we will undertake.
- We should not undertake the forklifts replacement project. This project meets our internal rate of return criteria and there are sufficient funds to undertake it.
- We should not undertake the forklifts replacement project. This project does not meet our internal rate of return criteria.
- We should not undertake the forklifts replacement project. While this project meets our internal rate of return criteria, we have insufficient funds for this project with the other projects we will undertake.

We should undertake the safety equipment project. This project meets our internal rate of return criteria and there are sufficient funds to undertake it.

6. Choose an option below:

- [Original text] We should undertake the safety equipment project. This project meets our internal rate of return criteria and there are sufficient funds to undertake it.
- [Delete text]
- We should undertake the safety equipment project. This project does not meet our internal rate of return criteria.
- We should undertake the safety equipment project. While this project meets our internal rate of return criteria, we have insufficient funds for this project with the other projects we will undertake.
- We should not undertake the safety equipment project. This project meets our internal rate of return criteria and there are sufficient funds to undertake it.
- We should not undertake the safety equipment project. This project does not meet our internal rate of return criteria.
- We should not undertake the safety equipment project. While this project meets our internal rate of return criteria, we have insufficient funds for this project with the other projects we will undertake.

We should undertake the solar electricity system project. This project meets our internal rate of return criteria and there are sufficient funds to undertake it.

7. Choose an option below:

- [Original text] We should undertake the solar electricity system project. This project meets our internal rate of return criteria and there are sufficient funds to undertake it.
- [Delete text]
- We should undertake the solar electricity system project. This project does not meet our internal rate of return criteria.
- We should undertake the solar electricity system project. While this project meets our internal rate of return criteria, we have insufficient funds for this project with the other projects we will undertake.
- We should not undertake the solar electricity system project. This project meets our internal rate of return criteria and there are sufficient funds to undertake it.

- We should not undertake the solar electricity system project. This project does not meet our internal rate of return criteria.
- We should not undertake the solar electricity system project. While this project meets our internal rate of return criteria, we have insufficient funds for this project with the other projects we will undertake.

The project with the highest rank is project A, the machine shop project.

8. Choose an option below:

- [Original text] The project with the highest rank is project A, the machine shop project.
- [Delete text]
- The project with the highest rank is project B, the press replacement project.
- The project with the highest rank is project C, the forklifts replacement project.
- The project with the highest rank is project D, the safety upgrade project.
- The project with the highest rank is project E, the solar electricity system project.

The project with the second-highest rank is project A, the machine shop project.

9. Choose an option below:

- [Original text] The project with the second-highest rank is project A, the machine shop project.
- [Delete text]
- The project with the second-highest rank is project B, the press replacement project.
- The project with the second-highest rank is project C, the forklifts replacement project.
- The project with the second-highest rank is project D, the safety upgrade project.
- The project with the second-highest rank is project E, the solar electricity system project.

The project with the third-highest rank is project A, the machine shop project.

10. Choose an option below:

- [Original text] The project with the third-highest rank is project A, the machine shop project.
- [Delete text]
- The project with the third-highest rank is project B, the press replacement project.
- The project with the third-highest rank is project C, the forklifts replacement project.
- The project with the third-highest rank is project D, the safety upgrade project.
- The project with the third-highest rank is project E, the solar electricity system project.

The project with the fourth-highest rank is project A, the machine shop project.

11. Choose an option below:

- [Original text] The project with the fourth-highest rank is project A, the machine shop project.
- [Delete text]
- The project with the fourth-highest rank is project B, the press replacement project.
- The project with the fourth-highest rank is project C, the forklifts replacement project.
- The project with the fourth-highest rank is project D, the safety upgrade project.
- The project with the fourth-highest rank is project E, the solar electricity system project.

The project with the lowest rank is project A, the machine shop project.

12. Choose an option below:

- [Original text] The project with the lowest rank is project A, the machine shop project.
- [Delete text]
- The project with the lowest rank is project B, the press replacement project.
- The project with the lowest rank is project C, the forklifts replacement project.
- The project with the lowest rank is project D, the safety upgrade project.
- The project with the lowest rank is project E, the solar electricity system project.

Exhibits

Excerpt from attorney's letter

Excerpt from Attorney's Letter
A new regulation (AW13908.78) goes into effect as of January 1, 20X1. Without additional safety measures, the acid wash department will have to discontinue operations. Please contact me for additional details.

Proposal from Sizzle Acid Protection, Inc.

Sizzle Acid Protection, Inc.

1200 Industrial Road
Fort Myers, FL
1-800-555-BURN

Acid remediation shower	$150,000
Acid neutralization system	47,000
Safety goggles (case of 144)	1,000
Employee safety signage	1,000
Initial training for employees	1,000
Total	$200,000

- Installation from December 10, 20X0, to December 25, 20X0, with 10 days of unlimited access from 7:00 a.m. to 6 p.m.
- Training finished by December 31, 20X1, on any non-holiday weekday of your choice.
- Guaranteed compliant with regulation AW13908.78 for 10 years, given no changes to the regulation.
- Offer valid until November 30.

Acid wash department selected information

Major Manufacturing - Acid Wash Department
Select Amounts ($ in 1,000s)
January 3, 20X0

Plant and Equipment	
Historical Cost	$2,000
Deprecation	1,500
Salvage Value	50

Anticipated amounts	20X1 (Year 1)	20X2–20X10 (Years 2-10)
Capacity	96%	98%
Sales dollars	683	709
Cost of goods sold	638	650
Sales less cost of goods sold	45	59

Accounting Department Worksheet Excerpts

Major Manufacturing Company
Comparison of Potential Investments
January 21, 20X0

Project	A	B	C	D	E
Investment	1,600,000	1,000,000	800,000	200,000	1,000,000
Estimated annual cash inflow (ACI)	381,500	323,500	159,400		65,000
Investment divided by ACI	4.2	3.1	5.0		15.4
Payback period (rounded)	4	3	5		15
IRR—see below (rounded)	20%	30%	15%		5%
Interest rate	10%	15%	20%	25%	30%
Present value of an annuity factor	6.1446	5.0188	4.1925	3.5705	3.0915
Present value of project A ACI	2,344,165	1,914,672	1,599,439	1,362,146	1,179,407
Net present value, project A	744,165	314,672	-561	-237,854	-420,593
Present value of project B ACI	1,987,778	1,623,582	1,356,274	1,155,057	1,000,100
Net present value, project B	987,778	623,582	356,274	155,057	100
Present value of project C ACI	979,449	799,997	668,285	569,138	492,785
Net present value, project C	179,449	-3	-131,716	-230,862	-307,215

Present Value Tables

Present Value of a $1 Single Sum (PVS)

Period	5%	10%	15%	20%	25%	30%
1	0.9524	0.9091	0.8696	0.8333	0.8000	0.7692
2	0.9070	0.8264	0.7561	0.6944	0.6400	0.5917
3	0.8638	0.7513	0.6575	0.5787	0.5120	0.4552
4	0.8227	0.6830	0.5718	0.4823	0.4096	0.3501
5	0.7835	0.6209	0.4972	0.4019	0.3277	0.2693
6	0.7462	0.5645	0.4323	0.3349	0.2621	0.2072
7	0.7107	0.5132	0.3759	0.2791	0.2097	0.1594
8	0.6768	0.4665	0.3269	0.2326	0.1678	0.1226
9	0.6446	0.4241	0.2843	0.1938	0.1342	0.0943
10	0.6139	0.3855	0.2472	0.1615	0.1074	0.0725
30	0.2314	0.0573	0.0151	0.0042	0.0012	0.0004
83	0.0174	0.0004	0.0000	0.0000	0.0000	0.0000

Present Value of a $1 Annuity (PVA)

Period	5%	10%	15%	20%	25%	30%
1	0.9524	0.9091	0.8696	0.8333	0.8000	0.7692
2	1.8594	1.7355	1.6257	1.5278	1.4400	1.3609
3	2.7232	2.4869	2.2832	2.1065	1.9520	1.8161
4	3.5460	3.1699	2.8550	2.5887	2.3616	2.1662
5	4.3295	3.7908	3.3522	2.9906	2.6893	2.4356
6	5.0757	4.3553	3.7845	3.3255	2.9514	2.6427
7	5.7864	4.8684	4.1604	3.6046	3.1611	2.8021
8	6.4632	5.3349	4.4873	3.8372	3.3289	2.9247
9	7.1078	5.7590	4.7716	4.0310	3.4631	3.0190
10	7.7217	6.1446	5.0188	4.1925	3.5705	3.0915
30	15.3725	9.4269	6.5660	4.9789	3.9950	3.3321
83	19.6514	9.9963	6.6666	5.0000	4.0000	3.3333

Document Review Simulation Solution

To: Miles Stand, CEO
From: Alice Abernathy
Re: Analysis of Investment Opportunities
Date: January 7, 20X0

There are five potential projects (A, B, C, D and E) being considered. The accounting staff and I have prepared the following table for your comparison. I have compared the investments, ranked them, and provided a recommendation for each. Please let me if I can be of any further assistance.

		Investment (all first year)	Net present value at 10%	Internal rate of return	Payback period (in years)
A.	Machine shop	$1,600,000	$744,000	20%	4
B.	Replace press	1,000,000	988,000	30%	3
C.	Replace forklifts	800,000	179,000	15%	5
D.	Upgrade safety equipment	200,000	150,000	25%	4
E.	Solar electricity system	1,000,000	(601,000)	5%	15
	Total	$4,600,000			

Adjustments:
1. The net present value of the safety equipment upgrade is $150,000.
2. The payback period of the safety equipment upgrade is 4 years.

Recommendations:
3. We should undertake the machine shop project. This project meets our internal rate of return criteria and there are sufficient funds to undertake it.
4. We should undertake the press replacement project. This project meets our internal rate of return criteria and there are sufficient funds to undertake it.
5. We should not undertake the forklifts replacement project. While this project meets our internal rate of return criteria, we have insufficient funds for this project with the other projects we will undertake.
6. We should undertake the safety equipment project. This project meets our internal rate of return criteria and there are sufficient funds to undertake it.
7. We should not undertake the solar electricity system project. This project does not meet our internal rate of return criteria.

Ranking of Projects:
8. The project with the highest rank is project B, the press replacement project.
9. The project with the second-highest rank is project D, the safety upgrade project.
10. The project with the third-highest rank is project A, the machine shop project.
11. The project with the fourth-highest rank is project C, the forklifts replacement project.
12. [Delete text]

Explanations

1. **The net present value of the safety equipment upgrade is $150,000.**

    Without the acid wash department upgrade, the entire department must cease operations; therefore, the sales and cost of goods sold of the acid wash department are included in determining the cash inflows of the project. The book value of the acid wash department is irrelevant. Deleting the text is inappropriate as the omission in the table should be corrected.

    The NPV of the project at 10% (the hurdle rate) is $150,000, and there is no concern about meeting the hurdle rate. Calculations follow.

    NPV of not upgrading: $50,000 (the salvage value)
    NPV of upgrading $149,804. This amount rounds to $150,000.

    The present value of the cash flows from the acid wash department for the next ten years offsets the upgrade cost. (As the information on costs shared by the manufacturing departments is not given, shared costs are not included in this determination, but they would make the cost of not upgrading greater, as these costs then would be borne by the other departments to a greater extent.)

    An annuity is defined as a series of equal payments. The cash inflows for the safety upgrade are not equal for all ten years. The cash inflows are equal for the second through the tenth years. To determine the present value of the cash inflows, they should be separated into two payment streams: (1) the present value of one payment of $45,000 at the end of one year [abbreviated as PVS ($45,000, 1 year)] and (2) the present value of nine equal payments of $59,000 for the second through tenth years [abbreviated as PVA ($59,000, years 2 through 10)]. To calculate the present value of nine equal payments of $59,000 for the second through tenth years, one may subtract the present value of a single sum of $59,000 for one year from the present value of an annuity of 59,000 for ten years. (There are other ways to separate the payment stream and arrive at the same amount for the present value of the cash inflows.)

    NPV (safety upgrade, 10%) = PVS ($45,000, 1 year, 10%) + PVA ($59,000, years 2 through 10, 10%) – investment = $40,910 + $308,894 - $200,000 = $149,804

    PVS ($45,000, 1 year, 10%) = ($45,000 × 0.9091) = $40,910
        PVS ($1, 1 year, 10%) = 0.9091 (from PVS table, 1 year row, 10% column)

    PVA ($59,000, years 2 through 10, 10%) = PVA ($59,000, 10 years, 10%) – PVS ($59,000, 1 year, 10%)
        PVA ($1, 10 years, 10%) = 6.1446 (from PVA table, 10-year row, 10% column)
        = ($59,000 × 6.1446) – ($59,000 × 0.9091)
        = $362,531 – $53,637 = $308,894

2. **The payback period of the safety equipment upgrade is 4 years.**

    Without the acid wash department upgrade, the entire department must cease operations; therefore, the sales and cost of goods sold of the acid wash department are included in determining viability of the project. The book value of the acid wash department is irrelevant. Deleting the text is inappropriate as the omission in the table should be corrected.

    The payback period is about 3.6 years. This amount rounds to 4 years. Calculations follow:

$200,000 cost – $45,000 year 1 cash flow = $155,000 amount remaining after 1st year.
$155,000 remaining investment / $59,000 cash flow for subsequent years = 2.6 years.
2.6 years +1st year = 3.6 years.

3. **(Project A) We should undertake the machine shop project. This project meets our internal rate of return criteria and there are sufficient funds to undertake it.**

   Given the high internal rate of return (IRR) and the sufficient funds, project A should be undertaken. The hurdle rate is 10%; this project has an internal rate of return (IRR) of 20%. The company can fund both projects B (at $1,000,000) and D (at $200,000)—both have higher IRRs—and still have sufficient funds available to invest in project A, which will require a $1,600,000 investment: $3,500,000 available – $1,000,000 project B – $200,000 project D = $2,300,000 funds available for project A.

4. **(Project B) We should undertake the press replacement project. This project meets our internal rate of return criteria and there are sufficient funds to undertake it.**

   Given the high internal rate of return and the sufficient funds, project B should be undertaken. The hurdle rate is 10%; this project has an internal rate of return (IRR) of 30%. As this project has the highest internal rate of return, Major would give this project top priority for funding (barring strategic considerations—which rarely appear on the exam and are not mentioned in this simulation).

5. **(Project C) We should not undertake the forklifts replacement project. While this project meets our internal rate of return criteria, we have insufficient funds for this project with the other projects we will undertake.**

   Major cannot fund all projects since it has only $3,500,000 and funding all projects would cost $4,600,000; Major does not want to issue new debt or equity. Although this project's internal rate of return (IRR) of 15% exceeds the hurdle rate of 10%, the funding of projects with higher IRRs (projects A at $1,600,000, B at $1,000,000, and D at $200,000) leaves insufficient funds available to invest in this project: $3,500,000 available – $1,600,000 project A – $1,000,000 project B – $200,000 project D = $700,000 < $800,000 needed for forklifts replacement.

6. **(Project D) We should undertake the safety equipment project. This project meets our internal rate of return criteria and there are sufficient funds to undertake it.**

   Given the high internal rate of return and the sufficient funds, project D should be undertaken. The hurdle rate is 10%; this project has an internal rate of return (IRR) of 25%. The company can fund project B at $1,000,000 (the only project with a higher IRR) and still have sufficient funds available to invest in project D, which will require a $200,000 investment: $3,500,000 available – $1,000,000 project B = $2,500,000 funds available for project D.

7. **(Project E) We should not undertake the solar electricity system project. This project does not meet our internal rate of return criteria.**

   The hurdle rate is 10%; this project has an internal rate of return (IRR) of 5%. As this project's internal rate of return (IRR) of 5% is beneath the hurdle rate of 10%, the issue of whether sufficient funds exist is irrelevant.

8. **The project with the highest rank is project B, the press replacement project.**

   Project B, the press replacement project, has an IRR of 30%—so it outranks all other projects under consideration. Project B's rank is higher than project D with an IRR of 25%, project A with an IRR of 20%, project C with an IRR of 15% and project E with an IRR of 5%. In this situation, the IRR model is appropriate to rank the projects. As the instructions were to rank each project that exceeds the hurdle rate, it is inappropriate to delete this text. While the profitability index is theoretically preferable to rank projects of differing sizes, in this scenario, the same ranking results from use of the profitability index and the IRR.

9. **The project with the second-highest rank is project D, the safety upgrade project.**

   Project D, the safety upgrade project, has an IRR of 25%, so it ranks beneath project B with an IRR of 30%, but higher than project A with an IRR of 20%, project C with an IRR of 15%, and project E with an IRR of 5%. In this situation, the IRR model is appropriate to rank the projects. As the instructions were to rank each project that exceeds the hurdle rate, it is inappropriate to delete this text.

10. **The project with the third-highest rank is project A, the machine shop project.**

    Project A, the machine shop project, has an IRR of 20%, so it ranks beneath projects with higher internal rates of return (IRR): project B with an IRR of 30% and project D with an IRR of 25%. This project has an IRR of 20%, so it ranks higher than project C with an IRR of 15% and project E with an IRR of 5%. In this situation, the IRR model is appropriate to rank the projects. As the instructions were to rank each project that exceeds the hurdle rate, it is inappropriate to delete this text.

11. **The project with the fourth-highest rank is project C, the forklifts replacement project.**

    Project C, the forklifts replacement project, has an IRR of 15%, so it ranks beneath projects with higher internal rates of return (IRR): project B with an IRR of 30%, project D with an IRR of 25% and project A with an IRR of 20%. In this situation, the IRR model is appropriate to rank the projects. As the instructions were to rank each project that exceeds the hurdle rate, it is inappropriate to delete this text.

12. **[Delete text]**

    As the instructions were to rank each project that exceeds the 10% hurdle rate, it is appropriate to delete this text—the rank is irrelevant for a project that does not meet minimum profitability criteria (5% IRR).

Lecture 3.26 – Financial Management – Class Questions – TBS

Written Communication 1

Several middle managers at SOMC Corp. have submitted detailed financial proposals outlining possible projects that top managers could choose to fund. Making these decisions, the top managers want to consider the total profitability of each project and the fact that SOMC's capital structure has changed in recent years. Write a memorandum to Olive McEvoy, the chief financial officer, explaining how the internal rate of return technique could be combined with SOMC's weighted-average cost of capital to help make their choices.

REMINDER: Your response will be graded for both technical content and writing skills. Technical content will be evaluated for information that is helpful to the intended reader and clearly relevant to the issue. Writing skills will be evaluated for development, organization, and the appropriate expression of ideas in professional correspondence. Use a standard business memo or letter format with a clear beginning, middle, and end. Do not convey information in the form of a table, bullet point list, or other abbreviated presentation.

To: Mrs. Olive McEvoy, CFO
    SOMC Corp.
From: CPA Candidate

Written Communication Solution 1

To: Mrs. Olive McEvoy, CFO
    SOMC Corp.
From: CPA Candidate

Thank you for your question regarding how the internal rate of return technique could be combined with SOMC's Weighted-average cost of capital to help make important business choices.

Top managers could choose among several possible projects and take into account SOMC's changing capital structure by computing each project's internal rate of return (IRR) and comparing those IRRs with the company's weighted-average cost of capital (WACC).

Companies may use several methods to help them choose among possible projects. However, some of those methods, like the payback period and the accounting rate of return, do not take into account total profitability. In contrast, the IRR method takes into account projects' total profitability by discounting all projected cash flows using a "hurdle" interest rate.

Companies may obtain funds from a variety of sources, including loans, bonds, preferred stock, and common stock. Since each source may have different costs, companies compute their WACCs to assess their overall (or weighted) cost of capital.

In turn, companies use their WACC to choose what projects to fund. Companies would not fund projects whose IRRs fall short of WACC since that would reduce common stockholders' wealth.

To choose which projects to fund, SOMC's top managers could apply techniques similar to those used by other companies, such as projecting cash flows, capital structures, and costs of funds; computing IRRs and WACCs, and choosing projects whose projected returns exceed the company's costs of capital. If you need any additional information or have questions, don't hesitate to contact me.

Sincerely,

CPA Candidate

_____

Written Communication 2

Grace Fulbright, a research analyst at Dragon Hedge Fund, is concerned that expected changes in interest rates may affect the performance of a portfolio that she is tracking. She has requested that you draft a memorandum explaining the yield curve, the theories that explain its shape, and how its shape may contain relevant information about the future.

REMINDER: Your response will be graded for both technical content and writing skills. Technical content will be evaluated for information that is helpful to the intended reader and clearly relevant to the issue. Writing skills will be evaluated for development, organization, and the appropriate expression of ideas in professional correspondence. Use a standard business memo or letter format with a clear beginning, middle, and end. Do not convey information in the form of a table, bullet point list, or other abbreviated presentation.

To: Miss Grace Fulbright, Research Analyst
    Dragon Hedge Fund
From: CPA Candidate

Written Communication Solution 2

To: Grace Fulbright, Research Analyst
    Dragon Hedge Fund
From: CPA Candidate

In our earlier conversation, you asked that I explain the yield curve, the theories that explain its shape, and how it may contain relevant information about the future.

The yield curve presents U.S. Treasury interest rates across various maturities. According to the liquidity preference theory, the yield curve should normally be upward sloping (longer-term interest rates being higher than shorter-term interest rates) since investors demand more compensation for long-term investments. According to the expectations theory, long-term interest rates reflect future expected short-term interest rates. According to the market segmentation theory, various participants in bond markets may focus on lending at different terms. Considering all theories jointly, an inverted yield curve (longer-term interest rates being lower than shorter-term interest rates) usually reflects investors' expectations of upcoming declines in economy-wide interest rates, usually because investors expect falling inflation rates or a recession.

The yield curve provides valuable information both about current interest rates and about investors' expectations of future economic conditions. If you have any further questions, please feel free to contact me.

Sincerely,

CPA Candidate

Written Communication 3

JAGD Corp. has long used as sources of capital all of the following: bank loans, new issues of bonds, and periodic issues of common stock. Joseph Heron, the Chief Financial Officer, has grown concerned about the company's growing debt levels and the fixed interest payments they entail. However, other managers are also concerned about diluting ownership in the company should a recently-developed product line prove particularly profitable. Write a memorandum explaining how issuing preferred stock may address all of those concerns.

REMINDER: Your response will be graded for both technical content and writing skills. Technical content will be evaluated for information that is helpful to the intended reader and clearly relevant to the issue. Writing skills will be evaluated for development, organization, and the appropriate expression of ideas in professional correspondence. Use a standard business memo or letter format with a clear beginning, middle, and end. Do not convey information in the form of a table, bullet point list, or other abbreviated presentation.

To: Mr. Joseph Heron, Chief Financial Officer
    JAGD Corp.
 From: CPA Candidate

Written Communication Solution 3

To: Mr. Joseph Heron, Chief Financial Officer
     JAGD Corp.
 From: CPA Candidate

Thank you for your question regarding sources of capital and how issuing preferred stock may work out well for your company. Issuing preferred stock would provide JAGD Corp with a source of funds that avoids both (1) the fixed payments and (2) diluting common stockholders' claims.

Companies may obtain funds from a variety of sources. Issuing new debt has the advantage that, should profits increase, existing common stockholders would reap those profits. However, debt has the disadvantage that if the project does not turn out to be successful, the company will still owe payments. Higher levels of debt increase risk. Issuing new common stock has the advantage that the company will not be legally committed to increased payments. If the company experiences higher profits, it will likely increase dividends, but not be legally required to do so. Disadvantages of issuing common stock include (1) that dividends are not tax deductible and (2) that new issues dilute profits.

Preferred stock combines advantages of debt and common stock. Should the company experience difficulties, it could postpone dividends to preferred stockholders. Should the company experience profits, payments to preferred stockholders will be capped.

To reduce its reliance on debt while not diluting profits, JAGD could issue preferred stock. Please feel free to contact me if you have any additional questions or concerns.

Sincerely,

CPA Candidate

Section 4 - Decision Making

Table of Contents

EXAM NOTE: Please refer to the AICPA BEC Blueprint in the Introduction of this book to find a listing of the representative tasks (and their associated skill levels—i.e., Remembering and Understanding, Application, and Analysis) that the candidate should be able to perform based on the knowledge obtained in this section.

Decision Making

Lecture 4.01 – Cost Accounting: Cost Definitions

A primary purpose of cost measurement is to allocate the costs of production (direct materials, direct manufacturing labor, and manufacturing overhead) to the units produced. It also provides important information for management decisions, such as product pricing decisions.

Cost Definitions

y = A + Bx   **[TC = Fixed + Var (X)]**

In this formula:
- The **y** is equal to **total cost** and is referred to as the *dependent variable* since its amount is dependent on the other factors.
- The **x** is equal to **volume** and is referred to as the *independent variable* since it can be increased or decreased at the company's discretion. This is also often referred to as the **cost driver** as the amount of costs incurred will be largely dependent on the volume of this variable.
- The **A** is equal to **fixed costs** and remains constant at any volume as long as the company is operating within a given range of volume.
- The **B** is equal to the **variable cost** per unit.

    Note: These cost assumptions only remain valid within the **Relevant Range**.

- **Mixed cost** (Semi-Variable – Fixed and Variable Component).
- **High-Low Method** – This method computes the slope for the variable rate based on the highest and lowest observations. The difference in cost is divided by the difference in activity to obtain the variable cost.

Hi-Low Method

Total Cost	Hours
$ 110,000	30,000
$ 80,000	20,000
$ 30,000	**/10,000 = $3hr**

Total Cost/Hours = $3 per hour
TC = F + V(X)

110 = F + 3(30,000)
 F = 20

TC = 20 + 3(X)

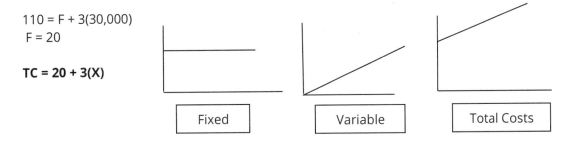

| Fixed | Variable | Total Costs |

Lecture 4.02 – Cost Classifications

Cost accounting refers to the calculation of the cost of manufactured inventory. There are three types of *Product costs* included:

- **Direct materials** – These are the materials that are physically included in the final manufactured product. For example, if a company is manufacturing metal paper clips, the only direct material is the metal. Some costs might include freight in, insurance in transit, storage, import duties and purchasing and receiving dept costs.
- **Direct labor** – These are the wages paid to those employees working with the direct materials to change them from their raw state to finished goods.
- **Overhead** – All other costs related to manufacturing are reported here. These include *indirect materials* (for example, sandpaper used to smooth edges of the paper clips and cleaning supplies to keep the assembly line in good condition) and *indirect labor* (for example, supervisors and maintenance workers in the factory building). Other examples of overhead include payroll taxes and fringe benefits for manufacturing employees, rent and depreciation on factory assets, lubricants, shop supplies and utilities to keep the factory in operation.

Direct materials and direct labor are known as the **prime costs** of manufacturing. Direct labor and overhead are known as the **conversion costs** of production.

Manufacturing costs are often called **product costs**, since they are matched to the product and not expensed until the product is sold. Costs that are not associated with manufacturing, such as selling, general, and administrative expenses, are often described as **period costs**, as they are *expensed* in the period incurred. *Normal spoilage* in a manufacturing process is treated as a product cost, while *abnormal spoilage* is expensed as a period cost.

- **Manufacturing costs** – Product costs (added to the cost of the finished product)
  - **DM** (Direct materials – an integral part of the product)
  - **DL** (Direct Labor – The labor to convert a raw material to a finished good)
  - **Manufacturing Overhead** (Mfg O/h) (all factory costs except DM & DL)
    - Indirect materials
    - Indirect labor
  - Prime costs   = DM + DL
  - Conversion costs = DL + MFG O/h
- **Non-MFG** costs – Period costs
  - Selling, General and Administrative costs (SG&A)
  - Marketing costs, freight out, re-handling costs
  - Abnormal spoilage
  - An expense in the period
- **Other Cost Classifications**
  - Relevant Costs - An anticipated future cost that differs among alternative plans.
  - Avoidable Costs – Costs that will not be incurred if a planned activity is changed or discontinued.
  - Marginal Costs – Additional costs incurred owing to one more output unit.

Cost Systems

- **Actual cost system** (DM, DL & Mfg O/h are all actual)
- **Standard cost system** (All costs based on standards)
- **Normal cost system** (DM & DL based on actual, Mfg O/h based on standards)

Lecture 4.03 – Predetermined Overhead Rate

Accounting for manufacturing overhead is an important part of a costing system. The distinguishing feature of manufacturing overhead is that while it must be incurred in order to produce goods, it cannot be directly traced to the final product as can direct material and direct manufacturing labor. Therefore, overhead must be applied, rather than directly charged, to goods produced.

$$\frac{\textbf{\textit{Estimated }} \textit{O/h costs }}{\textbf{\textit{Estimated }} \textit{DL \$/Hrs}} = \textit{Predetermined O/h rate X actual production} = \textbf{\textit{applied O/h}}$$

Applied O/h

WIP Control	300	
Factory O/h Applied		300

Actual O/h

Factory O/h Control	500	
Cash		500

Underapplied

Factory O/h Applied (a temporary account)	300	
Expense – *COGS* (Underapplied)	200	
Factory O/h Control		500

Lecture 4.04 – Flow of a Cost System

The **calculation of cost of sales** in a manufacturing company (one that manufactures the products that it sells) is more complicated than the equivalent computation for a merchandising company (one that purchases from outsiders the products that it sells).

- For a **merchandising** company, the calculation is:

  > Beginning inventory
  > + Purchases
  > = Cost of goods available for sale
  > - Ending inventory
  > = **Cost of goods sold**

- For a **manufacturing** company the *FLOW OF A COST SYSTEM* looks as follows:

Raw Materials	WIP	Finished Goods	Cost of Goods Sold
Beg RM	Beg WIP	Beg FG	CoGS
+ Purchases	+ DM Used	+ CoGM	+ Underapplied
= **Available**	+ DL	= **FG Available**	(Overapplied)
(Ending RM)	*Applied Mfg O/h*	(Ending FG)	= **CoGS**
= **Materials Used**	= **WIP Available**	= **CoGS**	
	(Ending WIP)		
	= **CoGM** (mfg/completed)		

To determine **Direct Materials used**, the calculation is:

Beginning direct materials inventory
+ Direct materials purchased
- Ending direct materials inventory
= Direct materials used

To determine **Cost of Goods Manufactured**, the calculation is:

Direct materials used
+ Direct labor incurred
+ Overhead applied
= Costs added to production
+ Beginning work-in-process inventory
- Ending work-in-process inventory
= Cost of goods manufactured

To determine **Cost of Goods Sold**

Beginning finished goods inventory
+ Cost of goods manufactured
= Cost of goods available for sale
- Ending finished goods inventory
= **Cost of Sales**

In the computation of cost of goods manufactured, **overhead is applied** to production. This is not the same as the actual overhead costs incurred during the period. The reason is that the matching principle requires an approach to overhead that systematically and rationally allocates it to the benefits, and companies normally do not have the same amount of production in every period.

> For example, assume a company is leasing factory equipment with rental payments of $500 per quarter ($2,000 per year) paid to the lessor. Over the course of the year, the company manufactures 1,000 units, so rental costs are $2,000 / 1,000 units = $2 per unit that year. Production is not paced evenly, however, since demand for the product varies through the year. Unit production and actual rent per unit each quarter are:
>
> | Quarter | 1st | 2nd | 3rd | 4th | Total |
> |---|---|---|---|---|---|
> | **Actual Rent** | 500 | 500 | 500 | 500 | 2,000 |
> | **Units** | 125 | 250 | 125 | 500 | 1,000 |
> | **Rent / Unit** | $4 | $2 | $4 | $1 | $2 |
>
> The problem with this approach is that the calculation of inventory cost per unit varies considerably from quarter to quarter, and it appears that rent is extremely high in the first and third quarters and extremely low in the fourth quarter. In fact, however, the rent is a stable amount. To follow the matching principle, more of the rent costs should be recognized in the periods of higher production. In this example, the simplest way is to apply rent at the rate of $2 per unit, which is the average over the course of the year:
>
> | Quarter | 1st | 2nd | 3rd | 4th | Total |
> |---|---|---|---|---|---|
> | **Units** | 125 | 250 | 125 | 500 | 1,000 |
> | **Rent / Unit** | $2 | $2 | $2 | $2 | $2 |
> | **Applied Rent** | 250 | 500 | 250 | 1,000 | 2,000 |
>
> In the first and third quarters, only $250 of rent is applied, even though $500 is paid, so the rent is underapplied by $250 in both of those quarters. In the fourth quarter, $1,000 is applied, even though $500 is paid, so the rent is overapplied by $500. By the end of the year, however, total applied and actual rent are the same, as long as actual production equals the number of units estimated at the beginning of the year, when the application rate of $2 was determined.

Overhead costs are not usually applied based on *units of production*, the method used in the example. One reason is that it can be difficult to determine the number of units that have been produced, especially with three different types of inventory: raw materials, work-in-process, and finished goods. Another is that most overhead costs are closely related to direct labor, so this might be a more accurate way to match costs. For example, payroll taxes and fringe benefit costs are overhead costs clearly associated with the amount of labor and not necessarily the productivity of those laborers. By applying overhead based on direct labor, it is more likely that applied overhead will be close to actual overhead.

The most common base selected is **direct labor hours**, which is usually easy for the company to determine, since these hours are necessary for wage computations. A company may also use **direct labor dollars**, though this requires the added step of applying wage rates to hours, and is not as popular as a method of allocating overhead as a result. For a company that is highly automated, overhead is occasionally computed based on **machine hours**, but this is quite rare on the CPA exam.

For example, assume the company paying $2,000 of rent on factory equipment and expecting to produce 1,000 units during the year also estimates that it requires approximately 2 hours for each unit to be produced, and expected wage rates to average $10 per hour. If the company chooses to apply overhead based on *direct labor hours*, then it will use:

$2,000 / 2,000 hours = $1 per direct labor hour

If the company chooses *direct labor dollars*, the result is:

$2,000 / $20,000 = 10% of direct labor cost

Lecture 4.05 – Cost Accounting – Class Questions

1. Sender, Inc. estimates parcel mailing costs using data shown on the chart below.

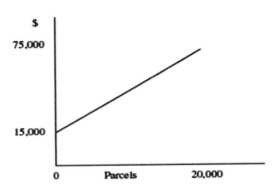

   What is Sender's estimated cost for mailing 12,000 parcels?

   a. $36,000
   b. $45,000
   c. $51,000
   d. $60,000

2. In a traditional job-costing system, issuing indirect materials to production increases which account?

   a. Materials (stores) control.
   b. Work in process control.
   c. Manufacturing overhead control.
   d. Manufacturing overhead applied.

3. In developing a predetermined variable factory overhead application rate for use in a process costing system, which of the following could be used in the numerator and denominator?

	Numerator	**Denominator**
a.	Actual variable factory overhead	Actual machine hours
b.	Actual variable factory overhead	Estimated machine hours
c.	Estimated variable factory overhead	Actual machine hours
d.	Estimated variable factory overhead	Estimated machine hours

Items 4 through 6 are based on the following information pertaining to Jobe Manufacturing Co.'s operations:

Inventories	Beginning	Ending
Direct materials	$45,000	$37,500
Work in process	22,500	15,000
Finished goods	67,500	90,000

Additional information for the period:

Direct materials purchased	$105,000
Direct manufacturing labor payroll	75,000
Direct manufacturing labor rate per hour	12.00
Factory overhead rate per direct labor hour	16.00

4. Prime cost was

    a. $112,500
    b. $150,000
    c. $180,000
    d. $187,500

5. Conversion cost was

    a. $112,500
    b. $175,000
    c. $180,000
    d. $212,500

6. For the month of March 20X3, cost of goods manufactured was

    a. $272,500
    b. $280,000
    c. $287,500
    d. $295,000

7. Birk Co. uses a job order cost system. The following debits (credits) appeared in Birk's work in process account for the month of April 20X3:

April	Description	Amount
1	Balance	$ 4,000
30	Direct materials	24,000
30	Direct manufacturing labor	16,000
30	Factory overhead	12,800
30	To finished goods	(48,000)

Birk applies overhead to production at a predetermined rate of 80% of direct manufacturing labor costs. Job No. 5, the only job still in process on April 30, 20X3, has been charged with direct manufacturing labor of $2,000. What was the amount of direct materials charged to Job No. 5?

    a. $ 3,000
    b. $ 5,200
    c. $ 8,800
    d. $24,000

Class Solutions

1. (c) When no units are mailed, the $15,000 in costs incurred would all be fixed costs. As a result, when 20,000 parcels are mailed, $15,000 of the total cost is fixed and the remaining $60,000 is variable, indicating that variable costs are $60,000/20,000 or $3 per parcel mailed. If 12,000 parcels are mailed, variable costs will be 12,000 x $3 or $36,000 and fixed costs will be $15,000 for a total of $51,000.

2. (c) In a traditional job-costing system, indirect costs are included in manufacturing overhead. When overhead is incurred, it is recognized with an increase to manufacturing overhead control. Answer (a) is incorrect because materials control would be increased when materials are purchased. Answer (b) is incorrect because work in process control is increased when direct materials or direct labor are charged to units being produced and when manufacturing overhead is applied to production. Answer (d) is incorrect because manufacturing overhead applied is increased when manufacturing overhead is allocated to units being produced.

3. (d) A predetermined variable factory overhead application rate is developed at the beginning of the period, prior to actual overhead costs being incurred and prior to the actual machine usage. As a result, it is calculated using estimated amounts for variable factory overhead in the numerator and machine hours in the denominator.

4. (d) Prime cost is the total of direct materials used and direct labor. Direct labor is given as $75,000. Adding direct materials purchased of $105,000 to beginning inventory of $45,000 gives direct materials available of $150,000. This is reduced by ending direct materials inventory of $37,500 to give direct materials used of $112,500. Prime costs are, therefore, $75,000 + $112,500 or $187,500.

5. (b) Conversion cost is direct labor plus manufacturing overhead applied. Direct labor is given as $75,000. At a direct labor rate of $12 per hour, 6,250 ($75,000/$12) hours were spend. Manufacturing overhead is applied at $16 per hour or ($16 x 6,250) or $100,000, resulting in total conversion costs of $75,000 + $100,000 or $175,000.

6. (d) Cost of goods manufactured is the cost of those goods that were completed during the period. It is calculated as beginning work-in-process inventory plus manufacturing costs incurred for the period, minus ending work-in-process inventory. Manufacturing costs incurred during the period consist of raw materials used, direct labor, and factory overhead. Raw materials used is beginning raw materials inventory of $45,000 plus purchases of $105,000 less ending inventory of $37,500 for a net amount of $112,500. If direct labor is $75,000 at a rate of $12 per hour, factory overhead would be calculated as $75,000/$12 x $16 or $100,000. Total manufacturing costs are $112,500 + $75,000 + $100,000 or $287,500. This is added to beginning work-in-process of $22,500 and reduced by ending work-in-process of $15,000 to give cost of goods manufactured of $295,000.

7. (b) Ending work in process, which consists exclusively of Job 5, is $4,000 + 24,000 + 16,000 + 12,800 - 48,000 or $8,800. Of that, conversion costs are $3,600, consisting of direct labor of $2,000 and manufacturing costs of (80% x $2,000) $1,600. As a result, the cost of direct materials is the difference of $8,800 - $3,600 or $5,200.

Lecture 4.06 – Variable & Absorption Costing

2 Income statements for a Manufacturing Co.

Absorption/Full costing/ GAAP	Direct/ Variable/Prime/CM/Internal
Sales	Sales
(Var COGS)	(Var COGS)
(Fix COGS)	(Var SGA)
Gross margin	CM (contribution margin)
(Var SGA)	**(Fix Mfg. Costs)**
(Fix SGA)	(Fix SGA)
Operating Income	Operating Income

Variable and absorption costing methods of accounting for fixed manufacturing overhead differ: under variable costing, fixed manufacturing overhead is expensed whereas under absorption costing, such amounts are treated as a product cost and inventoried. The treatment of fixed manufacturing overhead often results in different levels of net income between the absorption and variable costing methods. The differences are timing differences, which result from recognizing the fixed manufacturing overhead as an expense.

- **Variable costing** - *In the period incurred*
- **Absorption costing**- In the period in which the units to which fixed overhead has been applied are *sold*

Inventoriable Costs	Absorption Costing	Variable Costing
DM	Y	Y
DL	Y	Y
V O/h	Y	Y
F O/h	Y	**N**
V SGA	N	**N**
F SGA	N	**N**

Under direct (Variable) costing, whether a cost is included in inventory has nothing to do with whether it is expensed as a variable or fixed cost. Variable selling expenses are not included in inventory, but are included in the computation of contribution margin. Variable manufacturing costs are included in inventory and are included in the computation of contribution margin. Neither fixed manufacturing costs nor fixed selling expenses are included in inventory nor in the computation of contribution margin.

The calculation of operating income on a manufacturing company's income statement normally looks as follows, using what is commonly called **absorption costing:**

> Sales
> - Cost of sales
> = **Gross profit**
> - Selling and administrative expenses
> = Operating income

For internal purposes, a company may also prepare an income statement using the **direct costing** approach:

> Sales
> - Variable costs
> = **Contribution margin**
> - Fixed costs
> = Operating income

The direct costing statement differs in two ways: (1) variable selling expenses are matched to sales along with the variable manufacturing costs and (2) fixed overhead costs are expensed as incurred along with the fixed selling and administrative expenses. The first difference doesn't affect total operating income, since selling expenses are the result of sales, and will be the same amount in either statement. The second difference does affect total operating income, however, and is the reason direct costing statements *violate GAAP* and may only be used internally.

> For example, assume a company incurred $100 of fixed overhead during the year and produced 100 units, applying fixed overhead at the rate of $1 per unit produced (for simplicity, we're assuming overhead is applied based on units and not direct labor, but the results are effectively the same either way). If the company sells only 90 of the 100 units produced, then only $90 of the fixed overhead will be in cost of sales that year, and the remaining $10 will be absorbed into ending inventory on the balance sheet when using absorption costing. Under direct costing, however, the entire $100 is expensed as a fixed cost, causing operating income to be understated by $10. Direct costing normally understates income as inventory levels rise and overstates income as inventory levels fall, due to the different treatment of fixed overhead costs.

The difference in operating income will be equal to the fixed manufacturing overhead per unit multiplied by the increase or decrease in the units in inventory.
- When ending inventory *equals* beginning inventory, both methods will result in the same operating income.
- When ending inventory is *greater than* beginning inventory, absorption costing will result in higher operating income.
- When ending inventory is *lower than* beginning inventory, variable costing will result in higher operating income.

Lecture 4.07 – Variable & Absorption Costing – Class Questions

8. Cay Co.'s 20X1 fixed manufacturing overhead costs totaled $100,000, and variable selling costs totaled $80,000. Under direct costing, how should these costs be classified?

	Period costs	Product costs
a.	$ 0	$180,000
b.	$ 80,000	$100,000
c.	$100,000	$ 80,000
d.	$180,000	$ 0

9. Using the variable costing method, which of the following costs are assigned to inventory?

	Variable selling and administrative costs	Variable factory overhead costs
a.	Yes	Yes
b.	Yes	No
c.	No	No
d.	No	Yes

10. At the end of Killo Co.'s first year of operations, 1,000 units of inventory remained on hand. Variable and fixed manufacturing costs per unit were $90 and $20, respectively. If Killo uses absorption costing rather than variable (direct) costing, the result would be a higher pretax income of

 a. $0
 b. $20,000
 c. $70,000
 d. $90,000

Class Solutions

8. (d) Under direct costing, all fixed costs, including fixed manufacturing overhead, is considered a period cost. In addition, selling costs are always treated as period costs. As a result, the entire $180,000 would be reported as period costs.

9. (d) Under variable costing, variable manufacturing costs, including direct materials, direct labor, and variable manufacturing overhead, are treated as product costs and assigned to inventory. Fixed manufacturing costs and all selling, general, and administrative costs, variable or fixed, are recognized as expenses in the period incurred.

10. (b) Under the variable method, the $20,000 of fixed cost was charged to income, whereas with absorption costing the fixed costs were absorbed into inventory. Therefore, absorption costing results in a pretax income that is higher by $20,000. Under variable, or direct, costing, all fixed costs as well as all selling, general, and administrative costs are recognized as expense as incurred. This would include the $20,000 (1,000 units @ $20 per unit) of fixed manufacturing overhead incurred. Under absorption costing the $20,000 of fixed manufacturing overhead is included in inventory rather than expense, increasing income in that period by $20,000.

Lecture 4.08 – Cost Volume Profit

Cost-volume-profit (CVP) analysis provides management with profitability estimates at all levels of production in the relevant range (the normal operating range).

In making decisions about offering new products or services, companies often rely on cost-volume-profit analysis. The exam tests *three common applications* of this technique:
- Determining sales needed to break even
- Determining sales needed to achieve a particular dollar profit
- Determining sales needed to achieve a particular return on sales

> **Break Even in Units** $= \dfrac{\text{Fixed costs + Profit (Loss)}}{\text{SP-VC(CM)}}$

> **Break Even in Sales dollars** $= \dfrac{\text{Fixed costs + Profit (Loss)}}{\text{CM Ratio (cm/sales price)}}$

The information needed to apply this form of analysis is typically obtained from an income statement prepared using the direct costing approach.

 For example, assume a budget has been prepared for a product based on estimated sales of 100 units per period, selling price of $10 per unit, variable costs of $6 per unit, and fixed costs of $300 per period. A direct costing statement based on this information follows:

Units	100
Sales (10)	1,000
-Variable costs (6)	600
Contribution margin (4)	400
-Fixed costs	300
Operating profit	100

The **breakeven point** occurs when the operating profit is $0. Since fixed costs are always $300, contribution margin must also be $300 in order to achieve breakeven. To figure out the number of units that must be sold for contribution margin to equal fixed costs, the following formula is used:

Fixed costs / Contribution margin per unit = $300 / $4 = 75 units.

To figure out the number of dollars of sales needed, contribution margin can be expressed as a percentage of sales (or contribution margin per dollar of sales). In this information, that is 40% (either $4 / $10 or $400 / $1,000), so the formula is:

Fixed costs / Contribution margin percentage = $300 / 40% = $750.

Of course, these are related, since 75 units at a $10 selling price equals $750 in sales. Let's look at the breakeven statement next to the original budget:

Units	100	75
Sales (10)	1,000	750
-Variable costs (6)	600	450
Contribution margin (4)	400	300
-Fixed costs	300	300
Operating profit	100	-0-

Determining the level at which a **desired profit** is achieved is actually not much more complicated than determining the breakeven point. All that is needed is to increase contribution margin so that it exceeds the fixed costs by the desired profit. The formula for the sales in units is:

(Fixed costs + Desired profit) / Contribution margin per unit

The formula for the sales in dollars is:

(Fixed costs + Desired profit) / Contribution margin percentage

In the example, the sales in units needed for a $20 profit are:
($300 + $20) / $4 = $320 / $4 = 80 units.

Again, let's list the income statement next to the previous ones for budget and breakeven point.

Units	100	75	80
Sales (10)	1,000	750	800
- Variable costs (6)	600	450	480
Contribution margin (4)	400	300	320
- Fixed costs	300	300	300
Operating profit	100	-0-	20

Finally, to determine the point at which a **desired return on sales** is achieved, use an algebraic approach to desired profit:

(Fixed costs + Desired profit) / Contribution margin % = Sales

With a desired return on sales of 10%, the equation is expressed as:
$$(300 + 10\% \text{ of sales}) / 40\% = \text{Sales or}$$
$$(300 + .1x) / .4 = x \text{ or}$$
$$300 + .1x = .4x \text{ or}$$
$$300 = .3x \text{ or}$$
$$1,000 = x$$

This is the sales level of the original budget above, with a $100 profit that is 10% of sales.

The **Margin of Safety** is the excess of budgeted (or Actual) sales over the break-even volume of sales. It states the amount by which sales can drop before losses begin to be incurred in an organization. If, for example, a company had sales of $3,500,000 and a breakeven volume of $3,200,000, the margin of safety would be $300,000.

When a company that is operating at a profit experiences an increase in costs, whether variable or fixed, the breakeven point is increased and the margin of safety is decreased.

The Margin of Safety can also be expressed in percentage form. This percentage is obtained by dividing the Margin of Safety in dollar terms by total sales.
Total sales – Break even sales = *Margin of Safety*

Lecture 4.09 – Cost Volume Profit – Class Questions

11. At the breakeven point, the contribution margin equals total

    a. Variable costs.
    b. Sales revenues.
    c. Selling and administrative costs.
    d. Fixed costs.

12. Breakeven analysis assumes that over the relevant range

    a. Unit revenues are nonlinear.
    b. Unit variable costs are unchanged.
    c. Total costs are unchanged.
    d. Total fixed costs are nonlinear.

13. Del Co. has fixed costs of $100,000 and breakeven sales of $800,000. What is its projected profit at $1,200,000 sales?

    a. $ 50,000
    b. $150,000
    c. $200,000
    d. $400,000

14. In the budgeted profit/volume chart below, EG represents a two-product company's profit path. EH and HG represent the profit paths of products #1 and #2, respectively.

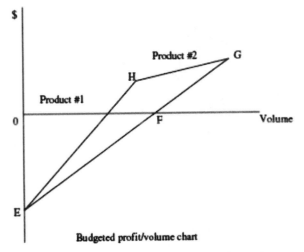

Budgeted profit/volume chart

Sales prices and cost behavior were as budgeted, actual total sales equaled budgeted sales, and there were no inventories. Actual profit was greater than budgeted profit. Which product had actual sales in excess of budget, and what margin does OE divided by OF represent?

	Product with excess sales	**OE/OF**
a.	#1	Contribution margin
b.	#1	Gross margin
c.	#2	Contribution margin
d.	#2	Gross margin

Class Solutions

11. (d) The contribution margin is the difference between sales revenues and all variable costs. When the contribution margin is equal to fixed costs, that means that sales revenue is equal to all variable and fixed costs and that the entity has achieved breakeven. Answer (a) is incorrect because if the contribution margin is equal to variable costs, this simply indicates that sales revenue is equal to 2 times variable costs, but that will only be breakeven if variable costs also equal fixed costs. Answer (b) is incorrect because the contribution margin cannot equal sales revenue unless there are no variable costs. Answer (c) is incorrect because some selling and administrative costs are variable and have already been deducted in calculating the contribution margin. This will only be equal to breakeven if the variable selling and administrative expenses were equal to fixed manufacturing costs.

12. (b) Breakeven analysis assumes that all costs and revenues are linear and that, over the relevant range, both fixed costs in total and variable costs per unit will remain constant. This includes the assumption that revenue per unit also will remain unchanged. Total costs do not remain unchanged since variable costs will increase or decrease as volume increases or decreases.

13. (a) If breakeven is when sales are $800,000 and fixed costs are $100,000, variable costs are the difference of $700,000 or 7/8 of sales. If sales were to increase to $1,200,000, variable costs, at 7/8, would be $1,050,000, resulting in a contribution margin of $150,000. This is reduced by fixed costs of $100,000 to give a profit of $50,000.

14. (a) If sales prices, cost behavior, and actual total sales were the same as budgeted, but profit was higher, that indicates that the product mix, the ratio of the products sold, must have changed. A higher profit indicates that higher quantities of the product with the higher contribution margin were sold and lower quantities of the product with the lower contribution margin were sold. The contribution margin is represented by the slope of the profit path, which is steeper for product #1 than for #2, indicating it has a higher profit and more of #1 would have been sold. The line OE represents fixed costs, which would be the loss at a volume of 0, while the line OF represents the volume at which profit is 0, indicating that the contribution margin is equal to fixed costs. As a result, OE/OF represents the contribution margin.

Lecture 4.10 – Special Decisions

Less common applications involve mere variations of the cost-volume-profit techniques:

- Determining whether a special order should be accepted.
- Determining whether to make or buy a product.
- Determining whether to sell a product or process it further.
- Determining whether to scrap or rework defective products.
- Determining whether to retain or eliminate a product line or division.

The general rule for these situations is to consider only the *relevant* revenues and costs (i.e., the revenues and costs that change between the alternatives). If the facility is at full capacity, an opportunity cost—the benefit (i.e., revenues – costs) forgone for an alternative not chosen—is involved.

The **Special Order** type of question typically involves an order at a lower than usual price, sometimes reducing regular sales. If the facility is not at full capacity, accepting a special order at a price lower than the absorption unit cost (including fixed costs) may make sense, as long as the variable costs are covered, because the total fixed costs already are borne by the regular units. When regular sales are impacted, this will not necessarily be the case.

For example, Flexco originally prepared an annual budget for a product based on estimated sales of 100,000 units with a per unit sales price of $100, variable manufacturing costs of $35, fixed manufacturing costs of $15, variable selling and administrative (S&A) costs of $20, and fixed S&A costs of $10, resulting in per unit operating income of $20. This budget does not use Flexco's full annual capacity of 105,000 units and neither increases nor decreases year-end inventory counts.

Big Mart offers to buy 10,000 units at $80 per unit; filling this order will not affect regular sale prices nor change fixed manufacturing costs and fixed and variable selling and administrative expenses; however, it will eliminate 5,000 units of regular sales, since Flexo has insufficient capacity for them. An analysis of revenues and costs that change shows that Flexo will increase its operating income by accepting the order:

Revenues due to special order ($80/unit x 10,000 units)	$800,000
Less: special order manufacturing costs ($35/unit x 10,000 units)	(350,000)
Less: reduction in revenues from regular sales ($100/unit x 5,000 units)	(500,000)
Plus: reduction in variable manufacturing costs ($35/unit x 5,000 units)	175,000
Plus: reduction in variable S&A costs ($20/unit x 5,000 units)	100,000
Increase in operating income	**$225,000**

A comparison of financial statements (*$ in 1,000s) for the two options will confirm this:

	Regular sales only			Total	=	Regular sales w/ order			+	Special order		
	#	$/#	$*	$*		#	$/#	$*		#	$/#	$*
Sales	100,000	100	10,000	10,300		95,000	100	9,500		10,000	80	800
Var. mfg.	100,000	35	3,500	3,675		95,000	35	3,325		10,000	35	350
Var. S&A	100,000	20	2,000	1,900		95,000	20	1,900				
Cont. margin			4,500	4,725				4,275				450
Fixed mfg.	100,000	15	1,500	1,500				1,500				
Fixed S&A	100,000	10	1,000	1,000				1,000				
Oper. Inc.			2,000	2,225				1,775				450

The fact that fixed manufacturing costs amount to $15 per unit and fixed S&A expenses amount to $10 per unit at a volume of 100,000 units indicates that fixed manufacturing costs are $1,500,000 per period, and fixed S&A expenses are $1,000,000 per period, regardless of the number of units produced and sold and regardless of whether or not a special order is accepted.

If Flexo does not accept the order and continues at a volume of 100,000 units at regular prices, revenues, costs and expenses will be as follows:

Revenue (100,000 units x $100/unit)	$10,000,000
Variable manufacturing costs (100,000 units x $35/unit)	3,500,000
Variable S&A expenses (100,000 units x $20/unit)	2,000,000
*Contribution margin	4,500,000
Fixed manufacturing costs ($1,500,000)	1,500,000
Fixed S&A expenses ($1,000,000)	1,000,000
Operating Income	$ 2,000,000

If Flexo does accept the order, the volume will consist of 10,000 units included in the special order and 95,000 units to be sold through normal channels, for a total of 105,000 units. Revenues, costs and expenses will be as follows:

Revenue regular (95,000 units x $100/unit)	$9,500,000
Revenue special (10,000 units x $80/unit)	800,000
Variable manufacturing costs (105,000 units x $35/unit)	3,675,000
Variable S&A expenses (95,000 units x $20 /unit)	1,900,000
*Contribution margin	4,725,000
Fixed manufacturing costs ($1,500,000)	1,500,000
Fixed S&A expenses ($1,000,000)	1,000,000
Operating Income	$2,225,000

*You might realize that this calculation can be further simplified. The contribution margin represents the amount that the sale of a unit contributes to covering fixed costs or, once covered, to profit. It is measured as the difference between the revenue that will be generated by the sale of a unit and the variable costs that will be incurred in relation to it.

Flexo's units sold at the normal sales price of $100 have a contribution margin of $45 per unit, taking into account variable manufacturing costs of $35 per unit and variable S&A expense of $20, for a total of $55. The units sold under the special order will have a sales price of $80 per unit and variable manufacturing costs of $35, resulting in a contribution margin that is also $45 per unit. There will be no variable S&A costs since the customer initiated the transaction and incremental selling and administrative expenses were not necessary.

As a result, if Flexo does not accept the special order, the contribution margin will be 100,000 units at $45, for a total of $4,500,000. If the special order is accepted, the contribution margin will consist of 95,000 units at $45 per unit, and 10,000 units at a contribution margin of $45 per unit, for a total of 105,000 units at $45 per unit, which is $4,725,000, an increase of $225,000.

Fixed costs, including both fixed manufacturing costs and fixed S&A expense, remain the same regardless of the number of units produced or sold as long as the volume falls within the entity's normal range of operations, referred to as the relevant range.

The **Make or Buy** type of question typically involves a component that can be produced in-house or by a subcontractor. The Sell or Process Further type of question typically involves a component that can be sold in an early stage or processed further before being sold. The Scrap or Rework type of question typically involves defective parts that could be either reworked and sold or merely sold for scrap. In analyzing these situations, add the opportunity cost of using the facilities for another purpose (if any) to the in-house costs.

> For example, Miller & Baker Company (MBC) uses 13,000 units of Part 1322 monthly. The per unit costs are $4 for direct material, $2 for direct labor, $2 for variable overhead, and $4 for fixed overhead (FOH). If MBC buys the parts, they will cost $13 apiece, but the company will eliminate $3 of FOH costs per unit. The remaining FOH remains regardless of whether MBC purchases or makes the part. The facilities used to manufacture Part 1322 alternatively could be used to manufacture Part 668 at a monthly profit of $50,000. An analysis of revenues and costs that differ between the two options indicates that it is more profitable to buy the part and use the facilities to manufacture Part 668:
>
> | | Make | Buy |
> | --------------------------------------- | --------- | --------- |
> | Direct material | $4 | |
> | Direct labor | 2 | |
> | Variable overhead | 2 | |
> | Fixed overhead subject to elimination* | 3 | |
> | Relevant unit costs | $11 | $13 |
> | Units | 13,000 | 13,000 |
> | Relevant costs for 13,000 units | $143,000 | $169,000 |
> | Opportunity cost of making Part 1322 | 50,000 | -0- |
> | Total relevant costs | $193,000 | $169,000 |
>
> *Note: The remaining $1 of FOH that cannot be eliminated is irrelevant to this decision.
>
> If the alternative equipment use for Part 668 were not an option ($50,000 opportunity cost), it would be $26,000 ($169,000 – $143,000) more profitable to make the part in-house; however, because of the $50,000 opportunity cost, it is $24,000 ($193,000 – $169,000) more profitable to buy the part and use the equipment to make Part 668.

Again, the **Sell or Process Further** type of question typically involves a component that can be sold in an early stage or processed further before being sold.

> For example, Sailor & Pirate Company (SPC) makes products X, Y, and Z jointly. Each product may be processed further or sold at the split-off point. Joint production costs of $100,000 are allocated using the relative-sales-value at split-off method. Additional per-unit information is as follows.
>
> | | X | Y | Z |
> | ------------------------- | ----- | ----- | ---- |
> | Sales value at spilt-off | $25 | $50 | $10 |
> | Additional processing cost| 20 | 10 | 15 |
> | Final sales value | $100 | $60 | $20 |

An analysis of revenues and costs that change for the two alternatives for each product indicates that it is most profitable to process product X further and sell product Z. For product Y, there is no difference.

	X	Y	Z
Final sales value	$100	$60	$20
Less: Sales value at spilt-off	25	50	10
Incremental revenue	75	10	10
Less: Incremental costs	20	10	15
Additional profit (loss)	$55	$0	$(5)

By processing product X further at a cost of $20, revenue will increase by $75 ($100 – $25), resulting in a net benefit of $55 ($75 revenue increase – $20 cost increase), making it more profitable to process product X further before sale. By processing product Y further at a price of $10, revenue will increase by $10 per unit ($60 – $50), resulting in no net difference between processing product Y further and selling it at the split-off point ($10 revenue increase – $10 cost increase). By processing product Z further at a cost of $15, revenue will increase by $10 per unit ($20 – $10), resulting in a net reduction in income of $5 per unit ($10 revenue increase – $15 cost increase). Product Z will not be processed further.

The joint production costs are irrelevant to this decision, as they will remain the same regardless of whether any of the products are processed further or not.

The **Scrap or Rework** type of question is another instance of sell or process further.

> For example, Sneak & Rogue Company (SRC) has 20,000 defective units of product Loot with a total cost of $18,000. As scrap, they can be sold for $1,500. If they are reworked for $10,000, they may be sold for $12,000. The rework option is the more profitable alternative, contributing more to net income than the scrap option.
>
> | | Scrap | Rework |
> | ------------------------ | ------- | ------- |
> | Incremental revenue | $1,500 | $12,000 |
> | Less: Incremental costs | 0 | 10,000 |
> | Additional profit (loss) | $1,500 | $ 2,000 |
>
> The total cost of the defective units before rework is irrelevant; this sunk cost is the same between the two alternatives.

The **Retain or Eliminate** type of question typically involves an unprofitable product line or division. One must consider whether the at-risk line or division helps the other more profitable divisions cover the fixed costs—generally allocated from corporate or administrative sources—that do not cease with the product line or division elimination. In other words, in some cases, the reason the product line or division is not profitable is due to costs allocated to that product line or division that will continue to be incurred after the product line is discontinued or the division is closed. If, for example, the CEO's salary is allocated among all four products that an entity manufactures, and one of the four products is discontinued, the CEO's salary will not be reduced proportionately. It will, instead, be allocated among the remaining products. As a result, when performing such an analysis, only those revenues and costs that will change should be considered.

For example, Roving Epicure Company (REC) has four product lines: quality fruits, game meats, fine wines, and fine cheeses. For the past three years, the fruit line has seen dwindling profits; this trend seems unlikely to reverse. Additional information (in 1,000s) is as follows.

Product line	Fruit	Meat	Wine	Cheese
Revenue	$4,000	$2,000	$6,000	$2,000
Variable costs	3,000	1,000	2,000	1,000
Contribution margin	1,000	1,000	4,000	1,000
Avoidable fixed costs	200	400	2,000	300
Unavoidable fixed costs	1,000	200	400	100
Net income	$(200)	$400	$1,600	$600

While the $200,000 of net loss from the fruit line can be eliminated, the $1,000,000 unavoidable fixed costs borne by the fruit line cannot be eliminated. These fixed costs remain to be allocated to the remaining product lines. In other words, even though the fruit product line appears to be unprofitable, it should be retained. If the fruit line is eliminated, revenues will be reduced by $4,000,000. Variable costs will be reduced by $3,000,000, and avoidable fixed costs of $200,000 will no longer be incurred. The unavoidable fixed costs will continue to be incurred and will be allocated to the other product lines. As a result, the reduction in revenues ($4,000,000) exceeds the reduction in costs ($3,200,000) by $800,000, thus reducing company profitability if the fruit product line is eliminated. The following chart is expressed in 1,000s:

Product line	With	Without	Reduction
Revenue	$14,000	$10,000	$4,000
Variable costs	7,000	4,000	3,000
Contribution margin	7,000	6,000	1,000
Avoidable fixed costs	2,900	2,700	200
Unavoidable fixed costs	1,700	1,700	0
Net income	$2,400	$1,600	$800

Lecture 4.11 – Special Decisions – Class Questions

15. A company with limited production resources that is currently using strategy C provides the following production information:

Strategy	Units produced Product X	Units produced Product Y
A	0	200
B	100	180
C	200	150
D	300	100
E	400	0

The company would encounter what opportunity cost if it doubled its production of Product X?

a. The cost of Product X would decrease by 50%.
b. Production of Product Y would double.
c. Production of Product Y would be eliminated.
d. Production of Product Y would not be affected.

16. In a lean accounting environment, a company accepts a special order to make 200 units of a product each month for the next two months for $130 per unit. The company normally sells the unit for $170 per unit with variable costs per unit at $80. The company plans to use excess capacity. By what amount would this special order increase profit?

a. $16,000
b. $20,000
c. $36,000
d. $52,000

17. The following information is available on Tackler Co.'s two product lines:

	Chairs	Tables
Sales	$180,000	$48,000
Variable costs	(96,000)	(30,000)
Contribution margin	84,000	18,000
Fixed costs:		
Avoidable:	(36,000)	(12,000)
Unavoidable:	(18,000)	(10,800)
Operating income (loss)	$ 30,000	($ 4,800)

Assuming Tackler discontinues the tables line and does not replace it, the company's operating income will

a. Increase by $4,800.
b. Increase by $6,000.
c. Decrease by $6,000.
d. Decrease by $10,800.

Class Solutions

15. (c) Under Strategy C, production of Product X is 200 units. If Product X production is doubled to 400 units, it is clear from Strategy E that production of Product Y would be eliminated. Therefore, the opportunity cost of doubling current production of Product X is the cessation of Product Y production. The validity of Answer (a) is indeterminable without additional information about costs. Neither answer (b) nor answer (d) are possible. Since the entity has limited capacity, a doubling of the production of Product X will, by necessity, require a decrease in the production of Product Y to zero.

16. (b) As a result of accepting this special order, the company will generate additional revenues of $52,000, consisting of 200 units per month for 2 months, or 400 units, at a sales price of $130 per unit. Variable costs will increase by $32,000 based on 400 units at $80 per unit, resulting in an increase in profit of $20,000. Fixed costs will neither increase nor decrease as a result of this transaction since the special order will be using excess capacity. A somewhat simpler approach to this problem is to merely calculate the contribution margin per additional unit ($130 price – $80 variable costs = $50) and multiply that by the 400 (200 x 2 months) additional units, for a total increase in profit of $20,000 ($50 x 400 units).

17. (c) If Tackler decides to discontinue the Tables product line, revenue will decrease by $48,000 and variable costs will decrease by $30,000, decreasing Tackler's contribution margin by $18,000. Avoidable fixed costs of $12,000 will also be eliminated, offsetting, in part, the $18,000 decrease in the contribution margin, resulting in a decrease in Tackler's operating income of $6,000. Although the reported loss for Tables was $4,800, the amount included a deduction of $10,800 for unavoidable fixed costs (costs that will continue to be incurred even if the Tables line is discontinued); the difference of $6,000 represents the amount that the Tables product line is contributing to the company's operating income.

Lecture 4.12 – Special Decisions – Class Questions – TBS

Fauna and Flora Industries, Inc., (F&F) is a food producer. It has several divisions encompassing many aspects of food and beverage production from developing new varieties of plants and domestic animals to large dairies, bakeries, and packing facilities.

F&F has just launched a new product, Frosted, so it is looking at the costs and cash flows associated with this project closely.

F&F is starting the process of pricing a new product, Freezed. As a starting point, F&F is looking at cost-plus pricing. F&F uses a standard minimum markup of 20% of gross margin for new products.

The dairy division needs 20,000 barrels of cheese culture #109 annually to use in its production cycle. If F&F buys the culture rather than producing it, the dairy division will eliminate $2 of fixed overhead cost per unit. The remaining fixed overhead will continue even if the culture is purchased from independent suppliers. The cost to buy a barrel of cheese culture #109 from an independent party is $44.

The aquatic division uses a joint process to produce product A, B, and C. Each product may be sold at its split-off point or processed further. Additional processing costs are all variable. Joint product costs are $200,000 and are allocated using the relative-sales-value at split-off method.

Management is considering eliminating the fresh product line from its produce division and keeping only the dried and frozen product lines.

Answer each question. Any information contained in an item is unique to that item and is not to be incorporated in your calculations when answering other items.

	Question	Amount
1.	What amount should be budgeted for cash payments to material suppliers during the period for the Frosted product?	
2.	Using variable costing, what is the budgeted income for the period for the Frosted product?	
3.	Using absorption costing, what is the budgeted income for the period for the Frosted product?	
4.	Actual results are as budgeted, except that only 60,000 of the 70,000 units produced were sold. Using absorption costing, what is the difference between the reported income and the budgeted net income for the Frosted product?	
5.	If a special order for 4,000 units of the Frosted product would cause the loss of 1,000 regular sales, what minimum amount of revenue must be generated from the special order so that net income is not reduced? (All cost relationships are unchanged.)	
6.	What is the minimum price that F&F is willing to assign to its new product, Freezed, rounded to the nearest penny?	

For item 7, determine and select from the choices below.
- A. Make
- B. Buy
- C. Either make or buy

For items 8 through 10, determine and select from the choices below.
- A. Sell
- B. Process further
- C. Either sell or process further

For item 11, determine and select from the choices below.
- A. Eliminate
- B. Keep

	Question	Answer
7.	Should F&F make or buy cheese culture #109?	
8.	Should F&F sell product A or process it further?	
9.	Should F&F sell product B or process it further?	
10.	Should F&F sell product C or process it further?	
11.	Should F&F eliminate or keep the fresh product line in the produce division?	

Exhibits:

Excerpt from the budget for the Frosted product for a 10-week period:

Sales price $11 per unit
Materials $ 3 per unit

Manufacturing conversion costs—Fixed $210,000
                    Variable $2 per unit

Selling and administrative costs—Fixed $45,000
                    Variable $1 per unit

Beginning accounts payable for materials $40,000

- Manufacturing and sales of 70,000 units are expected to occur evenly over the period.
- Materials are paid for in the week following use.
- There are no beginning inventories.

Excerpt from the cost sheet for Freezed:

Cost Sheet
Freezed

Direct material	$0.81
Direct labor	1.49
Variable overhead	0.51
Fixed overhead applied	0.86
Manufacturing cost, one barrel	$3.67

Excerpt from the cost sheet for cheese culture #109:

```
Cost Sheet
Cheese Culture #109

    Direct material                                $16.00
    Direct labor                                     8.00
    Variable overhead                               16.00
    Fixed overhead applied                           8.00
    Manufacturing cost, one barrel                 $48.00
```

Excerpts from the detail sheet for the aquatic division's products A, B, and C:

Product	Sales value at split-off	Additional processing costs	Final sales value
A	$ 75,000	$ 30,000	$ 150,000
B	150,000	30,000	180,000
C	30,000	45,000	60,000
Total	$255,000	$105,000	$390,000

Summary from the annual internal financial statements for the produce division

Product line	Dried	Fresh	Frozen	Total
Revenue (in 1,000s)	3,000	6,000	9,000	18,000
Variable costs	1,500	4,500	3,000	9,000
Contribution margin	1,500	1,500	6,000	9,000
Avoidable fixed cost	600	300	3,000	3,900
Unavoidable fixed costs	300	1,500	600	2,400
Fixed costs	900	1,800	3,600	6,300
Net income (in 1,000s)	600	(300)	2,400	2,700

Task-Based Simulation Solution

1. **$229,000** A manufacturing budget of 70,000 units for the 10-week period produced evenly indicates that the company will manufacture 7,000 units per week. Each unit requires materials of $3, indicating a weekly material cost of 7,000 units x $3/unit, or $21,000. Since materials are paid for in the week following use, the company will need to pay for the materials already used (i.e., $40,000 beginning accounts payable for materials) and for the materials used during the first 9 weeks of the 10-week period (9 x $21,000 = $189,000). Therefore, the total amount that should be budgeted for cash payments to material suppliers during the period is $229,000 ($40,000 + $189,000).

2. **$95,000** Under variable costing, only variable manufacturing costs are assigned to the product, and total fixed overhead is charged against revenues for the period. Thus, under variable costing, budgeted income for the period would be calculated as follows: Sales are 70,000 units x $11/unit = $770,000. Variable costs consist of materials of $3 per unit, conversion costs of $2 per unit, and selling and administrative costs of $1 per unit, for a total of $6 per unit x 70,000 units = $420,000. Fixed costs consist of fixed conversion costs of $210,000 and fixed selling and administrative costs of $45,000, for a total of $255,000. $770,000 sales – $420,000 variable costs – $255,000 fixed costs = $95,000 budgeted income.

3. $95,000   Under absorption costing, all manufacturing costs are assigned to the product, including fixed overhead. Thus, under absorption costing, the budgeted income for the period would be calculated as follows: Sales are 70,000 units x $11/unit = $770,000. Manufacturing costs consist of materials of $3 per unit, fixed conversion costs of $210,000/70,000, or $3 per unit, and variable conversion costs of $2 per unit, for a total of $8 per unit x 70,000 units = $560,000. Selling and administrative costs consist of variable costs of $1 per unit, or $70,000, and fixed costs of $45,000, for a total of $115,000. $770,000 sales - $560,000 manufacturing costs - $115,000 selling and administrative costs = $95,000 budgeted income. Note: Remember that the differences between variable and absorption costing are timing differences, which result from when the fixed manufacturing overhead is recognized as an expense: under variable costing, it is recognized in the period incurred; under absorption costing, it is recognized in the period in which the units to which fixed overhead has been applied are sold. Thus, under absorption costing, budgeted income for the period would be the same here as under variable costing because there is no difference in inventory since the company will both manufacture and sell 70,000 units during the period.

4. $20,000   Under absorption costing, all manufacturing costs are assigned to the product, including fixed overhead. Thus, under absorption costing, the reported income for the sale of 60,000 units in the period would be calculated as follows: Sales are 60,000 units x $11/unit = $660,000. Manufacturing costs are 60,000 units x $8/unit = $480,000. Selling and administrative costs would consist of variable costs of 60,000 units x $1/ unit, or $60,000, and fixed costs of $45,000, for total costs of $105,000. $660,000 sales - $480,000 manufacturing costs - $105,000 selling and administrative costs = $75,000 reported income. This is $20,000 lower than the $95,000 budgeted amount.

5. $29,000   Since all cost relationships will remain unchanged if the special order of 4,000 units is accepted, the company will not have either a savings or an additional cost in terms of the fixed costs. As a result of losing the sale of 1,000 units, the company will lose the contribution margin on those sales. This is the difference between the sales price of $11/unit and the variable costs, which total $6/unit, representing a loss of $5,000 ($5 x 1,000 units). In addition, the company will incur additional variable costs of 4,000 units x $6/unit = $24,000. In order to avoid reducing income, the company will need revenues of at least $24,000 + $5,000 = $29,000 from the special order.

6. $4.59   To convert the percentage markup on selling price (MOP) to a percentage markup on cost (MOC), the following formula is helpful: MOC = MOP / (100% - MOP). MOC = 20% / (100% - 20%) = 25%. The minimal selling price is the cost of the product plus the gross margin at 20% markup on selling price (or 25% markup on cost) $3.67 + ($3.67 x 0.25) = $4.5875, which rounds to $4.59. To prove this answer, use the markup on the computed selling price and compare the answer to the cost: $4.59 x (1 – 0.20) = $3.67.

7. Make The relevant costs to make the culture are $42 (direct material of $16, direct labor of $8, the variable overhead of $16, and the fixed overhead that can be eliminated of $2). This is cheaper than the purchase price of $44. The fixed overhead that cannot be eliminated is irrelevant to the decision.

8. Process further It is most beneficial to process product A further. This course of action results in an increase of $45,000 to net income. The joint production costs are irrelevant, as they do not differ between the alternatives.

	A	B	C
Final sales value	$150,000	$180,000	$ 60,000
Less: Sales value at split-off	75,000	150,000	30,000
Equals: Incremental revenue	$ 75,000	$ 30,000	$ 30,000
Less: Incremental cost	30,000	30,000	45,000
Difference	$ 45,000	$ 0	$(15,000)

9. Either sell or process further Financially, it is equally beneficial to either sell or process product B further. The decision has no impact on net income. The decision probably would be made based on qualitative or strategic factors. The joint production costs are irrelevant, as they do not differ between the alternatives. (Also see table in the explanation to item #8.)

10. Sell From a financial perspective, it is most beneficial to sell product C at the split-off point. This course of action avoids a reduction of $15,000 to net income. The joint production costs are irrelevant, as they do not differ between the alternatives. (Also see table in the explanation to item #8.)

11. Keep The fresh product line should not be eliminated because it contributes to covering the fixed costs of the division as a whole. The $1,500,000 of unavoidable fixed costs allocated to the fresh product line are irrelevant to this decision because they will continue regardless of the decision. Without the fresh product line, net income will decrease by $1,200,000, as outlined below. Alternatively, this difference may be derived by adding the unavoidable fixed costs back to the fresh product line's net loss (-$300,000 + $1,500,000 = $1,200,000).

Product line	Total division Keep fresh	Total division Eliminate fresh	Difference
Revenue (in 1,000s)	18,000	12,000	6,000
Variable costs	9,000	4,500	4,500
Contribution margin	9,000	7,500	1,500
Avoidable fixed cost	3,900	3,600	300
Unavoidable fixed costs	2,400	2,400	0
Fixed costs	6,300	6,000	300
Net income (in 1,000s)	2,700	1,500	1,200

Section 5 – Cost Accounting

Table of Contents

EXAM NOTE: *Please refer to the AICPA BEC Blueprint in the Introduction of this book to find a listing of the representative tasks (and their associated skill levels—i.e., Remembering and Understanding, Application, and Analysis) that the candidate should be able to perform based on the knowledge obtained in this section.*

Cost Accounting

Lecture 5.01 – Cost Accounting, Material & Labor Variances

Standard Costing

Standard costs are predetermined target costs which should be attainable under efficient conditions. Standard costs are used to aid in the budget process, pinpoint trouble areas, and evaluate performance. Cost accounting developed in response to internal concerns, rather than as a standardized tax or financial reporting framework with uniform terms. The industry (and hence, the CPA exam) commonly uses more than one name for some variances.

In setting internal goals for the efficient production of inventory, companies establish standards for the components that determine direct materials, direct labor, and overhead. At the end of the period, these standards are compared with actual results in order to determine **variances**.

The standards include:

- **Standard cost** – The unit purchase price of direct materials. Differences between standard cost and actual cost produce **direct materials price variances**.

- **Standard quantity** – The number of units of direct materials used to produce each unit of inventory. Differences between standard quantity allowed and actual quantity used produce **direct materials usage variances**.

- **Standard rate** – The hourly rate of pay for direct labor. Differences between standard rate of pay and actual rate of pay produce **direct labor rate variances**.

- **Standard hours** – The number of hours of direct labor used to produce each unit of inventory. Differences between standard hours allowed and actual hours used produce **direct labor efficiency variances**.

- **Predetermined overhead rate** (also called the standard fixed application rate, or **SFR**). The amount of overhead to apply (usually based on direct labor hours). Differences between applied overhead and actual overhead produce overhead variances. There are several different ways to compute overhead variances.

For example, assume a company manufactures collectible life-size figurines, which are sold for $1,000 each. Typically, a single figurine is completed in a day, and the **standard** costs involved in the manufacture of each figurine are:

Direct materials – 20 pounds of clay at $5 per pound

Direct labor – 5 hours of labor at $10 per hour

Overhead – Applied at $19 per direct labor hour

The estimated cost of manufacturing on a normal day (one figurine) is:

	Normal
Direct materials	$100
Direct labor	$50
Overhead	$95
Total cost	$245

Assume that, on a particular day, the company manufactures **two** figurines, and incurs the following **actual** costs:

Direct materials – 36 pounds of clay at $4 per pound

Direct labor – 12 hours of labor at $11 per hour

Overhead - $255

It is not appropriate to compare the normal costs with the actual costs, since the **normal costs are based on expected production** (one figurine). Instead, the actual costs are compared with **standard costs allowed based on actual production** (two figurines), as follows:

	Normal	Standard	Actual	Variance
Direct materials	100	200	144	56 F
Direct labor	50	100	132	32 U
Overhead	95	190	255	65 U
Total cost	245	490	531	41 U

The variances that result from actual costs being lower than standard costs are identified as *favorable* and those resulting from actual costs being higher are *unfavorable*.

The variances identified in the right column are not the ones usually requested on the exam. Instead, the 4 standards related to the direct costs each result in a variance:

Variance Analysis

(SAD → Standard – Actual = Difference)

DM	DM **Price** Variance = (purchasing)	AQ(SP – AP)	While in the factory, can I control the quantity used? YES (use Actual quantity)
	DM **Usage** Variance = (production)	SP(SQ – AQ)	While in the factory, can I control the price? NO (use Standard price)
DL	DL **Rate** Variance = (personnel)	AH(SR – AR)	While in the factory, can I control the hours worked? YES (use Actual quantity)
	DL **Efficiency** Var = (production)	SR(SH – AH)	While in the factory, can I control the pay rate? NO (use Standard price)

SQ × SH = Standard allowed for actual production

The **direct materials price variance (DMPV)** is the difference resulting from the actual cost per unit (AC) of the direct materials ($4 per pound) being different from the standard cost (SC) per unit ($5 per pound). It is based on the total quantity actually purchased (AQP). Assuming that the company maintains no inventories, it needs to purchase 36 pounds (if purchases are different from usage, the exam question will indicate that the calculation should be based on purchases). The variance is:

$$\textbf{DMPV} = AQP \times (SC - AC) = 36 \times (5 - 4) = 36 \times 1 = 36 \text{ F}$$

The **direct materials usage variance (DMUV)** is the difference resulting from the actual quantity used (AQU) of direct materials (36 pounds) being different from the standard quantity allowed (SQA) based on production (40 pounds for 2 figurines). It is based on the standard cost per unit, since there is already a separate price variance to take into account the effect of the actual cost per unit being different. (This also may be called the direct materials efficiency variance.) The variance is:

$$\textbf{DMUV} = SC \times (SQA - AQU) = 5 \times (40 - 36) = 5 \times 4 = 20 \text{ F}$$

The **direct labor rate variance (DLRV)** is the difference resulting from the actual rate of pay (AR) for the direct laborers ($11 per hour) being different from the standard rate of pay (SR) for those laborers ($10 per hour). The total difference is multiplied by the actual number of hours (AH) that the laborers worked (12 hours). The variance is:

$$\textbf{DLRV} = AH \times (SR - AR) = 12 \times (10 - 11) = 12 \times -1 = 12 \text{ U}$$

The **direct labor efficiency variance (DLEV)** is the difference resulting from the actual hours worked (12 hours) being different from the standard hours allowed (SH) based on actual production (10 hours for two figurines). The total difference is multiplied by the standard rate of pay, since there is already a separate variance that takes into account the effect of the actual rate of pay being different. (This also may be called the direct labor usage variance.) The variance is:

$$\textbf{DLEV} = SR \times (SH - AH) = 10 \times (10 - 12) = 10 \times -2 = 20 \text{ U}$$

Notice that the sum of the two unfavorable direct labor variances is $32 (DLRV $12 + DLEV $20), equal to the total direct labor variance.

Lecture 5.02 – Material & Labor Variances – Class Questions

1. Carr Co. had an unfavorable materials usage variance of $900. What amounts of this variance should be charged to each department?

	Purchasing	**Warehousing**	**Manufacturing**
a.	$0	$0	$900
b.	$0	$900	$0
c.	$300	$300	$300
d.	$900	$0	$0

2. The standard direct material cost to produce a unit of Lem is four meters of material at $2.50 per meter. During May 20X9, 4,200 meters of material costing $10,080 were purchased and used to produce 1,000 units of Lem. What was the material price variance for May 20X9?

    a. $400 favorable.
    b. $420 favorable.
    c. $ 80 unfavorable.
    d. $480 unfavorable.

Class Solutions

1. (a) The materials usage variance measures the actual amount of materials used versus the standard amount that should have been used given the level of output. Normally, the only department with controls over usage of materials is the manufacturing department. Purchasing would be responsible for a price variance, not a usage variance, and warehousing would have no control over either.

2. (b) At $2.50 per meter, 4,200 meters should cost $10,500. Since it only cost $10,080, the difference is a favorable material price variance of $420. The actual cost of materials was $10,080/4,200, or $2.40 per yard, and the variance can be calculated as AQ (SP – AP), or 4,200 ($2.50 - $2.40) = $420. Since the actual cost is lower than standard, it is favorable.

Lecture 5.03 – Overhead Variances

When companies apply a standard cost system to overhead, the amount of overhead applied will be determined on the basis of the standard amount of the allocation base that should have been used in the production process based on the number of units produced. If overhead is allocated, for example, on the basis of direct labor hours, overhead applied (OA) can be calculated as follows:

OA = SDLH × POHR

In the formula above, POHR is the predetermined overhead rate including both the variable and fixed components. It is calculated in a three-step process:

1. The total of the base is estimated. For example, if the company expects to produce 50,000 units at 2 standard direct labor hours per unit, the estimate for the base is 100,000 hours.

2. Second, total overhead is estimated on the basis of expected fixed overhead for the period and variable overhead per unit of the base. If, for example, the entity paid rent of $400,000 per year and utilities of $1 per hour, at 100,000 hours, total overhead would be $400,000 (rent) + $100,000 (utilities calculated as 100,000 hours at $1 per hour), for a total of $500,000.

3. Finally, total estimated overhead is divided by the number of units in the base to establish a rate. At $500,000 for 100,000 hours, the POHR would be $5 per hour ($500,000/100,000 DLH), which includes $4 per hour fixed and $1 per hour variable costs.

Many companies will further analyze overhead using a 2-variance, 3-variance, or 4-variance approach. The most common is the 3-variance approach, dividing the total variance into a Spending variance, an Efficiency variance, and a Volume variance.

The **overhead Spending variance** (OSV) measures whether the amount of variable overhead being spent per hour is more or less than the amount expected and whether the amount of fixed overhead incurred is more or less than the budgeted amount. The overhead spending variance is the difference between the amount of overhead that would be budgeted based on actual hours worked and the amount actually spent on overhead. It is calculated as follows:

OSV = (ADLH × PVOHR + Budgeted fixed overhead) - Actual overhead

In the above formula, if OSV is a positive number, the variance is favorable. The overhead spending variance can also be segregated into a fixed and a variable component.

In addition to spending, the total overhead variance includes a portion related to usage. The variable component is referred to as the overhead efficiency variance, which measures the extra variable overhead spent if the entity worked more hours than expected or the variable overhead saved if the entity worked fewer. The fixed component is referred to as the volume variance since it is better to spread fixed overhead over a greater number of units, resulting in a lower cost per unit, than a smaller number.

The **overhead Efficiency variance** (OEV) is similar to the labor efficiency variance. It measures whether the units manufactured required more or less than the number of hours expected. Since variable overhead is incurred with each direct labor hour spent, the amount can be calculated as follows:

OEV = PVOHR × (SDLH - ADLH)

In the formula above, PVOHR is the predetermined variable overhead rate. If OEV is a positive number, the variance is favorable.

The **overhead Production Volume variance** (OVV) is the one over which the manufacturing department has the least control. This is due to the fact that the variance measures whether the company produced as many units as expected. The amount can be calculated as follows:

OVV = (SDLH × PFOHR) – Budgeted fixed overhead

In the formula above, PFOHR is the predetermined fixed overhead rate which is calculated by dividing the budgeted fixed overhead by the standard direct labor hours based on expected production. When more units were produced than were anticipated, the amount of overhead applied will exceed the budgeted amount, resulting in a favorable volume variance.

The total of the Spending variance, the Efficiency variance, and the Volume variance is the total overhead variance.

Budget to Actual Comparison

    Budgeted overhead costs:
        Fixed Rent = $400,000 ($4 × 100,000 hrs)
        Variable Electricity = $1 × 100,000 hrs
            FBE = $4(100,000 hrs) + $1 (*X*) (Note: *X* = Actual production × actual Hrs, or Actual production × Std hrs allowed for actual production)

Actual costs:
        Fixed Rent = $390,000
        Variable Electricity = $1.01 (97,000 hrs)

Actual At Budget	50,000 units (2 hrs) =	100,000 hrs	Budget
	48,000 (2.02) =	97,000	Actual
	48,000 (2) =	96,000	Standard allowed for Actual production

Mfg O/H (4 numbers + 3 variances = **SEV**en)
Budgeted Overhead = $400,000 ($4 × 100,000 hrs)
Actual Hours = 97,000

	Actual	FBE @ Actual	FBE @ Standard	Applied
Fixed O/H	390,000	400,000	400,000	4(96,000)
Variable O/H	1.01(97,000)	1(97,000)	1(96,000)	1(96,000)

Spending	**E**fficiency	Volume / Non-controllable

One variance method	Net O/H variance
Two	Budget (Controllable)/Volume (Non-controllable)
Three	Spending / Efficiency / Volume
Four	Fix/Var Spending / Effic / Vol

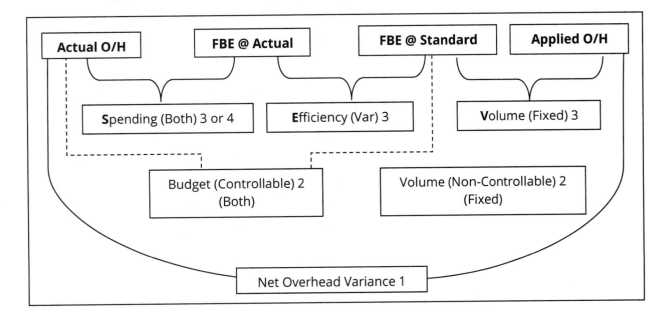

Lecture 5.04 – Overhead Variances – Class Questions

3. Which of the following standard costing variances would be least controllable by a production supervisor?

    a. Overhead volume.
    b. Overhead efficiency.
    c. Labor efficiency.
    d. Material usage.

4. Under the 2-variance method for analyzing overhead, which of the following variances consists of both variable and fixed overhead elements?

	Controllable (budget) Variance	Volume Variance
a.	Yes	Yes
b.	Yes	No
c.	No	No
d.	No	Yes

5. The following information pertains to Roe Co.'s 20X3 manufacturing operations:

Standard direct manufacturing labor hours per unit	2
Actual direct manufacturing labor hours	10,500
Number of units produced	5,000
Standard variable overhead per standard direct manufacturing labor hour	$3
Actual variable overhead	$28,000

Roe's 20X3 unfavorable variable overhead efficiency variance was

    a. $0
    b. $1,500
    c. $2,000
    d. $3,500

Class Solutions

3. (a) The overhead volume variance measures the difference between overhead applied, which is SH × POHR and budgeted OH based on actual production, which is SH × PVOHR (predetermined variable overhead rate) + budgeted fixed overhead. The variable overhead portion is the same in both amounts, making the volume variance equal to the amount of fixed overhead over- or under-applied. Fixed overhead is the factor that manufacturing would have the least control over. Answer (a) is incorrect because the overhead efficiency variance is a measure of the hours required for manufacturing, which is within the control of production. Answer (c) is incorrect because the labor efficiency variance is a measure of the hours required for manufacturing, which is within the control of production. Answer (d) is incorrect because the material usage variance is a measure of the amount of materials required for manufacturing, which is within the control of production.

4. (b) Under the 2-variance method, the controllable variance is the difference between actual overhead incurred and budgeted overhead based on actual volume produced, which would be standard hours (SH) × the predetermined variable overhead rate (PVOHR) plus budgeted fixed overhead. As a result, it includes both variable and fixed components. The volume variance measures the difference between fixed overhead applied, which is SH × PFOHR (fixed) and includes fixed overhead only.

5. (b) The variable overhead efficiency is the predetermined variable overhead rate multiplied by the difference between standard hours and actual hours. With 5,000 units produced at 2 standard hours per unit, there are 10,000 standard hours, compared to 10,500 actual, indicating 500 extra hours were spent in production. At a variable rate of $3 per hour, the result is an unfavorable variable overhead efficiency variance of $1,500.

Lecture 5.05 – Two Costing Systems: Job Order vs. Process Costing

Two methods of accumulating production costs in a manufacturing company and for allocating the costs to work in process, finished goods and cost of goods sold.

Job Order Costing

Job order costing is a system for allocating costs to groups of unique products. It is applicable to the production of customer-specified products. Each job becomes a cost center for which costs are accumulated. Job order costing is generally used when units are relatively expensive and when costs can be identified to specific units or batches of units. Because costs are traced to specific jobs, certain items that might otherwise be classified as manufacturing overhead (overtime premiums paid to accommodate a customer change order, for instance) are classified as direct costs.

- **Job order costing** – expensive, heterogeneous – cost based per **Job.**

Process Costing

Process costing, in contrast to job order costing, is applicable to a continuous process of production of the same or similar goods. Since the product is uniform, there is no need to determine the costs of different groups of products and each processing department becomes a cost center. Process costing is generally used when units are relatively inexpensive and when it is difficult to trace costs to specific units being produced, such as when units are mass-produced in large quantities.

- **Process costing** – inexpensive, homogeneous - costs per **Period.**
  - Equivalent "whole" units (80 × ¾ cc = 60 whole units) (cc = Conversion Cost)
    - **Weighted average method** (beginning + started)
    - **FIFO** (beginning first/ then started)

There are two methods of applying process costing to production. These are the weighted average method and FIFO.

Weighted Average

Under the weighted average approach, equivalent production for a period will include units that are **completed** during the period, considered whole units as to all costs, and units in process at the end of the period. The ending work-in-process will be converted into equivalent units based on the level of completion.

Total equivalent production will be divided into costs for the period to determine an average cost per equivalent unit. The costs included will be the costs associated with beginning inventory and the costs incurred during the period.

FIFO

Under the FIFO approach, equivalent production for a period will include the units that are **started and completed** during the period, considered whole units as to all costs. Both beginning and ending work-in-process inventory will be converted into equivalent whole units.

- For beginning inventory, the portion of the work that needed to be completed during the period will be multiplied by the number of units to determine equivalent production.

- For ending inventory, the percentage of completion will be multiplied by the number of units to determine equivalent production.

Total equivalent production will be divided into costs for the period to determine an average cost per equivalent unit. The costs included, however, will only be those costs that were incurred during the period.

Comparing Weighted Average to FIFO

The difference between weighted average and FIFO is the handling of beginning work-in-process inventory. When there is no beginning inventory, both will have the same result. When there is a beginning work-in-process inventory, the weighted average approach will yield a number of equivalent units that will be equal to or greater than equivalent production under FIFO.

- When costs are incurred at the end of the process, or at some point in the process that the beginning inventory had not yet reached, equivalent production will be the same under both approaches.
- When costs are incurred uniformly during the process, at the beginning of the process, or at some point in the process that the beginning inventory had already reached, equivalent production under weighted average would be greater than FIFO.

Weighted Average
TC/Total Equivalent Units = Cost per Unit

FIFO
*Costs **this Period**/Units Worked on **this period** = Cost per Unit*

Equivalent Production

One significant aspect of process costing is the computation of equivalent units. The objective is to analyze the period's production, including units completed and units partially completed, and determine the number of whole units the production is equivalent to.

The calculation of equivalent production will depend on the point in time at which costs are incurred.

- When costs are incurred at the beginning of the process, partially completed units will be considered equivalent to whole units as soon as they are started.

- When costs are incurred at a specific time during the process, such as when units are 40% complete, partially completed units will be considered equivalent to nothing until they reach that point and equivalent to whole units when that point is reached.

- When costs are incurred at the end of the process, partially completed units will be considered equivalent to nothing until completed, at which time they will be equivalent to whole units.

- When costs are incurred evenly throughout the process, the percentage of completion will be multiplied by the number of units in process to determine the number of equivalent whole units.

When a company has more than one manufacturing department, the costs are assigned to work-in-process and to goods transferred to the next department. In the subsequent department, the units transferred from a previous department are considered similar to a raw material that is added to the production cycle at the beginning of the process.

The Alexes Co. is the first of a two-stage production process. The following information concerns the conversion costs in May 20X3:

	Units	Conversion costs
Beginning work in process (60% complete)	30	$68
Units started	60	96
Spoilage — normal	0	$164
Units completed and transferred	50	
Ending work in process (80% complete)	40	

Using the Weighted-average and the FIFO methods, calculate equivalent whole units, the cost of goods completed and transferred, and ending inventory.

Weighted Average (Total Costs/Total Equivalent Whole units)

	units	% complete CC	Equivalent whole units	Costs
Beg. Units	30	60%		$ 68
Started	60			$ 96
Units to acct for	90			$ 164
Completed	50	100% =	50 × $2 = $100	
Spoilage	0			
End	40	80% Complete =	32 × $2 = $64 end / $164	
Units to acct for	90		82 equiv. units	**$164**

Same under Both → (points to End row)

W/A → What did you finish? Do not care where it came from.

TC/EU → EU = 50 completed + 40(0.8) = 82 equiv. Whole units

= $164/82 = $ 2 per unit

50 × $2 = $100 (COG completed)

32 × $2 =   64 (Ending Inventory)

      $164

FIFO (Costs incurred THIS PERIOD/Units actually worked on THIS PERIOD)

	units	% complete CC	Equivalent whole units	Costs
Beg. Units	30	60%		$ 68
Started	60			$ 96
Units to acct for	90			$ 164
Completed	50	30 × 40%=12 / 20 × 100%=20	12 × $1.5 = 18 / 20 × $1.5 = 30 / $48 / + started 68 / $116 Cogc	
Spoilage	0			
End	40	80% Complete =	32 × $1.5 = $48 end / $164	
Units to acct for	90		64 equiv. units	**$164**

Same under Both → (points to End row)

FIFO → What work did you perform *this period*?
  Costs this period/Units Worked on this period
  Units Worked on this period =

What did it take to make it 100% complete? Came in with 60%, so 40%.

The 30 units in beginning inventory were already 60% complete and the remaining 40% was required to complete them.

If 50 units were completed, 30 of which were from beginning inventory, there were 20 units that were started and completed in their entirety during the period.

Ending inventory is treated the same under FIFO as under weighted average. There are 40 units that are 80% complete.

Cost of goods completed will consist of:
- The costs in beginning inventory
- The cost to complete the units in beginning inventory (EU × cost per EU)
- The cost of units started and completed during the period (EU × cost per EU)

30 (from beginning)(.40) = 12 + 20(100%) = 32 + ending 40(.80) = 64 equiv. whole units
  = \$96/64 = \$1.5 × 32 = \$48+ 68 = 116 (COG completed)
            \$1.5 × 32 = 48 (Ending Inventory)
                  \$164.00

When a company produces large quantities of identical goods, it will often use **process costing** to determine the average cost per unit of products. When using this approach, costs are accumulated in work-in-process until the end of the period, and then a calculation is made of the cost per equivalent unit of products completed and incomplete at the end of the period.

For example, assume that a company had work-in-process at the beginning of the month of $30, associated with 2 units that were 50% complete at the time. During the month, it spent $150 and started an additional 8 units. At the end of the month, work-in-process consisted of 4 units that were 75% complete. Assume there was no spoilage in the production process.

The total cost in work-in-process before allocating is $30 + $150 = $180. With 2 units at the start and 8 more begun during the month, there were 10 units to account for at the end of the month. Since 4 were in process, 6 must have been completed. The **equivalent units** include the 6 that were completed and 4 × 75% = 3 equivalent units for the ending work-in-process, for a total of 9 equivalent units. The costs of $180 are allocated over 9 equivalent units at $20 per equivalent unit. Ending work-in-process is $20 × 3 equivalent units, or $60, and the remaining $120 must represent the costs associated with the 6 units completed and transferred to finished goods. To summarize:

	Units	Costs	Cost / EU	
Beg WIP (50%)	2	30		
Added	8	150		
To account for	10	180	180	
		EU		

	Units	Costs	Cost / EU	Allocation @ $20
End WIP (75%)	4	3		60
Completed	6	6		120
Accounted for	10	9	9	180
Cost / EU			20	

For costs added at the beginning of a process, the equivalent units are the same for work-in-process as they are for completed units. For example, if raw materials are added at the beginning of the process, the 4 units in process at the end of the month already have all the raw materials, and are assigned 4 equivalent units instead of 3.

Lecture 5.06 – Job Order vs. Process Costing – Class Questions

6. In a process cost system, the application of factory overhead usually would be recorded as an increase in

   a. Finished goods inventory control.
   b. Factory overhead control.
   c. Cost of goods sold.
   d. Work in process inventory control.

7. The Forming Department is the first of a two-stage production process. Spoilage is identified when the units have completed the Forming process. Costs of spoiled units are assigned to units completed and transferred to the second department in the period spoilage is identified. The following information concerns Forming's conversion costs in May 20X3:

	Units	Conversion costs
Beginning work in process (50% complete)	2,000	$10,000
Units started during May	8,000	75,500
Spoilage—normal	500	
Units completed and transferred	7,000	
Ending work in process (80% complete)	2,500	

   Using the weighted-average method, what was Forming's conversion cost transferred to the second production department?

   a. $59,850
   b. $64,125
   c. $67,500
   d. $71,250

Question numbers 8 and 9 are based on the following:

Dr. Oregano manufactures soft drinks. In the first department, a variety of ingredients are being mixed together while being heated at precise temperatures. The materials are added uniformly throughout the process and, when the process is complete, the output is transferred to the bottling department.

Dr. Oregano uses process costing to report manufacturing costs and summarized its operations for the month of April, 20X3, as follows:

	Gallons	Direct Materials
Beginning work in process	150,000	$ 108,000
Started during April	750,000	
Completed during April	600,000	
Ending work in process	300,000	
Raw materials cost incurred in April		$1,755,000

8. Beginning work in process inventory was 30% complete and ending work in process inventory was 40% complete. What were the equivalent gallons of production with regard to materials for April using the FIFO method?

    a. 450,000
    b. 675,000
    c. 705,000
    d. 720,000

9. What is the cost of goods that were transferred to the bottling department using the FIFO method?

    a. $1,443,000
    b. $1,551,000
    c. $1,560,000
    d. $1,863,000

10. In computing the current period's manufacturing cost per equivalent unit, the FIFO method of process costing considers current period costs

    a. Only.
    b. Plus cost of beginning work in process inventory.
    c. Less cost of beginning work in process inventory.
    d. Plus cost of ending work in process inventory.

Class Solutions

6. (d) Factory overhead applied is a cost of production that would be added to work-in-process inventory as it was incurred. Answer (a) is incorrect because amounts are charged to finished goods inventory control when goods are completed, and the cost is transferred out of work in process. Answer (b) is incorrect because manufacturing overhead control keeps track of actual manufacturing overhead costs, to be compared to amounts applied. Answer (c) is incorrect because amounts are charged to cost of goods sold when they are sold, and the cost is transferred out of finished goods.

7. (c) Under the weighted average method, total costs, including beginning inventory costs of $10,000 and costs incurred during the period of $75,500, or a total of $85,500, is allocated to output. Output consists of 7,000 units completed and transferred, 500 units that were completed but spoiled, and 2,500 units in ending inventory that are 80% complete. As a result, equivalent production would be 7,000 + 500 + (2,500 × 80%), or a total of 9,500 units. The cost per equivalent unit is then $85,500/9,500, or $9. The amount that will be transferred to the second department will include the cost of the completed units of $63,000 (7,000 @ $9) and the cost of the spoilage (500 @ $9), or $4,500, for a total of $67,500.

8. (b) Under FIFO, equivalent production consists of the work required to complete gallons in beginning inventory, gallons started and completed, and the work completed on ending inventory. If a total of 600,000 gallons were completed during the period and 150,000 gallons were in beginning inventory, there were apparently 450,000 gallons that were started and completed during the period. As a result, equivalent production is (150,000 × 70%) + 450,000 + (300,000 × 40%), or 675,000 gallons.

9. (b) Costs transferred to the bottling department will consist of the costs included in beginning inventory, the costs to complete beginning inventory, and the cost of gallons started and completed during the period. With costs of $1,755,000 incurred in April for equivalent production of 675,000 gallons, the cost per gallon is $2.60. The cost of gallons transferred will include the $108,000 from beginning inventory + $273,000 (150,000 × 70% × $2.60) + $1,170,000 (450,000 × $2.60) = $1,551,000.

10. (a) Under the FIFO method, equivalent production for the period consists only of the work done during the period. It includes work done to complete beginning inventory, inventory that was started and completed during the period, and the work completed on ending inventory. Since only work completed during the period is considered in computing equivalent production, only costs incurred during the period are included when determining the cost per equivalent unit.

Lecture 5.07 – Joint Product Costing

Joint products are two or more products produced together up to a split-off point where they become separately identifiable. They cannot be produced by themselves. When more than one product is being produced, certain costs are associated with the production of more than one product, and are known as **joint product costs**. These costs are allocated to the different products using an appropriate method. One method is called **Units of volume of output**, but this method is not as frequently tested.

The most popular is the **relative sales value at split-off** approach. The total sales value of the products involved is determined, and is reduced by separate costs incurred in the manufacture of each product after the split from the joint process. The result is the approximate sales value of each product at the point the joint process ended. This is referred to as the sales value at split-off or the synthetic sales value and is used to allocate the joint costs. Under the Relative Sales Value Method:

- The **sales value** of each joint product is determined by multiplying the amount produced by the sales price per unit.

- The sales value is reduced by **separable costs**. Separable costs are the costs incurred after the mutual manufacturing process is complete. They are the costs necessary to prepare a joint product to be sold. Not all joint products will have separable costs.

- The resulting reduced amount is considered the **relative sales value** of the joint product **at split-off point**. The split-off point is that point, at the conclusion of the joint manufacturing process, when individual joint products can be identified.

- The relative sales values for each of the joint products are combined to obtain a total amount.

The joint product costs to be allocated to a specific joint product will be determined by the relative sales value method using the following formula:

$$\frac{\text{Sales value of product at split-off}}{\text{Total of sales values of all products at split-off}} \times \text{Joint product costs}$$

Sometimes, in addition to joint products, companies may have by-products that result from a process. By-products are output from the joint process that do not contribute significantly to the firm's revenue and are not products that the company is manufacturing by intent. Joint costs may be allocated to **by-products** in a variety of ways:

- An amount equal to the net proceeds from the disposal of by-products may be allocated such that the by-products are sold at breakeven.

- Joint costs may be allocated to by-products in the same manner as to joint products using the relative sales value method, as if it were an additional joint product.

- No costs may be allocated to the by-product.

🖩 A company has joint product costs of $54,000 at split-off. There are 2 main products, A and B, and one by-product, Z. Division A has $30,000 of additional costs after split-off in order to sell all output for $80,000. Division B has $30,000 of additional costs after split-off in order to sell all output for $60,000. By-product Z has $1,000 of additional costs in order to sell for $5,000. How much of the joint product costs should be allocated to products A, B and by-product Z?

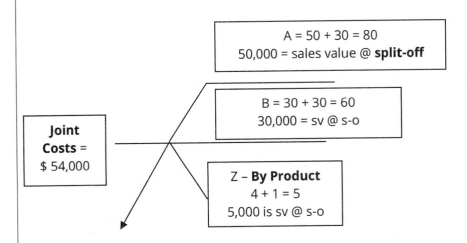

Sales-Value at Split-Off

Separable Costs (Work Backwards)
A → **$50,000** + $30,000 = $80,000
> If work on it more (put in an extra cost of $30,000), it could be worth $80,000.
> The $50,000 represents the synthetic sales value at split off.

B → **$30,000** + $30,000 = $60,000
> If work on it more (put in an extra cost of $30,000), it could be worth $60,000.
> The $30,000 represents the synthetic sales value at split off.

If we add those two synthetic values up, we get $50,000 + $30,000, or $80,000. We would then allocate the joint costs as follows:

A → 50,000/80,000 × (54,000)
B → 30,000/80,000 × (54,000)

Z → **$4,000** + $1,000 = $5,000
> Can use to offset cost or add to revenue.
> $54,000 – $4,000 = $50,000 Joint Costs to be allocated

- Product A would be allocated 50/80 × $50,000 = $31,250
- Product B would be allocated 30/80 × $50,000 = $18,750
  $50,000
- Product Z would show zero revenue as the $4,000 was reduced from the $54,000 of joint product costs that needed to be allocated between products A and B.

Assume a company produces a standard and deluxe version of a product. The standard version is produced starting in department A and finishing in department B. The deluxe version is produced starting in department A and finishing in department C. The total sales are $30 of the standard version and $50 of the deluxe. The costs incurred are $10 in department A, $6 in department B, and $34 in department C. While it is not a problem to determine total gross profit for the company, a breakdown by product line is more difficult, as the following schedule shows:

	Standard	Deluxe	Total
Sales	30	50	80
Separate costs	6	34	40
Sales value at split-off	24	16	40
Joint costs	?	?	10
Gross profit	?	?	30

Using the sales value at split-off approach, the standard version is allocated $24 / $40 = 60% of the joint costs of $10, or $6, and the deluxe version is allocated $16 / $40 = 40% of $10, or $4.

If one of the products resulting from production is considered a **by-product**, and is only being produced as an incidental result of production of the main product or products, then the net realizable value of the by-product is simply subtracted from the cost of production of the main. For example, oil refining involves the removal of impurities from crude oil. The impurities are actually useful in the manufacture of glue, so oil companies sell them and subtract the net proceeds (sales price less costs of disposal) from the cost of refining oil.

If there are two or more main products in addition to a by-product, the net realizable value of the by-product is subtracted from the joint product costs, which are then allocated to the main products based on relative sales value at split-off approach or a comparable method. Sometimes, rather than recognizing by-product market value as a reduction of production costs, it is recognized when sold and disclosed as ordinary income, other income, or as a contra to cost of sales.

Lecture 5.08 – Joint Product Costing – Class Questions

11. Lane Co. produces main products Kul and Wu. The process also yields by-product Zef. Net realizable value of by-product Zef is subtracted from joint production cost of Kul and Wu. The following information pertains to production in July 20X3 at a joint cost of $54,000:

Product	Units Produced	Market value	Additional cost after split-off
Kul	1,000	$50,000	$10,000
Wu	1,500	40,000	5,000
Zef	500	7,000	3,000

If Lane uses the net realizable value method for allocating joint cost, how much of the joint cost should be allocated to product Kul?

    a. $18,800
    b. $20,000
    c. $26,667
    d. $27,342

12. The diagram below represents the production and sales relationships of joint products P and Q. Joint costs are incurred until split-off, then separable costs are incurred in refining each product. Market values of P and Q at split-off are used to allocate joint costs.

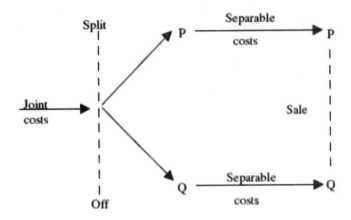

If the market value of P at split-off increases and all other costs and selling prices remain unchanged, then the gross margin of

	P	**Q**
a.	Increases	Decreases
b.	Increases	
c.	Decreases	Decreases
d.	Decreases	Increases

Class Solutions

11. (c) The requirement is to determine how to allocate joint cost using the net realizable value (NRV) method when a by-product is involved. NRV is the predicted selling price in the ordinary course of business less reasonably predictable costs of completion and disposal. The joint cost of $54,000 is reduced by the NRV of the by-product ($4,000) to get the allocable joint cost ($50,000). Sales value at split off is $50,000 - $10,000 = $40,000 for Kul and $40,000 - $5,000 = $35,000 for Wu. The computation is

	Sales value at split-off	Weighting	Joint cost allocated
Kul	$40,000	40,000/75,000 × 50,000	$26,667
Wu	$35,000	35,000/75,000 × 50,000	$23,333
	$75,000		$50,000

Therefore, $26,667 of the joint cost should be allocated to product Kul.

When a process results in joint products and by-products, the net realizable value of the by-products generally is subtracted from joint costs first, resulting in the net cost of the joint process. The by-product Zef has a sales value of $7,000, but requires separable costs of $4,000, resulting in a net realizable value of $4,000. This reduces joint costs of $54,000 so that only $50,000 will be allocated to the joint products based on their relative sales value at the split-off point. Kul has a sales value of $50,000 with separable costs of $10,000, resulting in a sales value at split-off of $40,000. Wu has a sales value of $40,000 with separable costs of $5,000, resulting in a sales value at split-off of $35,000. As a result, $26,667 ($40,000/$75,000 × $50,000) will be allocated to Kul.

12. (d) If the market value of P increases at split off, and joint costs are being allocated between products P and Q based on relative sales value at split off, that means that P will get MORE of the costs based on the ratio. Therefore, if more costs are allocated to P and all other costs and selling prices remain unchanged, then the gross margin (sales – costs) will decrease for P and increase for Q.

Lecture 5.09 – Cost Accounting – Class Questions – TBS

Ester, Inc., is a medical laboratory that performs tests for physicians. Ester recently hired Cat's-eye Consultants to evaluate its costs. Ester performs between 4,000 and 12,000 tests during a month.

For items 1 through 8, determine and select from the choices below both the category and behavior.

Category
- A. Direct material cost
- B. Direct labor cost
- C. Overhead cost
- D. General and administrative cost

Behavior
- F. Fixed
- V. Variable

Costs incurred by Ester	Category				Behavior	
	(A)	(B)	(C)	(D)	(F)	(V)
1. Office manager's salary	O	O	O	O	O	O
2. Cost of electricity to run laboratory equipment	O	O	O	O	O	O
3. Hourly wages of part-time technicians who perform tests	O	O	O	O	O	O
4. Cost of lubricant used on laboratory equipment	O	O	O	O	O	O
5. Cost of distilled water used in tests	O	O	O	O	O	O
6. Accelerated depreciation on laboratory equipment	O	O	O	O	O	O
7. Straight-line depreciation on laboratory building	O	O	O	O	O	O
8. Cost of expensive binders in which test results are given to physicians	O	O	O	O	O	O

For items 9 through 12, each calculate the numeric amount for each analysis item.

	Analysis item	Amount
9.	Contribution margin per unit	
10.	Breakeven point in units at low activity range	
11.	Breakeven point in units at high activity range	
12.	Number of units sold to achieve a gross profit of $160,000	

For items 13 through 15, determine and select from the choices below.
- A. Greater than the industry average
- B. The same as the industry average
- C. Less than the industry average

		Comparison to the industry average	
Analysis item	**(A)**	**(B)**	**(C)**
13. Variable costs at low activity range	○	○	○
14. Contribution margin at high activity range	○	○	○
15. Breakeven point at high activity range	○	○	○

Exhibits

Excerpt from report of Cat's-eye Consultants

At the low range of activity (100 to 4,999 tests performed):

Sales price per test	$60
Variable costs per test	20
Fixed costs	160,000

At the high range of activity (5,000 to 14,999 tests performed):

Sales price per test	$60
Variable costs per test	20
Fixed costs	200,000

Excerpt from report from Medical Testing Association

Compared to industry averages, at the 100 – 4,999 tests/month range of activity, Ester has a lower sales price per test than industry average, higher fixed costs than industry average, and the same breakeven point in number of tests performed as industry average.

Compared to industry averages, at the 5,000 – 14,999 tests/month range of activity, Ester's sales price per test and fixed costs are the same as industry averages, and Ester's variable costs are lower than industry averages.

Task-Based Simulation Solution

1. **Office manager's salary: General and administrative cost; Fixed.**

   The office manager is outside the production process; the office manager's salary is a general and administrative cost. The office manager's salary is constant regardless of the quantity of product produced (or tests performed). Direct material costs are the costs of material readily traced to the product (the tests). No salaries or wages are direct material costs. Direct labor costs are the costs of labor of those producing the product (the tests). The office manager is outside the production process. Overhead costs for testing are production costs.

2. **Cost of electricity to run laboratory equipment: Overhead cost; Variable.**

   Overhead costs are production costs that cannot be traced to specific units of production readily. The laboratory equipment is being used to produce product (or perform the tests). The cost of electricity to run the laboratory equipment cannot be traced to specific tests readily;

hence, it is an overhead cost. The cost of electricity to run laboratory equipment varies with the quantity of product produced (or tests performed). While there often is a base charge every month regardless of quantity used, the amount typically is miniscule in comparison to the usage charge. Direct material costs are the costs of material readily traced to the product (the tests). The laboratory equipment is being used to produce product. The cost of electricity to run the laboratory equipment cannot be traced to specific tests readily. Direct labor costs are the costs of labor of those producing the product (the tests). Electricity is not labor. The laboratory equipment is being used to produce product (or perform the tests). The cost of electricity to run the laboratory equipment is a manufacturing cost, not a general or administrative cost.

3.   **Hourly wages of part-time technicians who perform tests: Direct labor cost; Variable.**

Direct labor costs are the costs of labor of those producing the product (the tests). The technicians who perform tests are part of the production process. The technicians' wages can be traced to specific tests readily. The technicians' wages vary with the quantity of product produced (or tests performed). Direct material costs are the costs of material readily traced to the product (the tests). No salaries or wages are direct material costs. Overhead costs are production costs that cannot be traced to specific units of production readily. The technicians' wages can be traced to specific tests readily. The technicians' wages are a manufacturing cost, not a general or administrative cost.

4.   **Cost of lubricant used on laboratory equipment: Overhead cost; Variable.**

Overhead costs are production costs that cannot be traced to specific units of production readily. The laboratory equipment is being used to produce product (or perform the tests). The cost of lubricant used on the laboratory equipment cannot be traced to specific tests readily; hence, it is an overhead cost. The cost of lubricant used on laboratory equipment varies with the quantity of product produced (or tests performed). While there conceivably is a minimal amount of lubricant that must be used if the equipment is idle to maintain the equipment, the amount would be miniscule in comparison to the quantity used even during low-volume periods. Direct material costs are the costs of material readily traced to the product (the tests). The cost of lubricant used on the laboratory equipment cannot be traced to specific tests readily. Direct labor costs are the costs of labor of those producing the product (the tests). Lubricant is not labor. The cost of lubricant used on the laboratory equipment is a manufacturing cost, not a general or administrative cost.

5.   **Cost of distilled water used in tests: Direct material cost; Variable.**

Direct material costs are the costs of material readily traced to the product (the tests). The distilled water cost can be traced to specific tests readily. The distilled water cost varies with the quantity of product produced (or tests performed). Direct labor costs are the costs of labor of those producing the product (the tests) that is readily traced to the product. Distilled water is not labor. Overhead costs are production costs that cannot be traced to specific units of production readily. The distilled water cost can be traced to specific tests readily. The distilled water cost is a manufacturing cost, not a general or administrative cost.

6.   **Accelerated depreciation on laboratory equipment: Overhead cost; Fixed.**

Overhead costs are production costs that cannot be traced to specific units of production readily. The equipment is being used to produce product (or perform the tests) so its related depreciation is a manufacturing cost. The depreciation cannot be readily traced to specific units. The depreciation on the laboratory equipment is constant regardless of the quantity of product produced (or tests performed). The fact that it will be a different amount next year owing to the nature of accelerated depreciation is irrelevant to classification as fixed or variable. Only if the depreciation was based on a variable charge method would it be a variable cost. Direct material costs are the costs of material readily traced to the product (the tests). Depreciation cannot be readily traced to specific units. Direct labor costs are the costs of labor of those producing the product (the tests) that is readily traced to the product. Depreciation is not labor. The depreciation on the laboratory equipment is a manufacturing cost, not a general or administrative cost.

7. **Straight-line depreciation on laboratory building: Overhead cost; Fixed.**

Overhead costs are production costs that cannot be traced to specific units of production readily. The building is being used to produce product (or perform the tests) so its related depreciation is a manufacturing cost. The depreciation cannot be readily traced to specific units. The depreciation on the laboratory building is constant regardless of the quantity of product produced (or tests performed). Direct material cost: Direct material costs are the costs of material readily traced to the product (the tests). Depreciation cannot be readily traced to specific units. Direct labor cost: Direct labor costs are the costs of labor of those producing the product (the tests) that is readily traced to the product. Depreciation is not labor. The depreciation on the laboratory building is a manufacturing cost, not a general or administrative cost.

8. **Cost of expensive binders in which test results are given to physicians: Direct material cost; Variable.**

Direct material costs are the costs of material readily traced to the product (the tests). The binders are readily traced to specific units. The cost of binders for test results varies with the quantity of product produced (or tests performed). Direct labor costs are the costs of labor of those producing the product (the tests) that is readily traced to the product. Binders are not labor. Overhead costs are production costs that cannot be traced to specific units of production readily. The binders are readily traced to specific units. The cost of binders for test results is a manufacturing cost, not a general or administrative cost.

9. **$40**   The contribution margin per test is the difference between the sales price of $60 and the variable costs of $20, resulting in a contribution margin of $40 per test. This is the same in both activity ranges.

10. **4,000**   The breakeven point at the low range is equal to fixed costs of $160,000 in the low range divided by the contribution margin per unit of $40, resulting in a breakeven point of 4,000 units.

11. **5,000**   The breakeven point at the high range is equal to fixed costs of $200,000 in the high range divided by the contribution margin per unit of $40, resulting in a breakeven point of 5,000 units.

12. **9,000**   To achieve a gross profit of $160,000, Ester would have to sell enough units to cover variable costs, fixed costs, and provide the desired gross profit. The desired gross profit could not be achieved at the maximum capacity in the low range, indicating that Ester will have to operate in the high range to achieve the goal. The number of units required can be calculated by dividing the total of the desired gross profit of $160,000 and the fixed costs at the high range of $200,000 by the contribution margin per unit. The amount is $360,000/$40 per unit, or 9,000 units.

13. Variable costs at low activity range: C. Less than the industry average

The report from the Medical Testing Association states that, at the low range of activity, Ester has a lower sales price, higher fixed costs, and the same breakeven point in number of tests as others in the industry. The breakeven point is that point when the operating profit is $0; thus, at the breakeven point, contribution margin = fixed costs. As Ester's fixed costs are higher than average, Ester's contribution margin is higher than others. Contribution margin is the difference between the sales price and the variable costs. As Ester has a lower than average sales price, the higher contribution margin must be the result of lower than average variable costs.

14. Contribution margin at high activity range: A. Greater than the industry average

The report from the Medical Testing Association states that, at the high range of activity, Ester's sales price per test is the same as industry averages and Ester's variable costs are lower than industry averages. Contribution margin is the difference between the sales price and the variable costs. As Ester has the same sales price at the high range as others in the industry and has lower variable costs, Ester's contribution margin would be higher.

15. Breakeven point at high activity range: C. Less than the industry average

The report from the Medical Testing Association states that, at the high range of activity, Ester's sales price per test and fixed costs are the same as industry averages, and Ester's variable costs are lower than industry averages. Contribution margin is the difference between the sales price and the variable costs. The breakeven point is that point when the operating profit is $0; thus, at the breakeven point, contribution margin = fixed costs. With a higher contribution margin at the high range than others in the industry, along with the same fixed costs as others, Ester would have a lower breakeven point than others.

Section 6 – Planning, Control & Analysis

Table of Contents

EXAM NOTE: *Please refer to the AICPA BEC Blueprint in the Introduction of this book to find a listing of the representative tasks (and their associated skill levels—i.e., Remembering and Understanding, Application, and Analysis) that the candidate should be able to perform based on the knowledge obtained in this section.*

Planning, Control & Analysis

Lecture 6.01 – Master & Static Budgets

Managers use a variety of tools for their organization's internal financial planning, control, and analysis. **Strategic planning** refers to setting long-term overall goals and policies, which help guide the organization's long-run operations. **Tactical planning** focuses on short-term objectives and temporary techniques. Strategic planning often begins with preparing a **mission statement** identifying the organization's purpose and highest values. The next step in strategic planning is to identify goals and objectives that flesh out more fully the organization's mission. In the next step, specific **performance measures** are associated with each of the goals and objectives, so that the organization may measure its performance (i.e., whether it is achieving its goals and objectives). Finally, the organization will design **tactics**, i.e., the specific actions to be used to meet these goals.

To assist in their management, companies often use several specialized budgets. Companies use a **master budget** (a static budget for the company as a whole) to summarize various individual budgets. The two major budgets that the master budget summarizes are:

- **An operating budget**, or a projected (or budgeted or future) income statement with its various supporting schedules.

- **A financial budget**, comprising projected (or budgeted or future) capital budget, cash budget, balance sheet, and statement of cash flows. This budget is usually for 1 year, but could be a rolling budget as well.

Static budgets serve to analyze conditions for a specific level of activity (e.g., what would our labor costs be if our level of sales were X?). Thus, static budgets do not change (or are recalculated) each time some volume (e.g., of sales) changes. Static budgets are normally set up for extended periods of time (e.g., before each year begins). Large companies may set up static budgets for:
- A division within the company
- The company as a whole

Under **Kaizen budgeting**, managers make cost projections that incorporate their expectations for future improvements. Of course, if those improvements do not take place, the budget (goals) cannot be met. The term "Kaizen" generally refers to an originally Japanese management approach that focuses on continually identifying and implementing small improvements (instead of focusing on major breakthroughs or large structural changes).

Preparing a master budget
1. Estimate (future) sales volumes (this is the *First* step in budgeting).
2. Use sales volumes to estimate (future) revenues.
3. Use collection histories to estimate (future) collections.
4. Estimate the cost of sales based on the number of units sold.
5. Use current finished goods inventory, budgeted ending inventory, & cost of sales to estimate the number of units to be manufactured.
6. Use units manufactured to estimate the organization's (future) material needs, labor costs, & overhead costs.

7. Use material needs, current raw materials inventory, & budgeted ending inventory to budget (future) purchases.
8. Use purchase terms to estimate (future) payments.
9. Analyze expense & payment patterns to complete operating & cash flow budgets.

Budgeting Material Purchases & Payments

Units sold

+ Budgeted increase in finished goods

- Budgeted decrease in finished goods

= Units to be manufactured

× Units of raw material per unit of finished goods

= Units of raw material required for production

+ Budgeted increase in raw materials

- Budgeted decrease in raw materials

= **Budgeted raw material purchases**

+ Budgeted decrease in accounts payable

- Budgeted increase in accounts payable

= **Budgeted payments for raw materials**

Production Budget

Budgeted (or projected) sales
+ desired ending inventory of finished goods
Total needs
- beginning inventory of finished goods
Number of units to be produced

Note: Budgets must be prepared in the following order:
- Sales budget
- Production budget
- Direct/Raw materials purchases budget
- Cash Disbursements budget
- Budgeted financial statements (budgeted - Income statement, cash flow, balance sheet)

Flexible Budgeting

In contrast to static budgets, flexible budgets may be adjusted for changes in volumes. When organizations prepare budgets for internal use, they often use the direct costing method, since variable and fixed costs behave differently.

For example:

Sales (in dollars, not number of units)	1,000
-Variable costs	600
Contribution margin	400
-Fixed costs	300
Operating profit	100

If sales for a period turn out to be $1,500, one can readily modify the above statement. Sales increased from $1,000 to $1,500, or by 50%, and would be expected to also increase variable costs by 50%. One would not expect fixed costs to be affected. Thus:

Sales	1,000	× 1.5 =	1,500
-Variable costs	600	× 1.5 =	900
Contribution margin	400		600
-Fixed costs	300	=	300
Operating profit	100		300

Alternatively, the mathematics underlying a **flexible budget** can be most readily expressed using a linear function:

Y = a + (b * X)

- The capital letter "Y" is referred to as the **dependent variable**, or the item whose value is being estimated—in our example: expected total costs.
- The lower case letter "a" is referred to as "the constant" (or the intercept), and in our example stands for **fixed costs.**
- The capital letter X is referred to as the **independent variable**, or the item whose changes may have an impact on the value of the dependent variable (Y). In linear functions applied to flexible budgeting, the independent variable is often called the **cost driver**. In our example, the cost driver is sales. In other settings, the independent variables are often called "predictors" or "determinants."
- The lower case letter "b" is referred to as "the slope," and in our example stands for a **variable rate**, or the multiplier that reflects the effect of change in one unit of X on Y.

 In our example, when sales were $1,000, variable costs were $600, implying a variable rate (b) of 0.6 (i.e., variable costs / sales = $600 / $1,000, or 60% of sales). Fixed costs (a) are $300. Thus:

$$Y = 300 + (0.6 * X)$$

When sales are $1,000:

Expected total costs = 300 + (0.6 * 1,000) = 300 + 600 = 900

When sales are $1,500:

Expected total costs = 300 + (0.6 * 1,500) = 300 + 900 = 1,200

The **_advantage_ of flexible budgets** is that they can readily adapt to changes in variable costs that result from changes in sales levels.

Lecture 6.02 – Master & Static Budgets – Class Questions

1. The basic difference between a master budget and a flexible budget is that a master budget is

    a. Based on one specific level of production and a flexible budget can be prepared for any production level within a relevant range.
    b. Only used before and during the budget period and a flexible budget is only used after the budget period.
    c. Based on a fixed standard, whereas a flexible budget allows management latitude in meeting goals.
    d. For an entire production facility whereas a flexible budget is applicable to single departments only.

2. A 20X5 cash budget is being prepared for the purchase of Toyi, a merchandise item. Budgeted data are

Cost of goods sold for 20X5	$300,000
Accounts payable 1/1/X5	20,000
Inventory -1/1/X5	30,000
-12/31/X5	42,000

   Purchases will be made in twelve equal monthly amounts and paid for in the following month. What is the 20X5 budgeted cash payment for purchases of Toyi?

    a. $295,000
    b. $300,000
    c. $306,000
    d. $312,000

Class Solutions

1. (a) A master budget is prepared on the basis of the expected level of activity. A flexible budget is in the form of a formula with fixed costs remaining constant within a relevant range and variable costs increasing or decreasing depending on the level of activity. Answer (b) is incorrect because both master and flexible budgets can be used before the period to anticipate needs for financing or other resources, during the period to evaluate performance and make corrections, and after the period to evaluate performance. Answer (c) is incorrect because both a master budget and flexible budgets are prepared on the assumption that, within a relevant range, fixed costs will approach a standard amount and variable costs will vary by volume in accordance with a standard relationship. Answer (d) is incorrect because both master budgets and flexible budgets may be prepared for an individual department or an entire entity.

2. (c) If Toyi is anticipating cost of goods sold of $300,000 and an increase in inventory of $12,000, total purchases for the period will be $312,000 or $26,000 per month. During 20X5, Toyi will pay the beginning balance in accounts payable of $20,000 and will pay for purchases made in January through November: 11 × $26,000, or $286,000. As a result, total payments for merchandise will be $306,000 during 20X5, and accounts payable at 12/31 will be equal to December purchases of $26,000.

Lecture 6.03 – Correlation & Regression Analysis

To develop more relevant flexible budgets, companies may seek to identify which predictors to use as the X's for which Y's in their linear functions. For instance, sales might be the best predictor for a company's total costs. In contrast, direct labor hours might be the best predictor for manufacturing overhead costs. Managers may use a variety of techniques to assess the best predictors of their dependent variables. Using **Correlation Analysis**, one may calculate the **Correlation Coefficient** (or coefficient of correlation, ρ, or the lower-case Greek letter, Rho) between (only) two variables at a time (i.e., one's dependent variable and only one independent variable at a time). Values for ρ range between -1.0 and +1.0.

- The closer ρ is to -1 or to +1, the stronger the relationship between the two variables.
- A ρ close to -1 signals a very strong *inverse* relationship.
- A ρ close to +1 signals a very strong *direct* relationship.
- A ρ close to 0 signals a negligible relationship, and likely *no reliable relationship*, between the variables.

What is the relationship between the X & Y variable?

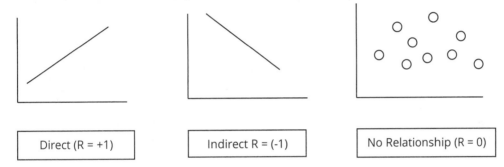

| Direct (R = +1) | Indirect R = (-1) | No Relationship (R = 0) |

Using **Regression Analysis** (i.e., a mathematical or statistical technique), one may test the relationship between one dependent variable and several independent variables (i.e., multivariate or multiple regression analysis). (One can also perform regression analysis with the dependent variable and only one independent variable, i.e., univariate or simple regression analysis). Regression analysis provides a streamlined approach to test which, among various independent variables, is the best predictor of the dependent variable. Regression analysis may also reveal that several independent variables are simultaneously each relevant (i.e., statistically significant) predictors of the dependent variable.

Using regression analysis to determine the best determinants, managers are likely to experiment with a variety of combinations of independent variables (i.e., a model specification). To compare model specifications, managers may use a variety of measures. One of the key measures of a model specification's "goodness of fit" is its **coefficient of determination** (R^2, pronounced R squared). R^2 is defined as the percentage of variation in the dependent variable explained by the variation in the independent variables, and is commonly expressed with values ranging between 0 and 1.

The **F-statistic** (with the "F" always a capital letter) is a measure of the statistical significance (relevance) of the model specification. The p-value (with the p always a lower case letter) attached to an F-statistic is the probability that the overall predicted relationship simply occurred by chance.

Regressions yield **t-statistics** (with the "t" always a lower case letter) (and attached p-value) for each independent variable, which indicate their individual statistical significance (or relevance) in predicting the dependent variable p-value.

Analysts using regression analysis customarily to interpret p-values smaller than 0.01 (1%) as associated with relationships that are very reliable; p-values between 0.01 and 0.05 as reliable; p-values between 0.05 and 0.10 as somewhat, perhaps, or borderline reliable; and p-values larger than 0.10 as not reliable.

Regressions also yield **coefficients** for each independent variable which may be readily interpreted (if statistically significant) as the impact of a change of unit in the independent variable on the dependent variable (i.e., the "b" in linear functions, or the variable rate in our earlier example). Thus, a coefficient of 0.6 would imply that one (or ten) extra dollar(s) of sales would yield 0.6 (or 6) dollars in total expected costs.

Responsibility Accounting

To reduce or eliminate defective units, to increase efficiency in the manufacturing process, and to reduce costs, companies seek to identify which parties within their organization are responsible for which tasks and seek to establish mechanisms to evaluate their performance. To evaluate managers' and divisions' performance, companies often apply **responsibility accounting**. In this terminology:

- The manager of a **cost center** is responsible for the costs incurred by that center.
- The manager of a **profit center** is responsible for both (1) the revenues earned and (2) the costs incurred by that center.
- The manager of an **investment center** is responsible for all of (1) the revenues earned, (2) the costs incurred, and (3) the capital investments from each center.

One way in which the performance of an investment center is evaluated is based on its **economic value added** (EVA). The EVA is equal to the earnings of the investment center over its cost of capital. It is calculated by first multiplying the cost of the investment center by the entity's weighted average cost of capital to determine the cost of capital, which is generally the minimum return that the investment center is expected to yield. Subtracting that amount from the investment center's operating profit gives the amount by which profits exceed the cost of capital and by which the investment center adds economic value to the entity.

Ideally, a manager should not be held responsible for costs that the manager cannot affect, such as costs that have somehow been allocated to that department, but that are directed by and incurred on behalf of either the corporate level or other divisions. Similarly, if the manager's own salary is determined by someone other than the manager, the manager should not be held responsible for that cost.

Modern budgets seek to identify cost drivers as accurately as possible (i.e., what variables affect what costs). An example of these efforts is the technique called **activity based costing (ABC)**. ABC seeks to group together costs that are affected by common factors. For example, depreciation, repairs, and maintenance might be grouped together as activities affected by machine hours (i.e., the usage of machines). In contrast, payroll taxes, employee wages, and benefits might be grouped together as activities affected by direct labor hours.

Under ABC, companies segregate manufacturing overhead into numerous overhead cost pools. Each pool will include costs that have common elements, usually the particular activity that will result in an increase in the costs included in that pool. The activity is the cost driver, or allocation base. One advantage of segregating costs in this manner is that it enhances the usefulness of **multiple regression analysis**, since it will yield both a greater number of potential cost drivers (which commonly enhances regression's ability to yield relevant results) and by ensuring that the boundaries across costs drivers are more sensible.

Costs may also be classified as either **Value-adding** or **Nonvalue-adding**. Value-adding costs are those that actually make the product itself or make it better for customers (such as engineering activity, direct manufacturing costs, the operation of production machinery, modifying products to better meet customers' specifications, or expenses that improve the product's endurance or performance, such as research & development). Costs are ultimately value adding if they result in specific outcomes that customers perceive as increasing the worth of a product or service, for which they would pay more. Nonvalue-adding costs (such as moving, handling, and storage of raw materials, factory utilities, or depreciation of manufacturing equipment) are costs that increase the cost of a product but that customers do not specifically value.

Service Department Costs

Large firms may include various **service departments** that incur overhead costs providing support to the production (or manufacturing) departments. Under the ABC approach, the firms seek to allocate the overhead costs incurred by service departments to the appropriate production departments.
- Under the **direct allocation** method, the firm allocates costs from each service department directly to, and only to, the production or operating departments.
- Under the **step allocation** method, the firm may allocate costs from a service department both to production/production departments and "temporarily or as a step" to the other service departments.
- The **reciprocal allocation** method is similar to the step allocation method except costs are allocated simultaneously among service departments. The high degree of complexity makes it unlikely that the CPA exam will test this method.

Under the **step allocation method**, the costs of individual service departments are allocated as follows:
1. The service departments are ranked, from the one performing services for the most other service departments to the one that performs the least.
2. The costs of the first service department are allocated to the remaining service departments and production/operating departments using appropriate allocation bases. Once the costs of a service department are allocated, that department is eliminated from the process.
3. The costs of the next service department are allocated to the remaining service and production departments. The process is repeated until the costs of the last (and thus of all) service departments have been allocated to production departments.

Most forms of regression analysis are too complicated for exam testing, but a simple technique known as the two-point, **high-low method** is occasionally tested. Under this method, a series of values of an independent and dependent variable (e.g., the monthly observations for one year) are reduced to the two data points associated with the high and low value periods for the cost driver (or independent variables). For instance, assume the highest month of sales was March and the lowest month July, with the following sales and cost figures:

Month	Sales	Total costs
March	600	400
July	500	360
Difference	100	40

Based on the differences (i.e., sales range from 500 to 600, or by 100, and total costs range from 360 to 400, or by 40), total costs change by 40/100 = 40% of the change in sales from the low to the high period. This method yields an estimate of the variable rate, or b. Using the data from March, with sales of $600, variable costs are 40%, or $240. Since total costs in March are $400, variable costs of $240 mean fixed costs are $160, and the resulting linear function is $Y = 160 + (.4 \times X)$.

Forecasting

Firms may use a wide variety of statistical techniques to assist them in developing the values and assumptions included in budgets. Some of these techniques are often referred to by several overlapping names.

- Regression analyses that incorporate not only company data, but also industry and/or economy-wide measures to estimate future sales and costs for a company are sometimes referred to as **econometric models** (economists use the terms *regression analysis* and *econometric models* interchangeably).
- The subset of regression (or econometric) techniques (or models) focusing on analyzing and forecasting data for a single firm over time (e.g., its sales or costs) are commonly referred to as **time series analysis (or models)**.

When adequate data is not available, or budgets are being developed where there is little or no historical information to use, the judgment of various experts may be thought through a method known as **Delphi** (this is a somewhat bemused reference to The Oracle at Delphi, who in Ancient Greece was sought out by those looking for the advice of the gods). Experts are questioned individually and the judgments of the experts are then examined, combined, and sent back to the experts recursively until a consensus arises. In the Delphi technique, the experts do not meet with each other (except sometimes in the final stage), so that their independent judgments aren't biased by the views of the other "oracles" interviewed. The Delphi technique avoids experts meeting to minimize the possibility of **groupthink**, i.e., the tendency of people at meetings to come to a consensus because of the pressures of conformity and fear of embarrassment, such that such consensus may fail to actually represent the best judgment of these same people individually.

Probability Analysis

Most planning techniques require estimates of the revenues and costs that will result from various decisions. In the real world, many decisions may lead to many different possible outcomes. Managers may use **probability theory** to develop the most sensible possible single estimates from the range of possibilities. A *probability distribution* describes the possible outcomes relating to a single action and the likelihood of occurrence of each possible outcome. To turn a probability distribution into a single expected value, one would multiply each of the possible outcomes by its likelihood (or probability, weight, or percentage) and sum the amounts.

> For example, if the decision to market a product is believed to have a 10% probability (chance) of resulting in sales of $100, a 40% probability of $200, a 30% probability of $300, and a 20% probability of $400. The calculation of expected value is as follows:
>
> | Revenue | Probability | Weighted Value |
> |:---:|:---:|:---:|
> | $100 | 10% | $10 |
> | 200 | 40% | 80 |
> | 300 | 30% | 90 |
> | 400 | 20% | 80 |
> | **Expected value** | 100% | $260 |

Lecture 6.04 – Correlation & Regression Analysis – Class Questions I

3. When production levels are expected to increase within a relevant range, and a flexible budget is used, what effect would be anticipated with respect to each of the following costs?

	Fixed costs per unit	Variable costs per unit
a.	Decrease	Decrease
b.	No change	No change
c.	No change	Decrease
d.	Decrease	No change

4. Using regression analysis, Fairfield Co. graphed the following relationship of its cheapest product line's sales with its customers' income levels:

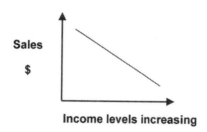

If there is a strong statistical relationship between the sales and customers' income levels, which of the following numbers best represents the correlation coefficient for this relationship?

    a.   -9.00
    b.   -0.93
    c.   +0.93
    d.   +9.00

5. Controllable revenue would be included in a performance report for a

	Profit center	Cost center
a.	No	No
b.	No	Yes
c.	Yes	No
d.	Yes	Yes

6. In an activity-based costing system, cost reduction is accomplished by identifying and eliminating

	All cost drivers	Nonvalue-adding activities
a.	No	No
b.	Yes	Yes
c.	No	Yes
d.	Yes	No

7. Nile Co.'s cost allocation and product costing procedures follow activity-based costing principles. Activities have been identified and classified as being either value adding or non-value-adding as to each product. Which of the following activities, used in Nile production process, is non-value-adding?

    a. Design engineering activity.
    b. Heat treatment activity.
    c. Drill press activity.
    d. Raw materials storage activity.

Class Solutions

3. (d) Within the relevant range, **total** fixed costs remain constant. As production levels increase, the same amount of fixed cost is spread over a greater number of units, and fixed costs **per unit** decrease. In contrast, variable costs **per unit** do not change within the relevant range.

4. (b) The correlation coefficient is a relative measure of the relationship between two variables. The range of the correlation coefficient is from -1 (perfect negative correlation) to +1 (perfect positive correlation). A correlation coefficient of zero means that there is **no** correlation between the two variables. Since the level of sales **increases significantly** as the level of income **decreases**, this relationship represents a strong **negative** correlation and a coefficient of correlation that should be close to -1. An answer of +0.93 is incorrect because that value is close to +1, implying a strong positive relationship. An answer of 9 is incorrect because correlation coefficients range between only -1 and 1, and thus cannot have a value of 9.

5. (c) Responsibility accounting allocates to responsibility centers those costs, revenues, and assets that are the responsibility of the manager to control. If a manager is only responsible for costs, the area of responsibility is called a cost center. If the manager is responsible for both revenues and costs, it is called a profit center. As a result, controllable revenue pertains to the profit center but not the cost center.

6. (c) Cost drivers are the factors that affect costs, such as the number of units being produced affecting the amount of raw materials used. Cost drivers cannot be eliminated as long as the entity is in operation. Non-value-adding activities, those that do not make the product more valuable to the customer or less expensive to provide, are identified and eliminated to reduce costs.

7. (d) Activity-based costing focuses on incorporating into product costs only those activities that provide value to the product. Design engineering is a fundamental activity needed to design a good product. Heat treatment activities would strengthen and protect the product being produced. A drill press activity alters the physical product as it moves on toward becoming a finished good. Raw materials storage activity does nothing to alter or improve the value of a product. It is a non-value-adding activity.

Lecture 6.05 – Correlation & Regression Analysis – Class Questions II

8. A company has an online order processing system. The company is in the process of determining the dollar amount of loss from user error. The company estimates the probability of occurrence of user error to be 90%, with evenly distributed losses ranging from $1,000 to $30,000. What is the expected annual loss from user error?

    a. $13,050
    b. $13,500
    c. $13,950
    d. $14,400

9. Macaw College allocates support department costs to its individual colleges using the step method. Information for July is as follows:

	Maintenance	Power
Costs incurred	$79,200	$43,200
Services percentages provided to:		
Maintenance	–	10
Power	20	–
School of Business	30	20
School of Humanities	50	70
Total	100	100

    What is the amount of July support department costs allocated to the College of Business?

    a. $32,400
    b. $36,880
    c. $38,340
    d. $39,300

10. Which of the following forecasting methods relies mostly on judgment?

    a. Time series models
    b. Econometric models
    c. Delphi
    d. Regression analysis

Class Solutions

8. (c) Expected value is the sum of possible outcomes multiplied by the probability of occurrence. A 90% likelihood of loss means a 10% likelihood of no loss; the 10% likelihood of zero loss is multiplied by $0. To calculate expected annual loss from user error, find the midpoint of the evenly distributed losses and multiply by the likelihood of losses. The midpoint of 1,000 and 30,000 is 15,500, calculated as (1,000 + 30,000)/2. Multiplying 15,500 by the 90% likelihood equals an expected annual loss from user error of $13,950.

9. (b) Under the step method, costs are allocated from one service department to operating departments and other service departments. Costs are not allocated to a department once costs are allocated from that service department. A percentage of use by a service department with costs already allocated is ignored; new ratios are derived using the relationships between the departments still accepting costs. This scenario (modeled after one from the AICPA) does not establish clearly which service department's costs are allocated first. The maintenance department (M) costs must be allocated first because if one assumes the power department (P) costs are allocated first, the answer ($39,960) does not appear as one of the options. In the table below, B and H represent the Schools of Business and Humanities, respectively.

Allocating P costs first	P $	M ratio	M $	B ratio	B $	H ratio	H $
Costs (in 1,000s)	$43.2		$ 79.20				
P ratio/allocation [1+2+7=10]	(43.2)	1/10	4.32	2/10	8.64	7/10	30.24
Subtotal	–0–		$83.52		$ 8.64		$30.24
M ratio/allocation [3+5=8]			(83.52)	3/8	31.32	5/8	52.20
Totals (not an answer option)	–0–		–0–		$39.96		$82.44

Allocating M costs first	M $	P ratio	P $	B ratio	B $	H ratio	H $
Costs (in 1,000s)	$79.2		$ 43.20				
M ratio/allocation [2+3+5=10]	(79.2)	2/10	15.84	3/10	23.76	5/10	39.60
Subtotal	–0–		$59.04		$23.76		$39.60
P ratio/allocation [2+7=9]			(59.04)	2/9	13.12	7/9	45.92
Totals	–0–		–0–		**$36.88**		$85.52

The step method allocates all the first service department costs to production departments and all remaining service departments before allocating the second service department costs.

10. (c) Delphi is a structured forecasting method based on the collective judgement of a group of experts. Each expert's judgment is involved; the forecasts will become more refined after each round–during which experts can revise their previous answers. It is used in novel situations where more objective approaches are unavailable. Answer (a): Time series models objectively analyze a sequence of previously observed data to predict future values, requiring relatively little reliance on judgment. Answer (b): Econometric models are statistical models applying economic theories. Some judgment is involved when selecting theories to apply, but the application of the theories is objective. Answer (d): Forecasting based on regression analysis predicts the dependent variable (y) based on the observed behavior of an independent variable (x). As long as the independent variable and other factors are determined, no subjective judgment is involved.

Lecture 6.06 – Performance Measures

Organizations use performance measures to monitor and manage various aspects of their performance for the organization as a whole and across its various subparts.

Organizations often use **Balanced Scorecards** to help ensure that they are following and implementing their mission and strategic plans. Balanced Scorecards commonly include *performance measures* that may be grouped across into various *perspectives*:

- **Financial perspectives** involve measures of profitability (return on investment, residual income, etc.), revenue, profit, or asset growth, and soundness (debt and equity ratios, etc.).
- **Customer perspectives** involve measuring customer satisfaction (such as through surveys) and retention.
- **Internal business process perspectives** involve measuring averages and variances in the cost, time (i.e., *cycle time*), and *number of defects* involved in producing and delivering a product or service. These perspectives may play a role in promoting **innovation** within organizations.
- **Learning and growth perspectives** seek to ensure that key drivers of organizations' long-term ability to carry out their mission (e.g., employees and their ability to use and access necessary technology) are not neglected in the pursuit of shorter-term objectives. To ensure this balance, organizations may, for instance, track their employees' satisfaction, training, and advancement.

A balanced scorecard commonly includes:

- **Strategic objectives** – A statement of the firm's goals and what is needed to achieve them.
- **Performance measures** – The quantitative methods to be used to determine how much of the strategic objectives are being reached (yardstick).
- **Baseline performance** – How well the firm is doing under each performance measure.
- **Targets** – The amount of improvement being sought for each performance measure.
- **Strategic initiatives** – What specific changes the firm will undertake to achieve its objectives (and targets).

Organizations may seek to identify **cause-and-effect linkages** across their initiatives and changes in various performance measures. These efforts may help to identify which performance measures are actually **performance drivers** (leading indicators) and which are **outcome performance measures** (lagging indicators). Organizations would thus be better able to focus on the drivers that are most critical to achieving their strategic objectives. **Data mining** may also be used, which is the sorting through data to identify patterns and establish relationships, to bring to light previously unidentified relationships. Some of the parameters include association, sequence or path analysis, classification, clustering and forecasting (predictive analytics).

Sunk costs are current costs associated with past decisions that are largely unavoidable, and that are thus largely irrelevant to such analyses.

Organizations using the balanced scorecard framework use **Strategy maps** (i.e., diagrams) to help identify cause-and-effect relationships:

Decision Trees - Managers constantly face decisions for which they cannot have all relevant information initially. As any project evolves, managers have to respond to changing prices, to sales and costs that differ from their initial projections, and to all sorts of new developments, including new investment alternatives, and whether to expand the project further or to retrench. Managers may use decision trees as graphical aids to highlight the chains of decisions that will or will not happen under various scenarios (e.g., if X happens, then the choices about Y are...).

Value-Based Management (VBM) seeks to examine all aspects of a company (as in a **financial scorecard**) to identify the **economic value added (EVA)** that different activities contribute. (EVA is defined as net operating profit after taxes minus the cost of capital). VBM seeks to determine each activity's financial value (or contribution) to the firm. However, if misapplied, VBM may focus on the activities for which it is easiest to link costs to value creation, and fail to reflect that some activities do lead to value creation, even if the links from cost to value creation are less easy to identify. For instance, cost cutting may yield value in the short term, but not in the long term. Similarly, research expenditures may yield value in the long term, or erratically, or through improvements that are shared with other departments but with enhancements in revenues never clearly credited to the research expenditures.

A *value chain* is the sequence of business processes through which a product or service becomes more valuable (or useful), by converting inputs into outputs.

Real Options Techniques treat each business investment decision (i.e., project) as the purchase of a series of options to be exercised as the project evolves. The value of these chains of options is not reflected when managers focus solely on expected cash flows.

Profitability Ratios

Return on Investment (based on assets) = Net income / Total assets or Average invested capital

DuPont ROI analysis: ROI = Return on sales × Asset turnover
- **Return on sales =** Net income / Sales
- **Asset turnover** = Sales / Total assets

Residual income = Operating profit – Interest on investment
- **Interest on investment =** Invested capital × required rate of return

Economic Value Added: EVA = Net operating profit after taxes (NOPAT) – Cost of Financing
- **Cost of financing =** (Total assets – Current Liabilities) × Weighted average cost of capital

Free Cash Flow = NOPAT + Depr + Amort – Capital expenditures – Net increase in working capital

Benchmarking

Benchmarking involves evaluating performance (producing products, delivering services, etc.) on an ongoing basis across subdivisions within an organization and relative to historical and current performance within and outside the organization. Organizations engage in benchmarking in part to identify "best practices" that may then be adopted more widely across the subdivisions of the organization. Common types of benchmarking include:
- **Internal benchmarking:** To track, for instance, how well various subdivisions within one firm carry out one task. Generally, the information is relatively easy to obtain. The disadvantage is that improvement may be limited to the best that one subdivision is doing;

external benchmarking may result in more dramatic improvements. For instance, reducing the employee time to process a vendor invoice and issue a check from 29 minutes to 14 minutes is impressive, until compared with 2 minutes to process an electronic funds transfer (EFT).

- **Competitive benchmarking:** To track how well one firm performs relative to its most direct competitors. This may yield dramatic improvements, but the information often is difficult to obtain; while some of this information is directly observable by the public, obtaining this information typically is very difficult as competitors have little incentive to assist and many incentives to protect their competitive advantages.
    - *Cross-sectional analysis:* exploring data for one time period for multiple firms (i.e., including one's firm and other firms) in the same industry.
    - *Time-series analysis:* exploring data for one firm over time.
    - *Panel data analysis:* exploring data for multiple firms over time (i.e., panel data analysis uses both multiple firms and multiple time periods).
- **Industry benchmarking:** To track one firm against its industry as a whole, instead of against only its direct competitors.
- **Generic benchmarking:** To track one firm against all firms, even if outside its industry. Benchmarking is likely to be more relevant the more alike the firms are that one compares against. Of course, obtaining data is usually easier the broader the category of firms one uses.

Quality Control

The International Organization of Standards (ISO) has developed a series of **ISO Quality Standards**).

- **ISO 9000 Series** – including five parts (9000 to 9004) focusing on the *quality* of products and services provided by firms.
- **ISO 14000 Series** – focusing on environmental goals.

According to the **Pareto Principle,** 80% of quality problems result from only 20% of the possible causes. Thus, firms should first focus on the most important causes of problems, and only later address less important cases.

Six-Sigma Quality is a statistical measure of the percentage of products that are in acceptable form (i.e., achieve the firm's quality goals), based on standard deviation measures (hence the name sigma). To achieve one sigma, 68% of products must be acceptable. To achieve six sigmas, 99.999997% of products must be acceptable. Six-sigma constitutes the practical hypothetical goal of perfection in manufacturing, with only 3.4 defects per million units.

Total quality management (TQM) is an entity-wide effort to continuously improve the ability to deliver high quality products and services by attending to systematic analysis; thus, it includes insights from suppliers as well as employees. It now is largely supplanted by six sigma and ISO programs; however, concepts from TQM often appear (in more evolved and formal versions) in implementation of these later perspectives.

Businesses may apply the **theory of constraints (TOC)** to maximize their operating income and overcome bottlenecks in their operations. Under TOC, if demand exceeds capacity for a resource, the resource is defined as a **bottleneck resource**. If capacity exceeds demand, the resource is defined as a **non-bottleneck resource**. TOC seeks to simultaneously maximize throughput contribution and minimize investment and operating costs.

- **Throughput contribution** equals revenues minus the direct materials cost of goods sold (COGS).
- **Investment** equals the cost of materials, work in process, inventories; research and development expenses; and (upfront) expenses on equipment and buildings.
- **Operating costs** equals employee compensation, rents paid, utilities (electricity, garbage collection, etc.), and depreciation (e.g., of equipment and buildings).

Cost of Quality

This philosophy argues that failures have causes, that preventing failures is cheaper than having to address failures after they take place, and that measuring a firm's performance in implementing the cost of quality philosophy can be achieved and will help the firm. The costs related to addressing quality issues rise the later in the production process that the firm deals with the quality problems. There are *four different stages* at which costs can be addressed:

- **Prevention costs** – seeking to prevent quality failures
  - Using high-quality materials
  - Inspecting the production process
  - Focusing engineering and design to improve quality
  - Providing training to employees that focuses on improving quality
  - Quality circles
  - Maintenance of equipment (machines, etc.)

- **Appraisal (or detection costs)** – expenses on detecting quality failures
  - Inspecting samples of materials, in-process, and finished goods
  - Obtaining information from customers

- **Internal failure costs** – expenses addressing quality failures that were detected after production but before they were shipped to customers
  - Disposing of scrap resulting from wasted materials
  - Reworking units to correct defects
  - Re-inspecting & retesting after rework

- **External failure costs** – expenses addressing defective products that reached customers
  - Warranty costs
  - Expenses addressing customer complaints
  - Product liability costs
  - Cost of product returns
  - Marketing to help maintain and/or improve the firm's image
  - Losses of future sales, your reputation

Costs of conforming to quality control standards are called **Conformance costs** = prevention + appraisal costs.

Costs of failure of quality controls are called **Nonconformance costs** = internal + external failure costs.

Lecture 6.07 – Performance Measures – Class Questions I

11. On a balanced scorecard, which of the following is considered an internal business process perspective?

    a. Number of defects in product that customers report
    b. Number of hours of employee training
    c. Percentage of employee advancement
    d. Percentage of employee retention

12. Apex Athletics, LLC, is manufacturer of premium athletic equipment and apparel. Apex is starting a value based management process. What is an activity for which it most likely will be difficult to trace to the economic value added to Apex?

    a. Cycle time reduction in manufacturing processes
    b. Design of products to reduce packaging and shipping costs
    c. Lead generation
    d. Sponsorship of after-school and summer youth programs in low-income neighborhoods.

13. At 20% of industry sales, Party Hearty, Inc., is one of the top three chains of party stores. These three chains cumulatively have 73% of industry sales. Party Hearty would like to perform benchmarking to determine the best practices for its processes, but is having difficulty obtaining data for benchmarking. For which form of benchmarking will Party Hearty find it easiest to obtain data?

    a. Competitive benchmarking
    b. Generic benchmarking
    c. Industry benchmarking
    d. Internal benchmarking

14. Which of the following quality costs generally are most difficult to quantify?

    a. Detection costs
    b. External failure costs
    c. Internal failure costs
    d. Prevention costs

Class Solutions

11. (a) The internal business perspective includes measuring the cost, time, and quality of producing and delivering a product or service. One example of this is the number of defects. Answers (b), (c), and (d): Employee advancement, training, and retention are considered part of the learning and growth perspective.

12. (d) As a manufacture of "premium" athletic equipment and apparel, Apex is unlikely to generate much future (and even less immediate) business among those participating in the low-income neighborhood programs; however, the social responsibility demonstrated by Apex's sponsorship of these programs may resonate with affluent consumers of its products. The extent to which sales are a result of consumers' appreciation of Apex social responsibility as opposed to those that would have occurred without such sponsorship is difficult to determine. Answer (a): Shorter cycle times equate to less time that inventory is held, reducing the holding costs (such as, property taxes and financing). Answers (b) and (c): Greater revenue, lower costs, and shorter cycles generally are easy to equate to economic value added.

13. (d) Internal benchmarking involves comparing various subdivisions within one company; presumably, the head office merely could instruct each subdivision to collect and report any required information that it does not already receive. Answer (a): Competitive benchmarking involves comparing processes with direct competitors. Competitors are unlikely to assist. Answer (b): Generic benchmarking involves comparing processes at all types of companies; at a minimum, this would involve researching sources of such information. Answer (c): Industry benchmarking involves comparing processes at all companies in the industry; at a minimum, this would involve researching sources of such information.

14. (b) External failure costs include such costs as the loss of reputation, product liability costs, and marketing to maintain or improvement of the company image. While estimated future sales form an input to determine the loss of reputation costs, it is itself an estimate. These costs are difficult to quantity. Answer (a): Detection costs include inspection costs and customer survey costs. These costs tend to be easy to separate from other costs and objectively calculated, making them relatively easy to quantify. Answer (c): Internal failure costs include the costs of wasted materials, reworking units to correct defects and re-inspecting and retesting after rework. These costs tend to be easy to separate from other costs and objectively calculated, making them relatively easy to quantify. Answer (d): Prevention costs include using materials of known quality, designing production processes to promote quality, monitoring production processes, and employee training. Compared to external failure costs—such as product liability and loss of reputation, prevention costs tend to be calculated objectively; this makes them relatively easy to quantify.

Lecture 6.08 – Performance Measures – Class Questions II

15. Last year a consulting company that solves computer network problems instituted a total quality management (TQM) program and produced the following summary cost-of-quality report:

	Year 1	Year 2	Change
Prevention costs	$ 200,000	$ 300,000	+50%
Appraisal costs	210,000	315,000	+50%
Internal failure costs	190,000	114,000	-40%
External failure costs	1,200,000	621,000	-48%
Total quality costs	$1,800,000	$1,350,000	-25%

Which of the following statements regarding the report is most likely correct?

  a. An increase in inspection costs was solely responsible for the decrease in quality costs.
  b. An increase in conformance costs resulted in a decrease in nonconformance costs.
  c. The increase in conformance costs indicated that the TQM program was not working.
  d. In the long run, increased conformance costs would cause total quality costs to increase.

16. A manufacturer that wants to improve its staging process compares its procedures against the check-in process for a major airline. Which of the following tools is the manufacturer using?

  a. Total quality management.
  b. Statistical process control.
  c. Economic value-added.
  d. Benchmarking.

Class Solutions

15. (b) An increase in prevention and appraisal costs, or the costs of conforming to quality standards, appears to have led to a decrease in costs associated with internal and external failure, or nonconformance costs. Answer (a): It is not likely that an increase in inspection costs was solely responsible for the decrease in quality costs, as there was most likely significant investment in non-inspection activities included in both the Prevention and Appraisal spending categories. Answer (c): The TQM program is working because overall quality costs are down as a result of increased investment in conformance. Answer (d): Given the dramatic short-term success of the TQM program, a long-term increase in total quality costs does not seem highly likely, as they most likely would have decreased.

16. (d) Benchmarking involves comparisons within or outside a firm in order to evaluate performance. Companies may engage in benchmarking to identify "best practices," which can then be implemented and used to set performance standards. Answer (a): Total quality management is a company-wide effort to continuously improve the ability to deliver high quality products and services. Answer (b): Statistical process control is a form of quality control that employs statistical techniques. Answer (c): Economic value-added refers to the value created in excess of an entity's required return.

Lecture 6.09 – Business Process Management (BPM)

This operations management approach seeks to align all aspects of an organization with the wants and needs of its clients. BPM is often called a "process optimization process." Business processes are the structured activities of an organization that produce a product or service. BPM promotes business effectiveness and efficiency while striving for innovation, flexibility, and integration with technology. Business processes are strategic assets that must be *understood, managed, and improved*. Under BPM, managers seek to recognize that processes have **human and technological aspects** and that the two aspects interact. BPM argues that understanding these interactions play a key role in improving processes.

The life-cycle of business process management includes:

1. **Design**
   This first phase identifies current processes and designs improvements for them. Of course, proper design may prevent problems later.

2. **Modeling**
   During this second phase, processes are tested under various "what if" scenarios before rolling them out to full production so that issues may be identified and addressed (i.e., redesigned).

3. **Execution**
   During the third phase, equipment and software are installed, employees are trained, and the new processes are implemented at full-production levels.

4. **Monitoring**
   Once new processes are implemented, they continue to be monitored (tested) yielding performance data.

5. **Optimization**
   Performance data (from the modeling or monitoring phases) is analyzed to identify areas for improvement (i.e., bottlenecks) that may be re-designed further. Re-design may variously involve centralizing or de-centralizing some activities as appropriate (some purchases may be cheaper in large quantities; others may require specialized knowledge or be subject to particular time constraints). Re-design may also involve bringing some processes inside the firm (i.e., acquiring a supplier) or outside the firm (**out-sourcing**) or outside the country (**off-shoring**, whether inside or outside the firm). Any re-design choice involves benefits, costs, and risks. For instance, the benefits of out-sourcing and off-shoring might include lower employee compensation and some tax benefits. However, they might also open the firm to the following risks:
   - Quality risk (less control over quality).
   - Language risk (e.g., customer service).
   - Information security risk (potential loss of control over confidential customer and company info).
   - Intellectual property risk (potential loss of control of information about the company's products and processes).
   - Public opinion risk (potential loss of reputation).
   - Social responsibility risk (concerns about the ethics of organizations the firm may work with in other countries).

Re-design is an on-going process. Each change opens the doors for new benefits, new risks, and the eventual need for further re-designs. For instance, firms may seek to minimize the risks listed above by setting up various procedures, such as operating agreements with their domestic and international partners.

Lecture 6.10 – Business Process Management (BPM) – Class Questions

17. General Looms hires a consultant to implement business process management. What best describes the consultant's goals?

    a. Identify General Looms' long-term goals and determine how best to reach them.
    b. Ensure that General Looms' objectives are met while the legitimate needs and concerns of all stakeholders are being addressed.
    c. Establish a code of conduct and encourage appropriate behavior by example.
    d. Align all aspects of General Looms with the wants and needs of its customers.

18. A consultant proposed that Trendy Gizmos, a U.S. manufacturer, have its electronic devices assembled in a factory in India. One member of the team considering the proposal is concerned about the potential loss of control over information about the company's products and processes. What best describes the team member's concerns?

    a. Social responsibility risk.
    b. Quality risk.
    c. Intellectual property risk.
    d. Information security risk.

Class Solutions

17. (d) Business process management involves the alignment of all aspects of a business with the wants and needs of its customers. Answer (a): Strategic planning is the identification of long-term goals and determination of how best to reach them. Answer (b): Corporate governance involves ensuring that an entity's objectives are met while the legitimate needs and concerns of all stakeholders are being addressed. Answer (c): Implementing internal control involves management establishing a code of conduct and encouraging appropriate behavior by example.

18. (c) Intellectual property risk is the risk that an entity could lose control of information about the entity's products and processes. Copyright and patent regulation and enforcement is not uniform internationally. Answer (a): Social responsibility risk concerns the ethics of business partners or working practices at the foreign site. Answer (b): Quality risk is due to less control over quality. Answer (d): Information security risk is the risk that an entity could lose control over confidential customer and entity information.

Lecture 6.11 – Planning, Control & Analysis – Class Questions – TBS

 The Uniform CPA Examination   CALC   EXCEL   AUTH. LIT   OVERVIEW   ? HELP    SUBMIT TESTLET

Gilligan, Inc. commenced operations on January 2, 20X3. Gilligan's three products (Aster, Begonia, and Cosmos) are produced in different plants located in the same community.

- Gilligan prepared standard absorption costing statements using full capacity (based on machine hours) to allocate overhead costs.
- Fixed costs are incurred evenly throughout the year.
- There is no ending work-in-process.
- Material price variances are reported when raw materials are taken from inventory.
- Apart from initial build-ups in raw materials, and finished goods inventories, production schedules are based on sales forecasts.

Gilligan uses the graph below to estimate Aster's total standard manufacturing cost.

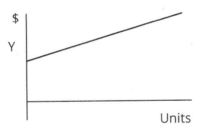

Based on this information and the information on the Resources tab, answer the following questions.

For items 1 through 13, determine whether the answer is **(Y)** yes or **(N)** no.

___ **1.** Should Gilligan include standard indirect material costs in standard fixed overhead costs?

___ **2.** Should Gilligan categorize the operation of production equipment as a value-adding activity?

___ **3.** If Gilligan's three products were produced in a single plant, would activity-based costing provide more useful total production cost information for Aster, Begonia, and Cosmos than traditional standard costing?

___ **4.** Is the regression analysis technique helpful in determining the variable cost component of Gilligan's manufacturing overhead costs?

___ **5.** In Gilligan's internal performance reports, should normal spoilage costs be reported in fixed manufacturing overhead costs?

___ **6.** The computation of Begonia's normal spoilage assumes 10 units in 1,000 contain defective materials and, independently, 15 units in 1,000 contain defective workmanship. Is the probability that is used in computing Begonia's normal spoilage less than 0.025?

___ **7.** Gilligan has contracted to sell units of Aster to a customer in a segregated market during the offseason. Ignore variances and the costs of developing and administering the contract. Standard cost patterns are unchanged, except that variable selling and administrative costs are one-half the standard rate. Gilligan will sell Aster at a price which recoups the variable cost of goods sold at the standard rate, plus variable selling and administrative costs at one-half of the standard rate. Will Gilligan break even on the contract?

___ **8.** Were the actual 20X3 direct labor hours used in manufacturing Aster less than the standard hours?

___ **9.** Would Aster's 20X3 operating income reported using absorption cost be lower than the amount reported using variable costing?

___ **10.** Was the total amount paid for direct materials put into process for the manufacture of Aster more than the standard cost allowed for the work done?

___ **11.** Gilligan is considering investing $60,000 in a 10-year property lease that will reduce Aster's annual selling and administration costs by $12,000. Gilligan's cost of capital is 12%. The present value factor for a 10-year annuity at 12% is 5.65. Is there a positive net present value for the lease investment?

___ **12.** Gilligan is considering investing $60,000 in a 10-year property lease that will reduce Aster's annual selling and administration costs by $12,000. Gilligan's cost of capital is 12%. The present value factor for a 10-year annuity at 12% is 5.65. Is the internal rate of return for the lease investment lower than the cost of capital?

___ **13.** Does Gilligan practice a just-in-time philosophy?

For item 14, select from the following list: **(A)** Increase, **(B)** Decrease, or **(C)** No effect.

___ **14.** If Gilligan sells $10,000 more of Begonia and $10,000 less of Cosmos, what is the effect on Gilligan's standard dollar breakeven point?

For items 15 through 18, select from the following list: **(A)** Aster, **(B)** Begonia, or **(C)** Cosmos

___ **15.** For which product is evaluation of investments by the payback method likely to be more appropriate?

___ **16.** For which product is the economic order quantity formula likely to be most useful when purchasing raw materials to be used in manufacturing?

___ **17.** Which product had the greatest actual return on investment?

___ **18.** Ignore 20X3 reported variances and assume that Gilligan used expected demand to allocate manufacturing overhead costs. Which product would be most likely to have a substantial percentage of under-applied or over-applied fixed manufacturing overhead costs on quarterly statements?

___ **19.** What is Aster's budgeted standard per unit cost for variable selling and administrative costs on sales of 75,000 units?

___ **20.** What is Aster's budgeted standard fixed selling and administrative costs on sales of 75,000 units?

___ **21.** What is Gilligan's standard breakeven point in sales dollars for the actual sales mix achieved?

___ **22.** What amount of Aster's direct material and direct manufacturing labor variances might be regarded, wholly or partially, as direct manufacturing labor employees' responsibility?

___ **23.** What amount does the Y represent on Aster's total standard manufacturing cost graph?

Exhibits

Excerpt from Gilligan's Utilization Study

	Aster	Begonia	Cosmos
* Manufacturing Capacity Utilization	75%	80%	70%
* Average Investment	$1,000,000	$800,000	$400,000
* Demand	Somewhat seasonal and moderately difficult to project more than 3 years	Constant and easy to project more than 3 years	Very seasonal and very difficult to project more than 3 years

Excerpt from Gilligan's internal 20X3 contribution margin income statement, based on standard costs

Gilligan, Inc.
20X3 CONTRIBUTION MARGIN INCOME STATEMENT

Products	Aster	Begonia	Cosmos	Total
Sales (Aster 80,000 units)	$1,200,000	$800,000	$500,000	$2,500,000
Standard Costs:				
Direct Material	180,000			
Direct Labor (Aster 20,000 hours)	240,000			
Variable Manufacturing Overhead	80,000			
Total Variable Manufacturing Costs	500,000	(Detail omitted)		
Less: Finished Goods Inventory 12/31/X3	100,000			
Variable Cost of Goods Sold	400,000			
Variable Selling and Administrative Costs	120,000			
Total Variable Costs	520,000			
Standard Contribution Margin	680,000	176,000	144,000	1,000,000
Fixed Manufacturing Overhead Costs	440,000			
Fixed Selling and Administrative Costs	140,000	(Detail omitted)		
Total Fixed Costs	580,000			
Standard Operating Income	100,000	35,000	25,000	160,000
Variances - Favorable **F**/ Unfavorable **U**:				
Direct Materials - Price	2,000 F			
Usage	16,000 U			
Direct Labor - Rate	12,000 U	(Detail omitted)		
Efficiency	24,000 U			
Manufacturing Overhead - Total	43,000 U			
Selling and Administrative - Total	7,000 U			
Operating Income, Net of Variances	$ -0-	$ 41,000	$ 36,000	$ 77,000

Task-Based Simulation Solution

1. N Indirect materials generally are treated as a variable overhead cost, rather than a fixed overhead cost. Greater amounts of indirect materials are used in periods of higher production, unlike fixed costs that are incurred evenly throughout the production period.

2. Y Production equipment is used in the manufacture of the product. As a result, the operation of production equipment is a value-adding activity.

3. Y Under traditional product standard costing, costs are allocated to production based on a single factor used to determine the predetermined overhead rate. In activity-based costing, different costs are allocated to production using different bases. It would be difficult to find a single base for allocating costs that would be appropriate for all three of these products. This circumstance suggests that activity-based costing would be more appropriate when the three products are produced in a single plant.

4. Y Regression analysis is a tool that can be used to determine the fixed and variable components of costs so that they can be estimated at various levels of production. Regression analysis would be helpful in determining the variable cost component of Gilligan's manufacturing overhead costs.

5. N In a manufacturing situation, normal spoilage occurs as a part of the production process. There is a relationship between the amount of spoilage incurred and the volume of production. Generally, more spoilage is experienced in periods of high production than in periods of low production. As a result, normal spoilage is a variable rather than a fixed cost.

6. Y A total of 1% of units contain defective materials and 1.5% contain defective workmanship. Some units will contain both types of defects. As a result, less than 2.5% of the units produced will be defective.

7. Y Gilligan is working at only 75% of capacity in the manufacture of Aster, indicating there is capacity to accept a special order that uses 25% or less of capacity in the manufacture of Aster. As standard cost patterns are unchanged—except the variable selling and administrative costs, indicating that there will be no additional fixed costs resulting from accepting the order, Gilligan would have to recover only variable costs to break even on the special order. If units can be sold for an amount equal to the standard variable cost of goods sold and one-half of the ordinary standard variable selling and administrative costs, when those will be the actual variable costs, Gilligan would break even on the sale.

8. N There is an unfavorable direct labor efficiency variance. This indicates that units took longer to produce than expected and that actual direct labor hours used exceeded the standard hours.

9. N Since this is Gilligan's first year of operations, there would be no beginning inventories; however, there are ending inventories. In periods in which inventory increases, a company will report a higher income under absorption costing than under variable costing. This is due to the fixed overhead being included in inventory under absorption costing and being expensed under variable costing.

10. Y Aster reported a favorable material price variance of $2,000 and an unfavorable usage variance of $16,000, resulting in an unfavorable net variance of $14,000. An unfavorable net variance indicates that, overall, more was paid for materials than the standard amount.

11. Y   The present value of the savings in selling and administrative costs would be $12,000 × 5.65 or $67,800. This is reduced by the investment of $60,000 to give a positive net present value of $7,800.

12. N   The present value of the savings at 12% is $12,000 × 5.65 or $67,800, which is greater than the investment of $60,000. The internal rate of return (IRR) on the investment would be the rate at which the present value would be equal to $60,000, making the internal rate of return on the investment greater than 12%. Since 12% is Gilligan's cost of capital, the IRR on the investment is higher than the cost of capital.

13. N   Under a just-in-time approach, a company would maintain low levels of inventory and production schedules would be based on demand. Gilligan's production schedules are based on sales forecasts rather than demand. This indicates that Gilligan is not following a just-in-time approach.

14. I   Begonia has a contribution margin ratio of 22% based on a contribution margin of $176,000 and sales of $800,000. Cosmos has a contribution margin ratio of 28.8% based on a contribution margin of $144,000 and sales of $500,000. The higher the proportion of sales of products with higher contribution margin ratios, the lower the breakeven point will be. Increasing sales of a product with a low contribution margin and decreasing sales of a product with a higher contribution margin will increase the breakeven point.

15. C   Demand for Cosmos is very difficult to project more than 3 years. Net present value and internal rate of return models rely heavily on forecasts for the entire life of a project, but the payback period model typically is concerned about only the early years of a project. Demand for Cosmos might not exist after 3 years. Gilligan would be concerned about at least being able to recover an investment within a 3-year period. As a result, the payback method would be most appropriately applied to Cosmos.

16. B   The economic order quantity formula is the square root of 2AP/S with A equal to annual demand for the product, P the cost of placing an order or setting up a production run, and S the cost of carrying a unit of inventory for one year. In order to apply the formula, demand must be predictable. Since it is easy to project demand for Begonia, the economic order quantity formula would be most useful applied to that product.

17. C   Return on investment (ROI) is operating income divided by average investment. Aster has an actual ROI of $0/$1,000,000 or 0%. Begonia has an actual ROI of $41,000/$800,000 = 5.125%. Cosmos has the highest actual ROI of $36,000/$400,000 = 9%.

18. C   When expected demand is used to allocate overhead costs, the same amount of fixed overhead (FOH) would be applied to each unit. In periods of high production, however, the actual FOH per unit is lower than in periods of low production. As a result, a product that is very seasonal, like Cosmos, would have large FOH variances during interim periods, even though the variances will offset one another over the year.

19. $1.50   Aster has standard variable selling and administrative costs of $120,000 based on production of 80,000 units. Since 75,000 units is within the same relevant range, the per unit standard variable selling and administrative costs would be the same as for 80,000 units, $120,000/80,000 or $1.50 per unit.

20. $140,000   Standard fixed selling and administrative costs for Aster is the same on sales of 75,000 units as on sales of 80,000 units. The standard fixed selling administrative costs for Aster at 80,000 units is $140,000.

21. $2,100,000   Gilligan has a contribution margin of $1,000,000 based on sales of $2,500,000, indicating a contribution margin ratio of 40%. With operating income of $160,000, fixed costs must be $840,000 (i.e., $2,500,000 sales - $1,500,000 variable costs = $1,000,000 contribution margin – $840,000 fixed costs = $160,000 operating income). The breakeven point in dollars is equal to fixed costs divided by the contribution margin ratio = $840,000/40% = $2,100,000.

22. $40,000   Direct labor employees may be responsible for variances relating to the use of raw materials and the efficiency of the manufacturing process. As a result, they may be partially or wholly responsible for the $16,000 unfavorable material usage variance and the $24,000 unfavorable labor efficiency variance, for a total of $40,000. As both of these variances are unfavorable, they do not offset each other. Direct labor employees generally are not considered responsible for the price of raw materials or assigning employees to tasks, and thus, determining the labor rate. Thus, neither the direct material price variance nor the direct labor rate (price) variance are their responsibility.

23. $440,000   Point Y intersects the cost axis at zero units. Thus, Y represents the amount of manufacturing costs that will be incurred if no units of Aster are produced. As a result, it is equal to Aster's fixed manufacturing costs of $440,000.

Lecture 6.12 – Planning, Control & Analysis – Class Questions – Written Communication

Written Communications 1

Katherine Olivier, the recent heir to Navarre Enterprises, a family-owned company, is considering applying professional management techniques to her company. Katherine would like you to prepare a memorandum explaining balanced scorecards. She is concerned that professional management techniques do not go against her family's and company's traditions.

REMINDER: Your response will be graded for both technical content and writing skills. Technical content will be evaluated for information that is helpful to the intended reader and clearly relevant to the issue. Writing skills will be evaluated for development, organization, and the appropriate expression of ideas in professional correspondence. Use a standard business memo or letter format with a clear beginning, middle, and end. Do not convey information in the form of a table, bullet point list, or other abbreviated presentation.

To: Mrs. Katherine Olivier, President
    Navarre Enterprises
From: CPA Candidate

Written Communication Solution 1

To: Mrs. Katherine Olivier, President
    Navarre Enterprises
From: CPA Candidate

Thank you very much for your question regarding how a balanced scorecard may benefit your company. A balanced scorecard seeks to focus an organization's attention on implementing its mission and strategic plans. Developed and used appropriately, a balanced scorecard would not go against the traditions of the Olivier family and Navarre Enterprises, but rather facilitate implementation of their core values.

The balance part of a balanced scorecard is due to using different perspectives in measurements: learning and growth, customer, internal business process, and financial. Financial perspectives involve profitability and fiscal soundness. Internal business process perspectives involve issues such as cycle time and quality. Customer perspectives involve customer retention and satisfaction. Learning and growth perspectives involve providing for the organization's long-term growth; this involves employee satisfaction and development.

Typically, a balanced scorecard includes strategic objectives, performance measures, performance baselines, performance targets, and strategic initiatives. Strategic objectives merely are what is needed to meet the firm's goals. Performance measures are the yardstick that is used to track how well those goals are met. These are determined in a variety of ways, such as regression analysis. The baseline is how the firm is doing initially; the target is the goal sought. The strategic initiatives are the specific means the firm is using to reach those targets.

Appropriate performance measures are determined in a variety of ways. Often firms seek cause and effect links between performance drivers and desired outcomes. Data mining also may be used to bring to light previously unidentified relationships. Regression analysis can help to evaluate proposed performance measures. The balanced scorecard should help the firm to focus on performance drivers that are most essential to achieving the strategic objectives.

A balanced scorecard should help reinforce an organization's values by tracking the progress of the organization's initiatives. If you have further questions, please feel free to contact me.

Sincerely,

CPA Candidate

Written Communications 2

Beatrix Benedict, the CFO of Canary Wharf Docks, is concerned that her CEO does not really understand what drives costs within their company and is, thus, not allocating resources appropriately. She has asked you to explain regression analysis and how she could use it to better ascertain what the cost drivers are within her company.

REMINDER: Your response will be graded for both technical content and writing skills. Technical content will be evaluated for information that is helpful to the intended reader and clearly relevant to the issue. Writing skills will be evaluated for development, organization, and the appropriate expression of ideas in professional correspondence. Use a standard business memo or letter format with a clear beginning, middle, and end. Do not convey information in the form of a table, bullet point list, or other abbreviated presentation.

To: Ms. Beatrix Benedict, CFO
    Canary Wharf Docks
From: CPA Candidate

Written Communication Solution 2

To: Beatrix Benedict, CFO
    Canary Wharf Docks
From: CPA Candidate

Thank you very much for your question regarding how regression analysis may benefit your company. Some firms use regression analysis to ascertain drivers for various outcomes. For instance, regression analysis can help ascertain what types of sales are driving what types of costs.

Regressions typically study the impacts of multiple variables (e.g., sales from various divisions within the company) on one variable (total costs). Beyond internal company data, regressions may also include macroeconomic factors. Regressions yield various measures to assess the relevance of the included variables as a group (e.g., F-statistics and R^2) and the size of the impact and relevance of individual variables (variable coefficients and t-statistics). Regressions help answer questions such as which of two potential cost drivers is more important.

Regression analysis may be very useful not only in helping one manager ascertain which factors are driving costs, but also in providing numerical estimates that are readily understandable by other managers. If you have any further questions, please feel free to contact me.

Sincerely,

CPA Candidate

Written Communications 3

MTDV, Inc. operates retail outlets across many cities, has detailed historical sales data for each individual outlet, and could obtain demographic data about each of the cities where it operates. The company is considering opening a new outlet in a region where it does not have any outlets at this point.

Teresa Highlander, the Chief Executive Officer of the company has asked you to write a memo outlining how they could estimate the sales they could expect in that new outlet, and some of the issues involved in such a calculation.

REMINDER: Your response will be graded for both technical content and writing skills. Technical content will be evaluated for information that is helpful to the intended reader and clearly relevant to the issue. Writing skills will be evaluated for development, organization, and the appropriate expression of ideas in professional correspondence. Use a standard business memo or letter format with a clear beginning, middle, and end. Do not convey information in the form of a table, bullet point list, or other abbreviated presentation.

To: Ms. Teresa Highlander, Chief Executive Officer
     MTDV Inc.
From: CPA Candidate

Written Communication Solution 3

To: Ms. Teresa Highlander
     MTDV Inc.
 From: CPA Candidate

Thank you for your question regarding how to forecast estimates of the new outlet you are considering opening. To estimate sales in an outlet in a new city, MTDV could use forecasting techniques. The reliability of these estimates will be greater the more that the region where the new outlet will be located is similar to the regions where MTDV already operates.

Forecasting techniques first assess the past relationships across variables, e.g., sales at individual outlets and demographic characteristics where the outlets are. Forecasting techniques next use those relationships to make projections. The techniques might take into account, for instance, that the new outlet is located in a city that is fairly small or with income levels that are slightly above average. Sales estimates will be more reliable if the city is similar to other cities where MTDV already operates, e.g., similar size, same proportion of young, vs. elderly residents, etc. Sales estimates will be least reliable if the city differs greatly.

MTDV could use forecasting techniques to project likely sales for its outlet in a new city. Forecasts for new outlets in regions where MTDV has not operated before will be less reliable. Please feel free to contact me if you have any additional questions or concerns.

Sincerely,

CPA Candidate

Section 7 – Information Technology

Table of Contents

EXAM NOTE: *Please refer to the AICPA BEC Blueprint in the Introduction of this book to find a listing of the representative tasks (and their associated skill levels—i.e., Remembering and Understanding, Application, and Analysis) that the candidate should be able to perform based on the knowledge obtained in this section.*

Information Technology

Lecture 7.01 – Information Technology Role in Business

The use of computers first focused on relieving humans of the tedious work involved in general recordkeeping and reporting. Now, regulatory requirements include electronic reporting. For instance, the IRS requires electronic submission of many business tax returns.

Transaction processing systems focus on relieving humans of the tedious work involved in general recordkeeping and reporting. **Management reporting systems** assist in the decision-making process within the organization. The most common business systems include:

- *Management information system* – (MIS) An organized assembly of resources and procedures required to collect, process, and distribute data for use in decision making.

- *Decision support system* – (DSS) An interactive system that provides the user with easy access to decision models and data, to support semi-structured decision-making tasks.

- Enterprise Resource Planning (ERP) is a packaged business software system that allows an organization to automate and integrate the majority of its business processes (sales, inventory management, planning and forecasting), share common data and practices across the entire organization, and produce and access information in a real-time environment. These systems span both transaction processing systems and management reporting systems. Examples of ERP include SAP, Oracle Financials, and J.D. Edwards.

- *Executive support information system* – Systems designed specifically to support executive work (nonroutine decision, helps answer questions regarding competitors and identify new acquisitions).

- *Analytical processing system* – software technology that enables the user to query (ask) the system, retrieve data and conduct analysis.

- *Expert system* – The most prevalent type of computer system that arises from the research of artificial intelligence. An expert system has a built-in hierarchy of rules, which are acquired from human experts in the appropriate field. Once input is provided, the system should be able to define the nature of the problem and provide recommendations to solve the problem.

Connectivity

The Internet and related Web technologies ushered in a paradigm shift from the computer as a number-crunching device to a communication tool. This paradigm shift was aided by significant declines in computing costs coupled with dramatic increases in computing power in the last several decades.

Since the introduction of smart phones in 2007, the Internet has driven another shift—from desktop devices to mobile devices and tablets. Thus, computing is being even more fully integrated into daily life.

For example, in the number-crunching phase, businesses started using computers to record the sales made each day at a store and then made by each cashier, then a computer at the store recorded each sale and concurrently updated the inventory files. In the communicating phase, the cashier's computer automatically contacts the credit card company to confirm that the customer's available credit limit is sufficient for the purchase. Businesses websites started with contact information and driving directions and evolved to online retail sites.

Obviously, businesses still are using the number-crunching aspect of computers. Indeed, automation of many tasks once performed by humans is ubiquitous. The communications aspect's applicability to accounting might be less obvious.

For example, decades ago, employees submitted physical copies of receipts and a printed expense report to the accounting department. An A/P clerk reviewed the report, coded expenses by category, confirmed expenses meet per diem and other limits, and requested supervisor approval. After the report was approved, the A/P clerk submitted a paper payment voucher. A check was issued for the employee to take to his or her bank and deposit.

Now, employees use smartphones to take a picture of any paper receipts. They might use the smartphone linked to a credit card to pay for expenses. Employees submit electronic copies of receipts to a website that "reads" the receipts, suggests likely categories, confirms that expenses meet *per diem* and other limits, and requests supervisor approval. After the report is approved, an A/P clerk reviews the categories (lodging, airfare, local transportation, meals, etc.) to ensure they are correct and submits an electronic payment voucher. An electronic payment is issued to the employee's bank account.

While these computers are keeping records, they also are communicating with each other: the employee's smartphone with the credit card company servers, the employee's tablet that gets an e-mail with a receipt from the taxi driver's smartphone, the employee's tablet and smartphone with the server hosting the expense website, the expense website server with the supervisor's laptop and the employer's servers, and the A/P clerk's desktop with the bank's servers.

A distributor's computer likewise can communicate with manufacturers' and retailers' computers, ordering and shipping product without each shipment being initiated directly by a human.

The ubiquitous nature of computers make it important that their systems are operating as designed.

Control Objectives for Information and Related Technology (COBIT)

ISACA (formerly Information Systems Audit and Control Association) has developed a framework, referred to as Control Objectives for Information and Related Technology (COBIT), for the governance and management of enterprise IT (Information Technology). In 2012, ISACA issued COBIT 5, the most recent iteration of the framework. The COBIT framework is business oriented in that it provides a systemic way of integrating IT with business strategy and business risk.

COBIT 5 helps enterprises of all sizes:
- Maintain high-quality information to support business decisions
- Achieve strategic goals and realize business benefits through the effective and innovative use of IT
- Achieve operational excellence through reliable, efficient application of technology
- Maintain IT related risk at an acceptable level
- Optimize the cost of IT services and technology
- Support compliance with relevant laws, regulations, contractual agreements and policies

COBIT 5 is based on 5 core principles around which an effective governance and management framework can be established, the goal of which is to maximize the benefit provided to stakeholders by their investment in information and technology.

The 5 core principles relate to:
- Meeting stakeholder needs
- End-to-end application
- Development of a single integrated framework
- Enabling a holistic approach
- Separating governance from management

Meeting Stakeholder Needs

The objective of an entity is to bring value to stakeholders, which may be in the form of financial return, as in the case of a "for profit" entity, or public service, as in the case of a not-for-profit entity. Regardless of how stakeholders define value, stakeholder needs are met through balancing the realization of benefits while optimizing risk and resource use. ISACA suggests the use of a "goal cascade" to customize COBIT 5 to create stakeholder value.

The goal cascade consists of 4 steps:

1. Factors influencing stakeholder needs are identified.

2. Stakeholder needs are translated into generic goals of the entity. COBIT 5 suggests 17 *generic entity goals* that fall into 4 categories. The list is comprehensive, although not intended to be all inclusive:
   - Financial
   - Customer
   - Internal
   - Learning and growth

3. IT-related goals are derived from the generic entity goals. COBIT 5 also suggests 17 IT goals that fall into the same 4 categories.

4. IT-related goals are next translated into what COBIT 5 refers to as **enabler** goals. Enablers are the processes, structures, and information that enable the entity to achieve its goals.

Financial goals include:
- Value of business investments
- Competitive products and services
- Safeguarding of assets
- Compliance
- Transparency

Customer goals include:
- Culture of customer service
- Service continuity and availability
- Ability to respond to change
- Strategic planning based on information model
- Optimization of costs of delivering products or services

Internal goals include:
- Optimizing functionality of business functions
- Optimizing process costs
- Management of change
- Productivity
- Compliance with policies

Learning and growth goals include:
- Capable, motivated personnel
- Culture of innovation

End-to-End Application

There are 2 respects in which COBIT 5 addresses the management and governance of IT applying an end-to-end approach to the enterprise.

- The system of governance for IT should "seamlessly" integrate into the system of governance for the enterprise as a whole.

- Systems for the governance and management of IT should apply to all components of the entity in which information is processed, both internally and externally.

Application of a Single Integrated Framework

COBIT 5 is considered a single integrated framework because it incorporates or aligns with other relevant standards and frameworks, allowing COBIT 5 to be applied to the enterprise as a whole.

Enabling a Holistic Approach

COBIT 5 describes 7 categories of enablers and indicates that each enabler requires inputs from, and delivers outputs to, other enablers that are necessary for the enablers to be fully effective. The categories are:
- Principles, policies, and frameworks, which apply to all other enablers
- Processes
- Organizational structure
- Culture, ethics, and behavior
- Information, which is also a resource
- Services, infrastructure, and applications, which are also resources
- People, skills, and competencies, which are also resources

Separating Governance from Management

COBIT 5 distinguishes between governance and management.

- Governance determines enterprise objectives, taking into account stakeholder needs, and sets direction for the entity.

- Management oversees the entity's activities toward achieving enterprise objectives in alignment with governance's direction.

- Ensures that stakeholders' needs, conditions and options are evaluated to determine balanced, agreed-on enterprise objectives to be achieved; setting direction through prioritization and decision making; and monitoring performance and compliance against agreed-on direction and objectives.

- Management plans, builds, runs and monitors activities in alignment with the direction set by the governance body to achieve the enterprise objectives.

IT Environment

The IT environment is largely dependent on the size of the company and the number of employees and type of computers involved. Historically, a few large computers were operated exclusively by IT personnel. With personal computers, tablets, and phones networked together, it now is not unusual for each employee in a company to use a computer on a daily basis.

- Large companies will have a separate IT department.
- Others will have many IT functions outsourced or partially outsourced and partially performed by end users.
- One characteristic of an IT environment is a reduction in the segregation of duties.

An IT department will normally include systems development and maintenance, operations, and other technical services.

Systems Development and Maintenance

Systems development and maintenance might include the following:

- A **systems analyst** designs the information system using systems flowcharts and other tools and prepares specifications for applications programmers, as well as acting as an intermediary between the users and programmers. Flowcharts are graphical representations of sequences of activities and decisions, and are useful for both documenting systems and procedures and for isolating control weaknesses.

- An **application programmer** writes, tests, and debugs programs that will be used in the system. The programmer also develops instructions for operators to follow when running the programs.

- A **database administrator** is an individual or department responsible for the security and information classification of the shared data stored on a database system. This responsibility includes the design, definition and maintenance of the database.

  Note: The *systems development life cycle* (SDLC) consists of the phases deployed in the development or acquisition of a new software system. SDLC is an approach used to plan, design, develop, test, and implement an application system or a major modification to an application system. Typical phases of the SDLC include the feasibility study, requirements study, requirements definition, detailed design, programming, testing, installation, and post-implementation review.

Operations in an IT Function

Operations might include data control, computer operations, and librarians.

- A **data control clerk** schedules jobs for the computer and manages the distribution of reports and other output. Data control clerks may be involved in coding activities, calculating and checking batch totals, and related clerical tasks.

- The data control department is responsible for collecting data for input into a computer's batch processing operations as well as the dissemination of the finished reports.

- Data entry includes keyboard entry, scanning, and voice recognition. When transactions are entered (batch data entry), they are just stacks of source documents to the keyboard operator. Deciphering poor handwriting from a source document is a judgment call that is often error prone. In online data operations, in which the operator takes information in person or by phone, there is interaction and involvement with the transaction and less chance for error.

- A **computer operator** is a person who operates a computer in a datacenter and performs such activities as commanding the operating system, mounting disks and tapes, and placing paper in the printer. Operators may also write the job control language (JCL), which schedules the daily work for the computer.

- **Librarians** are the individuals responsible for the safeguarding and maintenance of all program and data files.

Other Technical Services

Other technical services might include telecommunications, systems programming or technical support, and security administration.

- **Telecommunications** is responsible for maintaining and enhancing computer networks and network connections.

- A **systems programmer** or **technical support** is responsible for updating and maintaining the operating systems.

- **Security administration** is responsible for security of the system including control of access and maintenance of user passwords.

Lecture 7.02 – Systems Development Life Cycle (SDLC)

A traditional SDLC approach is made up of a number of distinct phases, each with a defined set of activities and outcomes. Designing and implementing a new information and control system provides an opportunity to reexamine business processes, making them more efficient and effective. When designing an information and control system, the designers should keep in mind the need for sustainability. The system should meet the entity's current needs while keeping in mind needs that may evolve in the future as well as environmental, social, economic, and resource considerations, as well as an evolving environment surrounding the governance of an entity. Generally, there are several SDLC steps:

1. **Feasibility Study**
   Determine the strategic benefits of implementing the system either in productivity gains or in future cost avoidance, identify and quantify the cost savings of a new system, and estimate a payback schedule for costs incurred in implementing the system. Further, intangible factors such as readiness of the business users and maturity of the business processes will also be considered and assessed. This business case provides the justification for proceeding to the next phase.

2. **Requirements Definition**
   Define the problem or need that requires resolution and define the functional and qualitative requirements of the solution system. This can be either a customized approach or vendor-supplied software package, which would entail following a defined and documented acquisition process. In either case, the user needs to be actively involved.

3. **Software Selection and Acquisition** (purchased systems) or **Software Design** (systems developed in-house)
   - **Purchased systems** – Based on the requirements defined, prepare a request for proposal (RFP) from suppliers of purchased systems. In addition to the functionality requirements, there will be operational, support, and technical requirements. These, together with considerations of the suppliers' financial viability and provision for escrow, will be used to select the purchased system that best meets the organization's total requirements (e.g., Salesforce).
   - **Systems developed in-house** – Based on the requirements defined, establish a baseline of system and subsystem specifications that describe the parts of the system, how they interface, and how the system will be implemented using the chosen hardware, software, and network facilities. Generally, the design also includes program and database specifications, and will address any security considerations. Additionally, a formal change control process is established to prevent uncontrolled entry of new requirements into the development process. (Change controls are discussed in more detail in another section.)

4. **Configuration (purchased systems) or Development (systems developed in-house)**
   - *Purchased systems* – Configure the system, if it is a packaged system, to tailor it to the organization's requirements. This is best done through the configuration of system control parameters, rather than changing program code. Modern software packages are extremely flexible, making it possible for one package to suit many organizations simply by switching functionality on or off and setting the parameters in tables. There may be a need to build interface programs that will connect the acquired system with existing programs and databases.

o **Systems developed in-house** – Use the design specifications to begin programming and formalizing supporting operational processes of the system. Various levels of testing also occur in this phase to verify and validate what has been developed. This would generally include all unit and system testing, as well as several iterations of user acceptance testing. **Scope creep** refers to uncontrolled changes or continuous growth in a project's scope; this can occur when the scope of a project is not properly defined, documented, or controlled.

5. **Final Testing and Implementation**
Establish the actual operation of the new information system, with the final iteration of user acceptance testing and user sign-off conducted in this phase. The system may also go through a certification and accreditation process to assess the effectiveness of the business application in mitigating risks to an appropriate level and providing management accountability over the effectiveness of the system in meeting its intended objectives and in establishing an appropriate level of internal control. User acceptance testing is considered more important in an object-oriented development process than in a traditional environment because of the implications of the inheritance of properties in hierarchies.

6. **Post-implementation**
Following successful implementation of a new or highly modified system, implement a formal process that assesses the adequacy of the system and projected cost-benefit or ROI measurements vis-à-vis the feasibility stage findings and deviations. In so doing, Information Systems (IS) project and end-user management can provide lessons learned and/or plans for addressing system deficiencies as well as recommendations for future projects regarding system development and project management processes followed.

7. The **Maintenance Phase** (some interpretations do not include this phase)
Monitoring and support of the new system, including ongoing training, help desk resources, and a system for making authorized and tested changes to the system.

Agile Project Management

Traditional project management (sequential IT development or waterfall methodology) generally completes each phase of the SDLC before the next is started. This can result in months of effort invested in a system that is a poor match to users' needs.

An agile methodology seeks a more efficient process than waterfall methodology. Scrum is probably the simplest form of agile implementation. Scrum emphasizes empirical feedback, team self-management, and the goal of developing properly tested product increments within short iterations. Whereas traditionally, programmers presented a complete application to users for acceptance testing, agile development is broken into sprints (typically 3-5 weeks, rather than 6-18 months). User stories are developed outlining probable scenarios. These stories form a backlog. The backlog is groomed (stories are refined and ordered based on how essential their function and estimated time to complete). Sprint goals are set at finishing a handful of user stories. As each sprint is finished, results are presented and feedback from users is sought. This feedback is used to further groom the backlog. The Scrum team (typically programmers, developers, and quality assurance specialists) evaluates its performance in the sprint and brainstorms on improvements in process as well as product to improve the results of the next sprint.

Big Data

Big data is information in such high volumes that is difficult for traditional information processing to collect and analyze. It is generated by the large volume of IT processing (social media use, cloud storage, website-tracking data, and ecommerce transactions). Instead of merely storing information for contractual, operational, reporting, and compliance purposes, big data is viewed as an asset that can mined to identify trends, enhance insight, and support decision making.

Data analysis (also called data analytics) is a process of examining, cleaning, organizing, and modeling data with the goal of support decision making.

Data mining is an analysis of data using tools which look for trends or anomalies without advance knowledge of the meaning of the data. It may involve the sorting through data to identify patterns and establish relationships, to bring to light previously unidentified relationships. Some of the parameters include association, sequence or path analysis, classification, clustering and forecasting (predictive analytics).

For example, Big Box, a large-scale retail store, analyzed receipt information to determine a few recurring shopping cart collections. One recurring companion purchase turns out to be beer and disposable baby diapers purchased between 3:30 and 6:30 p.m. Apparently, customers are stopping to purchase these staples on the way home from work. Big Box can use this insight to place products likely to appeal to customers purchasing these items in its stores near or between these staples.

As data mining can be used to address open-ended questions, it is very useful for auditing.

Data integration is the process of combining data from different sources (for example, from industry publications, customer surveys, invoices, etc.) in one collection for analysis.

Data visualization is the process of presenting data in a visual format, typically a diagram, chart, or word cloud. These presentations are limited only by the preparers' imaginations. A word cloud is a visual summary of text data, typically a circle or square of words or short phrases with frequency and importance indicated by size and color.

Product Life Cycle Impact

The Internet removes the physical constraints inherent in former economic models, giving rise to new paradigms. The sales cycle of a successful consumer item will grow to a peak. As its popularity declines, its physical shelf space will be assigned to a more popular item. Availability (and, hence, sales) will decrease to zero quickly. On the other hand, if the item is available online, demand will peter into a small, but sustainable, niche market. Conceivably, a small but ongoing demand will result in more cumulative sales over time than that of the initial peak.

In other words, a physical retail environment has limited space; it is logical to replace less popular items with more popular ones. In the physical world, sales would likely end abruptly, as demand for the item moves to the declining, almost-horizontal portion of the life-cycle curve—the tail end. In contrast, an electronic retail environment can hold less popular items indefinitely because warehouse storage space constraints are not a major concern. Also, the global reach of the Internet increases the likelihood that an extended sustainable niche market continues for less popular items. Search engines enable a large audience to find items in the "niche market" portion of the graph. The digital business model allows the tail end of the product life cycle to be long, giving rise to the phenomena of a long tail for product lives. For some products, the units sold in the long tail can be larger in total than in the mainstream period, especially for electronic products like movies or games.

The "Weighty Whale Superhero" Figurines Life Cycle graph illustrates to how a graph of demand for consumer items (clothing, books, music, videos, memorabilia, etc.) over time shows an upward curve in the introduction period, a large peak for the period when an item is popular, and a period when demand peters out.

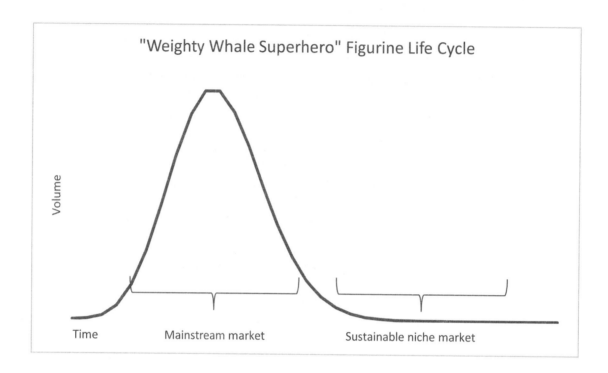

For example, Aquatic Adventurers, an animated superhero series, is cancelled after its fifth season. In Fenland—a town of 100,000 people—chances are not good that sufficient customers will purchase the remaining 80 Weighty Whale Superhero figurines that Fenland Toys has in stock at the time the cancellation is announced. A year after the show is cancelled, the chances are even less likely that Fenland Toys will be able to sell these products locally. Without the Internet, a sustainable niche market does not exist for long after the mainstream market subsides; Fenland Toys would dispose of the figurines at a loss to make room for products in high demand. With the Internet, the series' owners (or a movie webcasting network licensed by the owners) can show subscribers the existing episodes indefinitely. Also, Fenland Toys can offer the remaining figurines to billions of people. Even without the webcasting, Fenland Toys will be able to sell figurines to people nostalgic for the original broadcasts. With the webcasting, Fenland Toys will gain customers from people seeing the series online for the first time—conceivably years after the original broadcasts.

Lecture 7.03 – IT Role – Class Questions

1. Which of the following systems assists with nonroutine decisions, serves strategic levels of the organization, and helps answer questions regarding what a company's competitors are doing, as well as identifies new acquisitions that would protect the company from cyclical business swings?
    a. Executive support system
    b. Decision support system
    c. Transaction processing system
    d. Management information system

2. Optimizing functionality and process costs, management of change, productivity, and compliance with policies and procedures are goals related to which category described by COBIT 5?

    a. Customer.
    b. Internal.
    c. Financial.
    d. Learning and growth.

3. During a post implementation review of an accounting information system (AIS), a CPA learned that an AIS with few customized features had been budgeted and scheduled to be installed over nine months for $3 million (including hardware, software, and consulting fees). An in-house programmer was assigned as the project manager and had difficulty keeping the project on schedule. The implementation took 18 months, and actual costs were 30% over budget. Many features were added to the system on an ad-hoc basis, with the project manager's authorization. The end-users are very satisfied with the new system. The steering committee, however, is dissatisfied about the scope creep and would like a recommendation to consider before approving initiation of another large project. Based on those findings, the CPA should recommend implementing a

    a. Change control system.
    b. Contract management system.
    c. Budgeting system.
    d. Project timekeeping system.

4. According to COBIT 5, covering the enterprise from end-to-end means that COBIT 5:

    a. Applies to all of the different systems within the enterprise by the various components that process information.
    b. Involves a process for developing systems of governance from the time the enterprise is created and continuing throughout its life.
    c. Establishes systems for governance of IT, accounting, and enterprise governance.
    d. Integrates governance of enterprise IT with enterprise governance and management.

Class Solutions

1. (a) An executive support system is designed to support the work of executives, including making nonroutine decisions, answering questions about competitors, and identifying new acquisitions. Answer (b) is incorrect because a decision support system provides users with easy access to decision models and data. Answer (c) is incorrect because a transaction processing system is a set of procedures to be applied to the processing of a particular type of transaction. Answer (d) is incorrect because a management information system is an organized assembly of resources and procedures required to collect, process, and distribute data.

2. (b) Internal goals include optimizing functionality of business functions, optimizing process costs, management of change, productivity, and compliance with policies. Answer (a) is incorrect because customer goals include a culture of customer service, continuity and availability of service, ability to respond to change, information based strategic planning, and optimizing the cost of delivery. Answer (c) is incorrect because financial goals include value of business investments, competitive products and services, safeguarding of assets, compliance, and financial transparency. Answer (d) is incorrect because learning and growth goals include having well-trained and motivated personnel and a culture of innovation.

3. (a) A change control process is designed to minimize adverse effects resulting from changes. Change requests are made and analyzed. Decisions about making a requested change are made. If approved, the requested change is planned and implemented. The change is monitored to be sure it is implemented properly and also that the change is having the intended effects. Scope creep refers to incremental changes or continuous growth in a project's scope; this can occur when the scope of a project is not properly defined, documented, or controlled. (This topic also is discussed in the Corporate Governance section.) Answer (b) is incorrect because a contract management system generally is used to manage the contracts and the contract documents of independent contractors and suppliers; it is unlikely to highlight or prevent scope creep. Answer (c) is incorrect because a budget system generally has a role to play in project management, but is unlikely to highlight or prevent scope creep. Answer (d) is incorrect because a project timekeeping system may have a role to play in project management, but is unlikely to highlight or prevent scope creep.

4. (d) According to COBIT 5, covering the enterprise from end-to-end includes the seamless integration of the system for governing IT with the system for governing the enterprise and applying the systems for the governance and management of IT applying to all components of the enterprise that are involved in the processing of information, internally or externally. Answer (a) is incorrect because as a result, the components of the enterprise that process information would not use different systems. Answer (b) is incorrect because it relates to all aspects of the enterprise, not its duration. Answer (c) is incorrect because accounting is a component involved in the processing of information and would not be subject to a separate system of governance or management.

Lecture 7.04 – Electronic Commerce

Whenever a network allows one computer to initiate an action that will have an effect on the other, it is known as a **Value-Added Network (VAN)**.

Electronic Data Interchange (EDI)

Extranets have been established as VANs to enable a process of communication between suppliers and customers (trading partners) known as **Electronic Data Interchange (EDI).** This allows a company, for example, to have its inventory program automatically send an order to a supplier when quantities in stock of an item drop below a certain level. It is also possible to use the Internet rather than a traditional VAN for EDI (the advantage is that this would permit suppliers and customers to use the system without having previously established an extranet with each other). E-Commerce often involves electronic funds transfers (**EFT**), which can significantly reduce transaction costs. There are several **special considerations related to EDI:**

- **Strict standards** are needed for the form of data, so that it will be understood by the computers at both ends and to ensure completeness and accuracy. The critical nature of many EDI transactions, such as orders and payments, requires that there be positive assurances that the transmissions were complete. An example is the use of the ASCII format for text data.

- **Translation software** is needed by each computer so that it can convert data between the standard used for EDI and the form needed for processing internally. The process of identifying which field on the transmitted form corresponds to each field on the internal form is known as **mapping**.

- **Unauthorized access** to company computers and interception of transmissions are great dangers, requiring the use of **encryption** (application control) programs that make stolen data unreadable to someone without knowledge of the coding method and **firewall** programs that prevent access to the network without the explicit permission originating from the company computer. This is a particular concern with respect to EFT.

In an EDI environment **cryptography**, a public key certificate (also known as a *digital certificate or identity certificate*) is an electronic document which uses a digital signature to bind together a public key with an identity. Such information may include the name of a person or an organization, their address, and so forth. The certificate can be used to verify that a public key belongs to an individual.

There are numerous **advantages** associated with the use of EDI. It eliminates the need for human intervention and can be more efficient than other systems. When inventory is ordered automatically at the point that the reorder point is reached, it eliminates gaps and shortens the business cycle. In addition, payments are made and received automatically, which will tend to reduce accounts receivable balances.

Electronic commerce using **electronic data interchange** or **EDI** adds to the complexity of auditing. EDI enables:
- Communication without the use of paper
- Electronic funds transfers and sales over the Internet
- Simplification of the recording process using scanning devices
- Sending information to trading partners as transactions occur

E-Commerce Risks

Electronic commerce, as is true of any other form of commerce, depends on a level of trust between two parties. The challenges are proving to the buyer that the seller is who they say they are, proving to the buyer that their personal information remains confidential and that the seller cannot later refute the occurrence of a valid transaction. Some of the most important **elements at risk** are:

- *Confidentiality* – potential consumers are concerned about providing unknown vendors with personal information.

- *Integrity* – data, both in transit and in storage, could be susceptible to unauthorized alteration or deletion (i.e., hacking or the e-business system itself could have design or configuration problems).

- *Availability* – business may be conducted 24/7. Hence high availability is important with any system's failure becoming immediately apparent to customers or business partners.

- *Authentication and nonrepudiation* – the parties to an electronic transaction should be in a known and trusted business relationship, which requires that they prove their respective identities before executing the transaction in preventing man-in-the-middle attacks (i.e., preventing the seller from being an imposter). Then, after the fact, there must be some manner of ensuring that the transacting parties cannot deny that the transaction was entered into and the terms on which it was completed.

- *Power shift to customers* – the Internet gives consumers unparalleled access to market information and generally makes it easier to shift between suppliers.

E-commerce increases the risk of *improper use of information*. Controls might include:

- Security mechanisms and procedures that, taken together, constitute a security architecture for e-commerce

- Firewall mechanisms that are in place to mediate between the public network (the Internet) and an organization's private network

- A process whereby participants in an e-commerce transaction can be identified uniquely and positively

There is also the risk of *improper distribution* of transactions with information being electronically transmitted to an inappropriate company. Controls might include:
- Routing verification procedures
- Message acknowledgement procedures

Finally, there is a danger that orders and confirmations might be sent by an imposter (this is known as **spoofing)**, or transmitted files may be intercepted and altered maliciously by third parties before being sent to their destination. The controls might include:

- Echoing of transmitted documents back to the claimed sender so they know what the recipient has received in their name.

- **Digital signatures** on files and emails to prove the identity of the sender and to assure us that the information was unaltered in transmission (the Electronic Signatures in Global and National Commerce Act of 2000 permits the use of these in private contracts).

The reduction in the paper audit trail associated with EDI creates special challenges to the auditor.

- Detection risk may not be sufficiently reduced through substantive testing.

- Control risk must be reduced adequately to achieve an acceptable level of audit risk. Controls must be built into the system to insure the validity of information captured.

Cryptocurrency (or crypto currency) is a digital asset exchanged over the Internet outside of traditional banking and government institutions (Bitcoin for ex). Cryptocurrency is designed to work as a medium of exchange using blockchains to secure the transactions and to control the creation of additional units of the currency.

- Rather than governments controlling the supply of currency by printing more money or changing banking reserve requirements—resulting in inflation (or rarely, deflation), cryptocurrency is decentralized and has built-in restraints on how much may be created.

- Cryptocurrency networks use blockchains to maintain integrity. Blockchains are expanding chains of blocks (or records) that are linked and secured using cryptography. Each block typically contains a timestamp, a link to a previous block, and the transaction data. Inherently, blockchains resist data modification.

- The safety, integrity and balance of ledgers within cryptocurrency systems is maintained by a community of mutually distrustful parties, referred to as miners. Miners are members of the general public using their computers to help validate and timestamp transactions. Miners add transactions to the ledger in accordance with an algorithm. Collectively, miners provide security to the system, each having financial incentive to maintain accurate ledgers.

- Compared with traditional currencies held by financial institutions or kept as cash on hand, cryptocurrencies are less susceptible to seizure by law enforcement and somewhat more anonymous (different currencies have different degrees of anonymity). Due to this anonymity, there is a risk that crypto currencies may become tools for cyber criminals. Along with facilitating money laundering and tax evasion, cryptocurrencies also may grease the wheels of black markets (illegal drug trade or other illegal activity).

Lecture 7.05 – Electronic Commerce – Class Questions

5. Which of the following characteristics distinguish electronic data interchange (EDI) from other forms of electronic commerce?

    a. The cost of sending EDI transactions using a value-added network (VAN) is less than the cost of using the Internet.
    b. Software maintenance contracts are unnecessary because translation software for EDI transactions need not be updated.
    c. EDI commerce is ordinarily conducted without establishing legally binding contracts between trading partners.
    d. EDI transactions are formatted using strict standards that have been agreed to worldwide.

6. Which of the following allows customers to pay for goods or services from a website while maintaining financial privacy?
    a. Credit card
    b. Cryptocurrency
    c. Electronic check
    d. Sight draft

Class Solutions

5. (d) Since electronic data interchange requires computers to communicate with one another, it requires strict standards that have been agreed to worldwide, translation software installed on those computers involved, and encryption to prevent unauthorized access. Answer (a) is incorrect because the cost would not be lower than the Internet, since the cost of using the Internet is largely limited to the cost of access, but the Internet would not provide a reasonable level of security. Answer (b) is incorrect because translation software needs to be updated regularly, which is often facilitated with a software maintenance contract. Answer (c) is incorrect because entities will use the same types of arrangements, including legally binding contracts, when employing EDI, as used in other systems.

6. (b) The use of cryptocurrency (such as Bitcoin) allows a customer to pay for goods or services from a website while maintaining financial privacy. The cryptocurrency address is tracked, rather than a name. Cryptocurrency is designed to allow payments through an intermediary such that the transmission of sensitive credit or bank account information is not required. (a) The use of a credit card does not allow customers to pay for goods from a website while maintaining financial privacy. Using a credit card to pay for purchases from a website requires the purchaser to enter the credit card number, expiration date and, usually, a security code. (c) An electronic check is a type of electronic funds transfer that is essentially an electronic version of a paper check; it requires the drawer to provide the routing and account numbers. (d) A sight draft is similar to a check. The process of paying with a sight draft is very similar to paying with a check and requires the drawer of the draft to provide routing and account numbers.

Lecture 7.06 – Control Overview

One characteristic of an IT environment is a reduction in the segregation of duties. Although this might appear to create a potential problem:
- A computer has no incentive to conceal its errors.
- Functions often can be combined in an IT environment without weakening internal control.

In the operation of computer systems, management must focus on two broad types of controls:
- **General controls** – These relate to the overall integrity of the system. Controls include policies, procedures, and practices (tasks and activities) established by management to provide reasonable assurance that specific objectives will be achieved.
- **Application controls** – These are specific to individual programs and uses of the system.

General Controls – Overall Environment	**Application** (Program Controls)
Overall Computer Environment	Specific Program Controls
1) **Personnel Policies** • **_Systems_ = Development & Maintenance** (analysts, application programmer, database administrator) • **_Operations_ = Input** (data entry → make sure computer operator is computer illiterate); =**Output** (control clerk or librarian)	1) **Input** • Check Digit → Inputted correctly • Validity Check (Valid SS#) • Edit Test → #s in SS not letters • Limit Test → SS#'s not greater than 9 characters • Financial total • Record counts • Hash = A meaningless total • Nonfinancial totals
2) **File Security** • Back Up - Grandfather/father/son retention system • Lock Out • Read-Only	2) **Processing** • System & software documentation • Error-checking compiler • Test data • Change control-measures to ensure that changes to processing programs and production processes have minimal impact • System testing • User Acceptance Testing
3) **Contingency Planning** – Business Continuity/Disaster Recovery (hot/cold site) • Hot Site (Computer's ready to go) • Cold Site (No computer waiting) • Mirrored web server – off site	3) **Output** – Accurate • Distribution lists • Shredders • System testing
4) **Computer Facilities** – Fire/Insurance/smoke detectors/I.D. badges (Physical Controls)	
5) **Access Controls** (biometrics)	

Contingency planning refers to general controls that are designed to protect the information from accidental or intentional destruction or unauthorized alteration. This includes:

- **Backup & planned downtime controls**—Copies of files and programs should be maintained to allow reconstruction of destroyed or altered files. This may include copies on the same computer, backups to removable storage media, such as disks, and off-premises backups to computers and locations outside the company. Copies may be identical or the client may use the **grandfather/father/son** retention system, in which periodic saving of data versions allows the reconstruction of records by starting with an older file and reentering lost data since that time (the name comes from the general idea of saving at least two generations of older data so that, if the immediate version before the lost file is also lost, reconstruction can start two versions back with reentry of all data processed since that point). Since some downtime is inevitable, planned downtime allows maintenance so that unplanned downtime doesn't interrupt system operations.

- **Checkpoint**—Similar to grandfather/father/son, but at certain points, "checkpoints," the system makes a copy of the database and this "checkpoint' file is stored on a separate disk or tape. If a problem occurs, the system is restarted at the last checkpoint.

- **Business continuity and disaster recovery**—The company should have plans in place that will allow operations to be restored and continued in the event of physical destruction or disabling of the site of computer operations. This can be done by maintaining an alternate **hot site,** which has available computers and data ready to begin operations immediately in the event of the disaster, or a **cold site,** which has available space for operations but will require setup of computers and loading of data before operations can begin at that site. All critical applications need to be identified so a plan can be established. Establishment of an off-site **mirrored web server** is an effective way, particularly for an e-commerce company, to assure continuity of operations in the event of a natural disaster.
  - The configuration that represents the most complete disaster recovery plan should provide for an alternative processing site, backup and off-site storage procedures, identification of critical applications, and a testing of the plan.

Lecture 7.07 – Control Overview – Class Questions

7. Which of the following describes the primary purpose of a disaster recovery plan?

   a. To document how data will be backed up to expedite recovery.
   b. To document the location of off-site replacement facilities.
   c. To test how well prepared the company is to recover data.
   d. To specify the steps required to resume operations.

8. Which of the following terms refers to a site that has been identified and maintained by the organization as a data processing disaster recovery site but has not been stocked with equipment.

   a. Hot
   b. Cold
   c. Warm
   d. Flying start

Class Solutions

7. (d) A disaster recovery plan outlines procedures to follow in the event of a disaster. Answer (a) is incorrect because while documentation of data backup procedures may be included in the plan, it is not the primary purpose. Answer (b) is incorrect because while documentation of the off-site replacement facility locations may be included in the plan, it is not the primary purpose. Answer (c) is incorrect because while testing the plan is prudent, it is not the primary purpose of the plan.

8. (b) A cold site has available space for operations but will require setup of computers and loading of data before operations can begin at that site and can be used as a data processing recovery center in the case of a data processing disaster. Answer (a) is incorrect because a hot site can also be used as a data processing recovery center in the case of a disaster, but it is ready to go with computers set up and software loaded. Answer (c) is incorrect because there is no term such as a warm site to describe a data processing recovery center. Answer (d) is incorrect because there is no term such as a flying start site to describe a data processing recovery center.

Lecture 7.08 – General & Application Controls

General Controls

There are other general controls, in addition to contingency planning. Just as in a manual system, one of the **general controls** in an IT environment involves segregation of the incompatible duties of authorization, recording, and custody:

- **Authorization** - The development of new programs and changes to existing programs should be performed by **systems analysts** and **programmers**. These personnel should not be involved in the supervision of computer operations or the control and review of output. Systems analysts work with operating systems and compilers.

- **Recording** - **Data input clerks** and **computer operators** have the role of entering information into the computer and running the programs. These personnel should not have access to program code that would enable them to modify programs nor should they control the output.

- **Custody** - **Control clerks** and **librarians** obtain and review the output from computers to review exception reports indicating inappropriate functioning of the computer, send printouts and other output to the appropriate destinations, and maintain disks, tapes, or other storage units of data. These personnel should not have the ability to create or alter programs or to operate the computers that generate the information.

Clearly, general controls over **access** to computers and files are of great significance in evaluating internal control in an IT environment. This is particularly important in networks, since the data is distributed widely in such cases. Access to programs and data should require the entry of **passwords** or identification numbers (biometrics), and different levels of password authority should apply so that individuals only gain access to the programs and files that are compatible with their assigned responsibilities. It is also considered good practice to require that individual users change assigned passwords when new accounts are created.

Failure to remove user accounts when an employee leaves a client is a major security risk. An auditor can test these procedures by entering invalid passwords to see that they are rejected and verifying that valid passwords only provide compatible access. The systems access log should also periodically be reviewed to detect computer-related fraud. A **concurrent update control (concurrency control)** helps to address conflicts in a multi-user system, when two people, for example, are trying to purchase tickets at the same time. It will lock the other out, so as not to oversell the tickets.

Limiting access to an entity's computers and the data they hold is becoming an increasingly challenging problem. Measures, referred to as **cybersecurity**, are designed to protect computers against unauthorized access or attack. The National Institute of Standards and Technology (NIST), an agency of the U.S. Department of Commerce, released a framework for improving critical infrastructure cybersecurity.

Documentation of new programs and alterations to existing programs ensures that IT personnel are aware of the availability and proper use of programs and that changes in programming personnel during projects does not interfere with the ability of other employees to understand what has been done previously.

Hardware controls are built into the processing equipment by the manufacturer and provide reasonable assurance that data are not altered or modified as they are transmitted within the system. Binary computers can only think in terms of **bits** (binary digits) of information that are on or off ("1" or "0"). A series of 8 consecutive bits will produce a **byte** of information that represents a unit of human thought, such as a letter, number, or other character. Hardware controls may include:

- **Parity check -** In the storage of bytes, one bit will be a "dummy" bit that doesn't represent any actual information, but is turned on automatically when necessary so that the total number of bits in the on position is an odd number (in an odd-parity computer). When the computer is reading bytes of data from a chip or disk drive, a byte with an even number of bits turned on will be known to be functioning improperly.

- **Echo check (Echo control) -** When data is being transmitted from one computer to another, especially over telephone lines, distortions caused by static or other causes can cause information to be transmitted improperly. An echo check involves the data sent from one computer to another being transmitted back to the original one, which will verify that it has received what it sent. If the echoed data doesn't agree with the transmission, the packet of data is then resent.

Personal computers (also called microcomputers) present additional control risks since they are small and portable, making them easier to steal or damage. In a microcomputer environment, data and software are also more accessible, and individuals can more readily access unauthorized records and modify, copy, or destroy data and software. Also, individually installed applications make integration difficult in such an environment. A variety of controls can be employed in a microcomputer environment.

- Maintain an inventory listing of all microcomputer equipment and the purposes for which it is used.
- Keyboard locks can be built into the CPUs of microcomputers so that unauthorized users will not have access.
- Microcomputers and monitors can be secured to desks or fixtures to discourage theft.
- Passwords that are changed periodically limit the access of unauthorized users to sensitive data.
- Periodic backup of data on microcomputers enables recovery in the case of alteration or destruction of data.
- Sensitive information can be maintained in offline storage and kept in locked cabinets to prevent unauthorized access.

Application Controls

Application controls are those applied to specific business activities within a computerized processing system to achieve financial reporting objectives. Application controls are specific to each cycle and refer to a client's activities. Application controls relate to data input, data processing, and data output. They are designed to ensure the proper recording of transactions and to prevent or detect errors and fraud for transactions within these cycles. Because application controls are related to specific transactions, audit teams rely extensively on the effectiveness of these controls to mitigate the risk of material misstatement for account balances or classes of transactions. Application controls include:

- **Preventive controls** are designed to prevent errors and fraud.
- **Detective controls** are designed to detect errors and fraud (e.g., reviewing the audit log).
- **Corrective controls** allow individual users to follow up on detected errors and fraud.

Input Controls

Input controls are designed to provide reasonable assurance that data received for processing by the computer department have been properly authorized and accurately entered or converted for processing. These controls also provide the opportunity for entity personnel to correct and resubmit data initially rejected as erroneous. Errors can be avoided through:
- Observational controls
- Use of point-of-sale devices, such as scanners, to gather and record data automatically
- The use of preprinted recording forms can minimize errors.
- Data transcription controls, such as preformatted screens, can minimize errors when converting data to machine-readable form.
- Automated log-off of inactive users is an effective way to prevent unauthorized access to sensitive data. Many banking institutions use these measures.

As data is being entered, it should be subject to various *forms of verification (Logic Tests)*. These might include:

- **Field checks -** Data is validated as to the correct length, character types, and format accepted. For example, an entry of a license plate might be verified for type (alphanumeric, so that only letters and numbers are acceptable) and length (not longer than 7).

- **Validity checks -** Data is compared with a list of acceptable entries to be sure it matches one of them. For example, a field to accept the two-letter state abbreviation will be checked against a file that lists all the acceptable choices, so that an entry of OG for the state will be rejected as invalid.

- **Limit tests -** Numbers are compared to limits that have been set for acceptability. For example, the entry of a pay rate may be compared to the current minimum wage on the lower side and $50 per hour on the upper side to be sure the number entered makes sense. This is sometimes called a reasonableness test, and is the closest computer equivalent to human judgment in reviewing information.

- **Check digits -** Numbers with no obvious meaning, such as identification numbers, are often designed so that one of the digits is determined by a formula applied to the rest of the number. The computer applies the formula when a number is entered to determine if it is an acceptable one. This control makes it difficult for someone to invent a fake number if they do not know the formula, since the program will recognize a number that isn't designed so that the check digit is correct. The check digit can actually be either a number or letter, and can be placed in any consistent position in the overall identification. For example, many states have driver licenses that start with a letter which is derived from a formula applied to the numbers which follow it, and a person trying to create a fictional license will only have a 1 in 26 chance of correctly guessing the letter that should be in the first position based on the numbers.

When using batch processing of data, the data input clerk will often prepare manual **control totals** to be compared with computer-generated totals of entered information in order to ensure accuracy of inputs. These totals include:
- **Record count -** The total number of records entered into the program during a period.
- **Financial total -** The total dollar amount of entries that are financial in nature.
- **Hash total -** The total of values (such as Social Security numbers) which cannot be meaningfully added together, but which serve as a way to verify the correct entry of these values.

For example, assume that the checks written during a particular day are being entered into a checkbook program, and that the data input clerk is working from the following sheet to make the entries:

Check Number	Payee	Amount	Account Code
1001	Philipp Corporation	$ 500.00	307
1002	Rog Enterprises	$3,000.00	602
1003	Ruiz Company	$ 600.00	302
3006		$4,100.00	1211

After the data input clerk enters each of the checks, the computer will then indicate:
   Checks Entered = 3 (record count)
   Check Number total = 3006 (hash total)
   Amount total = $4,100.00 (financial total)
   Account Code total = 1211 (hash total)

The data input clerk would have also determined these numbers by computing them from the input sheet, and the agreement of the clerk's totals with those of the program will indicate all lines most likely have been entered correctly.

A program may also perform **edit checks** on batch-processed data to verify that each individual entry is appropriate, and generate a list of rejected transactions for review by the control clerk.

Processing Controls

Once data is input, processing controls are designed to provide reasonable assurance that data processing has been performed accurately without any omission or duplicate processing of transactions. Many processing controls are similar in nature to input controls, but they are used in the processing phases, rather than at the time input is verified. The most fundamental processing control a client can implement is periodically testing and evaluating the processing accuracy of its programs.

- Systems and software documentation allows system analysts to verify that processing programs are complete and thorough.
- Computer programs can be tested using error testing compilers to ensure that they do not contain programming language errors.
- Test data exposes the program to one sample of each type of exception condition likely to occur during its use.
- System testing can be used to make certain that programs within the system are interacting properly.

Output Controls

Output controls represent the final check on the results of computerized processing. Output controls are concerned with detecting errors rather than preventing errors. These controls should be designed to provide reasonable assurance that only authorized persons receive output or have access to files produced by the system.

Auditing Issues

Although the existence of an electronic system does not change the basic objectives of an audit engagement, it has a major impact on the approach used to achieve those objectives.

Computer software cannot replace the judgment of the auditor. The responsibility for determining the acceptable level of audit risk and assessing the component risks remains with the auditor.

Differences

AU-C 315 summarizes the **differences** as follows:
- **Benefits of IT**
  - Consistency – Computers process data the same way every time.
  - Timeliness – Electronic processing and updating is normally more efficient.
  - Analysis – Data can be accessed for analytical procedures more conveniently (with proper software).
  - Monitoring – Electronic controls can be monitored by the computer system itself.
  - Circumvention – Controls are difficult to circumvent when programmed properly, and exceptions are unlikely to be permitted.
  - Segregation of duties – Security controls can prevent the performance of incompatible functions by the same individual or group through security controls in applications, databases, and operating systems.

- **Risks of IT**
  - Overreliance – Without clear output, IT systems are often assumed to be working when they are not.
  - Access – Disclosure, destruction and alteration of large amounts of data are possible if unauthorized access occurs.
  - Changes in programs – Severe consequences without detection are possible if unauthorized program changes occur.
  - Failure to change – Programs or systems are sometimes not updated for new laws, rules, or activities.
  - Manual intervention – Knowledgeable individuals can sometimes alter files by bypassing the appropriate programs.
  - Loss of data – Catastrophic data loss is possible if appropriate controls aren't in place.

Risks

There are **two risks** of major concern to the auditor:
- **Unauthorized access** to a computer system can cause more damage to the accounting system as a whole than in a manual system where it is difficult for one person to access all the different records of the system.
- The **audit trail** is an electronically visible trail of evidence enabling one to trace information contained in statements or reports back to the original input source.

  An **audit trail** is also important to the client for the proper functioning of the system during the year, since such a trail allows monitoring of activities, providing a deterrent to fraud and making it possible to answer queries by examining the source data. The auditor should establish the reliability and extent of the audit trail.

Audit Efficiency

When examining a company in an IT environment, the auditor may decide to use a **generalized audit software package**. This refers to a series of programs that can be used for general processes, such as record selection, matching, recalculation and reporting and might include:
- Programs to **access client files** for purposes of testing. For example, the auditor's program may access computerized inventory files to determine the location of inventory,

perform analytical procedures (such as calculating inventory turnover), or review dates of last purchase and sale in order to identify obsolete or slow-moving inventory.

- **Source code comparison** programs that can detect unauthorized changes made by the client in programs that the auditor is testing. For example, after the auditor has verified the proper functioning of a copy of the payroll program provided to them by the client for testing, this program would compare the tested program with the one being used by the client to process an actual payroll period to be sure the files are identical.

- Programs that duplicate common functions of client software that can be used to perform **parallel simulation**, in which the auditor inputs client data to the auditor's program (created by the auditor) to see if it produces the same results as the client's program. For example, the auditor might obtain the raw data for an actual payroll period and run it through a payroll program included in the generalized audit software package to see if the checks and payroll records produced are identical to the checks and records generated by the client's program.

- Programs to produce **spreadsheets** for working trial balances and similar audit needs.

When the client has a program that the auditor wishes to verify and for which there is no appropriate equivalent program available to the auditor, techniques involving the direct use of the client program are necessary. One approach is known as the **test data** approach, in which the auditor will develop simulated transactions to enter into the client's program. Characteristics of this approach include:
- The auditor can include both valid and invalid transactions to verify that the program processes appropriate data correctly and rejects inappropriate transactions.
- The auditor only needs to design simulated transactions for those **valid and invalid conditions** that interest the auditor.
- Only **one example** of each valid and invalid condition needs to be included (since computer programs are consistent in the way they handle items), making this an efficient method of testing.

The auditor should obtain audit evidence about the accuracy and completeness of information produced by the entity's information system when that information is used in performing audit procedures. The primary **advantage** of IT as it relates to an audit is that a computer is not subject to **random errors** as is a human. Thus, an auditor who has **verified** that a computer program is working properly will **not** have to **test individual transactions** to be sure the computer is following directions consistently: it will always follow its program. An audit of a computerized system can, therefore, rely more heavily on internal control structure and reduce the need for substantive testing, making the audit potentially more efficient.

It is possible to create **embedded audit modules** in the DBMS so that information wanted by an auditor during annual engagements can be easily accessed. One difficulty in this idea is that these modules should be included in the design of the system itself, forcing the outside auditor to be involved in consulting on the design, and may impair the auditor's independence.

One danger is that the client may provide the auditor with a program to verify which isn't the actual program used by the client. To avoid this, the auditor will often include the **test data** in an **integrated test facility**, including the simulated data (fictitious transactions) along with actual data during a program run. For example, the auditor may add simulated payroll data to the actual data for a pay period, so that the testing occurs at the same time the actual employee information is being processed (of course, the simulated data is specially coded so as not to be permanently mixed with the real data).

If it isn't practical to use an integrated test facility, the auditor may use an approach known as **controlled reprocessing,** in which the auditor supervises the entry of actual client data into the client program to reproduce the results of a previous run of the program by the client. After verifying that the results are identical to the previous run, the auditor knows that the program is the actual one used, and can enter the test data into it at a separate time.

To summarize the techniques available:

	Data	**Program**
Test Data (Phony Data) – theoretically only have to check one above and one below credit limit.	Auditor	Client's
Controlled reprocessing	Client's	Client's (but Auditor's computer)
Integrated Test Facility (ITF) (Dummy division or file & fictitious transactions)	Auditor & Client's	Client's
Transaction Tagging	Client's information with a tag	Client's
Parallel Simulation	Client's	Auditor's (Going around their system)

	Actual Client Data	**Simulated Data**
Actual Client Program	Controlled Reprocessing	Test Data (Integrated Test Facility)
Program Purchased Separately by Auditor	Parallel Simulation	No Relevance to Audit of Client

Trust Services

Trust Services are governed by SSAE (Statements on Standards for Attestation engagements) and represent attest engagements in which a CPA assesses a client's commercial internet site and reports on whether the system meets one or more of the following **principles:** Security; Availability for operation; Processing integrity; Online privacy; and Confidentiality. For each Principle reported, the auditor considers each of the following **4 criteria:** Policies; Communications; Procedures; and Monitoring.

Both WebTrust and SysTrust are designed to incorporate a seal management process by which a seal (logo) may be included on a client's website as an electronic representation of the practitioner's unqualified WebTrust report. If the client wishes to use the seal (logo), the engagement must be updated at least annually. Also, the initial reporting period must include at least two months. Any of the 5 types of opinions may be issued as discussed in the audit report section.
- **Websites (WebTrust)** – An assurance function designed to reduce the concerns of Internet users regarding the existence of a company and the reliability of key business information placed on its website.
- **Information systems (SysTrust service)** – An assurance function that reviews an entity's computer system to provide confidence to business partners and customers concerning the security, privacy, and confidentiality of information in addition to system availability and processing integrity.

System and Organization Controls (SOC) Reports

Service organizations are entities that provide services—such as payroll or web-hosting—to other entities. SOC for Service Organizations reports are issued by an independent CPA to assist service organizations in building trust and confidence in the service provided and controls related to those services. There are three types of such services.

SOC 1® – SOC for Service Organization: ICFR

Report on Controls at a Service Organization Relevant to User Entities' Internal Control over Financial Reporting

Reports prepared in accordance with AT-C 320, *Reporting on an Examination of Controls at a Service Organization Relevant to User Entities' Internal Control Over Financial Reporting*, are intended to meet the needs of user entities and user auditors in considering the controls at the service organization and their impact on the user entities' financial statements. *User entities* are entities that use the service organizations' services. *User auditors* are the auditors of user entities. Use of these reports is **restricted** to the management of the service organization, user entities, and user auditors. There are two types of reports for ICFR engagements:

- Type 1 – Report on the fairness of the presentation of management's **description** of the service organization's system and the **suitability of the design of the controls** to achieve the related control objectives included in the description as of a specified date.

- Type 2 - Report on the fairness of the presentation of management's **description** of the service organization's system and the **suitability of the design and operating effectiveness of the controls** to achieve the related control objectives included in the description throughout a specified period.

SOC 2® – SOC for Service Organizations: Trust Services Criteria

Report on Controls at a Service Organization Relevant to Security, Availability, Processing Integrity, Confidentiality or Privacy

These reports are designed to meet the needs of users that seek **detailed** information and assurance about the controls at a service organization relevant to security, availability, and processing integrity of the systems the service organization uses to process users' data and the confidentiality and privacy of the information processed by these systems. The emphasis within SOC 2 reports is not on ICRF, but the operational fitness of the system. These reports can play an important role in:
- Oversight of the organization
- Vendor management programs
- Internal corporate governance and risk management processes
- Regulatory oversight

Similar to a SOC 1 report, there are two types of reports, with similar differences: A type 1 report is on management's **description** of a service organization's system and **the suitability of the design of controls**. A type 2 report is on management's description of a service organization's system and **the suitability of the design and operating effectiveness of controls**. Use of these reports are **restricted**.

SOC 3® – SOC for Service Organizations: Trust Services Criteria for General Use Report

These reports are intended to meet the needs of users who seek assurance about the controls at a service organization relevant to security, availability, processing integrity confidentiality, or privacy, but do not seek or have the knowledge required to make effective use of the detail in a SOC 2 Report. Since SOC 3 reports are **general-use reports**, they can be freely distributed. The most common examples of a SOC 3 report are WebTrust and SysTrust.

Lecture 7.09 – General & Application Controls – Class Questions

9. When a client's accounts payable computer system was relocated, the administrator provided support through a dial-up connection to a server. Subsequently, the administrator left the company. No changes were made to the account payable system at that time. Which of the following situations represents the greatest security risk?

    a. User passwords are not required to be in alpha-numeric format.
    b. Management procedures for user accounts are not documented.
    c. User accounts are not removed upon termination of employees.
    d. Security logs are not periodically reviewed for violations.

10. General controls in an information system include each of the following, **except**

    a. Information technology infrastructure.
    b. Security management.
    c. Software acquisition.
    d. Logic tests.

11. A company began issuing handheld devices to key executives. Each of the following factors is a reason for requiring changes to the security policy, except

    a. Storage of sensitive data.
    b. Portability of the device.
    c. Vulnerability of the device.
    d. Convenience of the device.

12. Which of the following classifications of security controls includes smoke detectors, generators, security guards, and ID badge?

    a. Technical.
    b. Physical.
    c. Administrative.
    d. Logical.

13. An entity has the following invoices in a batch:

Invoice #	Product	Quantity	Unit price
201	F10	150	$ 5.00
202	G15	200	$10.00
203	H20	250	$25.00
204	K35	300	$30.00

Which of the following most likely represents a hash total?

    a. FGHK80
    b. 4
    c. 204
    d. 810

14. A retail store uses batch processing to process sales transactions. The store has batch control total and other control checks embedded in the information processing system of the sales subsystem. While comparing reports, an employee notices that information sent to the subsystem was not fully processed. Which of the following types of controls is being exercised by the employee?

    a. Preventive.
    b. Corrective.
    c. Detective.
    d. Input.

15. Which of the following controls is a processing control/Input control designed to ensure the reliability and accuracy of data processing?

	Limit test	**Validity check test**
a.	Yes	Yes
b.	No	No
c.	No	Yes
d.	Yes	No

16. Passenger 1 and passenger 2 are booking separately on an airline website for the last available seat on a flight. Passenger 1 presses the enter key a few seconds before passenger 2, thus locking out passenger 2 and obtaining the last seat. This locking is a form of which of the following types of control?

    a. Concurrent update control.
    b. Compensating control.
    c. Data entry control.
    d. Operational data control.

17. A systems engineer is developing the input routines for a payroll system. Which of the following methods validates the proper entry of hours worked for each employee?

    a. Check digit.
    b. Capacity check.
    c. Sequence check.
    d. Reasonableness check.

18. An auditor most likely would test for the presence of unauthorized computer program changes by running a

    a. Program with test data.
    b. Check digit verification program.
    c. Source code comparison program.
    d. Program that computes control totals.

19. Processing data through the use of simulated files provides an auditor with information about the operating effectiveness of control policies and procedures. One of the techniques involved in this approach makes use of

    a. Controlled reprocessing.
    b. An integrated test facility.
    c. Input validation.
    d. Program code checking.

Class Solutions

9. (c) If user accounts are not removed upon termination of employees, those employees would continue to have access to computer programs and data, creating a security risk. Answer (a) is incorrect because not requiring passwords to be an alpha-numeric format does not create an additional security risk as long as passwords are constructed to make them difficult to figure out. Answer (b) is incorrect because the documentation of security procedures does not make them more or less effective. It is their execution that is significant. Answer (d) is incorrect because although a practice of not reviewing security logs for violations may allow violations to recur, it is not as significant a security risk as allowing terminated employees to have access.

10. (d) Logic tests are application controls. They depend on specifics found at the application level. Information technology infrastructure, security management, and software acquisition procedures are applicable to the entire computer system, not a particular application. Answer (a) is incorrect because information technology infrastructure is applicable to the entire computer system, not a particular application. Answer (b) is incorrect because security management is applicable to the entire computer system, not a particular application. Answer (c) is incorrect because software acquisition procedures are applicable to the entire computer system, not a particular application.

11. (d) Storage of sensitive data, portability of the device, and vulnerability of the device are all security considerations which merit changes to the security policy. Convenience is not. The question asks for the exception. Answer (a) is incorrect because storage of sensitive data merits changes to the security policy. Answer (b) is incorrect because portability of a device merits changes to the security policy. Answer (c) is incorrect because vulnerability of a device merits changes to the security policy.

12. (b) Smoke detectors, generators, security guards, and ID badges are all forms of physical security, because they protect assets from physical damage or intrusion.. Answer (a) is incorrect because technical controls are performed or managed by a computer, such as a firewall. Answer (c) is incorrect because administrative controls involve the exercise of authority by people. Answer (d) is incorrect because logical controls employ instructions on what is logical in a given situation; for instance, a logical access control would not allow even a high-ranking official stationed on the east coast with no travel plans to access a west coast facility.

13. (d) A hash total is a total of values where the total is not a meaningful financial amount but it can be used to verify that all items in that field of a batch have been entered correctly. The total of the invoice numbers, for example, is 810, which indicates that it is likely that all of the invoice numbers were entered correctly. Answer (a) is incorrect because FGHK80 is not a total but rather an accumulation of the letters from the product numbers and the total of the product numbers. Answer (b) is incorrect because 4 is the number of invoices being entered, which is a meaningful total, not a hash total. Answer (c) is incorrect because 204 is the number of the last invoice and is not a total.

14. (c) Detective controls detect error and fraud that has occurred already. Answer (a) is incorrect because preventive controls ensure mistakes are not made; a batch control total is determined after sales have been made for a period of time—not soon enough to prevent errors and fraud. Answer (b) is incorrect because corrective controls permit users to resolve detected errors and fraud. Answer (d) is incorrect because Input controls operate at the time of input, not when the information has been incorporated into a batch.

15. (a) A limit check is used to determine that data entered falls within acceptable limits, indicating a potential error when it does not. A validity check test compares certain data to acceptable values, indicating a potential error when there is not a match. Both are designed to ensure the reliability and accuracy of data processing.

16. (a) A concurrent update control, also referred to as a concurrency control, is one that updates data on a real-time basis and is particularly useful when multiple users have access to limited resources. This control allows users to access the resources, such as seats on an airline flight, as long as there are resources available, usually on a first-come, first-served basis, but will lock out all remaining users once capacity has been filled. Answer (b) is incorrect because a compensating control is a data security measure that compensates for some other security measure that is deemed too difficult or impractical to implement. Answer (c) is incorrect because a data-entry control validates data. Answer (d) is incorrect because operational data control is not a commonly used term.

17. (d) A reasonableness check would be the best input validation technique to use in this situation, because based on the entity's policies for using full-time and part-time workers and regarding overtime, the number of hours entered for any given employee should fall within a relatively narrow range. Answer (a) is incorrect because a check digit might be used to determine if all employee I.D. numbers were appropriate, but would not provide meaningful information about hours. Answer (b) is incorrect because a capacity check is a term commonly used in warehouse management and cellular networks and is generally a procedure used for physical storage or network operations, not data storage. Answer (c) is incorrect because a sequence check is used to validate that a correct expected sequence of numbers in an entry or that all records in a sequence, such as pre-numbered payroll checks, are accounted for.

18. (c) To detect unauthorized program changes, an auditor would need to examine the source code or program documentation to determine whether such changes were made. Answer (a) is incorrect as test data is data developed and entered to test a program's operation. Answer (b) is incorrect as a check digit is a digit added to an identification number to verify that other digits in the number are entered correctly; verifying such a digit does not confirm that no unauthorized program changes were made. Answer (d) is incorrect as a control total is designed to test a batch of data, not to detect unauthorized program changes.

19. (b) Under the integrated test facility approach, fictitious and real transactions are processed, using the client's system. The auditor then reviews the client system's processing of the data to evaluate the effectiveness of its control environment. Controlled reprocessing involves reprocessing client data through the client's programs under the control of the auditor. Input validation and program code checking are application control procedures.

Lecture 7.10 – Glossary – Transaction Processing

Acquaintance with these terms is necessary to understand exam IT questions sufficiently well to answer them correctly, although most of this information is tested directly on the AICPA exam only infrequently.

Artificial Intelligence

Artificial intelligence is computer learning, planning, and solving problems, when the computer perceives its environment and executes actions designed to reach a goal. It generally includes competing at strategic games (such as chess), understanding human speech, and complex tasks (such as driving a car). Machine learning involves algorithms that can learn from data and make predictions on data in a reiterative fashion.

Transaction Processing

The processing of transactions can take place in one of two general ways:
- **Online Transaction Processing (OLTP), online real-time (OLRT) processing**
- **Batch processing**

OLTP means that the database is updated as soon as a transaction is received (**immediately**). Online transaction processing keeps business records up-to-date the moment transactions are keyed or transmitted into a system. This produces records that are as up-to-date as possible, but poses a problem of requiring that computers be continually running and accessible at all points-of-transaction. This is a good method to be used by retail businesses. With the common presence of computers, this has become the default processing method for most business activity.

Batch processing involves gathering information and then entering transactions in a group (usually dollar fields) to the computer periodically. This allows for greater control over the input process, including more possibility for verifying data entry with control totals and authorization before input. The major difficulty is associated with the **delay** between the transactions and the input, which can result in accounting records not accurately reflecting the current situation.

As an example of the choice between the two approaches, a bank is going to use OLTP for the processing of cash withdrawals, since it is critical that these be immediately reflected in the depositor's balance and errors can be easily reversed later with little harm to the bank. On the other hand, a bank would prefer to use batch processing for deposits to be sure that increases in depositors" balances are authorized and checked carefully for accuracy before accounts are updated. Unauthorized postings of deposits could allow a depositor to withdraw large sums of money and delays in posting would be of little negative consequence to the bank itself. As a practical matter, batch processing tends to be used for large (such as bank deposits over $5,000) or sporadic (such as payroll preparation) transactions.

Networks

In the early days of computers, each device was so expensive that a company rarely had more than one and all activity had to take place on that single computer. Although different people could connect to that single computer using **remote terminals**, these were simply input and output devices (essentially equivalent to just the keyboard and monitor on a current desktop). All activity had to take place on the one computer, known as **centralized processing**. Today, computers are so reasonably priced that, in many businesses, employees each are assigned their own computers (whether a laptop, tablet, or smartphone). This allows the allocation of a large volume of computer tasks to different employees and computers at different locations, known as **distributed processing**. Since the data utilized by the company is no longer on a single computer, it is necessary for them to be able to connect to each other in some way to form a **network.**

In a computer network, computers are connected to one another to enable sharing of peripheral devices, sharing data, and programs stored on a **file server.** A file server is a high capacity disk storage device or a computer that stores data centrally for network users and manages access to that data. File servers can be dedicated so that no process other than network management can be executed on that server while the network is available. Non-dedicated file servers allow the standard user applications to run while the network is available.

Networks allow various user departments to share information files maintained in **databases**. Databases should:
- Provide departments with information that is appropriate
- Prevent access to inappropriate information

Network configurations allow the linking of computers in different ways:

- **Local area networks (LANs)** Communications networks that serve several users within a specified geographical area. A personal computer LAN functions as distributed processing in which each computer in the network does its own processing and manages some of its data. Shared data are stored in a file server that acts as a remote disk drive for all users in the network. Good management controls, such as access codes and passwords, are essential.

- **Wide area networks (WANs)** Computer networks connecting different remote locations that may range from short distances, such as a floor or building, to extremely long transmissions that encompass a large region or several countries.

- **Value-added network (VAN)** – Links computer files of different companies together. As a result, it is necessary to have increased security for data transmissions to make certain that others will not have access to inappropriate entity information.

- **Virtual Private Network (VPN)** – Allows users to access network resources from remote locations; may or may not be incorporated as part of a larger cloud computing strategy.

The need for solid physical transmission media in LANs has been overcome through the development of **wireless local area networks (WLANs).** Short-range radio transmission allows different computers to communicate with each other and share printers, Internet connections, and other devices. The two prominent standards for WLANs are **Wi-Fi** (also known as 802.11) and **Bluetooth**. Any devices that are in the vicinity of each other and which follow the same standard can communicate. In addition to computers, cell phones and personal digital assistants (PDAs) are often equipped to use one or both standards.

Clearly, unauthorized access is a major danger with WLANs and both **encryption of data** and **passwords** (a technical security control) to connect to the system are critical security needs to prevent others with wireless devices from accessing the system. On the other side, businesses such as hotels and restaurants have sometimes installed Wi-Fi connections for the benefit of guests and patrons to allow them high-speed Internet access (sometimes requiring logging into a network at a fee and sometimes at no charge to encourage visitors).

Networking would get very complicated if every computer in a network had to be able to directly connect to every other computer in the network (in order for 10 different computers in an office to be connected this way in a LAN, there would have to be 45 different cables!). Even in the case of a wireless network, a computer would have to be able to distinguish all the different signals coming from different computers.

Topology refers to the shape of a network, or the network's layout. How different nodes in a network are connected to each other and how they communicate are determined by the network's topology. To simplify the process, the communication is normally organized (and can be visualized) in one of the following ways:

- **Bus** – A common path or channel between hardware devices, which can be located between components internal to a computer or between external computers in a communications network.

- **Star** – There is one computer (central hub) to which all other computers connect, so that all data is first received and then sent from that one computer (in email systems, this will allow copies of all messages to be stored on a single computer while still allowing communication among all of the others).

- **Ring** – Each computer is connected to its two closest neighbors in a closed loop, and information is transferred through each intermediate computer to get to the intended destination (notice there will be two directions that can be used, so an interruption of a single connection won't bring down the network).

- **Tree** – Groups of star-configured networks are organized in branches with one computer at the base, so that computers that are on the same branch can connect to each other without going through the root computer, but computers on different branches may have to go through the root computer.

- **Mesh** - Devices are connected with many redundant interconnections between network nodes. In a pure mesh topology, every node has a connection to every other node in the network.

Networks may involve any size group from two (as in the case of many home networks) to the entire world (in the case of the Internet).

An **Intranet** is a network that is limited to the computers of a single company.

An **Extranet** is similar to an Intranet, since it is primarily for users within a single company, but select customers and vendors are able to participate as well.

The **Internet** is a worldwide network that allows virtually any computer system to link to it by way of an electronic gateway. The Internet facilitates data communication services including:
- Remote login
- File transfer
- Electronic mail (Email)
- Newsgroups

The networking of different computers allows more than just the transfer of information from one to another. It also allows one computer to be used to operate the other. In **client/server computing**, the users of **client** computers will be able to access a **server** computer and can be given the ability to add, edit, or delete data on the server, or even to operate programs running on the server as well as transfer files between their client and the server. The physical device used by an employee to access these resources, usually a computer, also is called a **workstation**. The server doesn't, in effect, have any particular user since it is being operated by the users on the client computers, and a server computer doesn't even need a display monitor or keyboard, except for initial set up. **Virtualization** is a method used to create multiple virtual machines for clients to access on a single physical server.

The development of the Internet has also created many opportunities and challenges when it comes to the use and protection of information. One example is the emergence of **mobile computing**. This allows individuals to use various devices to obtain access to data and information from whatever location they are at. Another is the rapidly spreading influence of **social media**. Social media enables individuals to create, share, and exchange information and ideas in virtual communities and networks. Social media has proven an effective tool for:

- Market research
- Communication
- Sales promotions
- Relationship development (match.com)
- E-commerce

Cloud computing is a model that allows organizations to use the Internet to access and use services and applications that run on remote third-party technology infrastructure, rather than rely on in-house platform solutions (e.g., Spotify, Youtube, our online course). Cloud computing is the integration of virtual machines, remote services for hardware and software, and Web access. Working in the cloud can mean simply using remote server for data storage or using a browser to access Web-based applications. Because cloud computing utilizes third-party hardware and software, it usually has lower upfront costs for equipment and maintenance. Cloud computing is generally not the best way to secure sensitive corporate information, as there are security risks to transmitting information over the Internet. Common implementations of cloud computing involve off-the-shelf software that is not developed or modified in-house, with generally limited configuration and program modification options.

Collaborative computing allows users to connect, communicate and work on projects and documents together in real time. Examples include instant messaging (google chat), video conferencing, multicasting, email applications, groupware systems, just to name a few.

Gamification refers to applying game elements and digital game design techniques to solving problems and making decisions that are not generally associated with games. This may include business problems or challenges related to social impact.

Geolocation is information about your physical, real-world location that can be associated with. an IP or MAC address. This information can be used by applications to show how nearby your friends or employees are, get directions to a restaurant or customer, or to **geotag** your photos.

World Wide Web To make use of the Internet more user-friendly, a framework for accessing documents was developed known as the World Wide Web.
- *Hypertext Transfer Protocol (HTTP)* – The language commonly understood by different computers to communicate via the Internet.
  - *Transmission Control Protocol and Internet Protocol (TCP/IP)* – an IP is a unique computer address and a TCP/IP is a communications protocol designed to network dissimilar systems, such as viewing a webpage.
- *Document* – A single file on any computer that is accessible through the Internet.
- *Page* – The display that results from connection to a particular Internet document.

- *Uniform Resource Locator (URL)* – The "address" of a particular page on the Internet.
- *Web Browser* – A program that allows a computer with a particular form of operating software to access the Internet and which translates documents for proper display.
- *Server* – The computer that is "sending" the pages for display on another computer.
- *Client* – The computer that is "receiving" the pages and seeing the display.
- *Upload* – Sending information from a client to a server computer.
- *Download* – Sending information from a server to a client computer.
- *HTML (HyperText Markup Language)* and *XML (Extensible Markup Language)* are specialized programming languages used to create websites.

Networks and Control Risk

To minimize control risk, a network should have some form of security that limits access to certain files to authorized individuals.

- Certain individuals may have *read only* access to files.
- Others will be authorized to alter the data in the files, such as *read/write*.

A **virus** is a program with the ability to reproduce by modifying other programs to include a copy of itself. A virus may contain destructive code that can move into multiple programs, data files or devices on a system and spread through multiple systems in a network. A **Trojan horse** is a purposefully hidden malicious or damaging code within an authorized computer program. Unlike viruses, they do not replicate themselves, but they can be just as destructive to a single computer.

- A **worm** is a program that duplicates itself over a network so as to infect many computers with viruses.
- A **hoax virus** is a widely distributed email message warning of a virus that doesn't exist.
- A **killer application** simply refers to a program that is extremely useful, and is not anything dangerous.
- **Phishing** (brand spoofing or carding) is the act of sending an email to a user falsely claiming to be an established legitimate enterprise in an attempt to scam the user into surrendering private information that will be used for identity theft.

Ransomware is an unauthorized program used by cybercriminals to extort money that restricts access to data until a ransom is paid and a digital key is entered.

Antivirus software is a software application deployed at multiple points in an IT architecture. It is designed to detect and potentially eliminate virus code before damage is done and repair or quarantine files that have already been infected.

Unauthorized downloads of "pirated" software from the Internet can also create risks of lawsuits and criminal prosecutions (e.g., movies, programs and music).

A tool for establishing security is a **firewall**, which prevents unauthorized users from accessing data. A firewall can be in the form of a computer program (software) or a physical device that blocks the transmission media being used (hardware). A **network firewall** is designed to prevent unauthorized access to the company computers, while **application firewalls** protect individual programs. Network firewalls are easier and cheaper to implement, but if penetrated, leave the computers at severe risk. Application firewalls need to be installed for each individual program the company wishes to protect, but allow additional user authentication procedures to protect the program and data and make access more difficult.

Lecture 7.11 – Glossary – Hardware & Software

Hardware

Hardware is the physical electronic equipment. Common components include:

- **Central Processing Unit** or **CPU** – The principal hardware component that processes programs.

- **Memory** – The internal storage space or **online storage**, often referred to as **random access memory** or **RAM.**

- **Primary Storage** – Computer memory which is used to store programs that must be accessed immediately by the CPU.

- **Offline Storage** –Devices used to store data or programs externally, including magnetic tape, flash drives, thumb (usb) drives, digital video disks (DVDs), and compact disks (CDs).

- **File Server** – A high capacity disk storage device or a computer that stores data centrally for network users and manages access to that data. File servers can be dedicated so that no process other than network management can be executed while the network is available. File servers can also be non-dedicated so that standard user applications can run while the network is available.

- **Input and Output Devices** – Devices that allow for communication between the computer and users, such as a terminal with a screen and a keyboard, scanners, microphones, wireless hand-held units, barcode readers, point-of-sale registers, optical character readers, mark sense readers, light guns, printers, speakers, floppy disk drives, CD and DVD drives, magnetic tape drives, and magnetic disk drives.

- **Router** – A specialized device that receives data packets from one computer and sends it toward its destination in the most efficient manner possible. The Internet, in fact, primarily consists of a series of routers used to transmit information among all the different computers of the world that are connected to the Internet at any one time. When a computer in California connects to a website in Australia, the two computers aren't actually connected to each other, and there might be 10 computers between them acting as intermediary routers. When parts of the Internet go down, due to a power outage or other difficulty, most people never notice because the routers find another way (route) to get the information to its destination.

- **Gateway** – This is a device (router, firewall) on a network that serves as an entrance to another network. In order for a home or business to connect to the Internet, for example, it must connect to a gateway computer at their Internet Service Provider (ISP), which is the first router in the process of connecting to the rest of the Internet.

Storage Devices

Magnetic tape – Inexpensive form of storage used primarily for backup, since only **sequential** access to data is possible.

Magnetic disks – Permanent storage devices inside a computer (including hard drives) that allow **random** access to data without the need to move forward or backward through all intervening data. Some systems use **RAID** (redundant array of independent disks), which includes multiple disks in one system so that data can be stored redundantly and the failure of one of the disks won't cause the loss of any data.

Transportable forms of storage - In increasing order of capacity, these include:
- Floppy disks
- Zip disks
- Compact disks (CDs)
- Optical disks (DVDs)
- Thumb drives

Input (Data-entry) and Output Devices

- Visual display terminal (keyboard and monitor)
- Mouse (including stylus, mousepad, joystick, and light pen)
- Touch-sensitive screen
- Magnetic tape reader
- Magnetic ink character reader
- Scanner
- Automatic teller machine
- Radio frequency data communication
- Point-of-sale recorder
- Voice/retina recognition
- Electronic data interchange
- Barcode readers

Software

Software consists of programs and supporting documentation that enable and facilitate use of the computer. Software controls the operation of the hardware and the processing of data. Software is either system software or application software.

- **System software** is made up of the programs that run the system and direct its operations, comprised of the operating system and utility programs. **An operating system (OS)** is a set of system software programs in a computer that regulate the ways application software programs use the computer hardware and the ways that users control the computer. Examples of commonly used operating systems are Windows and UNIX. Such programs may be designed to allow functions such as:
  - **Multiprocessing –** The simultaneous operation of multiple programs on a single computer.
  - **Windowing –** The ability to display the output of different programs on the monitor or portions of the monitor at the same time, as well as easily switch the display from one program to another (whichever program is set to accept and process the next click of the mouse or keyboard is known as the active window).

- **Application software** is designed to perform specific tasks for the company.

- **Utility** programs are used for sorts, merges, and other routine functions to maintain and improve the efficiency of a computer system. Specialized **security software** is a type of utility program used to control access to the computer or its files.

- **Library** programs are limited programs used by other programs, such as a random number generator.

- **A query program** is an application that counts, sums and retrieves items from a database based on user criteria.

- **Algorithms** are instruction sets used in programs to define and control processes.

- **Communication software** handles transmission of data between different computers.

- **Protocol –** Rules determining the required format and methods for transmission of data.

- **Heuristic** refers to software that can learn and modify its operations, such as a spell-checking program that can accept new words in its dictionary.

- Almost all commercially marketed software is copyrighted, but not necessarily copy-protected.

- **Open source** is a software development model with free access to programs created and supported by developers and users. The program source code is freely available to download, modify, and adapt to meet specific needs. The growing use of powerful collaborative and networking tools (social networks, blogs, news feeds and aggregators, podcasts, and collaborative content management) fuels the development of open source software.

Programming Languages

- **Source program** is in the language written by the programmer (high level languages resemble English while assembly languages are close to direct machine instructions).

- **Object program** is in a form the machine understands (on-off or 1-0).

- **Compiler** is a program that converts source programs into machine language.

- **Fourth Generation Programming Languages (4GL)** are commonly used in the development of business applications, and are distinguished by their use of "natural language" commands, making them self-documenting.

- **2 popular programming languages**
  - **C++** (pronounced "see plus plus") is a general-purpose programming language with high-level and low-level capabilities. It is a statically typed, free-form, multi-paradigm, usually compiled language supporting procedural programming, data abstraction, object-oriented programming, and generic programming.
  - **Java** is a programming language originally developed by Sun Microsystems and released in 1995. Java applications are typically compiled to bytecode, although compilation to native machine code is also possible. At runtime, bytecode is usually either interpreted or compiled to native code for execution, although direct hardware execution of bytecode by a Java processor is also possible.
    - Java derives much of its syntax from C and C++ but has a simpler object model and fewer low-level facilities. **JavaScript**, a scripting language, shares a similar name and has similar syntax, but is not directly related to Java.

- **HTML** (HyperText Markup Language) and **XML** (Extensible Markup Language) are specialized programming languages used to create websites.

- **eXtensible Business Reporting Language (XBRL)** is an open, market driven computer language that allows for the free electronic exchange of business and financial data. Instead of treating financial information as a block of text (e.g., standard Internet page or Word document), it provides a computer-readable identifying tag for each individual item of data. For example, "net income" has its own unique tag and a computer could immediately generate a comparison of net income for multiple companies or periods. XBRL eliminates the costly process of manual data comparison as computers can select, analyze, store, and exchange data in XBRL documents. Another benefit to XBRL is that it reduces the chance of errors when generating reports.

- o XBRL can handle data in different languages and accounting standards.
- o XBRL is built upon XML (Extensible Mark-up Language).
- o The SEC **mandated** that all public companies file financial statements in XBRL.
- o Her Majesty's Revenue and Customs (HMRC), the department of the British Government responsible for the collection of taxes, mandated all corporations' tax submissions use iXBRL ("inline" XBRL).

Data Structure

Data structure refers to the relationships among files in a database and among data items within each file. Since computers do not actually think and visualize, but are simply electronic machines, the storage of data is in the form of switches. Switches are typically associated as a data link layer device. They enable local area network (LAN) segments to be created and interconnected, which also has the added benefit of reducing the collision of domains in Ethernet-based networks. The term **binary** refers to the fact that the switches have only two possible positions. Binary computers can only think in terms of **bits** (binary digits) of information that are *on or off ("1" or "0")*. A series of 8 consecutive bits will produce a **byte** of information that represents a unit of human thought such as a letter, number, or other character. The manner in which data is described includes the following terms:

- **Bit** – A single switch in a computer that is either in the on (1) or off (0) position

- **Byte** – A group of 8 bits representing a character.

- **Character** – A letter, number, punctuation mark, or special character.

- **Alphanumeric** – A character that is either a letter or number.

- **Field** – A group of related characters representing a unit of information (such as a phone number or a city name).

- **Record** – A collection of related information treated as a unit. Separate fields within the record are used for processing the information (such as the name, address, and telephone number of one employee).
  - o Primary key – The field in a record that can be used to uniquely identify that record (such as the social security number field for an employee). It must be a field that has a value for every record, and is never the same in two different records (a name would not be a good idea as a primary key, since two people might have the same name).
  - o Secondary key – A key that might be able to uniquely locate a record when the primary key is unknown (the employee name, in this example, typically would to find a unique record, but isn't guaranteed to do so as the social security number would be).

- **File** – A group of logically related records (such as the contact info for all the employees).
  - o Master file – A permanent source that is used as an ongoing reference and that is periodically updated.
  - o Detail file – A file listing a group of transactions which may be used to update a master file. This is also frequently called a transaction file.

- **Database** – A stored collection of related data needed by organizations and individuals to meet their information processing and retrieval requirements (such as a payroll database that might have a file for contact info, a file with rate and withholding information, a file indicating hours worked, etc.).

- **Table** - A set of data elements (values) that is organized using a model of vertical <u>columns</u> (which are identified by their name) and horizontal <u>rows</u>. A table has a specified number of columns, but can have any number of rows. Users making database queries (a common audit technique) often need to combine several tables to get the desired information.

- **Data definition file** – A file that describes the logical structure of a database, including the titles and descriptions of the fields stored in each file and the relationships that exist between the data in the different files (for instance, indicating that the employee ID field in the file of hours worked is linked to one specific record in the contact info file which will have that same employee ID field). The data definition file should be included along with all the other files in the database to allow programs to read and understand all the files in the database.

A **database management system (DBMS)** is a software system that controls the organization, storage and retrieval of data in a database. The DBMS consists of a program and accompanying database that is used to keep track of information in an organized and efficient manner.

The program and database should be independent of one another, so that the database could be accessed by another user without needing the same program. One reason for this is that the database may be stored on a single file server (such as a website), while different users can use the database from their own client computer. Another reason is that the company may want to limit the access of some users to specific parts of the database, or allow some users to only read and not change data. This also might be done with a program that sets different access levels based on passwords, connection method, or other means. Yet a third reason is that the program maintenance can be performed more readily.

Data normalization is the process of organizing a database for minimum redundancy. While the details of DBMS design are too complicated to expect exam testing, it should be noted that an important goal of the DBMS should be to minimize the repetition and redundancy in the database, both to enhance efficiency and remove the danger of information being stored inconsistently in different places.

For example, the name and address of each employee is stored only in the contact info file and not included with the rate file or the hours worked file (the last two include the employee ID, but not the name). This way, only one file is updated when an employee changes his or her name or address. It is easy to generate reports (such as paychecks) by taking information from the three different files and grouping them together with the necessary computations.

Lecture 7.12 – Glossary – Class Questions

20. An entity doing business on the Internet most likely could use any of the following methods to prevent unauthorized intruders from accessing proprietary information except

    a. Password management
    b. Data encryption
    c. Digital certificates
    d. Batch processing

21. Cloud computing can best be defined as a model that

    a. Streamlines business processes onto a well-secured and highly available in-house e-commerce platform to optimize customers' online experience.
    b. Is designed for rapid application deployment by making several virtual servers run on one physical host.
    c. Allows users to access network resources from remote locations through a virtual private network.
    d. Allows organizations to use the Internet to access and use services and applications that run on remote third-party technology infrastructure.

22. In an effort to recognize improvement opportunities, a company is reviewing its in-house systems. The best reason for the company to consider switching to cloud computing as a solution is that it

    a. Is the best way to secure sensitive corporate information.
    b. Is accessible only from within the company on its Intranet.
    c. Usually has lower upfront costs for equipment and maintenance.
    d. Provides better program modification options.

23. Which of the following is the primary advantage of using a value-added network (VAN)?

    a. It provides confidentiality for data transmitted over the Internet.
    b. It provides increased security for data transmissions.
    c. It is more cost effective for the company than transmitting data over the Internet.
    d. It enables the company to obtain trend information on data transmissions.

Class Solutions

20. (d) Batch processing is simply a system under which transactions are periodically entered into the system in groups, rather than as they occur as in a real-time system. It does not specifically prevent unauthorized intruders from accessing proprietary information. Answer (a) is incorrect because password management provides assurance that only those with a valid password will have access, preventing unauthorized intruders. Answer (b) is incorrect because data encryption prevents unauthorized intruders from being able to understand data that they are not authorized for without obtaining the codes to decrypt the information. Answer (c) is incorrect because digital certificates provide identifying information to determine if a user is authorized to have access.

21. (d) Cloud computing is a model that allows organizations to use the Internet to access and use services and applications that run on remote third-party technology infrastructure, rather than rely on in-house platform solutions. Answer (a) is incorrect because cloud computing is a model that allows organizations to use the Internet to access and use services and applications that run on remote third-party technology infrastructure; it is not inherently secure. Answer (b) is incorrect because virtualization is a model that is designed for rapid application deployment by making several virtual servers run on one physical host. Answer (c) is incorrect because users may access network resources from remote locations through a virtual private network (VPN); a VPN may or may not be incorporated as part of a larger cloud computing strategy.

22. (c) Cloud computing utilizes third-party hardware and software, so it usually has lower upfront costs for equipment and maintenance. Answer (a) is incorrect because cloud computing is generally not the best way to secure sensitive corporate information, as there are security risks to transmitting information over the Internet. Answer (b) is incorrect because cloud computing allows information to be accessed by companies and their clients over the Internet, not via a company intranet. Answer (d) is incorrect because common implementations of cloud computing involve off-the-shelf software that is not developed or modified in-house, with generally limited configuration and program modification options.

23. (b) A value added network links the computer files of different companies, which requires increased security over data transmissions. Answer (a) is incorrect because since it shares files, it does not provide confidentiality. Answer (c) is incorrect because it is probably not as cost effective as transmission of data over the Internet, the cost of which would be generally limited to the cost of Internet access, but it provides a layer of security that transmission over the Internet cannot. Answer (d) is incorrect because it does not necessarily provide trend information.

Lecture 7.13 – Information Technology – Class Questions

Written Communication

3WAT, Inc. is discussing the data-storage possibilities for their highly mobile workforce. Currently, data is stored on laptop hard drives and is not centrally available. Management is concerned about data security, accessibility, and costs.

Prepare a memo to management discussing various options for data storage for a highly mobile workforce including advantages, disadvantages, and costs.

REMINDER: Your response will be graded for both technical content and writing skills. Technical content will be evaluated for information that is helpful to the intended reader and clearly relevant to the issue. Writing skills will be evaluated for development, organization, and the appropriate expression of ideas in professional correspondence. Use a standard business memo or letter format with a clear beginning, middle, and end. Do not convey information in the form of a table, bullet point list, or other abbreviated presentation.

To: Management of 3WAT, Inc.
RE: Data security and accessibility for a mobile workforce
From: CPA Candidate

Written Communication Solution

To: Management
RE: Data security and accessibility for a mobile workforce

In response to your expression of concern regarding the security, accessibility, and cost of your data storage, I have summarized some of the alternatives.

One possibility would be to continue your current approach of distributed processing. Under this approach, each individual involved in the processing of data has that data needed to perform their duties on their laptop computer. This is probably the most cost-effective alternative since your employees already have the laptop computers and it would require no additional capital investment.

It is also, unfortunately, a poor alternative when it comes to security and accessibility. Security is a particular challenge because laptop computers are often lost or stolen. In addition, unless the employee is very conscientious about maintaining anti-virus and anti-malware protection, risks become greater. Accessibility is also a challenge since each computer will have its unique data, which might be shared through email, or transferred through temporary storage devices like flash drives. Not only is this potentially cumbersome but it also entails the risk that an individual may not be working from the most recent data.

Another alternative would be to establish a network, either a local area network (LAN) or a wide area network (WAN), depending on the distances that your employees travel. This would involve creating a central storage area for all data, referred to as a server, that your employees would be able to access from remote locations. This is potentially an expensive alternative. The acquisition of the server will require an initial capital investment and, depending on decisions you make as to accessibility and security, there may be additional costs.

In order to make certain your data is secure in a LAN or WAN environment, you will have to make certain it is protected from unauthorized intruders, as well as from your own employees who should only have access to that data that is appropriate based on their authority and responsibilities. This can be done through the development of firewalls and establishing an identification system, such as the use of passwords. In addition, encryption of data can prevent an intruder from being able to obtain anything usable to them.

A LAN or WAN environment provides excellent accessibility to data. As long as employees can obtain a connection to the server, they will be able to access whatever data their password allows them access to. Since the data is centralized, all parties will always be dealing with the same, most recent data. Due to the mobility of your employees, obtaining a connection will probably require the use of wireless technology. One possibility is the use of Wi-Fi, which either requires that employees be within range of a portal or have a device, which also requires an initial investment as well as a monthly cost that gives them access from remote locations.

Another alternative would be to store data in a remote location that is independently operated. This alternative provides many of the advantages of a LAN or WAN environment, with comparable access to data and comparable means of obtaining security. Although it would be more costly than continuing with your distributed processing system, it would not require the initial outlay for a server and the related software support, other than establishing appropriate protocols for security purposes.

I hope this provides you enough information to provide a basis for considering your alternatives. Please contact me if I may address any additional questions or concerns.

Sincerely,

CPA Candidate

Section 8 – BEC Final Review

Table of Contents

Lecture 8.01 – BEC Final Review

YOU FINISHED YOUR BEC COURSE...NOW WHAT?
A quick guide to the final days leading up to, and following, the exam

I. FINAL REVIEW
Now is the time to make connections and solidify your understanding of the topics you found most challenging, and to review the most heavily tested topics on the exam.

- ❏ Reread your course notes and review bookmarked lectures.

- ❏ Review your Course Overview page in the Interactive Practice Questions (IPQ) software. Make sure to go through any unanswered questions and review any questions you have answered incorrectly or bookmarked for final review.

- ❏ A great way gear up for the upcoming exam is by adding a Roger CPA Review Cram Courses to your studies. The Cram Course works very well as a final review, as it is designed to reinforce your understanding of the most heavily tested CPA Exam topics.

- ❏ Take at least one full practice exam using the CPA Exam Simulator in your IPQ. This will help you hone your test taking strategy, time management and self-discipline under exam-like conditions, while continuing to expose you to the material.

II. DAY OF THE EXAM

- ❏ Get a good night's rest before heading into your exam.

- ❏ Arrive to the Prometric testing center at least 60 minutes before your appointment so you have time to park, check-in, and use the restroom before your exam begins.

- ❏ Bring your Notice to Schedule (NTS) and two forms of acceptable identification (see Intro for more details).

- ❏ Proceed through check-in: store belongings, get fingerprinted, have photo taken, sign log book, get seated, write your Launch Code (from your NTS) on your noteboard.

- ❏ Don't stress. You've prepared for this; now, just breathe and power through!

III. DURING THE EXAM

- ❏ Remember your BEC Exam time strategy, and jot down the times at which you want to be at your benchmarks:

  - o Allocate 75 seconds per multiple choice question
  - o Allocate 10 - 15 minutes for each written communication question
  - o Allocate 15-25 minutes for each task-based simulation, depending on complexity
  - o Take the standard 15-minute break after the 3rd testlet – it does not count against your time
  - o (Remember that any other break will count against your time)

BEC: 4 Hour Exam					
Testlet 1	Testlet 2	Testlet 3	B r e a k	Testlet 4	Testlet 5
31 MCQs	31 MCQs	2 TBSs		2 TBSs	3 WCs
45 min	45 min	50 min		50 min	50 min

❑ You will be given 10 minutes to review the welcome screens and exam instructions. You should already be familiar with these screens after taking the AICPA Sample Test, and can bypass them during your exam.

❑ Once you begin testing, make sure to read each question carefully, paying close attention to the keywords that dictate the question's intention (e.g. *except, is greater than*).

❑ Take note if your questions are getting more difficult. That's a good sign! A progressively harder exam indicates that you are performing well.

IV. AFTER THE EXAM

❑ Remember, it is normal to not feel great after you're done with your exam. It's a tough exam and designed to challenge your confidence and competencies.

❑ Relax and celebrate! You've earned it.

❑ Your scores will be released within a couple of weeks (see Intro for table).

❑ GOOD LUCK!!!

Section 9 – Document Review Simulations (DRS) Appendix

Table of Contents

Document Review Simulations (DRS) Appendix

Lecture 9.01 – DRS Introduction – Part 1

Lecture 9.02 – DRS Introduction – Part 2

Document review Simulations Overview

In 2016, the CPA Exam introduced a new type of Task-based simulation known as Document Review Simulations (DRS). These problems were added to the AUD, FAR and REG exams in 2016, and were added to the BEC exam in conjunction with the CPA Exam changes effective April 1, 2017.

What is a DRS?

DRS are designed to simulate tasks that the candidate will be required to perform as a newly licensed CPA (based on up to two years' experience as a CPA). Each DRS presents a document that has a series of highlighted phrases or sentences that the candidate will need to determine are correct or incorrect. To help make these conclusions, numerous supporting documents, or resources, such as legal letters, phone transcripts, financial statements, trial balances and authoritative literature will be included. The candidate will need to sort through these documents to determine what is, and what is not, important to solving the problem.

A DRS is one of many formats of Task-based simulation available to the examiners. There is no guarantee that the exam of any one candidate will have a DRS or any other particular format.

Why have DRS been added to the CPA Exam?

The AICPA conducted a Practice Analysis from 2014-2015 in which one main finding was clear: firms are expecting newly licensed CPAs on their staff to perform at a higher level—and they aren't. So, the AICPA is raising the bar with a revamped CPA Exam that more authentically tests candidates on the tasks and skill level that will be required of them as newly licensed CPAs. The introduction of DRS in 2016 was the first step in this larger initiative, with additional changes that become effective on April 1, 2017.

What do DRS test?

Up until recently, the CPA Exam has only tested candidates on the skill levels *Remembering & Understanding* and *Application* (skill levels based on Bloom's Taxonomy of Educational Objectives). To meet industry demands for the CPA Exam to test at a higher skill level, the CPA Exam is pivoting to test the higher order skills *Analysis* and *Evaluation* (Evaluation in AUD only). As a direct correlation to this exam evolution, DRS problems are designed to test these higher order skills by requiring candidates to analyze and evaluate documents they might see in the work force.

How a DRS works

As shown below, the DRS will present several buttons and exhibits:

- **Authoritative Literature**: Which is available on all task-based simulations (except in BEC)
- **Help**: Explanation of how to answer the problem
- **Exhibits**: A series of supporting documents which may, or may not, help candidates complete the problem

Notice the highlighted items within the main document. These represent the specific sentences or phrases that the candidate is required to analyze.

EXHIBITS

- Excerpt from attorney's letter
- Acid Wash Department Selected Information
- Proposal from Sizzle Acid Protection, Inc.
- Present Value Tables
- Accounting Department Worksheet Excerpts

To revise the document, click on each segment of underlined text below and select the needed correction, if any, from the list provided. If the underlined text is already correct in the context of the document, select "original text." If the underlined text is extraneous, select "delete text."

To: Miles Stand, CEO
From: Alice Abernathy
Re: Analysis of Investment Opportunities
Date: January 7, 20X0

There are five potential projects (A, B, C, D and E) being considered. The accounting staff and I have prepared the following table for your comparison. I have compared the investments, ranked them, and provided a recommendation for each. Please let me if I can be of any further assistance.

		Investment (all first year)	Net present value at 10%	Internal rate of return	Payback period (in years)
A.	Machine shop	$1,600,000	$744,000	20%	4
B.	Replace press	1,000,000	988,000	30%	3
C.	Replace forklift	800,000	179,000	15%	5
D.	Upgrade safety equipment	200,000	---	25%	---
E.	Solar electricity system	1,000,000	(601,000)	5%	15
	Total	$4,600,000			

Adjustments:

- The net present value of the safety equipment upgrade is $200,000.
- The payback period of the safety equipment upgrade is non-existent, as this project will not recoup the expenditure.

Recommendations:

- We should undertake the machine shop project. This project meets our internal rate of return criteria and there are sufficient funds to undertake it.
- We should undertake the press replacement project. This project meets our internal rate of return criteria and there are sufficient funds to undertake it.
- We should undertake the forklifts replacement project. This project meets our internal rate of return criteria and there are sufficient funds to undertake it.
- We should undertake the safety equipment project. This project meets our internal rate of return criteria and there are sufficient funds to undertake it.

To address each item within the problem, click on the highlighted phrase to see answer options. Each item will include the option to leave original text, delete text, or edit the text using the provided edit choices.

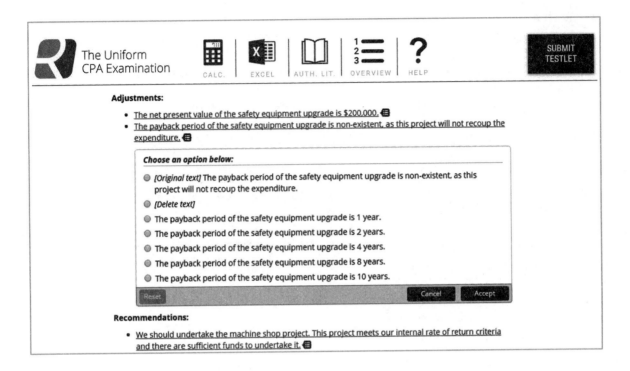

Once an item has been answered, a checkmark icon will appear next to the item in the document.

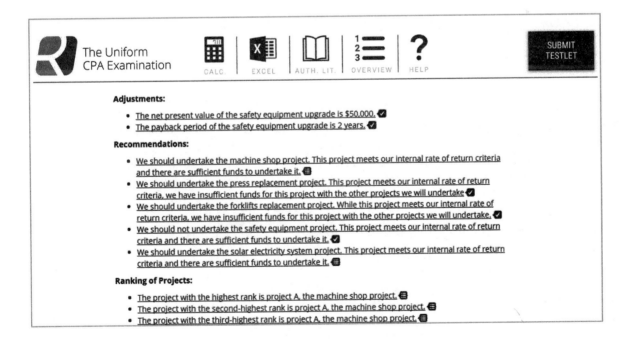

Approaching a BEC DRS

Step 1 – Get the lay of the land. YOU are the CPA – what is being asked of you? Skim over all the content in the Document Review Simulation to find out. You could be asked to do any of the following:

- Review the work of others – use your professional judgment, professional skepticism, and technical expertise to identify issues or correct errors. ← likely for BEC!
- Plan the work of others.
- Analyze and choose the best course of action from various alternatives presented. ← very likely for BEC!
- Address a client's technical questions and requests. ← likely for BEC!
- Draw on knowledge that is more extensively tested in a different exam section – detailed FAR knowledge may be expected for an BEC DRS, for instance. ← very likely for BEC!

Step 2 – Mentally note the gist of the DRS. "OK, this problem is about me, the CPA, reviewing the work of a staff member. Specifically, I must review a capital budgeting memo a staff member has drafted, review the accompanying documentation, and make changes to the memo as necessary."

Step 3 – Note the DRS subquestions. Briefly note down each DRS subquestion on your scratch whiteboard – you bought a handheld whiteboard just for CPA Exam study, right? Use your own shorthand. For instance, you might write:

1	determine NPV for D
2	" payback period for D
3	recommend projects
4	"
5	"
6	"
7	"
8	rank projects
9	"
10	"
11	"
12	"

Step 4 (Optional) – Choose an order of attack. Consider customizing the order in which you approach questions. It won't always be possible to tell, but if a few subquestions appear to be more time-consuming than others, consider moving them to the back of the queue. We don't know for sure, but we suspect each DRS subquestion is worth exactly as much as all the others—there are no bonus points for getting the most time-consuming ones right. Therefore, do the easiest ones first.

In this particular DRS, it seems we must determine the NPV and payback period in order to address the other items, so we will do items number 1 and 2 first. It might help to rank projects before making recommendations—so we will answer items 8 through 12 next. Finally, we will answer items 3 through 7.

Step 5 – Attack each subquestion one at a time. In either the default or custom order, work on each subquestion one at a time in order to be as efficient as possible to avoid getting overwhelmed. Remember that the necessary information for any one subquestion will almost certainly be contained across multiple documents.

Try to focus strictly on one subquestion at a time, but if you find yourself spending too much time on any one subquestion, make a tactical decision to skip it and move on to the next one. You may even decide to leave that subquestion undone and only return to it after completing other TBSs in your TBS testlet.

Check off each subquestion on your list as you complete it.

Step 6 – Go through a process of elimination for each subquestion.

Each DRS subquestion is similar to a multiple-choice question. The process of elimination, therefore, is a great tactic to employ. You can first eliminate **documents** and then **answer choices**.

Read the subquestion and all of its answer choices first.

For instance, the subquestion with default text "The net present value of the safety equipment upgrade is $200,000." appears to be about the net present value (NPV) of the safety equipment upgrade for the acid wash department. Briefly skim over each document in the Exhibits. Note any documents that clearly have no information about the net present value of the safety equipment upgrade for the acid wash department, and **ignore them**. Then hone in on the documents that do appear relevant.

As you focus on the relevant documents, eliminate answer choices one by one. That does not work well for this question; we must perform a calculation to know which is correct.

Follow this process of elimination for each subquestion, first eliminating documents, then answer choices. Even in cases (such as this one) where you're not sure there is a clear "winner" answer choice, you will at least have eliminated some irrelevant resources and the clear losers and given yourself a fighting chance.

To address the subquestion, we have to calculate the NPV of project D.

Several items in the available documentation are relevant to this subquestion.
- The first document is an excerpt from an attorney's letter. It relates to the additional safety measures required in the acid wash department.
- The second document is a bid from a contractor to install the additional safety measures required in the acid wash department.
- The third document is selected information on the acid wash department.
- The fifth document is a pair of present value tables. These contain information we need to calculate the net present value of a project.

The initial investment amount for project D (safety upgrades) comes from the second document. Apparently, Major must forego the revenues from the acid wash department unless the safety measures are installed—we know this from the attorney's letter, so the cash flows from the revenues (less the costs of goods sold) are used to evaluate this project—we get these from the third document. The present value factors come from the fifth document. We determine the NPV (at the 10% hurdle rate provided in the scenario) to be approximately $150,000 (see BEC Section 3 for details). Deleting the text is inappropriate as the omission in the table should be corrected.

NPV (safety upgrade, 10%) = PVS ($45,000, 1 year, 10%) + PVA ($59,000, years 2 through 10, 10%) – investment = $40,910 + $308,894 - $200,000 = $149,804

PVS ($45,000, 1 year, 10%) = ($45,000 x 0.9091) = $40,910

PVS ($1, 1 year, 10%) = $0.9091 (from PVS table, 1 year row, 10% column)

PVA ($59,000, years 2 through 10, 10%) = PVA ($59,000, 10 years, 10%) – PVS ($59,000, 1 year, 10%)
PVA ($1, 10 years, 10%) = 6.1446 (from PVA table, 10 year row, 10% column)
= ($59,000 x 6.1446) – ($59,000 x 0.9091)
= $362,531 - $53,637 = $308,894

The response to be selected will be, "The net present value of the safety equipment upgrade is $150,000."

This elimination process will be more useful for other subquestions in this DRS than it was for the first one. For instance, for subquestions 3 through 7, several similar responses can be eliminated for all projects. Consider the following:

- [Delete text] The instructions from the CFO ask for a recommendation for each project—this response will be inappropriate for all five subquestions concerning recommendations.

- We should undertake the _____ project. This project does not meet our internal rate of return criteria. If a project does not meet the IRR criteria, it should not be undertaken.

- We should undertake the _____ project. While this project meets our internal rate of return criteria, we have insufficient funds for this project with the other projects we will undertake. If we do not have funds for a project, it cannot be undertaken.

- We should not undertake the _____ project. This project meets our internal rate of return criteria and there are sufficient funds to undertake it. If a project does meets the IRR criteria and there are sufficient funds to undertake it, it should be undertaken.

We have eliminated half of the responses for these five subquestions.

Sample BEC DRS

Scroll down to complete all parts of this task.

Major Manufacturing will receive a windfall. Of this money, $3,500,000 is not earmarked for taxes, dividends, or an investment. Shareholders are not eager for an increase either in dividends or debt. Money not used for investment will be distributed to shareholders. Generally, the hurdle rate is 10%. As an S corporation, Major does not pay any income taxes.

Miles Stand, the CEO, asked the accounting staff to provide a table of the potential investments in Major's operations to Alice Abernathy so that she could compare the investments, rank each of them that exceeds the hurdle rate, and make a recommendation as to which investments or combination of investments, if any, are appropriate. Unfortunately, the accounting staff neglected to finish the chart for project D and Alice is unsure of how to complete it, so she needs you to look over the documents and help straighten out her memo.

Major has four manufacturing departments. Work in each department is finished at the fiscal year-end for extensive cleaning and repairs, so there is no work-in-process inventory at the fiscal year-end. Materials move through only one manufacturing department.

Amend the summary memo that Alice has drafted, as appropriate. Round the net present value to the nearest $1,000. Round the payback period to the closest year.

To revise the document, click on each segment of underlined text below and select the needed correction, if any, from the list provided. If the underlined text is already correct in the context of the document, select "original text." If the underlined text is extraneous, select "delete text."

To: Miles Stand, CEO
From: Alice Abernathy
Re: Analysis of Investment Opportunities
Date: January 7, 20X0

There are five potential projects (A, B, C, D and E) being considered. The accounting staff and I have prepared the following table for your comparison. I have compared the investments, ranked them, and provided a recommendation for each. Please let me if I can be of any further assistance.

		Investment (all first year)	Net present value at 10%	Internal rate of return	Payback period (in years)
A.	Machine shop	$1,600,000	$744,000	20%	4
B.	Replace press	1,000,000	988,000	30%	3
C.	Replace forklifts	800,000	179,000	15%	5
D.	Upgrade safety equipment	200,000	---	25%	---
E.	Solar electricity system	1,000,000	(601,000)	5%	15
	Total	$4,600,000			

Adjustments:

1. <u>The net present value of the safety equipment upgrade is $200,000.</u>

2. The payback period of the safety equipment upgrade is non-existent, as this project will not recoup the expenditure.

Recommendations:

3. We should undertake the machine shop project. This project meets our internal rate of return criteria and there are sufficient funds to undertake it.

4. We should undertake the press replacement project. This project meets our internal rate of return criteria and there are sufficient funds to undertake it.

5. We should undertake the forklifts replacement project. This project meets our internal rate of return criteria and there are sufficient funds to undertake it.

6. We should undertake the safety equipment upgrade project. This project meets our internal rate of return criteria and there are sufficient funds to undertake it.

7. We should undertake the solar electricity system project. This project meets our internal rate of return criteria and there are sufficient funds to undertake it.

Ranking of Projects:

8. The project with the highest rank is project A, the machine shop project.

9. The project with the second-highest rank is project A, the machine shop project.

10. The project with the third-highest rank is project A, the machine shop project.

11. The project with the fourth-highest rank is project A, the machine shop project.

12. The project with the lowest rank is project A, the machine shop project.

Items for Analysis

The net present value of the safety equipment upgrade is $200,000.

1. Choose an option below:

- [Original text] The net present value of the safety equipment upgrade is $200,000.
- [Delete text]
- The net present value of the safety equipment upgrade is $0.
- The net present value of the safety equipment upgrade is $50,000.
- The net present value of the safety equipment upgrade is $100,000.
- The net present value of the safety equipment upgrade is $150,000.

The payback period of the safety equipment upgrade is non-existent, as this project will not recoup the expenditure.

2. Choose an option below:

- [Original text] The payback period of the safety equipment upgrade is non-existent, as this project will not recoup the expenditure.

- [Delete text]

- The payback period of the safety equipment upgrade is 1 year.

- The payback period of the safety equipment upgrade is 2 years.

- The payback period of the safety equipment upgrade is 4 years.

- The payback period of the safety equipment upgrade is 8 years.

- The payback period of the safety equipment upgrade is 10 years.

We should undertake the machine shop project. This project meets our internal rate of return criteria and there are sufficient funds to undertake it.

3. Choose an option below:

- [Original text] We should undertake the machine shop project. This project meets our internal rate of return criteria and there are sufficient funds to undertake it.

- [Delete text]

- We should undertake the machine shop project. This project does not meet our internal rate of return criteria.

- We should undertake the machine shop project. While this project meets our internal rate of return criteria, we have insufficient funds for this project with the other projects we will undertake.

- We should not undertake the machine shop project. This project meets our internal rate of return criteria and there are sufficient funds to undertake it.

- We should not undertake the machine shop project. This project does not meet our internal rate of return criteria.

- We should not undertake the machine shop project. While this project meets our internal rate of return criteria, we have insufficient funds for this project with the other projects we will undertake.

We should undertake the press replacement project. This project meets our internal rate of return criteria and there are sufficient funds to undertake it.

4. Choose an option below:

- [Original text] We should undertake the press replacement project. This project meets our internal rate of return criteria and there are sufficient funds to undertake it.

- [Delete text]

- We should undertake the press replacement project. This project does not meet our internal rate of return criteria.

- We should undertake the press replacement project. While this project meets our internal rate of return criteria, we have insufficient funds for this project with the other projects we will undertake.

- We should not undertake the press replacement project. This project meets our internal rate of return criteria and there are sufficient funds to undertake it.

- We should not undertake the press replacement project. This project does not meet our internal rate of return criteria.

- We should not undertake the press replacement project. While this project meets our internal rate of return criteria, we have insufficient funds for this project with the other projects we will undertake.

We should undertake the forklifts replacement project. This project meets our internal rate of return criteria and there are sufficient funds to undertake it.

5. Choose an option below:

- [Original text] We should undertake the forklifts replacement project. This project meets our internal rate of return criteria and there are sufficient funds to undertake it.

- [Delete text]

- We should undertake the forklifts replacement project. This project does not meet our internal rate of return criteria.

- We should undertake the forklifts replacement project. While this project meets our internal rate of return criteria, we have insufficient funds for this project with the other projects we will undertake.

- We should not undertake the forklifts replacement project. This project meets our internal rate of return criteria and there are sufficient funds to undertake it.

- We should not undertake the forklifts replacement project. This project does not meet our internal rate of return criteria.

- We should not undertake the forklifts replacement project. While this project meets our internal rate of return criteria, we have insufficient funds for this project with the other projects we will undertake.

We should undertake the safety equipment project. This project meets our internal rate of return criteria and there are sufficient funds to undertake it.

6. Choose an option below:

- [Original text] We should undertake the safety equipment project. This project meets our internal rate of return criteria and there are sufficient funds to undertake it.

- [Delete text]

- We should undertake the safety equipment project. This project does not meet our internal rate of return criteria.

- We should undertake the safety equipment project. While this project meets our internal rate of return criteria, we have insufficient funds for this project with the other projects we will undertake.

- We should not undertake the safety equipment project. This project meets our internal rate of return criteria and there are sufficient funds to undertake it.

- We should not undertake the safety equipment project. This project does not meet our internal rate of return criteria.

- We should not undertake the safety equipment project. While this project meets our internal rate of return criteria, we have insufficient funds for this project with the other projects we will undertake.

We should undertake the solar electricity system project. This project meets our internal rate of return criteria and there are sufficient funds to undertake it.

7. Choose an option below:

- [Original text] We should undertake the solar electricity system project. This project meets our internal rate of return criteria and there are sufficient funds to undertake it.

- [Delete text]

- We should undertake the solar electricity system project. This project does not meet our internal rate of return criteria.

- We should undertake the solar electricity system project. While this project meets our internal rate of return criteria, we have insufficient funds for this project with the other projects we will undertake.

- We should not undertake the solar electricity system project. This project meets our internal rate of return criteria and there are sufficient funds to undertake it.

- We should not undertake the solar electricity system project. This project does not meet our internal rate of return criteria.

- We should not undertake the solar electricity system project. While this project meets our internal rate of return criteria, we have insufficient funds for this project with the other projects we will undertake.

The project with the highest rank is project A, the machine shop project.

8. Choose an option below:

- [Original text] The project with the highest rank is project A, the machine shop project.

- [Delete text]

- The project with the highest rank is project B, the press replacement project.

- The project with the highest rank is project C, the forklifts replacement project.

- The project with the highest rank is project D, the safety upgrade project.

- The project with the highest rank is project E, the solar electricity system project.

The project with the second-highest rank is project A, the machine shop project.

9. Choose an option below:

- [Original text] The project with the second-highest rank is project A, the machine shop project.

- [Delete text]

- The project with the second-highest rank is project B, the press replacement project.

- The project with the second-highest rank is project C, the forklifts replacement project.

- The project with the second-highest rank is project D, the safety upgrade project.

- The project with the second-highest rank is project E, the solar electricity system project.

The project with the third-highest rank is project A, the machine shop project.

10. Choose an option below:

- [Original text] The project with the third-highest rank is project A, the machine shop project.

- [Delete text]

- The project with the third-highest rank is project B, the press replacement project.

- The project with the third-highest rank is project C, the forklifts replacement project.

- The project with the third-highest rank is project D, the safety upgrade project.

- The project with the third-highest rank is project E, the solar electricity system project.

The project with the fourth-highest rank is project A, the machine shop project.

11. Choose an option below:

- [Original text] The project with the fourth-highest rank is project A, the machine shop project.

- [Delete text]

- The project with the fourth-highest rank is project B, the press replacement project.

- The project with the fourth-highest rank is project C, the forklifts replacement project.

- The project with the fourth-highest rank is project D, the safety upgrade project.

- The project with the fourth-highest rank is project E, the solar electricity system project.

The project with the lowest rank is project A, the machine shop project.

12. Choose an option below:

- [Original text] The project with the lowest rank is project A, the machine shop project.

- [Delete text]

- The project with the lowest rank is project B, the press replacement project.

- The project with the lowest rank is project C, the forklifts replacement project.

- The project with the lowest rank is project D, the safety upgrade project.

- The project with the lowest rank is project E, the solar electricity system project.

Exhibits

Excerpt from attorney's letter

> **Excerpt from Attorney's Letter**
>
> A new regulation (AW13908.78) goes into effect as of January 1, 20X1. Without additional safety measures, the acid wash department will have to discontinue operations. Please contact me for additional details.

Proposal from Sizzle Acid Protection, Inc.

Sizzle Acid Protection, Inc.

1200 Industrial Road
Fort Myers, FL
1-800-555-BURN

Acid remediation shower	$150,000
Acid neutralization system	47,000
Safety goggles (case of 144)	1,000
Employee safety signage	1,000
Initial training for employees	1,000
Total	$200,000

Installation from December 10, 20X0, to December 25, 20X0, with 10 days of unlimited access from 7:00 a.m. to 6 p.m.
Training finished by December 31, 20X1, on any non-holiday weekday of your choice.
Guaranteed compliant with regulation AW13908.78 for 10 years, given no changes to the regulation.
Offer valid until November 30.

Acid wash department selected information

Major Manufacturing - Acid Wash Department
Select Amounts ($ in 1,000s)
January 3, 20X0

Plant and Equipment	
Historical Cost	$2,000
Deprecation	1,500
Salvage Value	50

Anticipated amounts	20X1 (Year 1)	20X2–20X10 (Years 2-10)
Capacity	96%	98%
Sales dollars	683	709
Cost of goods sold	638	650
Sales less cost of goods sold	45	59

Accounting Department Worksheet Excerpts

Major Manufacturing Company
Comparison of Potential Investments
January 21, 20X0

Project	A	B	C	D	E
Investment	1,600,000	1,000,000	800,000	200,000	1,000,000
Estimated annual cash inflow (ACI)	381,500	323,500	159,400		65,000
Investment divided by ACI	4.2	3.1	5.0		15.4
Payback period (rounded)	4	3	5		15
IRR—see below (rounded)	20%	30%	15%		5%
Interest rate	10%	15%	20%	25%	30%
Present value of an annuity factor	6.1446	5.0188	4.1925	3.5705	3.0915
Present value of project A ACI	2,344,165	1,914,672	1,599,439	1,362,146	1,179,407
Net present value, project A	744,165	314,672	-561	-237,854	-420,593
Present value of project B ACI	1,987,778	1,623,582	1,356,274	1,155,057	1,000,100
Net present value, project B	987,778	623,582	356,274	155,057	100
Present value of project C ACI	979,449	799,997	668,285	569,138	492,785
Net present value, project C	179,449	-3	-131,716	-230,862	-307,215

Present Value Tables

Present Value of a $1 Single Sum (PVS)

Period	5%	10%	15%	20%	25%	30%
1	0.9524	0.9091	0.8696	0.8333	0.8000	0.7692
2	0.9070	0.8264	0.7561	0.6944	0.6400	0.5917
3	0.8638	0.7513	0.6575	0.5787	0.5120	0.4552
4	0.8227	0.6830	0.5718	0.4823	0.4096	0.3501
5	0.7835	0.6209	0.4972	0.4019	0.3277	0.2693
6	0.7462	0.5645	0.4323	0.3349	0.2621	0.2072
7	0.7107	0.5132	0.3759	0.2791	0.2097	0.1594
8	0.6768	0.4665	0.3269	0.2326	0.1678	0.1226
9	0.6446	0.4241	0.2843	0.1938	0.1342	0.0943
10	0.6139	0.3855	0.2472	0.1615	0.1074	0.0725
30	0.2314	0.0573	0.0151	0.0042	0.0012	0.0004
83	0.0174	0.0004	0.0000	0.0000	0.0000	0.0000

Present Value of a $1 Annuity (PVA)

Period	5%	10%	15%	20%	25%	30%
1	0.9524	0.9091	0.8696	0.8333	0.8000	0.7692
2	1.8594	1.7355	1.6257	1.5278	1.4400	1.3609
3	2.7232	2.4869	2.2832	2.1065	1.9520	1.8161
4	3.5460	3.1699	2.8550	2.5887	2.3616	2.1662
5	4.3295	3.7908	3.3522	2.9906	2.6893	2.4356
6	5.0757	4.3553	3.7845	3.3255	2.9514	2.6427
7	5.7864	4.8684	4.1604	3.6046	3.1611	2.8021
8	6.4632	5.3349	4.4873	3.8372	3.3289	2.9247
9	7.1078	5.7590	4.7716	4.0310	3.4631	3.0190
10	7.7217	6.1446	5.0188	4.1925	3.5705	3.0915
30	15.3725	9.4269	6.5660	4.9789	3.9950	3.3321
83	19.6514	9.9963	6.6666	5.0000	4.0000	3.3333

Solution to BEC DRS

This question is asking the candidate to determine what projects to recommend, their ranking, and to correct some figures in the provided information. Items in the memo that are not underlined are presumed to be appropriate. As a result, the candidate need not address them.

1. The first underlined item indicates "The net present value of the safety equipment upgrade is $200,000." and, when clicked upon, the following choices appear:

    *   [Original text] The net present value of the safety equipment upgrade is $200,000.

    *   [Delete text]

    *   The net present value of the safety equipment upgrade is $0.

    *   The net present value of the safety equipment upgrade is $50,000.

    *   The net present value of the safety equipment upgrade is $100,000.

    *   The net present value of the safety equipment upgrade is $150,000.

To determine what correction, if any, needs to be made, the candidate will have to review the available documentation.

   *   The first document is an excerpt from an attorney's letter. It relates to the additional safety measures required in the acid wash department.

   *   The second document is a bid from a contractor to install the additional safety measures required in the acid wash department.

   *   The third document is selected information on the acid wash department.

   *   The fourth document does not appear to relate to the acid wash department.

   *   The fifth document is a pair of present value tables. These contain information we need to calculate the net present value of a project.

The initial investment amount for project D (safety upgrades) comes from the second document. Apparently, Major must forego the revenues from the acid wash department unless the safety measures are installed—we know this from the attorney's letter, so the cash flows from the revenues (less the costs of goods sold) are used to evaluate this project—we get these from the third document. The present value factors come from the fifth document. We determine the NPV (at the 10% hurdle rate provided in the scenario) to be approximately $150,000 (see BEC Section 3 for details). Deleting the text is inappropriate as the omission in the table should be corrected.

NPV (safety upgrade, 10%) = PVS ($45,000, 1 year, 10%) + PVA ($59,000, years 2 through 10, 10%) – investment = $40,910 + $308,894 - $200,000 = $149,804

PVS ($45,000, 1 year, 10%) = ($45,000 x 0.9091) = $40,910
         PVS ($1, 1 year, 10%) = $0.9091 (from PVS table, 1 year row, 10% column)

PVA ($59,000, years 2 through 10, 10%) = PVA ($59,000, 10 years, 10%) – PVS ($59,000, 1 year, 10%)
         PVA ($1, 10 years, 10%) = 6.1446 (from PVA table, 10 year row, 10% column)
         = ($59,000 x 6.1446) – ($59,000 x 0.9091)
         = $362,531 - $53,637 = $308,894

The item to be selected will be:

   *   ***The net present value of the safety equipment upgrade is $150,000.***

2. The next underlined item indicates "The payback period of the safety equipment upgrade is non-existent, as this project will not recoup the expenditure." The choices are:

- [Original text] The payback period of the safety equipment upgrade is non-existent, as this project will not recoup the expenditure.

- [Delete text]

- The payback period of the safety equipment upgrade is 1 year.

- The payback period of the safety equipment upgrade is 2 years.

- The payback period of the safety equipment upgrade is 4 years.

- The payback period of the safety equipment upgrade is 8 years.

- The payback period of the safety equipment upgrade is 10 years.

As we have done most of the work evaluating the safety upgrade project already, we don't have to do much to address this item. Using the same documents, we determine the payback period is about 3.6 years—which rounds to 4 years. Calculations follow:

$200,000 cost – $45,000 year 1 cash flow = $155,000 amount remaining after 1st year.
$155,000 remaining investment / $59,000 cash flow for subsequent years = 2.6 years.
2.6 years +1st year = 3.6 years.

Deleting the text is inappropriate as the omission in the table should be corrected.

The item to be selected will be:
- ***The payback period of the safety equipment upgrade is 4 years.***

3. The next underlined item indicates "We should undertake the machine shop project. This project meets our internal rate of return criteria and there are sufficient funds to undertake it." The choices are:

- [Original text] We should undertake the machine shop project. This project meets our internal rate of return criteria and there are sufficient funds to undertake it.

- [Delete text]

- We should undertake the machine shop project. This project does not meet our internal rate of return criteria.

- We should undertake the machine shop project. While this project meets our internal rate of return criteria, we have insufficient funds for this project with the other projects we will undertake.

- We should not undertake the machine shop project. This project meets our internal rate of return criteria and there are sufficient funds to undertake it.

- We should not undertake the machine shop project. This project does not meet our internal rate of return criteria.

- We should not undertake the machine shop project. While this project meets our internal rate of return criteria, we have insufficient funds for this project with the other projects we will undertake.

To determine what correction, if any, needs to be made, the candidate will have to review the available documentation.

- Besides the table in the memo, the only document that refers to this project is the Accounting Department Worksheet Excerpts; however, everything you need is in the table itself, along with the NPV and the payback period you calculated for project D.

As there is more money required to fund all the projects than is available, we must compare them and decide on the most profitable projects.

While, generally, it is best to concentrate on one item at a time, this simulation does not lend itself to that approach.

Knowing that project E has an IRR of only 5%, which does not meet the hurdle rate, we are left with $3,500,000 to invest and projects requiring $4,600,000 – $1,000,000 = $3,600,000. Let's go ahead and rank the projects. As the directions say to rank the projects that exceed the hurdle rate, we know that we can now ignore project E and rank the other projects by their IRR. So, after a seemingly slow start, we can address five subquestions (8 through 12) in short order.

4. The underlined item indicates "The project with the highest rank is project A, the machine shop project." The choices are:

- [Original text] The project with the highest rank is project A, the machine shop project.

- [Delete text]

- The project with the highest rank is project B, the press replacement project.

- The project with the highest rank is project C, the forklifts replacement project.

- The project with the highest rank is project D, the safety upgrade project.

- The project with the highest rank is project E, the solar electricity system project.

Project B has the highest IRR of 30%. Deleting the text is inappropriate as the instructions were to rank the projects exceeding the hurdle rate.

The item to be selected will be:
- ***The project with the highest rank is project B, the press replacement project.***

5. The underlined item indicates "The project with the second-highest rank is project A, the machine shop project." The choices are:

- [Original text] The project with the second-highest rank is project A, the machine shop project.

- [Delete text]

- The project with the second-highest rank is second-highest B, the press replacement project.

- The project with the second-highest rank is second-highest C, the forklifts replacement project.

- The project with the second-highest rank is second-highest D, the safety upgrade project.

- The project with the second-highest rank is second-highest E, the solar electricity system project.

Project D has the second-highest IRR of 25%. Deleting the text is inappropriate as the instructions were to rank the projects exceeding the hurdle rate.

The item to be selected will be:
- ***The project with the second-highest rank is project D, the safety upgrade project.***

6. The underlined item indicates "The project with the third-highest rank is project A, the machine shop project." The choices are:

   - [Original text] The project with the third-highest rank is project A, the machine shop project.
   - [Delete text]
   - The project with the third-highest rank is project B, the press replacement project.
   - The project with the third-highest rank is project C, the forklifts replacement project.
   - The project with the third-highest rank is project D, the safety upgrade project.
   - The project with the third-highest rank is project E, the solar electricity system project.

Project A has the third-highest IRR of 20%. Deleting the text is inappropriate as the instructions were to rank the projects exceeding the hurdle rate.

The item to be selected will be:
- ***[Original text] The project with the third-highest rank is project A, the machine shop replacement project.***

7. The underlined item indicates "The project with the fourth-highest rank is project A, the machine shop project." The choices are:

   - [Original text] The project with the fourth-highest rank is project A, the machine shop project.
   - [Delete text]
   - The project with the fourth-highest rank is project B, the press replacement project.
   - The project with the fourth-highest rank is project C, the forklifts replacement project.
   - The project with the fourth-highest rank is project D, the safety upgrade project.
   - The project with the fourth-highest rank is project E, the solar electricity system project.

Project C has the fourth-highest IRR of 15%. Deleting the text is inappropriate as the instructions were to rank the projects exceeding the hurdle rate.

The item to be selected will be:
- ***The project with the fourth-highest rank is project C, the forklifts replacement project.***

8. The last underlined item indicates "The project with the lowest rank is project A, the machine shop project." The choices are:

   - [Original text] The project with the lowest rank is project A, the machine shop project.

   - [Delete text]

   - The project with the lowest rank is project B, the press replacement project.

   - The project with the lowest rank is project C, the forklifts replacement project.

   - The project with the lowest rank is project D, the safety upgrade project.

   - The project with the lowest rank is project E, the solar electricity system project.

Clearly, project E is the lowest ranked project, but we do not select, "The project with the lowest rank is project E, the solar electricity system project." Our instructions were to rank all of the projects that meet the minimum profitability criteria of exceeding the hurdle rate. A project with an IRR of 5% does not meet these criteria, so we will merely delete the text.

As a result, the item to be selected will be:
   - **[Delete text]**

At long last, we return to the start of the recommendations (subquestion 3).

Simply, we recommend the projects in the same order as the ranking, until we run out of capital to invest. Major has sufficient capital to invest in projects A, B, and D. While project C meets the minimum profitability requirements, Major doesn't have enough capital available to fund it. Project E does not meet the minimum profitability requirements; Major would not invest in project E even if it had extra capital.

9. Again, the underlined item indicates "We should undertake the machine shop project. This project meets our internal rate of return criteria and there are sufficient funds to undertake it." The choices are:

   - [Original text] We should undertake the machine shop project. This project meets our internal rate of return criteria and there are sufficient funds to undertake it.

   - [Delete text]

   - We should undertake the machine shop project. This project does not meet our internal rate of return criteria.

   - We should undertake the machine shop project. While this project meets our internal rate of return criteria, we have insufficient funds for this project with the other projects we will undertake.

   - We should not undertake the machine shop project. This project meets our internal rate of return criteria and there are sufficient funds to undertake it.

   - We should not undertake the machine shop project. This project does not meet our internal rate of return criteria.

   - We should not undertake the machine shop project. While this project meets our internal rate of return criteria, we have insufficient funds for this project with the other projects we will undertake.

We have sufficient capital to invest in projects A, B, and D.

The item to be selected will be:

- ***[Original text] We should undertake the machine shop project. This project meets our internal rate of return criteria and there are sufficient funds to undertake it.***

10. The underlined item for number 4 indicates "We should undertake the press replacement project. This project meets our internal rate of return criteria and there are sufficient funds to undertake it." The choices are:

- [Original text] We should undertake the press replacement project. This project meets our internal rate of return criteria and there are sufficient funds to undertake it.

- [Delete text]

- We should undertake the press replacement project. This project does not meet our internal rate of return criteria.

- We should undertake the press replacement project. This project meets our internal rate of return criteria; we have insufficient funds for this project with the other projects we will undertake.

- We should not undertake the press replacement project. This project meets our internal rate of return criteria and there are sufficient funds to undertake it.

- We should not undertake the press replacement project. This project does not meet our internal rate of return criteria.

- We should not undertake the press replacement project. While this project meets our internal rate of return criteria, we have insufficient funds for this project with the other projects we will undertake.

We have sufficient capital to invest in projects A, B, and D.

The item to be selected will be:

- ***[Original text] We should undertake the press replacement project. This project meets our internal rate of return criteria and there are sufficient funds to undertake it.***

11. The underlined item for number 5 indicates "We should undertake the press replacement project. This project meets our internal rate of return criteria and there are sufficient funds to undertake it." The choices are:

- [Original text] We should undertake the press replacement project. This project meets our internal rate of return criteria and there are sufficient funds to undertake it.

- [Delete text]

- We should undertake the press replacement project. This project does not meet our internal rate of return criteria.

- We should undertake the press replacement project. While this project meets our internal rate of return criteria, we have insufficient funds for this project with the other projects we will undertake.

- We should not undertake the press replacement project. This project meets our internal rate of return criteria and there are sufficient funds to undertake it.

- We should not undertake the press replacement project. This project does not meet our internal rate of return criteria.

- We should not undertake the press replacement project. While this project meets our internal rate of return criteria, we have insufficient funds for this project with the other projects we will undertake.

We have sufficient capital to invest in projects A, B, and D. While project C meets the minimum profitability requirements, we haven't enough capital available to fund it. Deleting the text is inappropriate as a recommendation is required.

The item to be selected will be:

- ***We should not undertake the press replacement project. While this project meets our internal rate of return criteria, we have insufficient funds for this project with the other projects we will undertake.***

12. The underlined item for number 6 indicates "We should undertake the safety equipment project. This project meets our internal rate of return criteria and there are sufficient funds to undertake it." The choices are:

- [Original text] We should undertake the safety equipment project. This project meets our internal rate of return criteria and there are sufficient funds to undertake it.
- [Delete text]
- We should undertake the safety equipment project. This project does not meet our internal rate of return criteria.
- We should undertake the safety equipment project. While this project meets our internal rate of return criteria, we have insufficient funds for this project with the other projects we will undertake.
- We should not undertake the safety equipment project. This project meets our internal rate of return criteria and there are sufficient funds to undertake it.
- We should not undertake the safety equipment project. This project does not meet our internal rate of return criteria.
- We should not undertake the safety equipment project. While this project meets our internal rate of return criteria, we have insufficient funds for this project with the other projects we will undertake.

We have sufficient capital to invest in projects A, B, and D.

The item to be selected will be:
- ***[Original text] We should undertake the safety equipment project. This project meets our internal rate of return criteria and there are sufficient funds to undertake it.***

13. The underlined item for number 7 indicates "We should undertake the solar electricity system project. This project meets our internal rate of return criteria and there are sufficient funds to undertake it." The choices are:

- [Original text] We should undertake the solar electricity system project. This project meets our internal rate of return criteria and there are sufficient funds to undertake it.
- [Delete text]
- We should undertake the solar electricity system project. This project does not meet our internal rate of return criteria.
- We should undertake the solar electricity system project. While this project meets our internal rate of return criteria, we have insufficient funds for this project with the other projects we will undertake.
- We should not undertake the solar electricity system project. This project meets our internal rate of return criteria and there are sufficient funds to undertake it.
- We should not undertake the solar electricity system project. This project does not meet our internal rate of return criteria.
- We should not undertake the solar electricity system project. While this project meets our internal rate of return criteria, we have insufficient funds for this project with the other projects we will undertake.

Project E does not meet the minimum profitability requirements; we would not invest in it even if we had extra capital. Deleting the text is inappropriate as a recommendation is required.

As a result, the item to be selected will be:

- ***We should not undertake the solar electricity system project. This project does not meet our internal rate of return criteria.***

Subquestions 8 through 12 already were addressed.